AutoCAD 2016

For Architectural Design

Tutorial Books

© Copyright 2015 by Tutorial Books

This book may not be duplicated in any way without the express written consent of the publisher, except in the form of brief excerpts or quotations for the purpose of review. The information contained herein is for the personal use of the reader and may not be incorporated in any commercial programs, other books, database, or any kind of software without written consent of the publisher. Making copies of this book or any portion for purpose other than your own is a violation of copyright laws.

Limit of Liability/Disclaimer of Warranty:

The author and publisher make no representations or warranties with respect to the accuracy or completeness of the contents of this work and specifically disclaim all warranties, including without limitation warranties of fitness for a particular purpose. The advice and strategies contained herein may not be suitable for every situation. Neither the publisher nor the author shall be liable for damages arising here from.

Trademarks:

All brand names and product names used in this book are trademarks, registered trademarks, or trade names of their respective holders. The author and publisher are not associated with any product or vendor mentioned in this book.

Download Resource Files from:

www.tutorialbook.info

For Technical Support, contact us at:

online.books999@gmail.com

Table of Contents

Scope of this Book vii

Part 1: Creating 2D Architectural Drawings 1

Tutorial 1: Starting AutoCAD 2015 1
Tutorial 2: Inserting Hand Sketches 3
    Scaling the Hand Sketches 4
    Saving the Document 12
Tutorial 3: Creating Layers 12
Tutorial 4: Creating Grid Lines 15
Tutorial 5: Creating Walls 18
Tutorial 6: Creating Doors and Windows 24
Tutorial 7: Creating Stairs 38
Tutorial 8: Creating the First Floor Plan 41
    Creating the Sliding Doors 45
    Creating the Balcony 47
Tutorial 9: Creating Kitchen and Bathroom Fixtures 48
    Creating Bathroom Fixtures 52
    Adding Furniture Blocks 57
Tutorial 10: Adding Hatch Patterns and Text 59
    Adding Text Labels 60
Tutorial 11: Creating Elevations 61
    Creating Windows and Doors in the Elevation View 71
    Creating the Opposite Elevation 76
    Creating the Front and Rear Elevations 81
    Hatching the Elevation Views 93
Tutorial 12: Adding Dimensions 95
Tutorial 13: Creating Grid Bubbles 97
Tutorial 14: Layouts and Title Block 99
    Creating the Title Block on the Layout 100
    Creating Viewports in the Paper space 101
    Creating layouts for the other views 104
    Changing the Layer Properties in Viewports 104
Tutorial 15: Printing 105

Part 2: Creating 3D Architectural Model 106

Tutorial 1: Importing 2D Drawings 107
Tutorial 2: Creating 3D Walls 108

Tutorial 3: Create the Ceiling.. 120
Tutorial 4: Creating Doors on the Ground Floor 125
Tutorial 5: Creating 3D Windows 135
Tutorial 6: Creating 3D Stairs 143
Tutorial 7: Modeling the First Floor... 147
Tutorial 8: Creating the Balcony... 153
Tutorial 9: Creating the Staircase on the first floor 163
      Creating Railing.. 167
Tutorial 10: Creating the Roof 175
Tutorial 11: Creating the Terrain surface 178

Part 3: Rendering...186

Tutorial 1: Adding Materials 186
Tutorial 2: Adding Cameras 192
Tutorial 3: Adding Lights.. 193
Tutorial 4: Rendering.. 195

Scope of this Book

The *AutoCAD 2015 for Architectural Design* book helps users to learn AutoCAD in a project-based approach. It is written for students and engineers who are interested to learn AutoCAD 2016 for creating two dimensional architectural drawings and three dimensional models. The topics covered in this book are as follows:

- Part 1, "Creating 2D Architectural Drawings", helps you to create architectural floor plans and elevations. Also, you will learn to add dimensions and annotations, and then print drawings

- Part 2, "Creating 3D Architectural Models", teaches you to create three dimensional models using the 2D drawings.

- Part 3, "Rendering", teaches you to locate the model on the live map, add materials to the objects, add lights and camera, and then generate photorealistic images.

Part 1: Creating 2D Architectural Drawings

In this chapter, you will learn to do the following:
- Starting AutoCAD 2015
- Inserting Hand Sketches
- Creating Layers
- Creating Grid Lines
- Creating Wall
- Doors Windows, and Stairs
- Kitchen and Bathroom fixtures
- Blocks and Hatch Patterns
- Adding Text
- Creating Elevations
- Adding Dimensions
- Layouts and Title Block
- Printing Drawings

In this chapter, you will learn to create architectural drawing shown below.

Tutorial 1: Starting AutoCAD 2015

- Click **Autodesk > AutoCAD 2015** icon on the windows grid. If you are working in Windows 7, click **Start > All Programs > Autodesk > AutoCAD 2015 > AutoCAD 2015**.
- To start a new document, click **Get Started > Templates > acadiso.dwt**.

The components of the AutoCAD user interface are shown in figure given next:

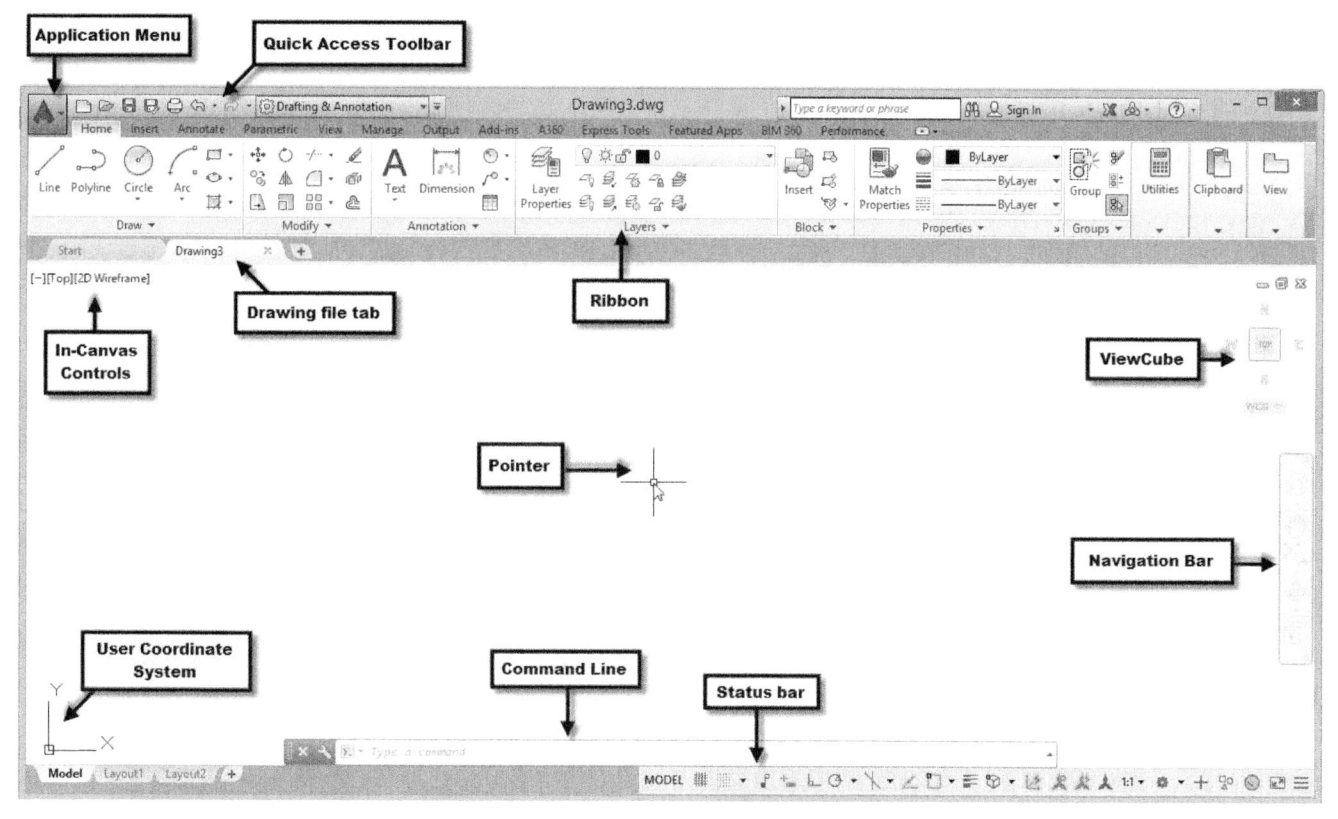

- On the Status bar, click **Workspace Switching > Drafting & Annotation**.

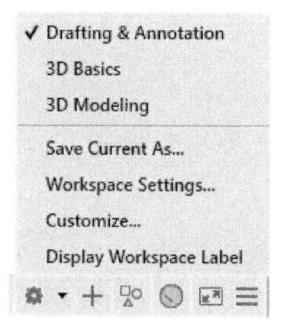

- On the Status bar, click the **GRIDMODE** icon to turn off the grid.

- Type UN in the command line and press Enter.
- On the **Drawing Units** dialog, select **Type > Decimal**. Select **Precision > 0.0000**. Set the **Insertion Scale** to **Millimeters**, and click **OK**.
- Right click and select the **Options** from the shortcut menu; the **Options** dialog appears on the screen and it allows you to change the settings of the user interface and various functionalities.
- On the **Options** dialog, click the **Selection** tab, and set the Pickbox size, as shown.

- Click **OK** to close the **Options** dialog.

Tutorial 2: Inserting Hand Sketches

In this tutorial, you will insert the scanned images of Hand sketches.

- Download the Reference files from the companion website, and unzip them.
- On the ribbon, click **Insert** tab **> Reference** panel **> Attach**.

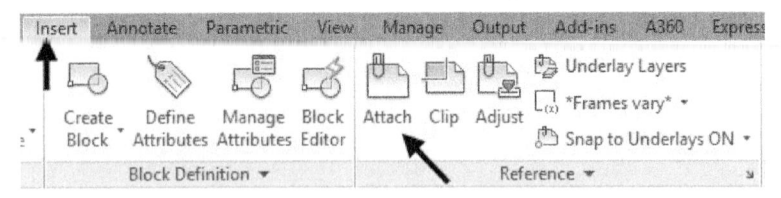

- On the **Select Reference file** dialog, set the **File of type** as **All image files**.
- Go to the location of the Reference files and double click on the **ground floor.jpg** file.
- On the **Attach Image** dialog, check the **Specify on Screen** option under the **Insertion point** section, and then click **OK**.
- Click at an arbitrary point in the graphics window, drag the pointer toward right, and then click. The image is inserted into the graphics window.
- Likewise, insert the **first floor.jpg** file.

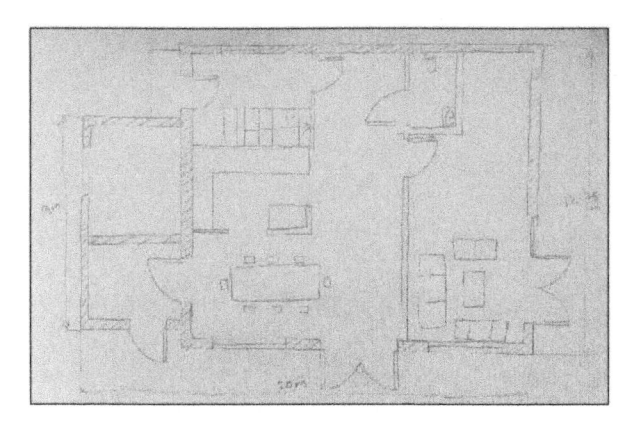

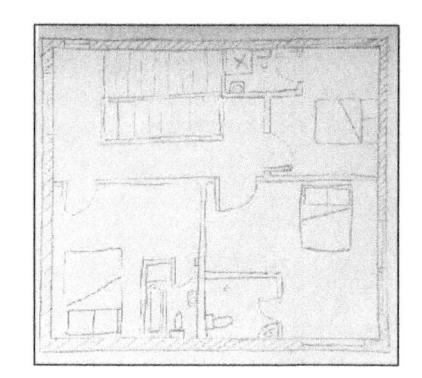

- Select the boundary edge of an image to display the **Image** tab on the ribbon. On the **Image** tab, adjust the **Fade** value to 50.

- Likewise, adjust the **Fade** value of the other image. Press Esc to deselect the image files.

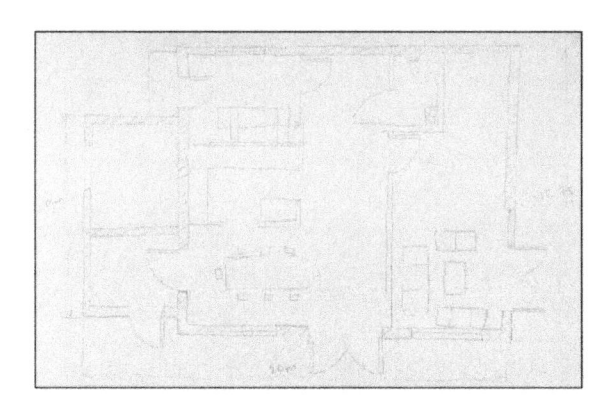

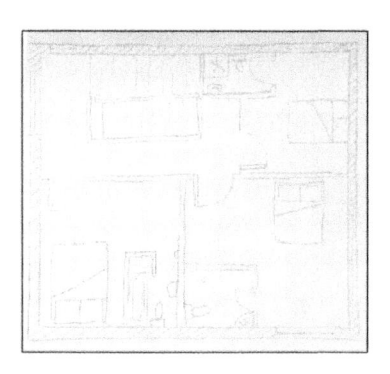

Scaling the Hand Sketches

Now, you need to scale the images as per the actual dimensions of the drawing. To do so, you need to create a reference line of 9000 mm (Length of the garage), and then scale the **groud_floor.jpg** image with respect to it.

- On the Navigation Bar, click **Zoom drop-down > Zoom Window**.

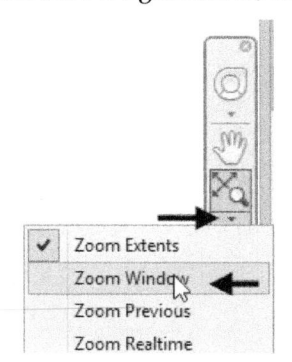

- Create a rectangular window on the left portion of the ground floor image.

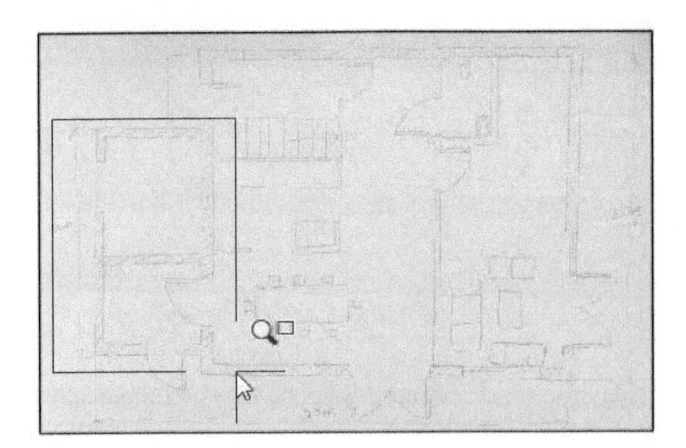

- On the status bar, activate the ORTHODMODE (F8) icon. The Orthomode will allow you to draw vertical or horizontal lines only.
- On the ribbon, click **Home** tab > **Draw** panel > **Line** (or) press **L** and Enter.

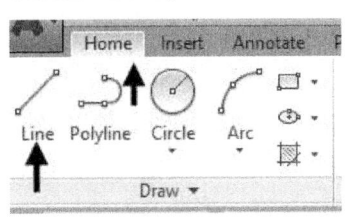

- Specify the start point of the line on the bottom left corner of sketch, as shown.

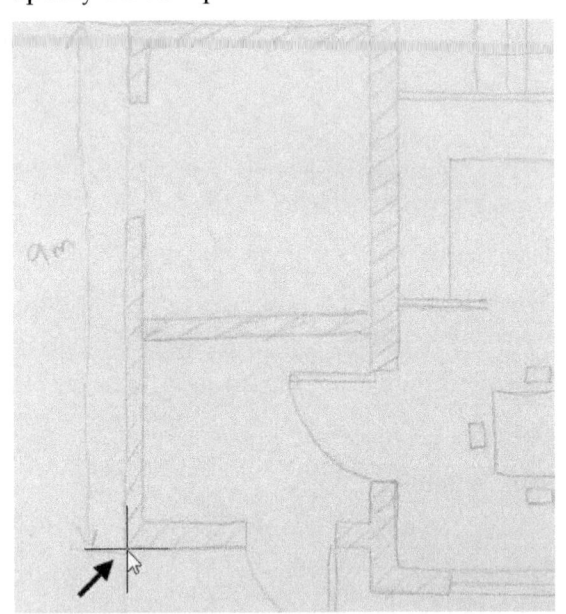

- Move the pointer up, type 9000, and press Enter.
- On the ribbon, click **Home** tab > **Modify** panel > **Scale**. The **Scale** tool is used to increase or decrease the size of an object.

5 | AutoCAD 2016 For Architectural Design

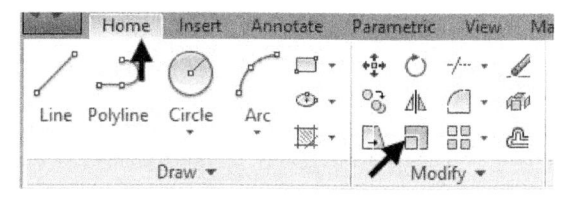

- Select the boundary of the ground floor image and press Enter.
- Select the lower end point of the line to define the base point.

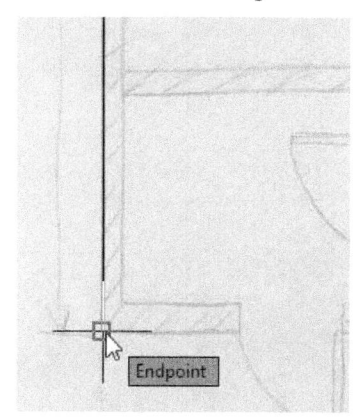

- Select **Reference** from the Command line.

Now, you need to specify the reference length by selecting two points

- Select the lower end point of the vertical line to define the start point of the reference length.
- Move the pointer up and select the second point, as shown. The reference length is defined.

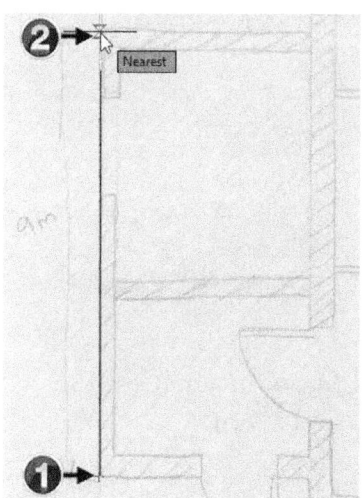

- On the Navigation Bar, click **Zoom drop-down > Zoom All**. All the objects in the graphics window will be visible.
- Move the pointer up and select the top end point of the vertical line. The ground floor image is scaled up to the reference length.

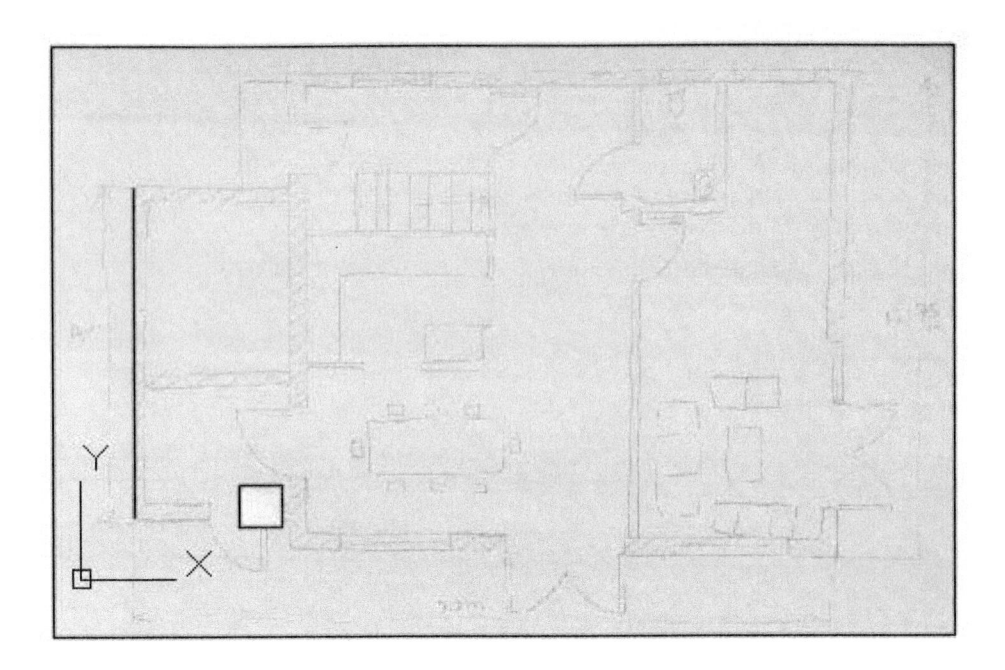

Notice that the first floor image is overlapping with the ground floor image. You need to move it outside using the **Move** tool.

- Select the first floor image. On the ribbon, click **Home** tab > **Modify** panel > **Move**. Select the bottom left corner of the image to define the base point. Move the pointer horizontally toward right, and click outside the ground floor image.

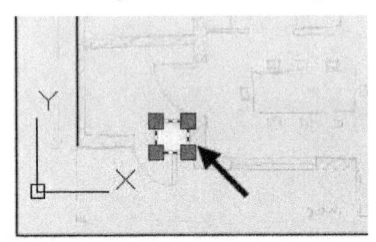

- Likewise, move the ground floor image such that it is positioned in the first quadrant of the user coordinate system.

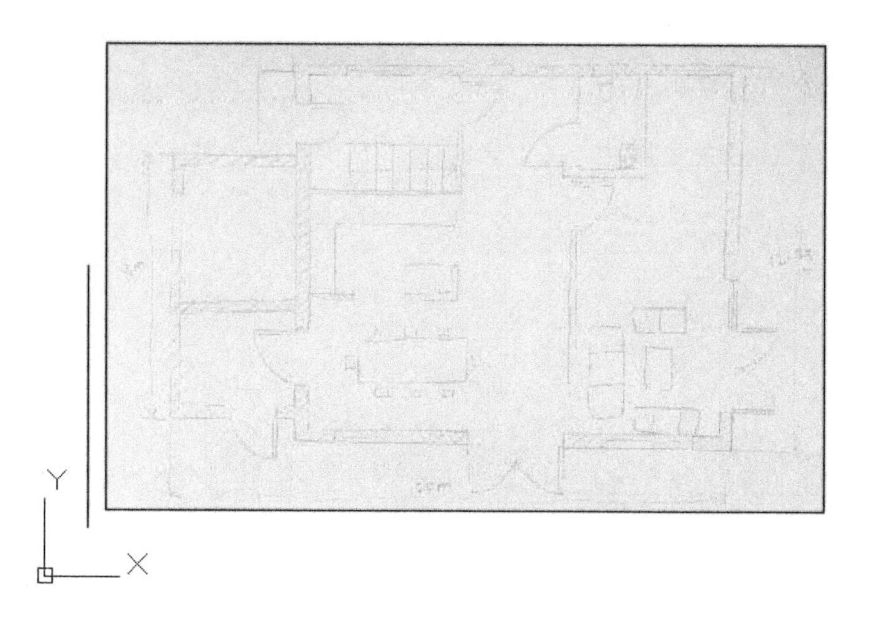

- Zoom in to the first floor image.
- Type L and press Enter to activate the **Line** command. Select the lower left corner of the hand sketch, as shown.

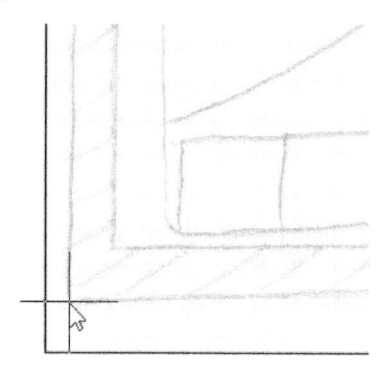

- Move the pointer upward, type 12750, and press Enter. Press Esc to deactivate the **Line** command.
- Scale the left wall of the first floor hand sketch using the newly created line.

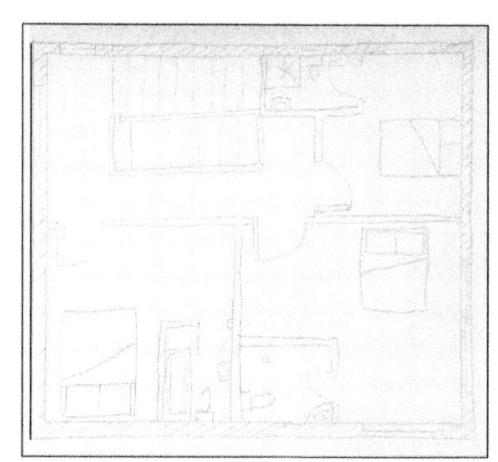

Now, you need to create a base point to be used as a reference.

- Activate the **Line** command and select the corner of the wall, as shown. Move the pointer downwards and click outside the image.

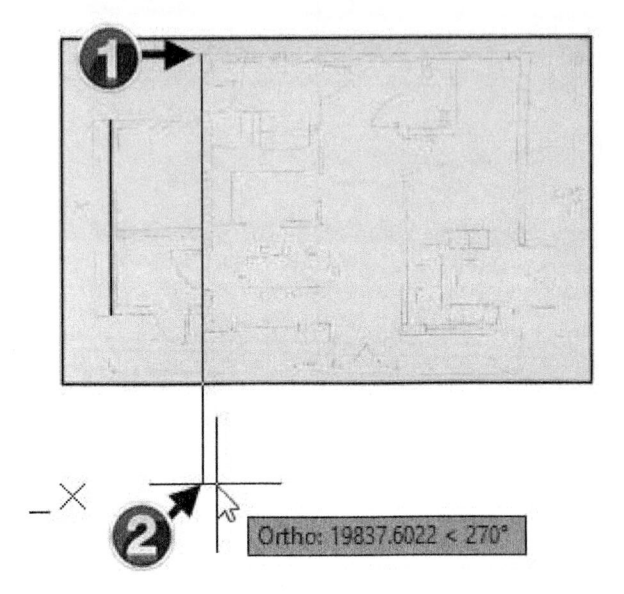

- On the ribbon, click **Home > Draw > Circle drop-down > Center, Radius**.

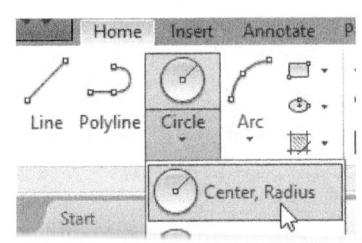

- Select the lower endpoint of the newly created line to define the center of the circle. Move the pointer outwards and click at an arbitrary point. A circle is created.

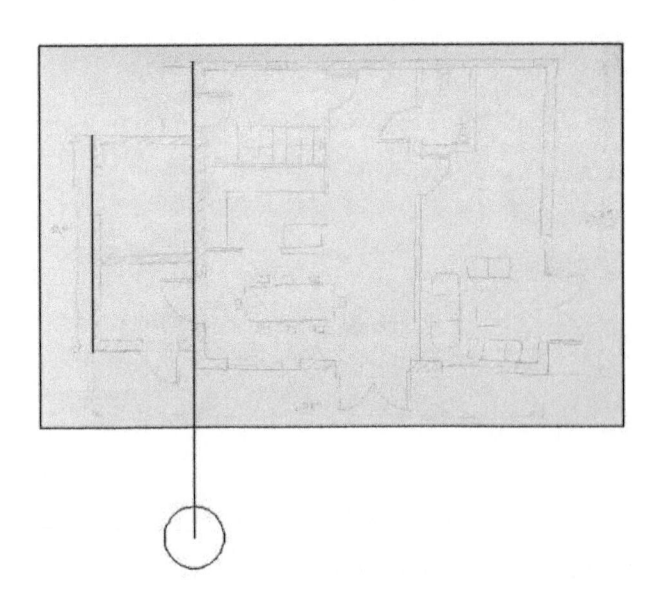

- On the status bar, click the down arrow next to the **Object Snap** icon, and select the **Quadrant** option.

9 | AutoCAD 2016 For Architectural Design

- Activate the **Line** command and select the left quadrant point of the circle. Move the pointer toward right and select the right quadrant point of the circle.

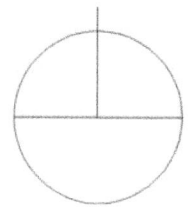

- Select the vertical line and place the pointer on the grip. Select the **Lengthen** option from the menu. Move the pointer downward and select the lower quadrant point of the circle.

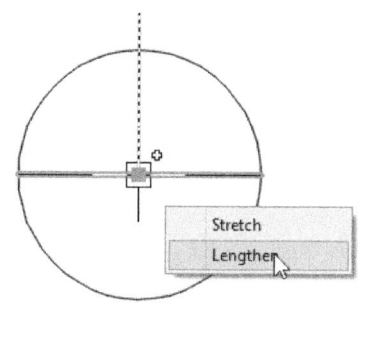

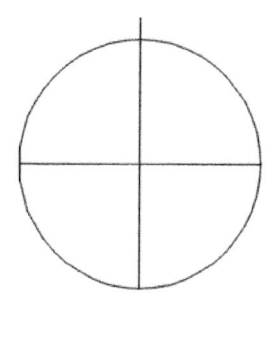

- Select the vertical line on the first floor image and press Delete. Select all the entities of the base point.

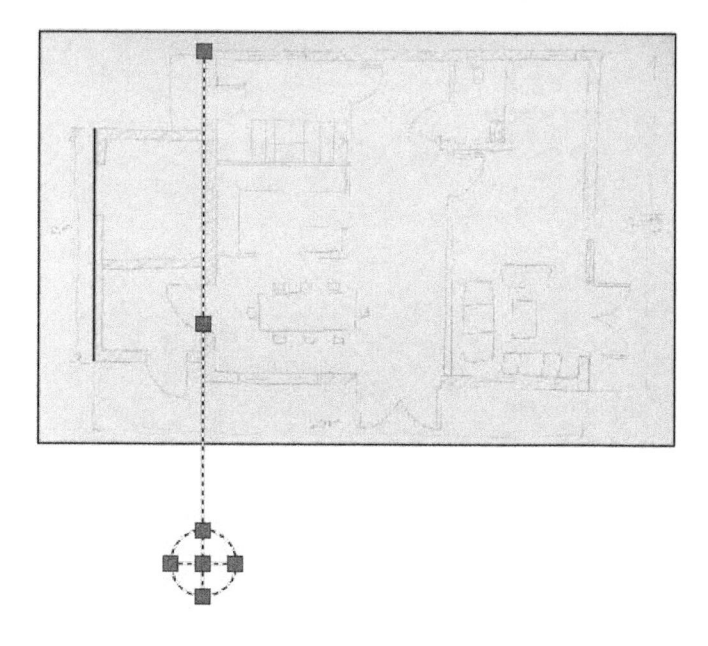

- On the ribbon, click **Home > Modify > Copy**. Select the center point of the circle to define the base point. Move the pointer toward right. Roll the mouse wheel forward to zoom into the first floor image.
- Select the extreme left wall edge to place a copy of the base reference.

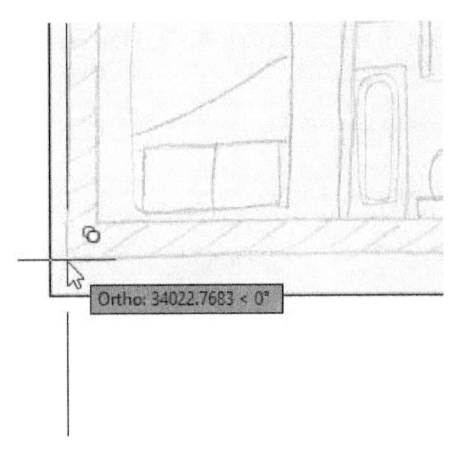

- On the **Home** tab of the ribbon, expand the **Draw** panel and click the **Construction Line** icon.

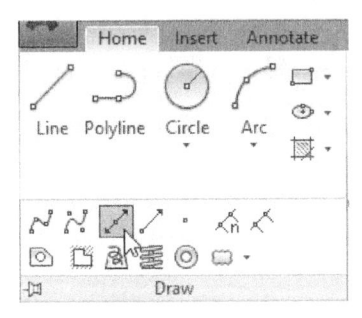

- Select **Hor** from the command line. Place the horizontal construction on the extreme top horizontal edge of the ground floor image.

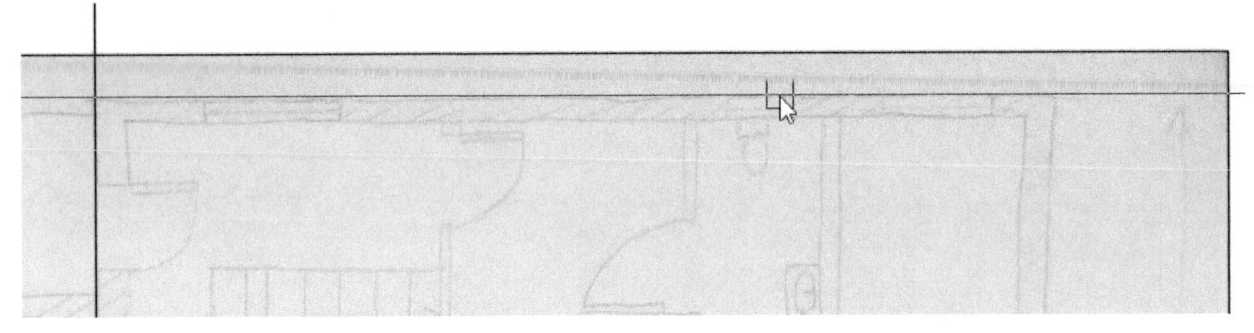

- Press Esc to deactivate the **Construction Line** command.
- Type **M** and press Enter to activate the **Move** command. Select the first floor image file and press Enter.
- Zoom in to the first floor image and select a point on the extreme top edge for plan.

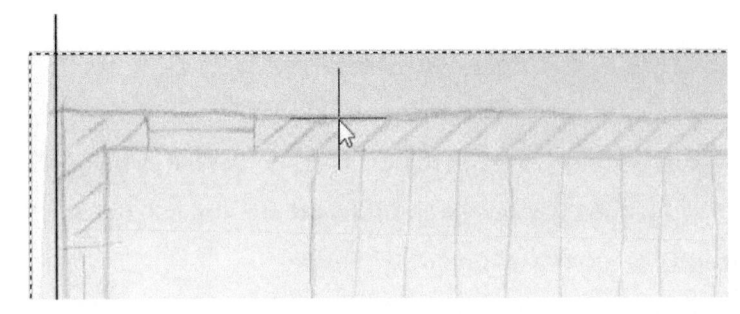

- Move the pointer upward and select the construction line. The image is aligned with the ground floor image.

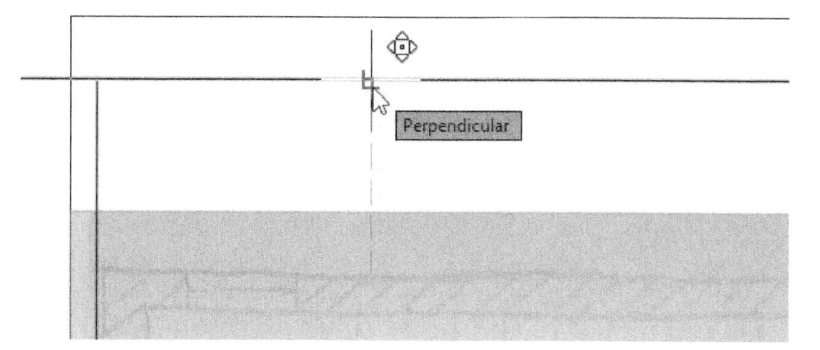

- Delete the construction line.

Saving the Document
- Click the **Save** icon on the **Quick Access Toolbar**.
- On the **Save Drawing As** dialog, use the **Save in** drop-down to define the location of the drawing.
- Click the **Create New Folder** icon on the **Save Drawing As** dialog.
- Type **Tutorial 1** in the **File name** box, and click **Save**.

Tutorial 3: Creating Layers

Layers are very important for grouping objects in a drawing. They are like a group of transparent sheets that are combined into a complete drawing. The figure below displays a drawing consisting of object lines and dimension lines. In this example, the object lines are created on the 'Object' layer, and dimensions are created on the layer called 'Dimension'. You can easily turn-off the 'Dimension' layer for a clearer view of the object lines.

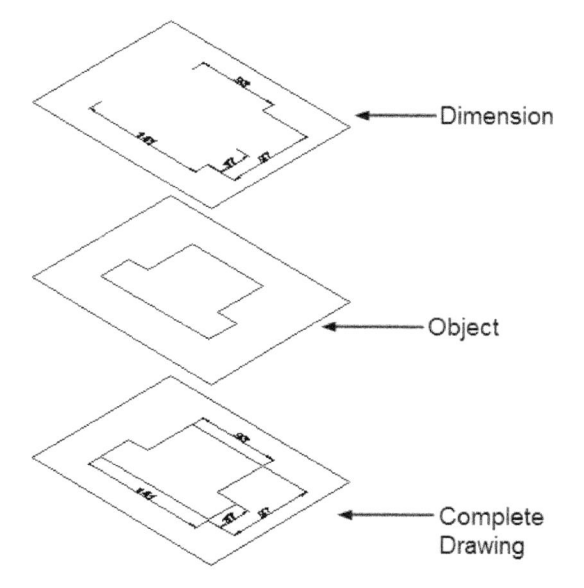

New layer — Alt + N

You can assign properties such as name, color, line weight (thickness), and linetype to a layer. The properties can vary for each layer.

- On the ribbon, click **Home tab > Layers panel > Layer Properties** .
- On the Layer Properties Manager, click **New Layer** icon located at the top left corner. Type A-WALL in the **Name** box, and press Enter.

The naming framework for layers according to United States National CAD standards is shown below.

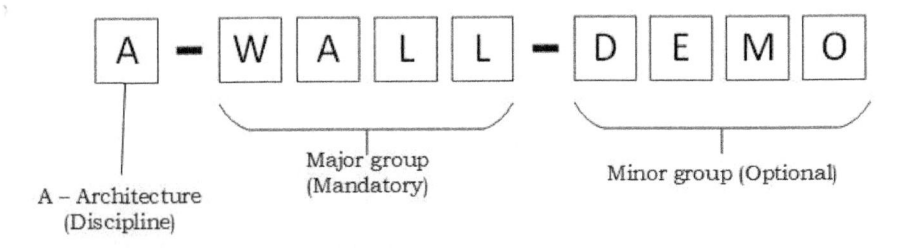

A – Architecture (Discipline)
Major group (Mandatory): WALL
Minor group (Optional): DEMO

- On the Layer Properties Manager, click the square in the **Color** column of the **A-WALL** row. On the **Select Color** dialog, select the **Cyan (4)** from the **Index color** section. Click **OK**.

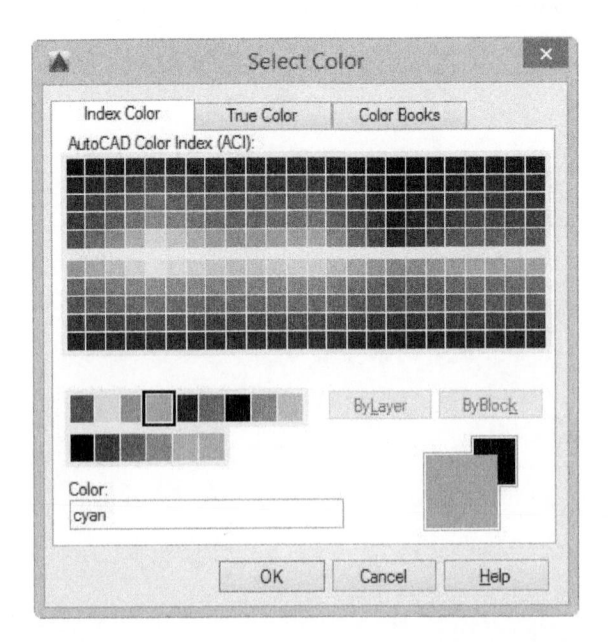

13 | AutoCAD 2016 For Architectural Design

The color assigned to a layer will determine the lineweight (thickness) of the object when you print the drawing. This condition is valid only when you use color-dependent plot style. However, you can define your own lineweight if you use a Named plot style. You can set lineweights for each color. The lineweights for different colors in this example are given below.

Color	Lineweight
Color 9	0.05 mm
Color 8	0.09 mm
Red	0.1 mm
Yellow	0.2 mm
Green	0.4 mm
Cyan	0.5 mm
Blue	0.7 mm
Magenta	1.0 mm

- Create a new layer with the A-GRID and assign the Index color 9 to it.
- On the Layer Properties Manager, click in the **Linetype** column of the **A-GRID** row. Click the **Load** button on the **Select Linetype** dialog. On the **Load or Reload Linetypes** dialog, select the DASHED linetype from the **Available Linetypes** list. Click **OK**. Select **DASHED** linetype from the **Loaded Linetypes** list and click **OK**.
- Create other layers and assign colors, as shown. Close the **Layer Properties Manager** by clicking X symbol on the top left/right corner.

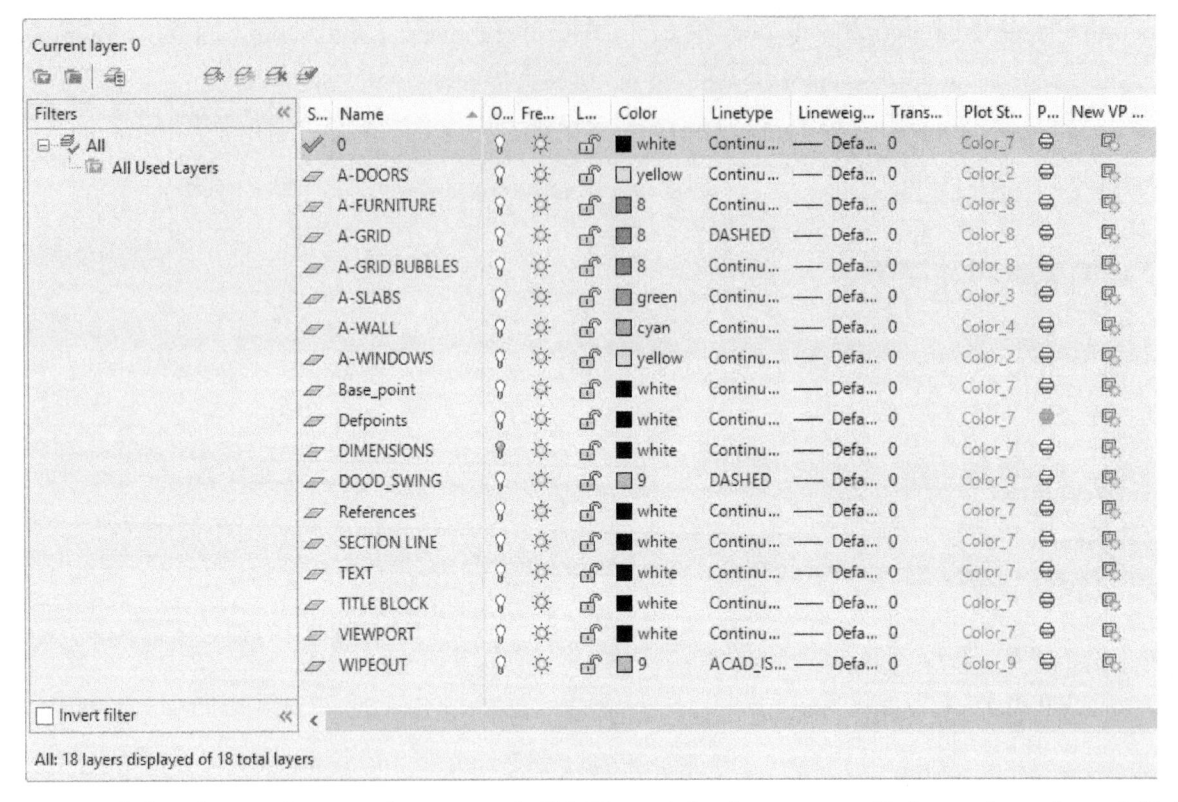

S...	Name	O...	Fre...	L...	Color	Linetype	Lineweig...	Trans...	Plot St...	P...	New VP
✓	0	☼	☀	🔓	■ white	Continu...	—— Defa...	0	Color_7	🖨	🗔
	A-DOORS	☼	☀	🔓	□ yellow	Continu...	—— Defa...	0	Color_2	🖨	🗔
	A-FURNITURE	☼	☀	🔓	■ 8	Continu...	—— Defa...	0	Color_8	🖨	🗔
	A-GRID	☼	☀	🔓	■ 8	DASHED	—— Defa...	0	Color_8	🖨	🗔
	A-GRID BUBBLES	☼	☀	🔓	■ 8	Continu...	—— Defa...	0	Color_8	🖨	🗔
	A-SLABS	☼	☀	🔓	■ green	Continu...	—— Defa...	0	Color_3	🖨	🗔
	A-WALL	☼	☀	🔓	■ cyan	Continu...	—— Defa...	0	Color_4	🖨	🗔
	A-WINDOWS	☼	☀	🔓	□ yellow	Continu...	—— Defa...	0	Color_2	🖨	🗔
	Base_point	☼	☀	🔓	■ white	Continu...	—— Defa...	0	Color_7	🖨	🗔
	Defpoints	☼	☀	🔓	■ white	Continu...	—— Defa...	0	Color_7	🖨	🗔
	DIMENSIONS	☼	☀	🔓	■ white	Continu...	—— Defa...	0	Color_7	🖨	🗔
	DOOD_SWING	☼	☀	🔓	■ 9	DASHED	—— Defa...	0	Color_9	🖨	🗔
	References	☼	☀	🔓	■ white	Continu...	—— Defa...	0	Color_7	🖨	🗔
	SECTION LINE	☼	☀	🔓	■ white	Continu...	—— Defa...	0	Color_7	🖨	🗔
	TEXT	☼	☀	🔓	■ white	Continu...	—— Defa...	0	Color_7	🖨	🗔
	TITLE BLOCK	☼	☀	🔓	■ white	Continu...	—— Defa...	0	Color_7	🖨	🗔
	VIEWPORT	☼	☀	🔓	■ white	Continu...	—— Defa...	0	Color_7	🖨	🗔
	WIPEOUT	☼	☀	🔓	■ 9	ACAD_IS...	—— Defa...	0	Color_9	🖨	🗔

- Select the two image references and click **Home** tab > **Layers** panel > **Layer** drop-down > **References** on the ribbon. The images are moved to the References layer. You can Turn OFF/ON the image references by clicking the bulb icon of the **References** layer in the **Layer** drop-down.

- Likewise, move the base points to the **Base point** layer.

Tutorial 4: Creating Grid Lines

Creating grid lines is a good starting point of an architectural design. They help you to create components of the architectural drawing easily and accurately. Now, you will create gird lines on the A-GRID layer.

- On the ribbon, click **Home** tab > **Layers** panel > **Layer** drop-down > **A-GRID**.

- On the ribbon, click **Home** tab > **Modify** panel > **Offset**. Type 160 and press Enter. Select the base point line of the ground floor. Move the pointer toward right and click to create an offset line.

- Select the offset line and click **Home** tab > **Layers** panel > **Layer** drop-down > **A-GRID** on the ribbon. The offset line is moved to the A-GRID layer.

- Select the offset line, type PR and press Enter (or) click the inclined arrow located on the bottom right corner of the **Properties** panel. On the **Properties** palette, under the **General** section, set the **Linetype scale** to 20. The linetype scale of the selected line is set to 20. Click the **Auto-hide** icon on the **Properties** palette to hide it.

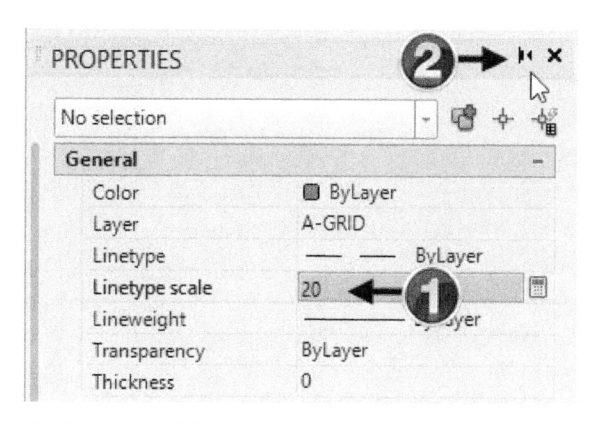

- Activate the ORTHOMODE (F8) icon on the status bar.
- On the ribbon, click **Home** tab > **Utilities** panel > **Measure**. Select a point on the base point line of the ground floor plan. Move the pointer toward right and select the inner wall edge, as shown. The measurement shows a distance of 5644. Press Esc to deactivate the **Measure** tool.

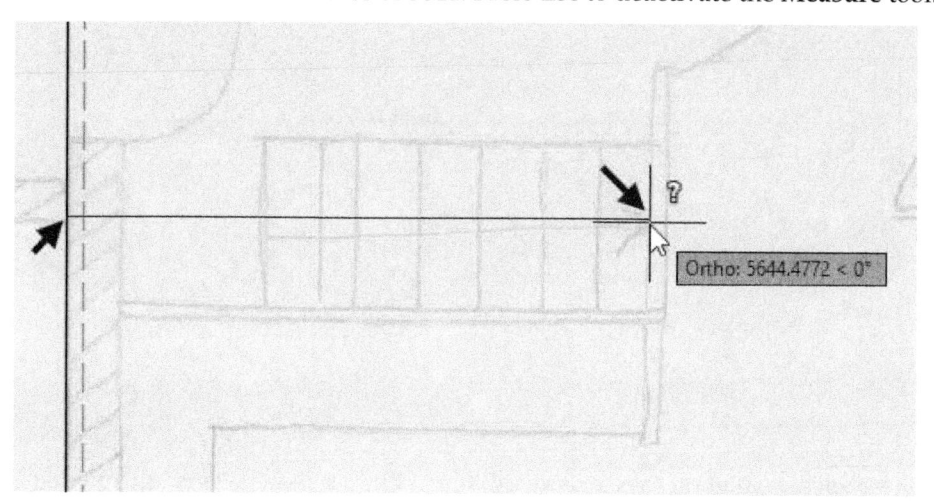

- Type O and press Enter. Type 5600 and press Enter to define the offset distance. Select the first grid line, move the pointer toward right and click. Select **Exit** from the command line.

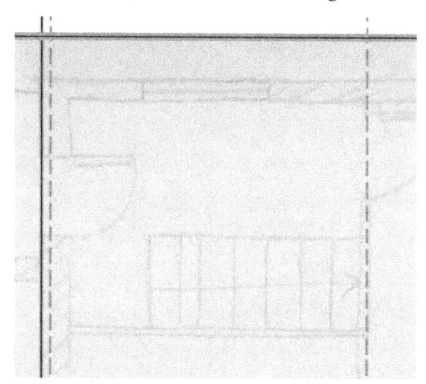

- Likewise, create other grid lines by offsetting the first one. You can use the **Measure** tool to measure the offset distances.

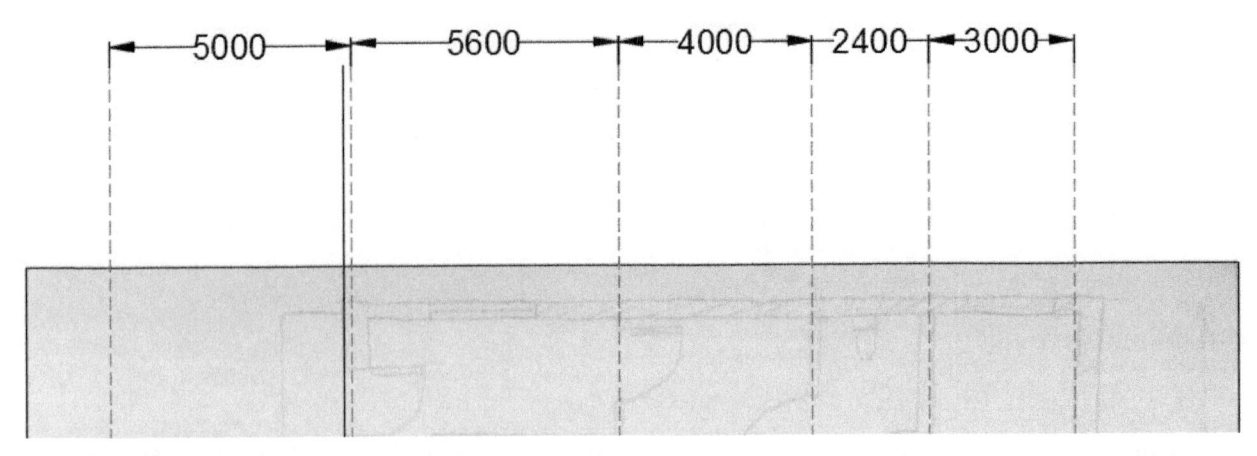

- Select the second grid line from the right hand side. Click the lower end point grip and move the pointer upward. The length of the line is reduced.
- Likewise, drag down the upper end point grip to shorten the grid line, as shown.

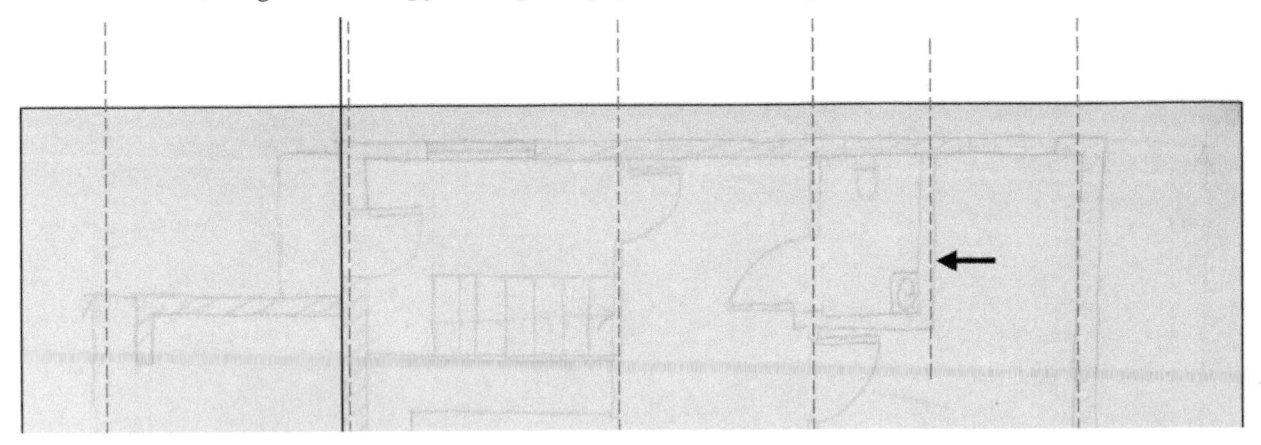

- Type L and press Enter. Select a point on the extreme right grid line, as shown. Move the pointer toward left and click outside the image.

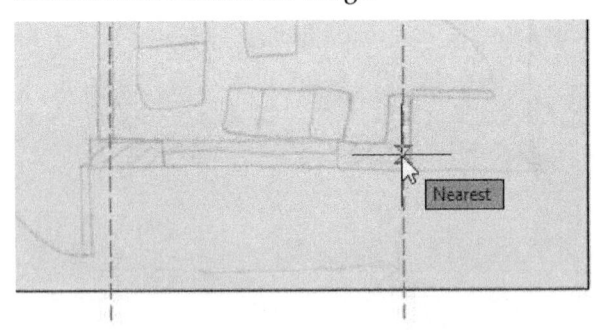

- Select the horizontal grid line and drag the endpoints to stretch it outside the image.

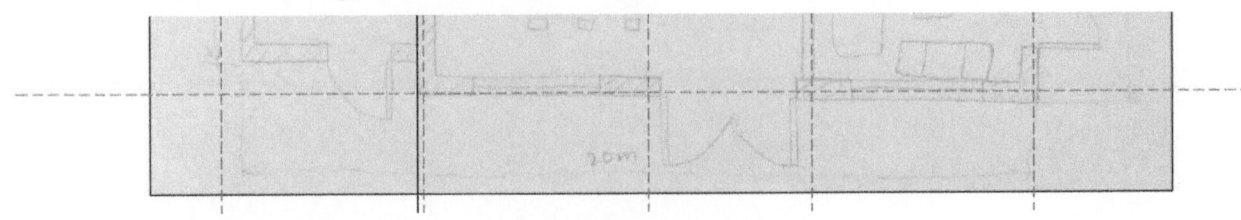

- Create other horizontal gird lines by using the **Offset** tool.

AutoCAD 2016 For Architectural Design

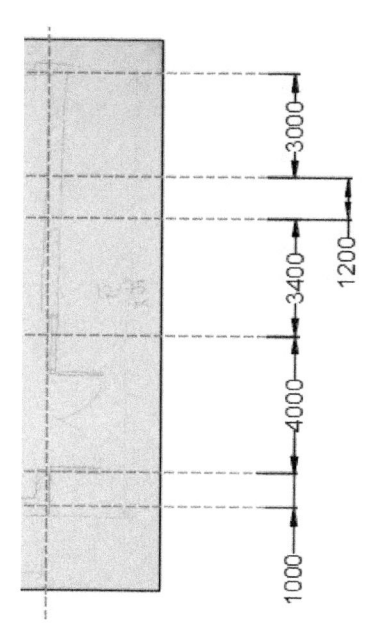

- Modify the grid lines by using the line grips.

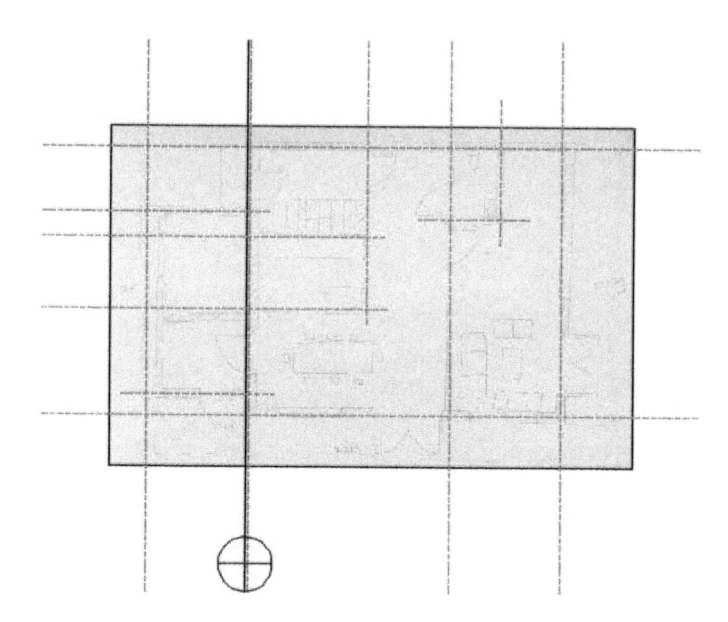

Tutorial 5: Creating Walls

AutoCAD offers many tools to create walls. Now, you will learn to create walls using various tools.

- On the ribbon, click **Home** tab > **Layers** panel > **Layer** drop-down > **A-WALL**.
- On the ribbon, click **Home** tab > **Modify** panel > **Offset**. Select the **Layer** option from the command line. Select the **Current** option from the command line. Type 160 in the command line and press Enter. Select the top most grid line, as shown. Move the pointer downwards and click to create an offset line in the current layer. Again, select the same grid line, move the pointer upward and click to create another offset line.

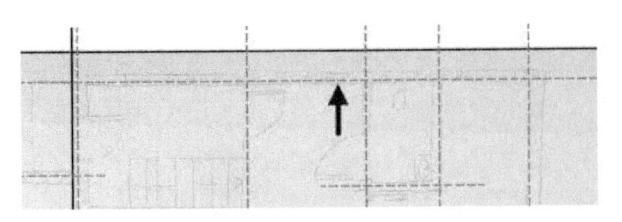

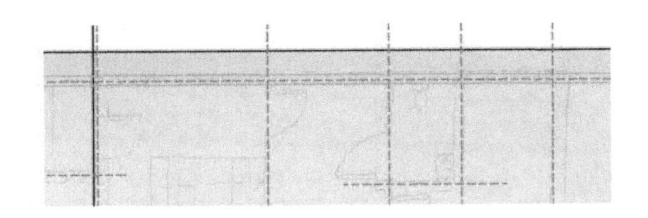

- Likewise, create other offset lines, as shown.

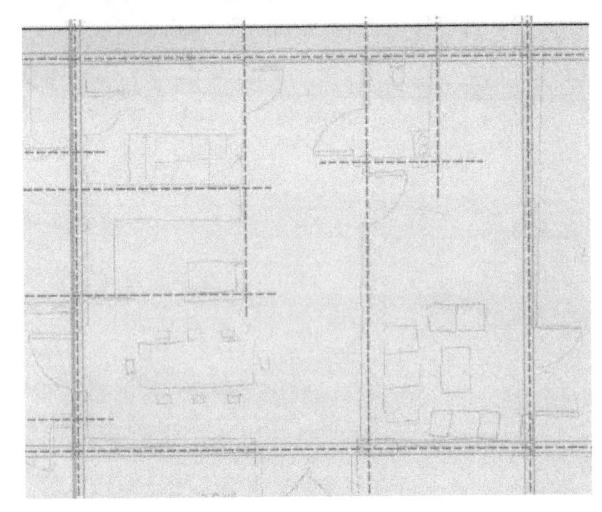

- On the ribbon, click **Home** tab > **Modify** panel > **Fillet**. Select the offset lines forming a corner, as shown. Note that you need to click on the portions of the lines forming the inside corner.

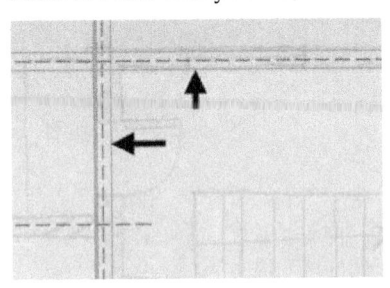

- Likewise, fillet the other corners, as shown.

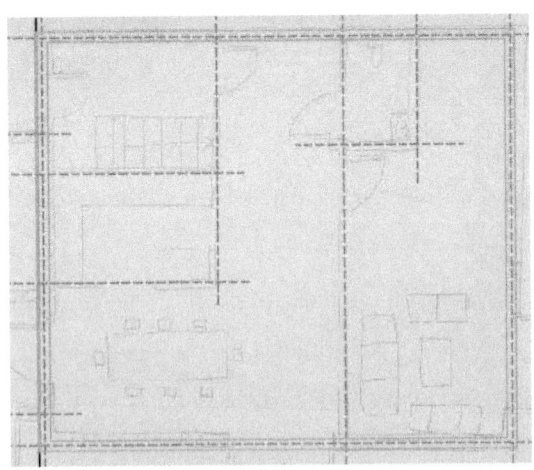

- On the status bar, click the down arrow next to the **Object Snap** icon and select **Intersection** from the menu.

- On the ribbon, click **Home** tab > **Draw** panel > **Polyline**. Zoom to the left hand side of the drawing and select the intersection point between the grid line of the garage and the wall edge. Select the other intersection points, as shown.

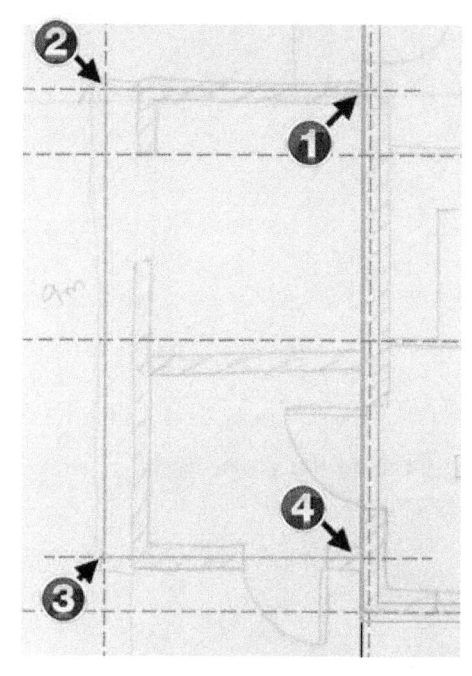

- Type O and press Enter. Again, press Enter to accept 160 as the offset distance. Select the polyline, move the pointer up and click. Again, select the polyline, move the pointer downward, and click. Press Esc to deactivate the **Offset** tool.

- Select the polyline coinciding with the grid line and press Delete.

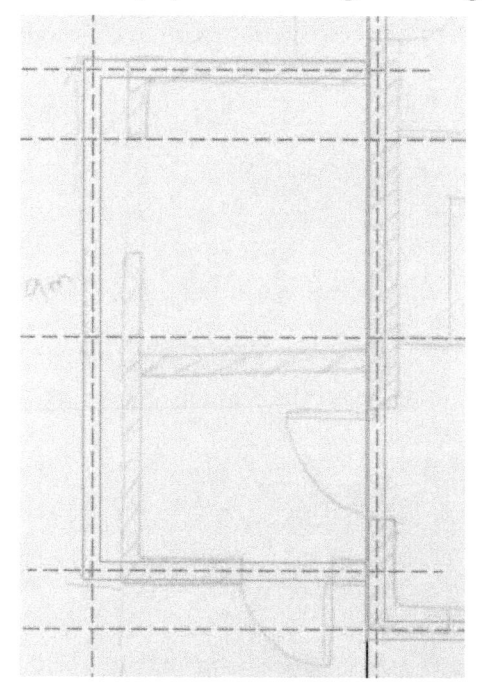

- Use the **Offset** tool to create a wall in the garage, as shown.

- On the ribbon, click **Home** tab > **Modify** panel > **Trim**. Select the two polylines, as shown. Press Enter to accept the selected entities as trimming boundaries. Select the portions to be trimmed, as shown. Press Esc to deactivate the **Trim** command.

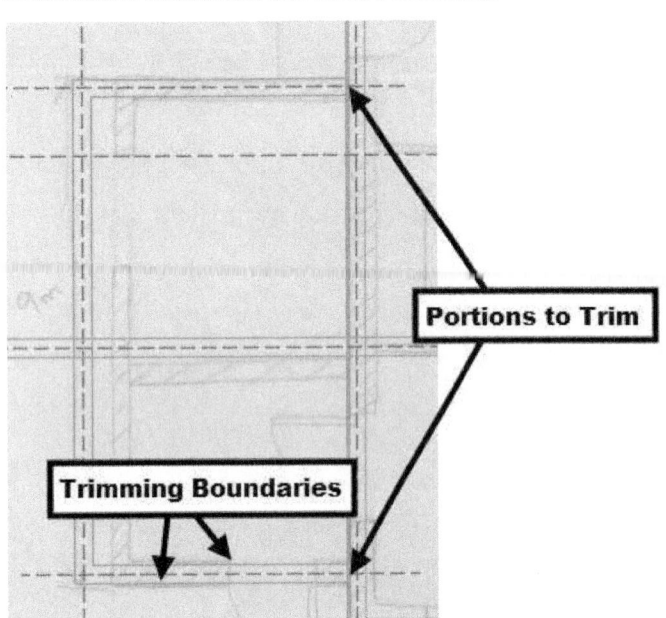

- On the ribbon, click **Home** tab > **Modify** panel > **Trim**. Select the inner edges of the walls, as shown. Press Enter to accept the selected entities as trimming boundaries. Select the portions to trim, as shown. Press Esc to deactivate the **Trim** command.

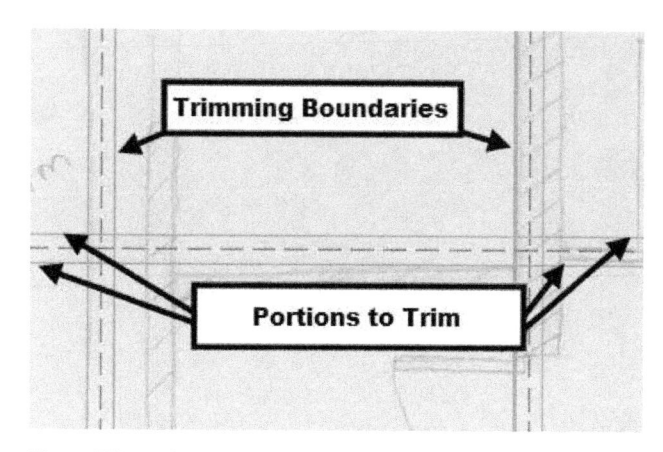

- Type TR and press Enter. Select the edges of the horizontal wall, and press Enter. Select the portions of the wall edges, as shown. Press Esc to deactivate the **Trim** tool.

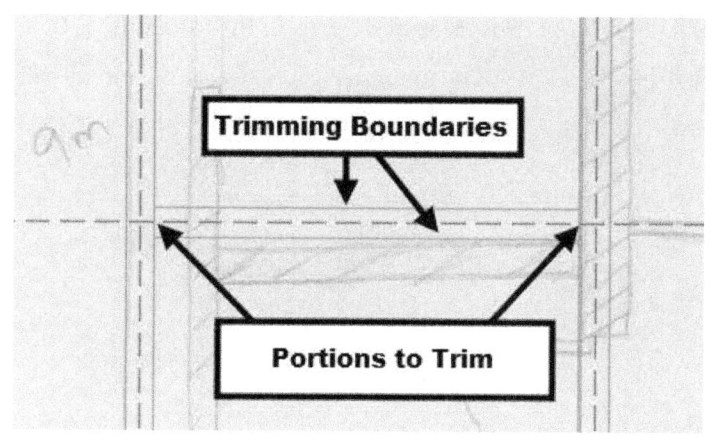

- Type ML and press Enter to activate the MULTILINE command. This command creates two parallel lines when you specify points in the graphics window.
- Select **Justification** from the command line. Select the **Zero** option to create the multi lines on both sides of the origin point. The **Top** and **Bottom** options align the origin point with the top and bottom lines, respectively.
- Select the **Scale** option from the command line. Type 150 and press Enter to define the distance between the lines. Select the start and end points of the multi-line, as shown. Press Esc.

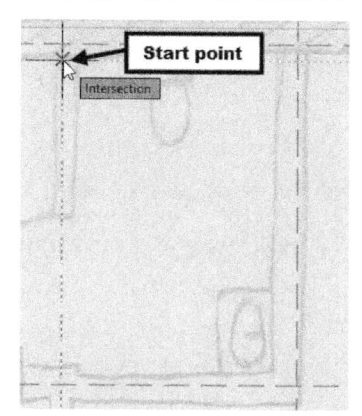

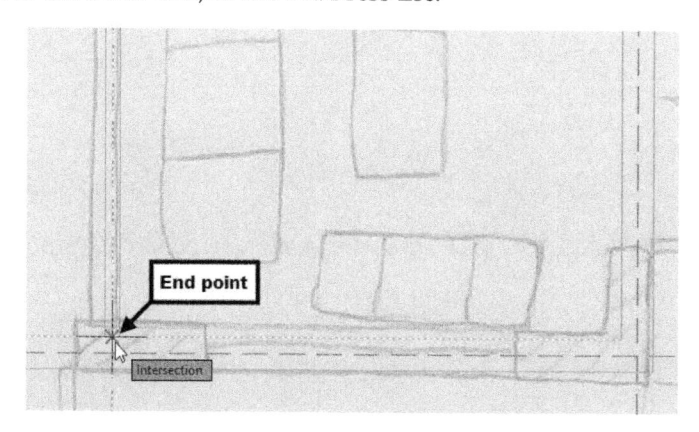

- Activate the MULTILINE command and create the bathroom wall, as shown.

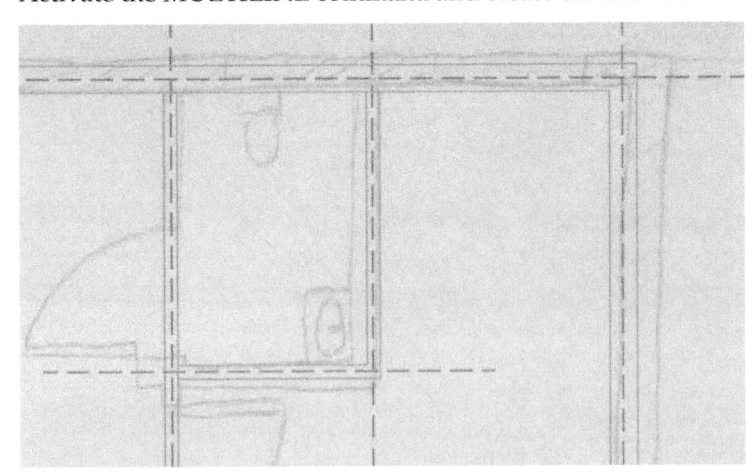

- Type **MLEDIT** in the command line and press Enter. Select **Open Tree** from the **Multiline Edit Tools** dialog. Select the two multi-lines in the order, as shown. The open tree is created at the intersection. Press Esc to deactivate the MLEDIT command.

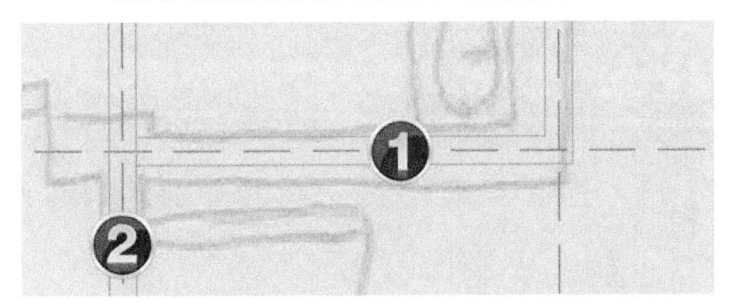

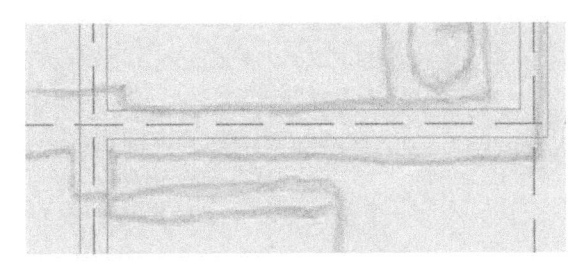

- Likewise, create the other walls and trim the unwanted portions at the intersections, as shown.

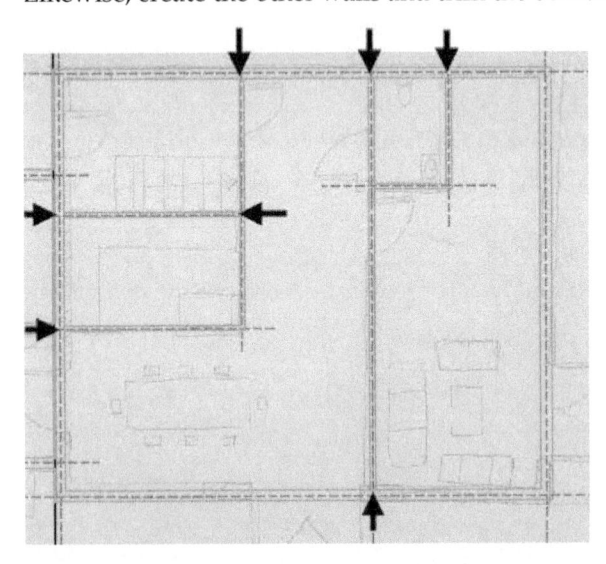

- On the ribbon, click **Home** tab > **Modify** panel > **Explode**. Select the multi-lines and press Enter. The multi-lines are exploded into individual lines.

Tutorial 6: Creating Doors and Windows

- On the ribbon, click **Home** tab > **Layers** panel > **Layer** drop-down > **A-DOORS**.
- On the ribbon, click **Home** tab > **Draw** panel > **Rectangle**. Define the first corner of the rectangle by selecting an arbitrary point in the empty space.
- Select **Dimensions** from the command line. Type 65 and press Enter to define the length of the rectangle. Type 100 and press Enter to define the width of the rectangle. Move the pointer up and click to create the rectangle.

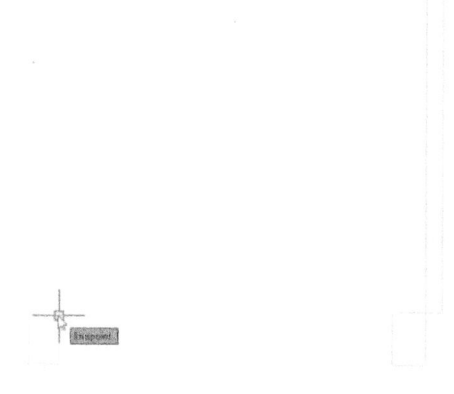

- Type REC and press Enter. Select the top right corner of the rectangle to define the first corner of the rectangle. Select **Dimensions** from the command line. Type 30 and press Enter to define the length of the rectangle. Type 610 and press Enter to define the width of the rectangle. Move the pointer up and click to create the rectangle.

- Select the small rectangle and click **Home** tab > **Modify** panel > **Copy** on the ribbon. Make sure that the **Endpoint** option is checked on the **Object Snap** menu of the status bar.
- Select the bottom left corner of the rectangle to define the base point. Move the pointer toward right, type 675, and press Enter.

24 | AutoCAD 2016 For Architectural Design

- On the ribbon, click **Home** tab > **Layers** panel > **Layer** drop-down > **DOORS_SWING**.
- On the ribbon, click **Home** tab > **Draw** panel > **Arc** drop-down > **Start, Center, End**. Specify the start, center, and end points of the arc, as shown.

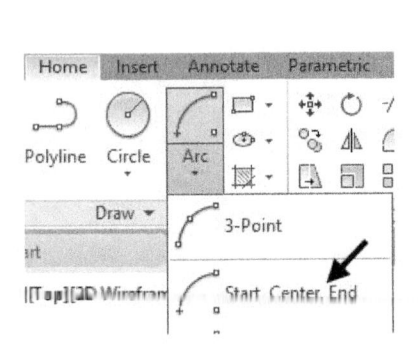

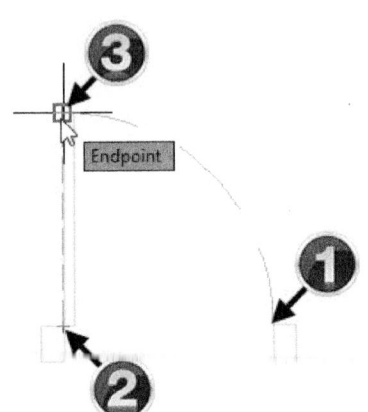

- Select the arc and press CTRL+1. On the **Properties** palette, under the **General** section, set the Linetype scale. Press Esc.

- On the ribbon, click **Home** tab > **Layers** panel > **Layer** drop-down > **A-WALL**. Create two vertical lines of 320 length, as shown.

25 | AutoCAD 2016 For Architectural Design

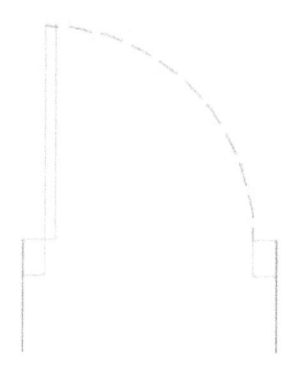

Now, you need to use the **Wipeout** tool to hide the wall edges at the door openings.

- On the ribbon, click **Home** tab > **Layers** panel > **Layer** drop-down > **WIPEOUT**. On the **Home** tab of the ribbon, expand the **Draw** panel and click the **Wipeout** icon. Select the endpoints of the vertical lines in the order, as shown. Select **Close** from the command line.

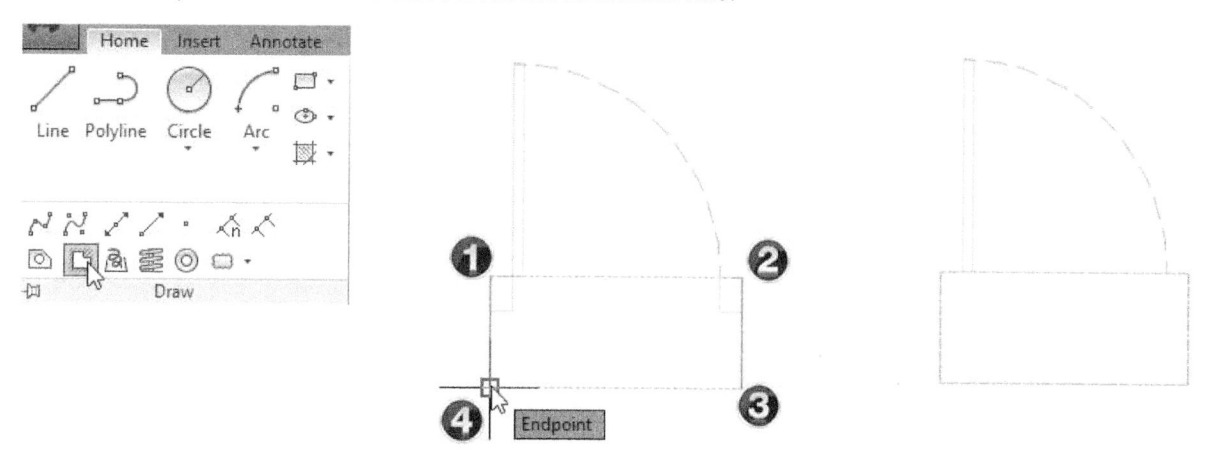

- Select the wipeout frame, right click, and select **Draw Order > Send to Back**. The wipeout is sent back, and the wall edges and door frame are displayed.

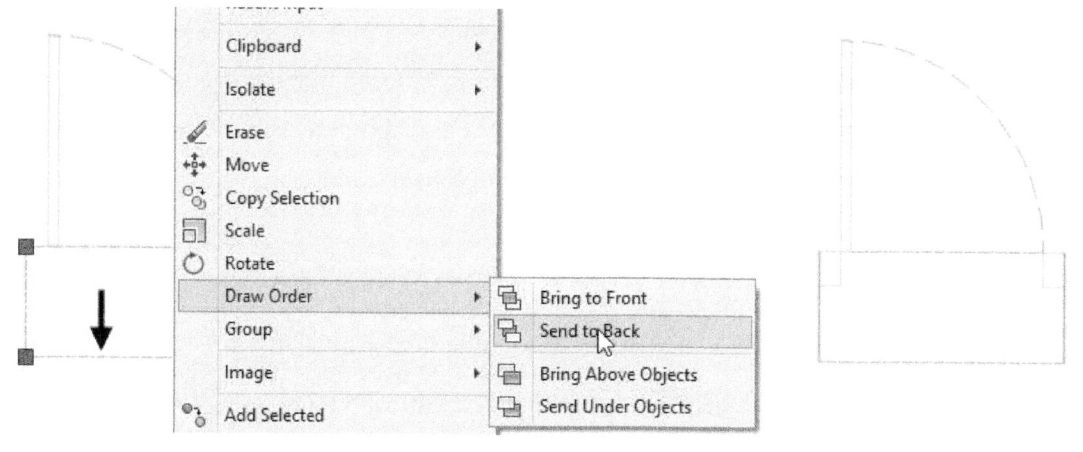

You need to make sure that the wipeout thickness is more than the wall thickness.

- Select the wipeout to highlight its grips at the corners. Select the top right corner grip of the wipeout and move the pointer vertically upward. Type 10 and press Enter. Likewise, extend the top left corner grip by 10 mm upwards.

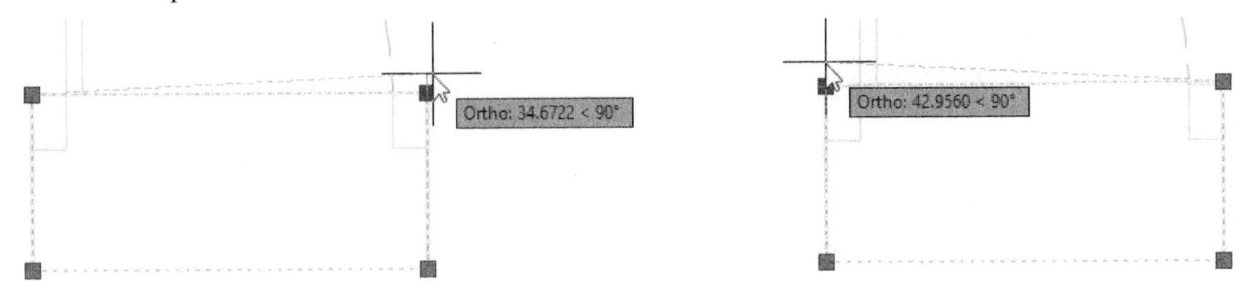

- Likewise, extend the wipeout in the opposite direction.
- On the ribbon, click **Insert** tab > **Block Definition** panel > **Create Block** > **Write Block**. On the **Write Block** dialog, click the **Select objects** icon. Specify the first and second corners of the selection window covering all the entities of the door. Click the **Pick point** icon and select the top left corner point of the wipeout frame. The base point of the block is defined.

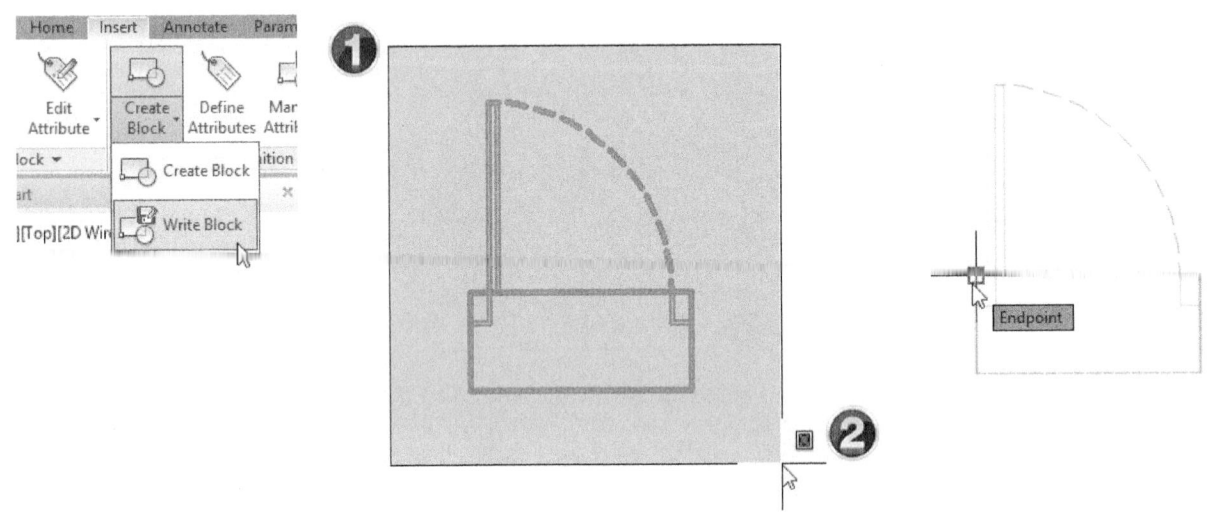

- Click the icon next to the **File name and path** box. Go to the folder location where you saved the **Tutorial 1** drawing file. Type **Single_Door** in the **File name** box and click **Save**. Select **Convert to block** from the **Objects** section and click **OK**. The selected objects are converted into blocks.

Now, you need to convert the block into a dynamic block. By doing so, you can change the size, shape and orientation of the block, dynamically.

- On the ribbon, click **Insert** tab > **Block Definition** panel > **Block Editor**. On the **Edit Block Definition** dialog, select **Single_Door** from the **Block to create or edit** list, and click **OK**. The **Block Editor** window appears.
- On the Block Authoring Palettes, click the **Parameter** tab and select **Linear**. Specify the start and

AutoCAD 2016 For Architectural Design

endpoints of the linear parameter, as shown. Move the pointer toward left and position the parameter. Select the **Distance 1** parameter and press CTRL+1 to open the **Properties** palette. On the **Properties** palette, under the **Property Labels** section, set the **Distance name** to **Wall Thickness**.

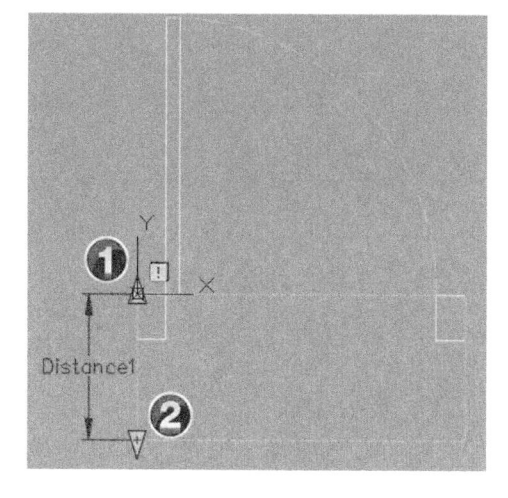

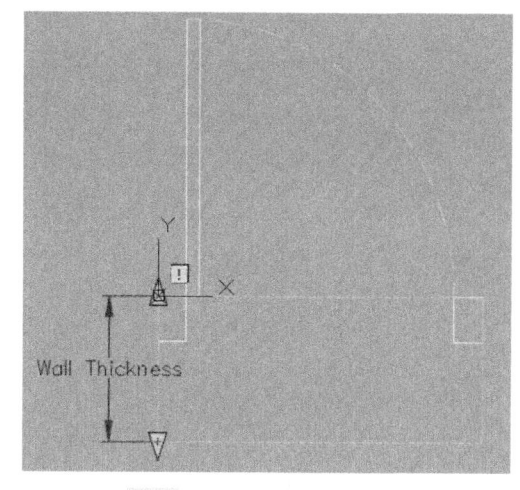

- On the Block Authoring Palettes, click the **Actions** tab and select **Stretch**. Select the **Wall Thickness** parameter. Select the endpoint of the **Wall Thickness** parameter. Specify the first corner of the stretch frame, as shown. Press and hold the left mouse button and drag the pointer. Click to specify the opposite corner of the stretch frame, as shown. Select the two vertical lines and press Enter to specify the objects to be stretched. The **Stretch** action appears at the bottom of the **Wall Thickness** parameter.

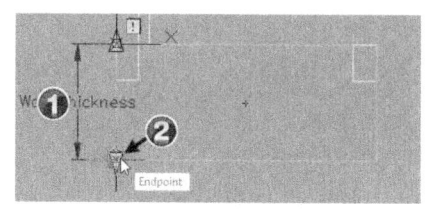

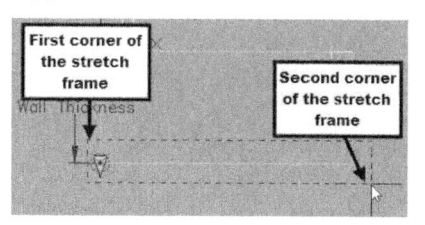

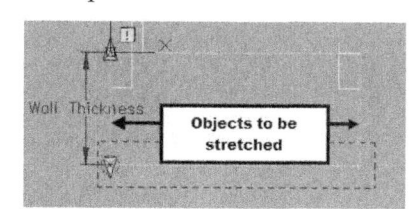

- On the **Block Editor** tab of the ribbon, click **Open/Save** panel > **Test Block**. Select the vertical line of the door and drag the arrow grip. Notice that the wall thickness changes, dynamically. On the ribbon, click the **Close Test Block** icon.

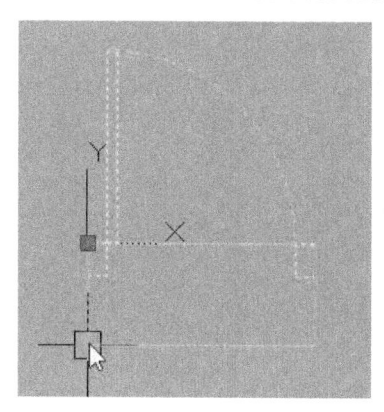

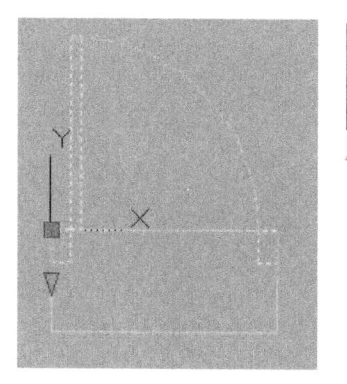

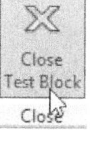

- Create a **Linear** parameter between the inside edges of the door frames, and then change its name to Door

28 | AutoCAD 2016 For Architectural Design

Width. On the Block Authoring Palettes, click **Action** tab > **Stretch**. Select the Door Width parameter, and then select its end point. Create the stretch frame on the right side of the block, as shown. Select the right vertical line, door frame, and wipeout frame as the objects to stretch. Press Enter.

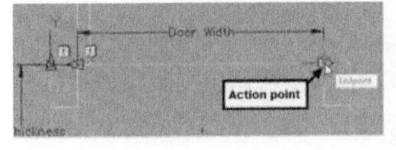

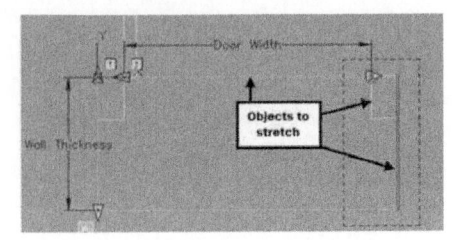

- On the Block Authoring Palettes, click **Action** tab > **Scale**. Select the Door Width parameter and the arc. Press Enter to create the **Scale** action.

- On the Block Authoring Palettes, click **Action** tab > **Stretch**. Select the Door Width parameter, and then select its end point. Create the stretch frame on the top portion of the door panel, as shown. Select the door panel and press Enter.

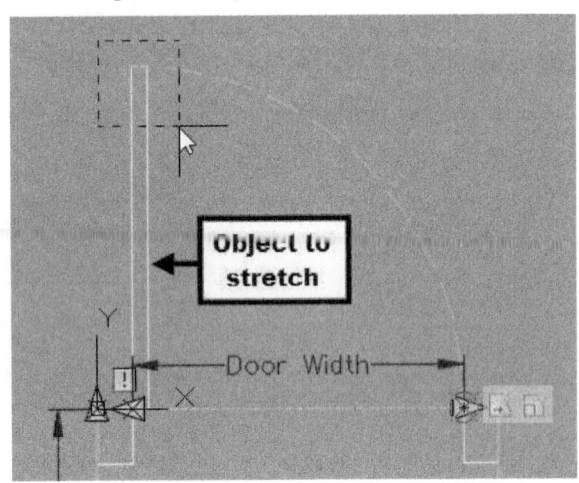

- On the **Block Editor** tab of the ribbon, click **Open/Save** panel > **Test Block**. Select the block and drag the arrow pointing toward right. Notice that the door width and door swing are modified. However, the door panel is skewed. Click **Close Test Block** on the ribbon.

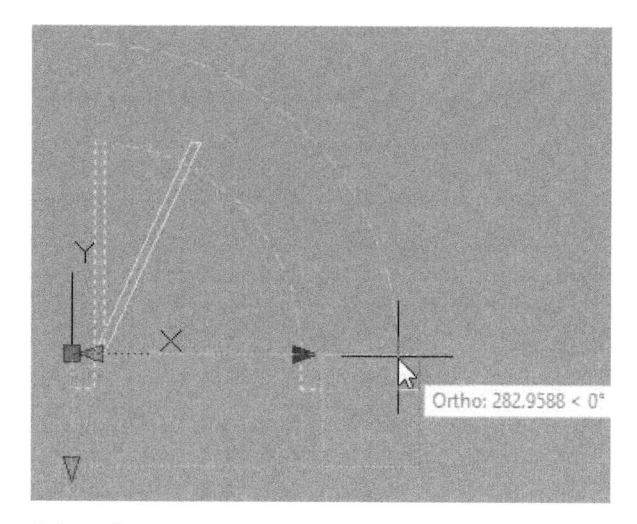

- Select the extreme right **Stretch** icon. On the **Properties** palette, under the **Overrides** section, change the **Angle offset** value to 90. Press Esc. Open the **Test Block Window** and drag the arrow grip pointing toward right. Notice that the block changes as desired. However, the size of the door can be changed to any non-standard value. Click **Close Test Block** on the ribbon.

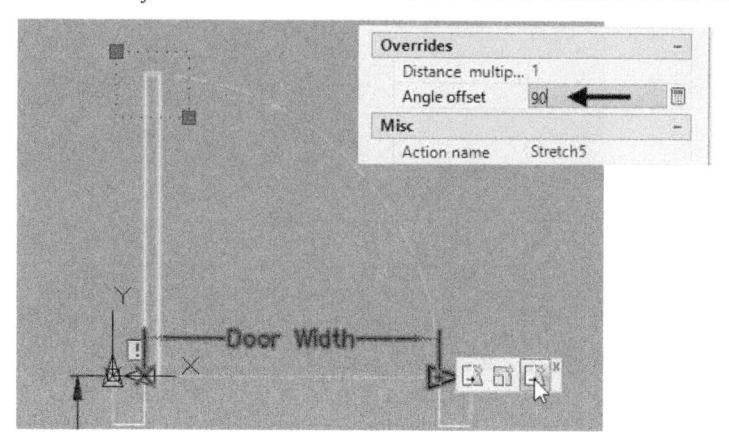

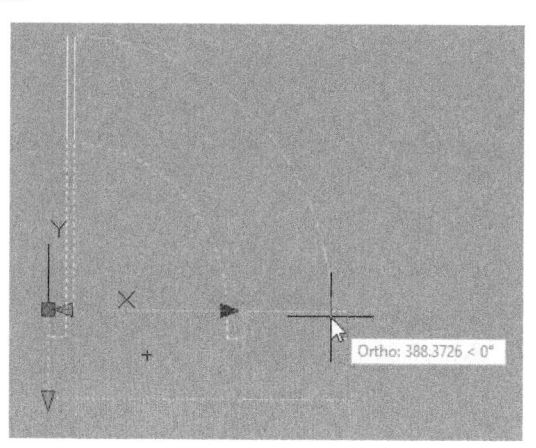

If you want the door to have some standard sizes, you need to change the **Dist type** of the Door Width parameter to **List**.

- Select the Door Width parameter. On the **Properties** palette, under the **Value Set** section, change the **Dist type** to **List**. Click in the **Dist value list** box and select the icon located next to it. On the **Add Distance Value** dialog, type 826 in the **Distance to add** box and press Enter. Likewise, add other values to the list, as shown. Click **OK** to close the dialog.

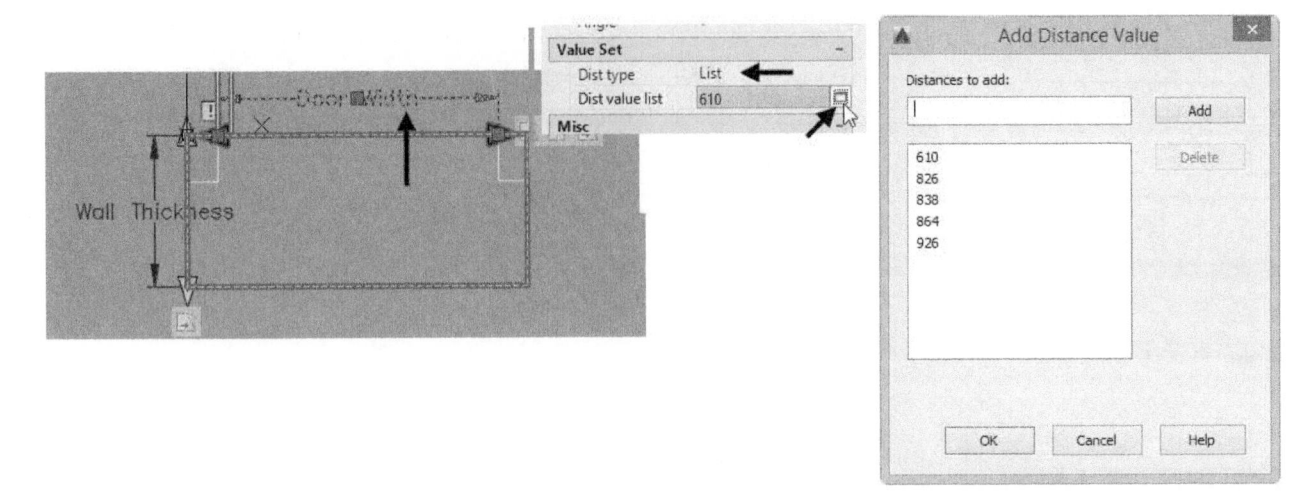

- Open the Test Block Window and modify the Door Width parameter. Notice the intervals displayed while dragging the stretch arrow. You can change the door width using the intervals. Click **Close Test Block** on the ribbon.

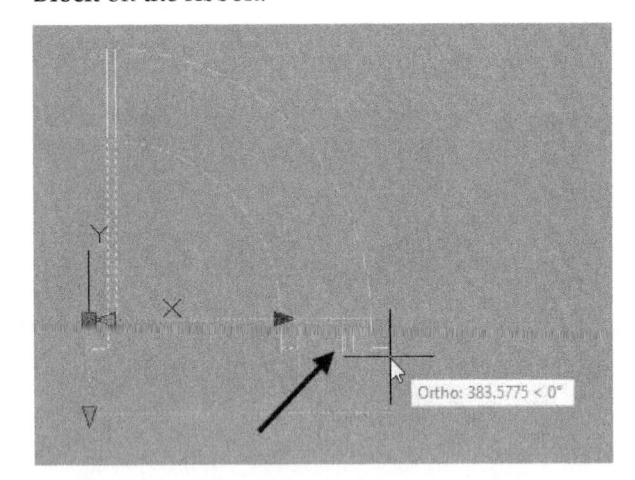

- Click **Close Block Editor** on the ribbon. Click **Save the changes** on the **Block-Save Parameter changes?** Dialog.
- On the ribbon, click **Home** tab > **Layers** panel > **Layer** drop-down > **A-DOOR**.
- On the ribbon, click **Insert** tab > **Block** panel > **Insert** drop-down > **Single_Door**. Select **Rotate** from the command line, type 90 and press Enter. Select the intersection point between the grid and the bathroom wall, as shown. Select the base point of the block and move the pointer up. Type 375 and press Enter.

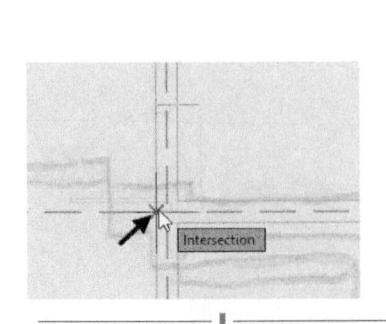

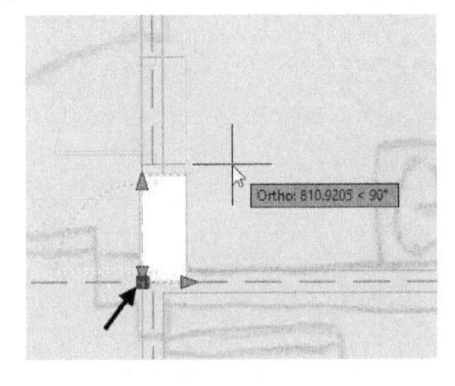

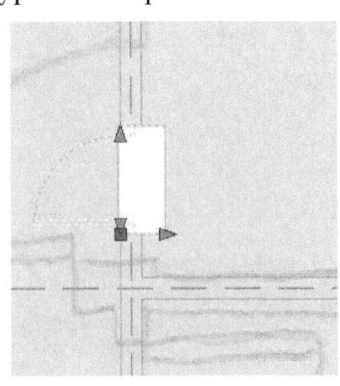

31 | AutoCAD 2016 For Architectural Design

- Click the stretch arrow pointing toward right. Drag the pointer toward left and select a point on the wall edge, as shown.

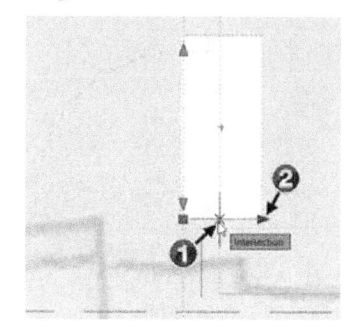

- Click the stretch arrow pointing upwards. Drag the pointer upward and click at the interval, as shown.

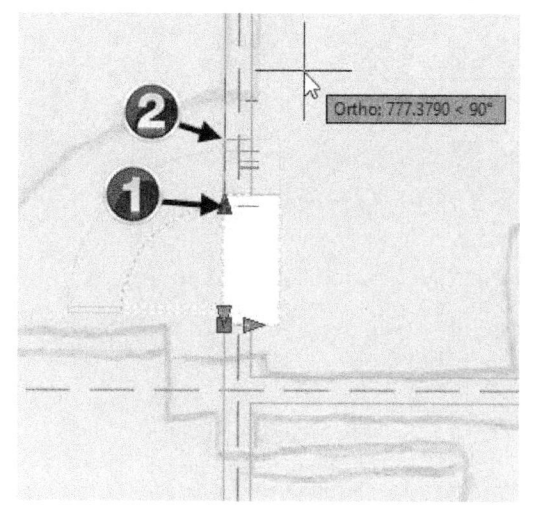

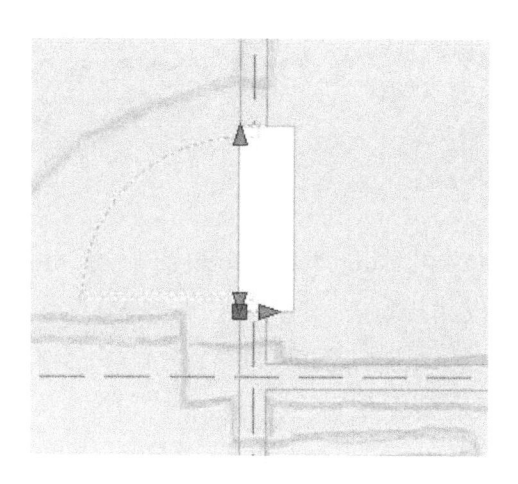

- On the **Home** tab of the ribbon, expand the **Draw** panel and click the Wipeout icon. Select **Frame** from the command line. Select the **OFF** option to turn off the wipeout frame.

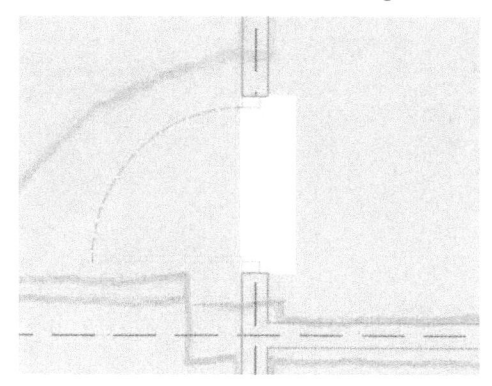

- Likewise, insert other instances of the Single_Door blocks, as shown. Note that you need to flip the Single_Door block at the utility room.

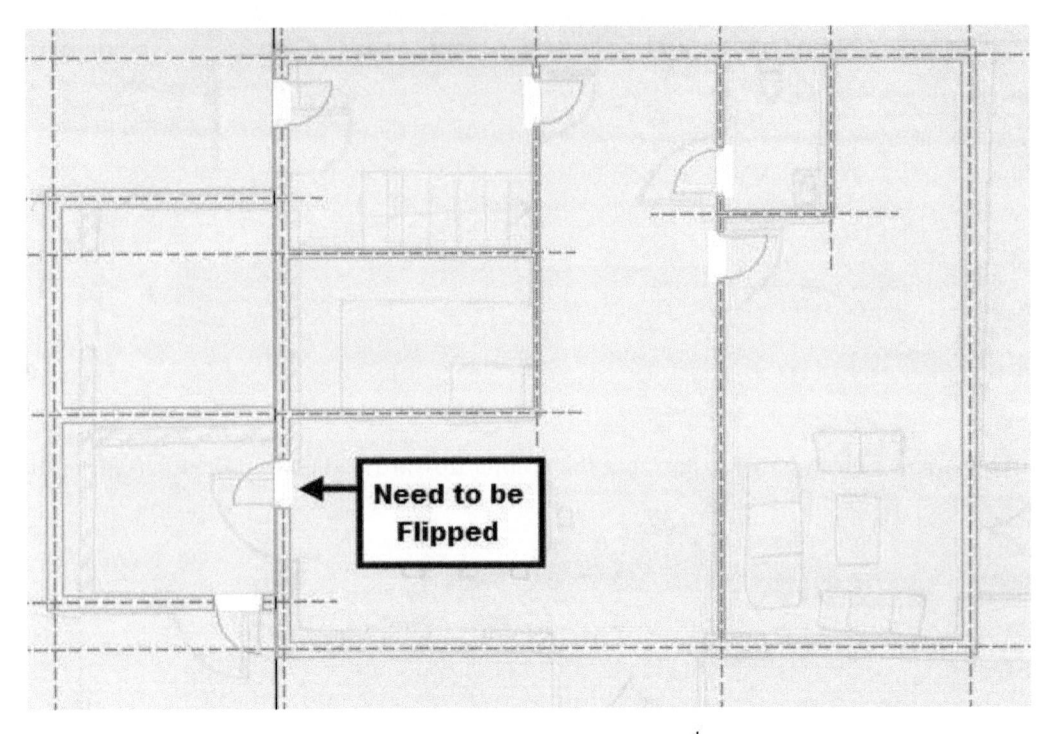

- On the ribbon, click **Home** tab > **Modify** panel > **Mirror**. Select the door to be flipped and press Enter. Select the base point of the door. Move the pointer horizontally toward left and click to define the mirror line. Select **Yes** from the command line delete the source objects.

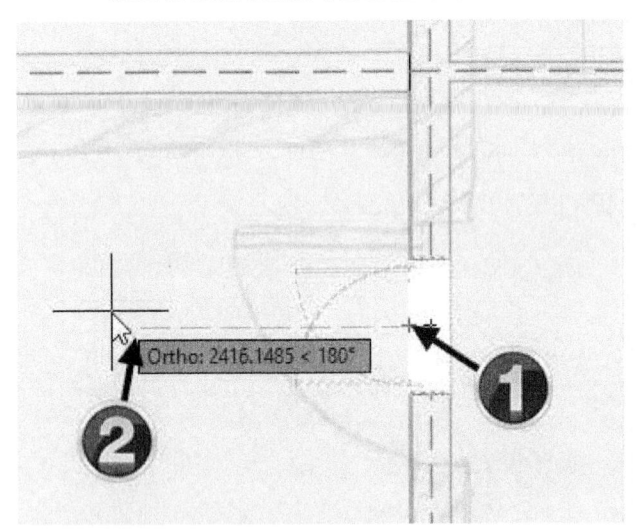

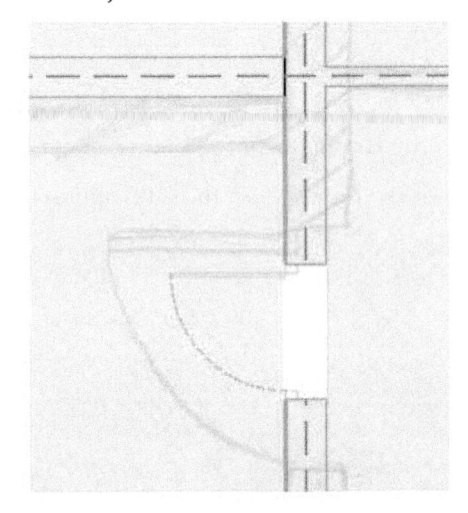

Now, you need to create double doors.

- Select the Single_Door block available in the empty area. On the ribbon, click **Home** tab > **Modify** panel > **Explode**. The block is exploded and individual objects are selectable.
- Select the right vertical line and rectangle, and then press **Delete**. Select the other objects of the door expect the wipeout. On the ribbon, click **Home** tab > **Modify** panel > **Mirror**. Select the start point of the arc, move the pointer, and click to define the mirror line. Select **No** from the command line to retain the source objects.

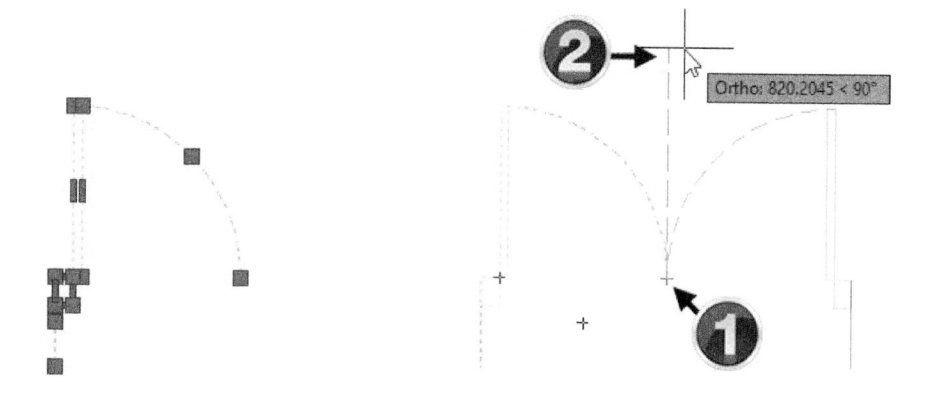

- Place the pointer in the lower portion of the door. The wipeout frame is highlighted. Select the wipeout frame and press Delete.
- On the ribbon, click **Home** tab > **Layers** panel > **Layer** drop-down > **WIPEOUT**. Type REC in the command line and press Enter. Specify the first and second corners of the rectangle, as shown.

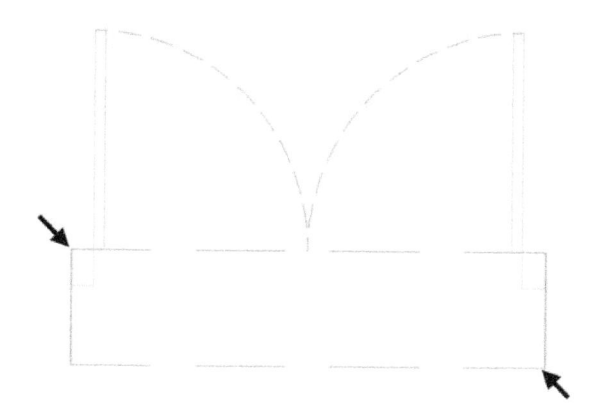

- Select the rectangle to display the grips on it. Select the midpoint grip of the lower horizontal line and move the pointer downward. Type 10 and press Enter. Likewise, stretch the rectangle in the upward direction.

- Type WIPEOUT in the command line and press Enter. Select **Polyline** from the command line. Select the rectangle, and select **Yes** to erase the source object.
- Place the pointer on the lower portion of the door to highlight the wipeout frame. Select the wipeout frame, right click and select **Draw order > Send Back**.

- Create the Double_Door block from the objects. Type BE and press Enter. Select Double_Door from the **Block to create or edit** list, and click **OK**. The Block Editor window appears.
- Create two Linear parameters, as shown. Apply the Stretch action to the Wall Thickness parameter.

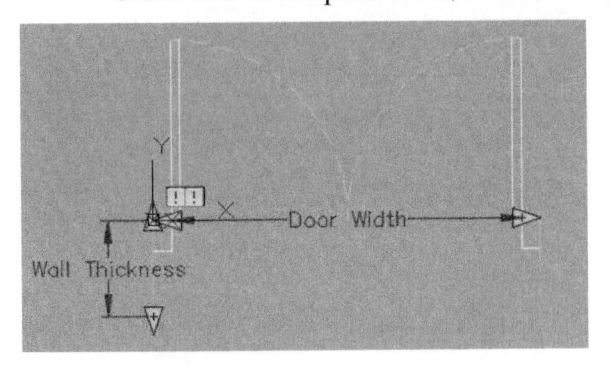

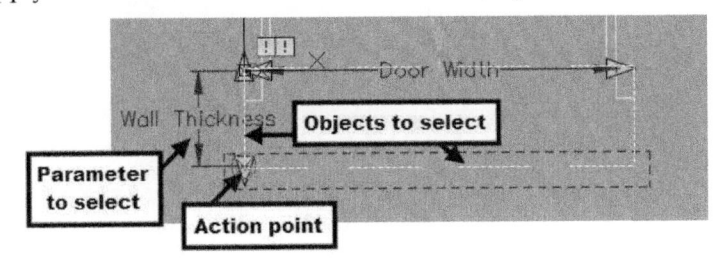

- Apply the Stretch action to the Door Width parameter, as shown.
- Apply the Scale action to the Door Width parameter and select the objects, as shown.

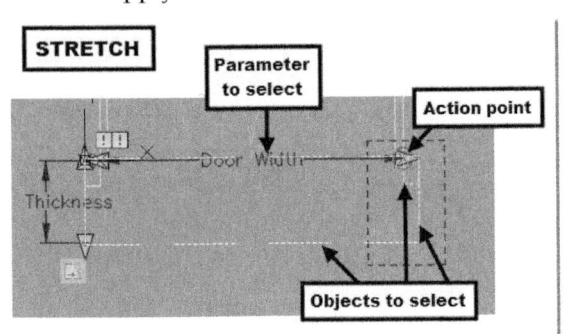

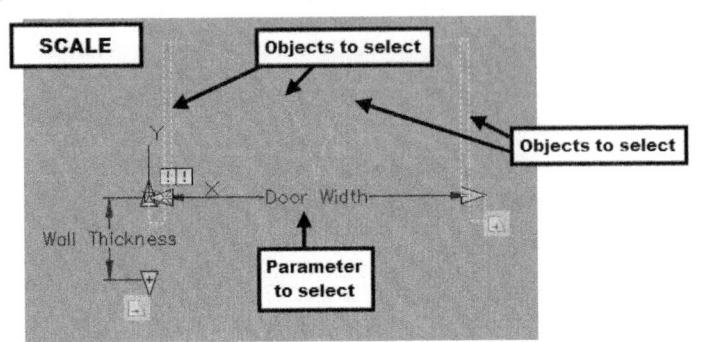

- Select the Door Width parameter. On the **Properties** palette, under the **Value set** section, change the **Dist type** to **List**. Click in the **Dist value list** box and select the icon located next to it. On the **Add Distance Value** dialog, type 1652 in the **Distance to add** box and press Enter. Likewise, add 1220, 1676, 1728, and 1852 to the list, as shown. Click **OK** to close the dialog.
- Test the block, save it, and close the **Block Editor**.
- On the ribbon, click **Insert** tab > **Block** panel > **Insert** drop-down > **Double_Door**. Select **Rotate** from the command line. Type 270 and press Enter. Select the point on the outer edge of the extreme right wall. Click and drag the arrow pointing downward. Click on the bottom most interval.

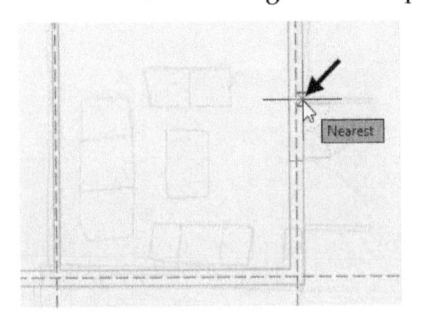

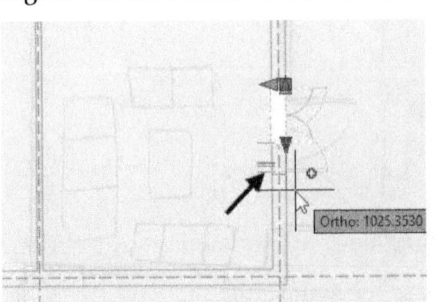

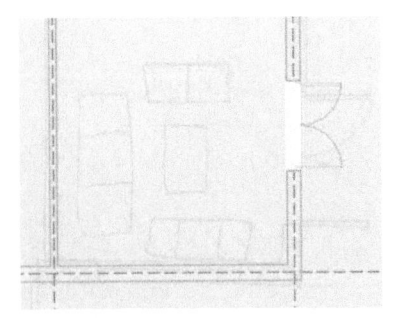

- Likewise, insert another instance of the block, as shown.

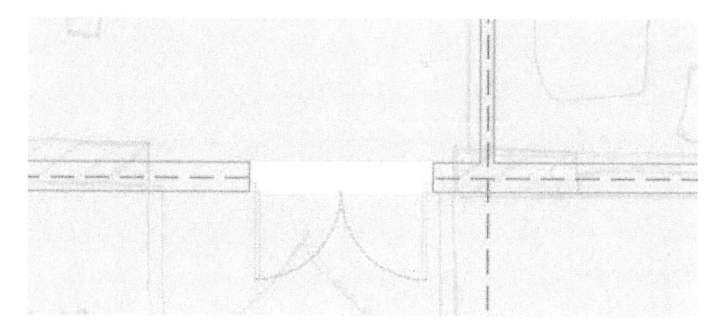

- Create two vertical lines and a wipeout, as shown. Create the 'Opening' block from the objects. Use the top left corner point as the base point.

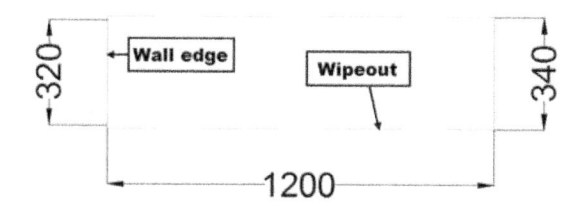

- Type BE and press Enter. Create two Linear parameters, as shown.

- Apply the Stretch action to the Wall Thickness parameter.

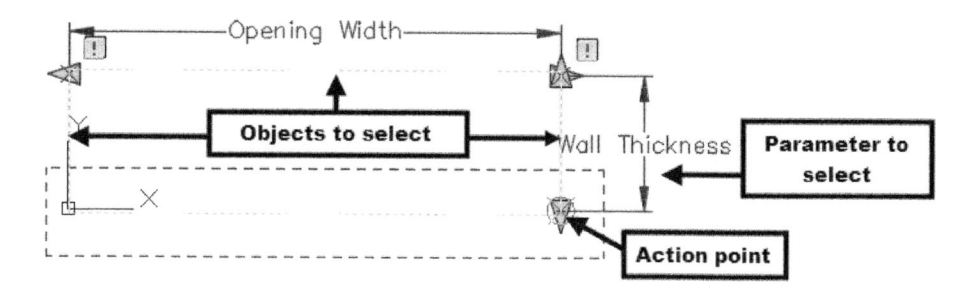

- Apply the Stretch action to the Opening Width parameter, save the block, and close the Block Editor.

36 | AutoCAD 2016 For Architectural Design

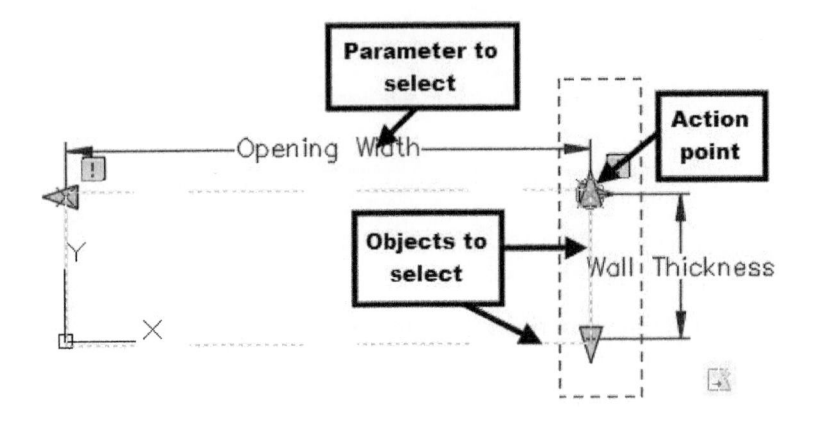

- On the ribbon, click **Home** tab > **Layers** panel > **Layer** drop-down > **A-DOOR**. Insert the Opening block into the drawing at the locations shown in figure.

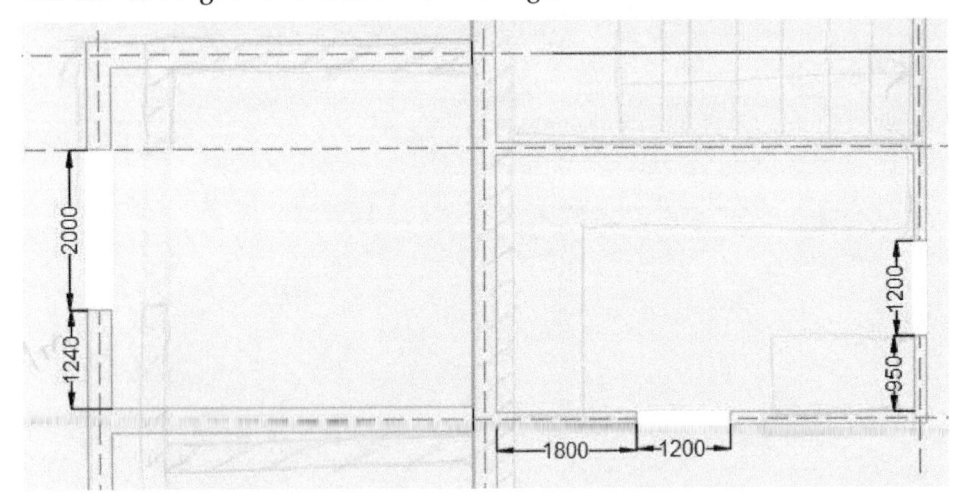

- On the ribbon, click **Home** tab > **Layers** panel > **Layer** drop-down > **A-WINDOW**. Create the 'Window' block, as shown. Use the top left corner as the base point.

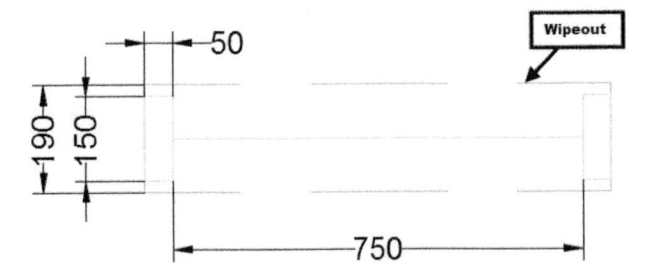

- Open the 'Window' block in the Block Editor. On the **Block Editor** tab of the ribbon, click the **Coincident** tool on the **Geometric** panel. Click the left end point of the horizontal line. Click on the middle portion of the vertical connected to the horizontal line. The **Coincident** constraint is created between the left endpoint of the horizontal line and the midpoint of the vertical line. Likewise, create the **Coincident** constraint between the right endpoint of the horizontal line and the midpoint of the vertical line connected to it.

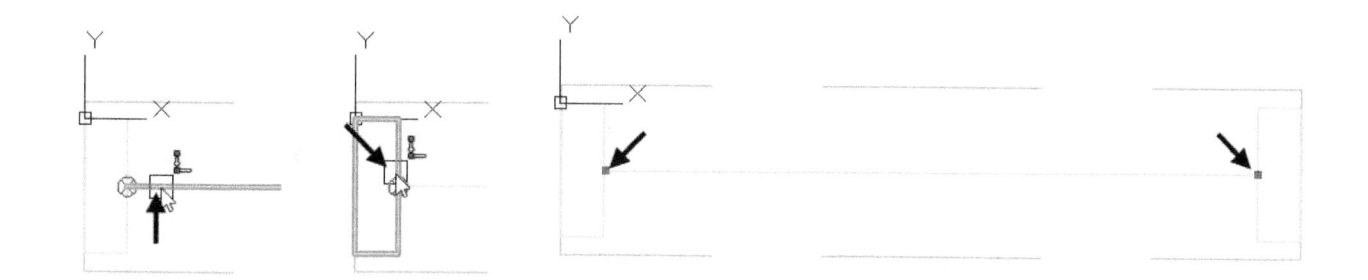

- On the **Block Editor** tab of the ribbon, click the **Horizontal** tool on the **Geometric** panel. Select the horizontal line located at the center.

- Create two linear parameters and apply the Stretch actions to them. Test the block, save it, and close the Block Editor.

- Insert the window blocks at the locations shown in figure. Also, change the window lengths.

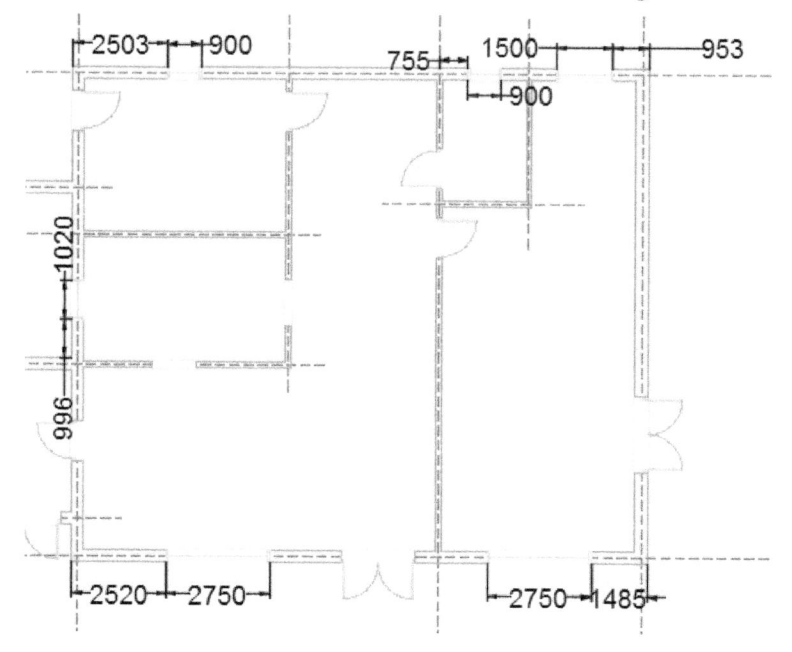

Tutorial 7: Creating Stairs

- On the ribbon, click **Home** tab > **Layers** panel > **Layer** drop-down > **A-STAIRS**.
- Type O in the command line and press Enter. Type 1732 and press Enter to define the offset distance. Zoom into the top left corner of the drawing. Select the edge of the horizontal wall, as shown. Move the pointer up and click to create the offset line.

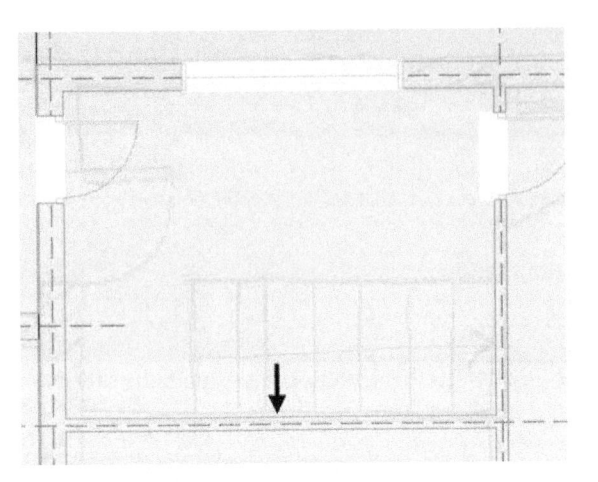

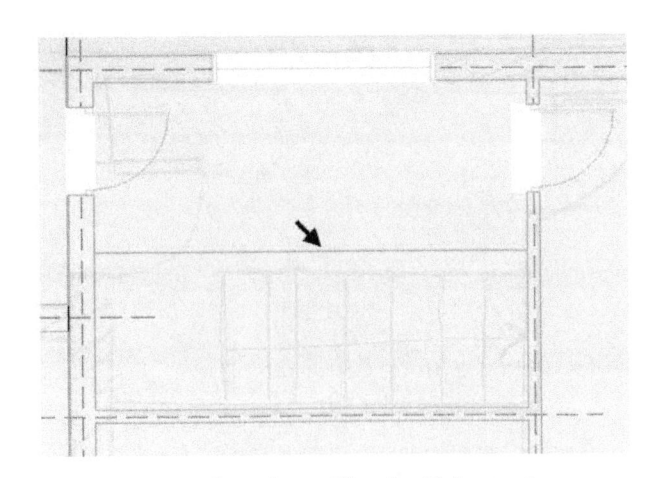

- Likewise, create other offset lines, as shown. The offset distances are also given. Use the **Trim** tool remove the unwanted portions of the lines, as shown.

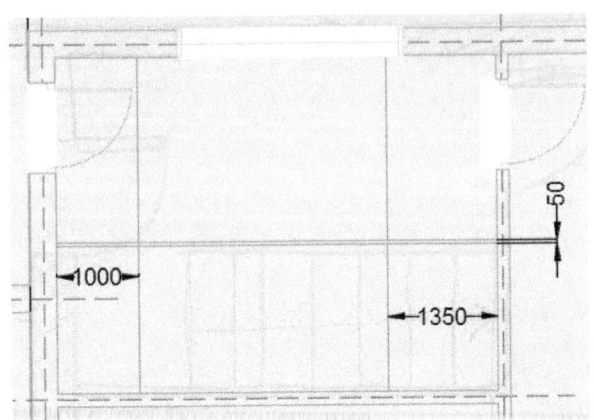

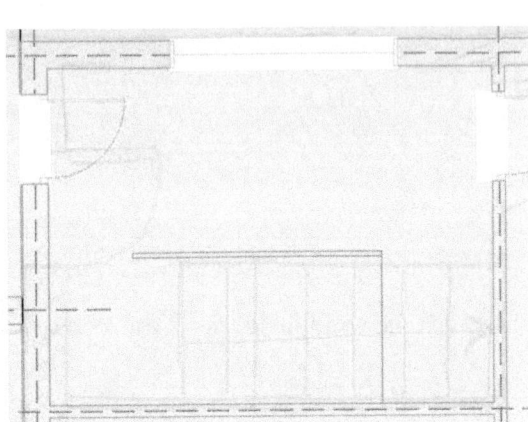

- On the **Home** tab of the ribbon, expand the **Modify** panel and click the **Break at Point** tool. Select the line shown in figure. Specify the break point, as shown. The selected line is broken at the selected point.

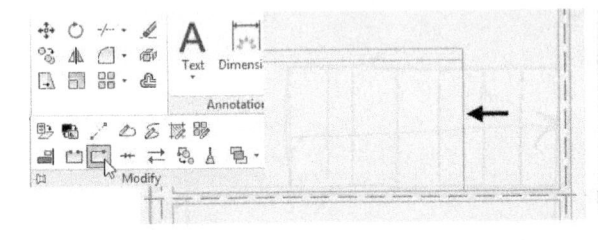

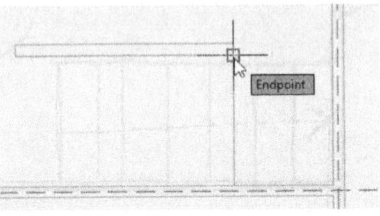

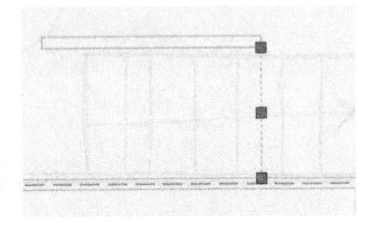

- On the ribbon, click **Home** tab > **Modify** panel > **Array** drop-down > **Rectangular Array**. Select the line that was broken in the previous step, and press Enter. On the **Array Creation** tab of the ribbon, change the **Columns** and **Rows** value to 10 and 1, respectively. Change the **Between** value on the **Columns** panel to -300. Click **Close Array** on the **Array Creation** ribbon tab.

39 | AutoCAD 2016 For Architectural Design

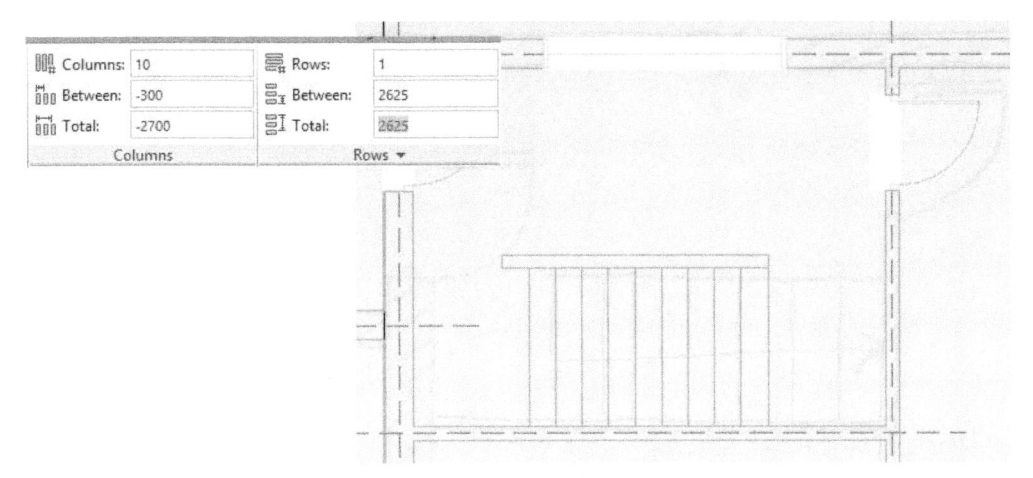

- On the ribbon, click **Home** tab > **Layers** panel > **Layer** drop-down > **CALLOUTS**. Draw a circle and lines, as shown. Assume the dimensions.

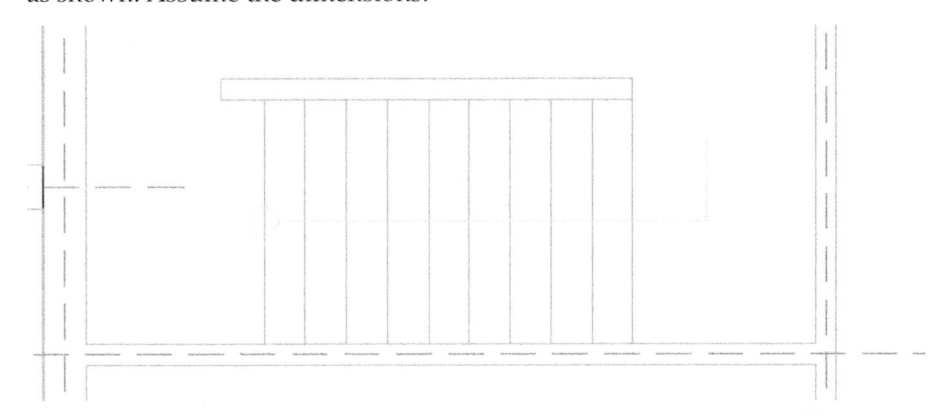

- On the status bar, click the down arrow next to the **Polar Tracking** icon and select **30**. Type L in the command line and press Enter. Select the endpoint of the line drawn in the last step. Move the pointer toward bottom left and click to create an inclined line. Press Enter twice. Specify the start point of the new line, as shown. Place the pointer on the endpoint of the inclined line. Move the pointer horizontally toward right at intersection of the trace lines. Press Esc.

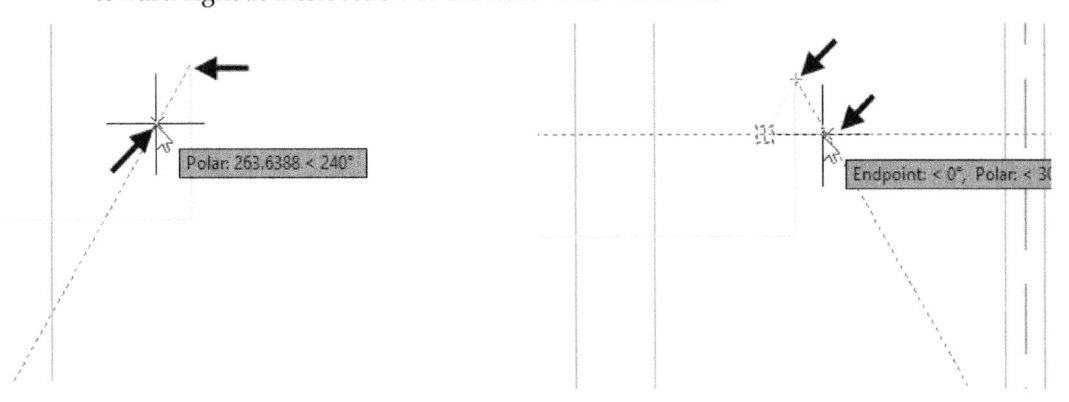

- On the **Home** tab of the ribbon, expand the **Annotation** panel and click the **Text Style** icon. On the **Text Style** dialog, click the **New** button. Type **Callout** in the **Style Name** box and click **OK**. Type 200 in the **Height** box and **Width Factor** to 0.75. Click the **Set Current** button, and then close the dialog.

- On the ribbon, click **Home** tab > **Annotation** panel > **Text** drop-down > **Single Line**. Type STAIR UP and press Esc.

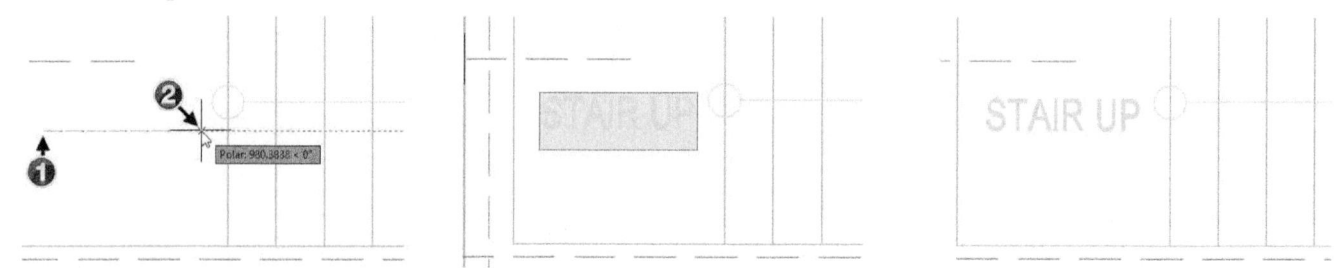

Tutorial 8: Creating the First Floor Plan

Now, you will create the upper floor plan by using the walls of the ground floor plan.

- On the ribbon, click **Home** tab > **Layers** panel > **Layer** drop-down. Click the bulb icon of the **References** layer. The image references are turned OFF.
- On the Status bar, activate the ORTHOMODE (F8) icon. Also, turn ON the **References** layer.
- Select all the objects of the ground floor plane including the grid lines. Right click and select **Copy Selection**. Select the base point of the ground floor. Move the pointer toward right and select the base point of the first floor.
- Delete the unwanted inner walls, garage walls, doors, and windows. The plan after deleting the unwanted entities is shown next.

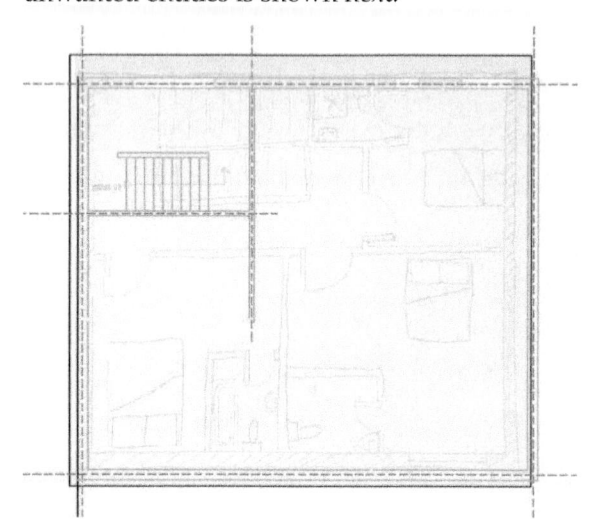

- Create grid lines by using the Offset tool.

41 | **AutoCAD 2016 For Architectural Design**

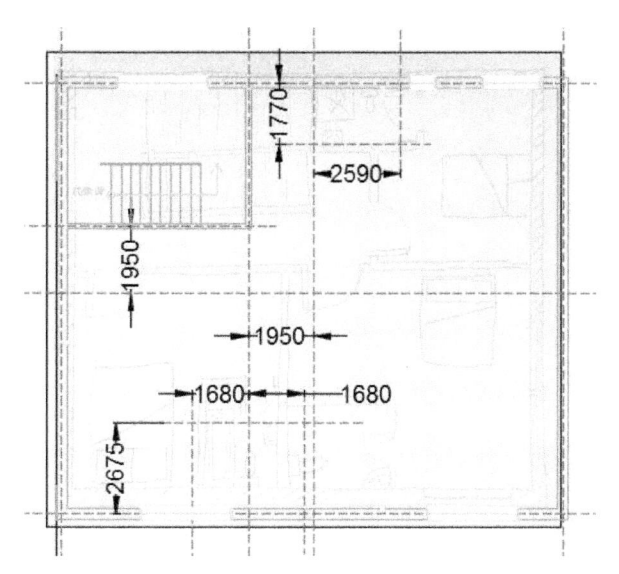

- Create the inner walls using the grid lines. Also, trim the wall intersections.

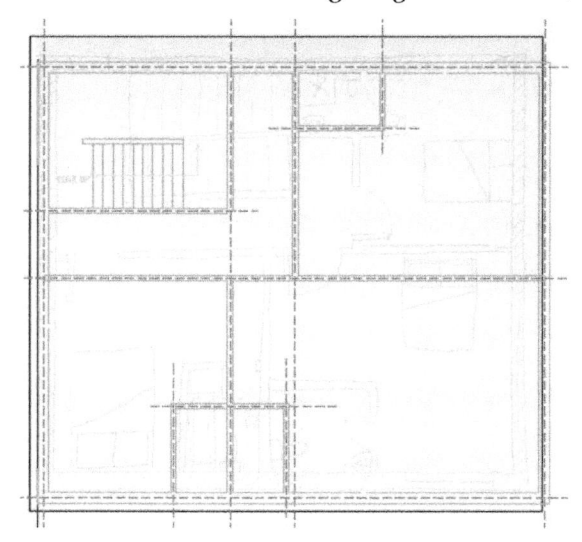

- Zoom to the bottom portion of the drawing and notice a gap on the wall. Select the line on the right side of the gap and press **Delete**. Select the line on the left side of the gap, drag its endpoint grip, and then select the endpoint of the vertical line at the corner.

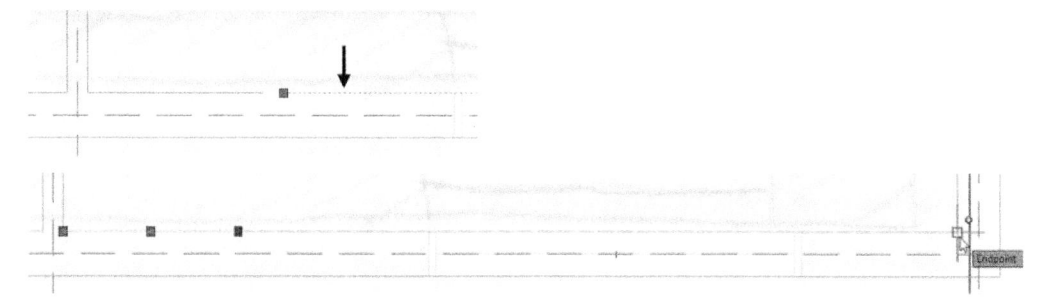

- Likewise, remove the gaps on other walls.
- Add doors and windows to first floor plan.

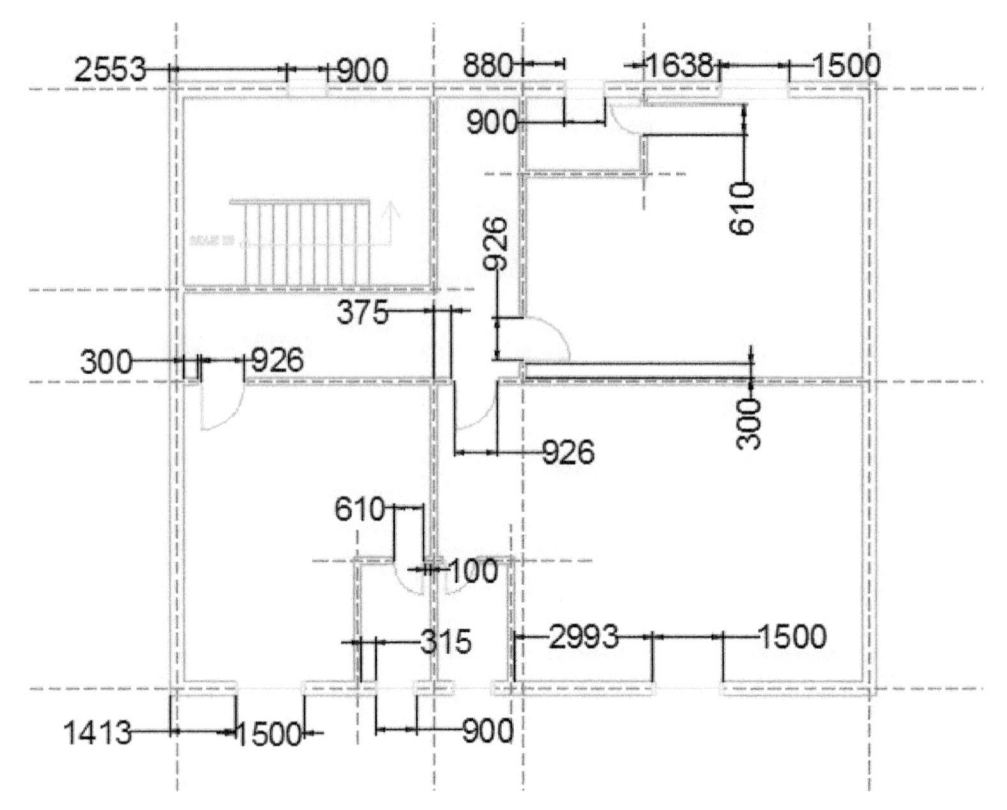

- On the ribbon, click **Home** tab > **Layers** panel > **Layer** drop-down > **A-STAIR**. Zoom to the stairs portion on the first floor plan and select the stairs. Type MI and press Enter. Specify the start and end points of the mirror line, as shown. Select **No** from the command line to retain the source objects.

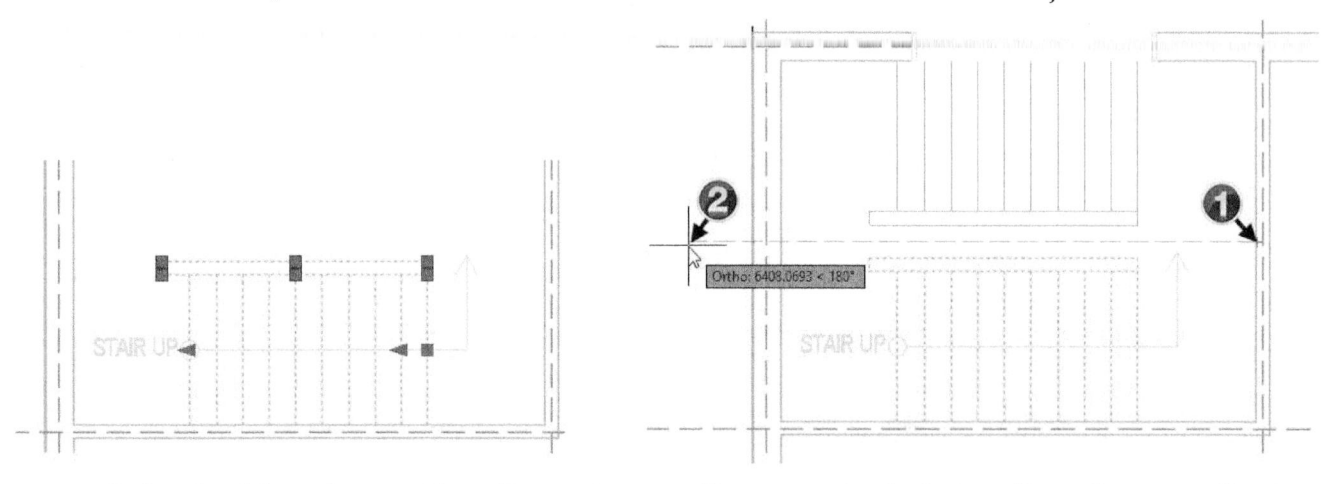

- Delete the right end caps of the railings and create a line connecting both the railings. Create an offset line on the left side of the newly created line. The offset distance is 50 mm.

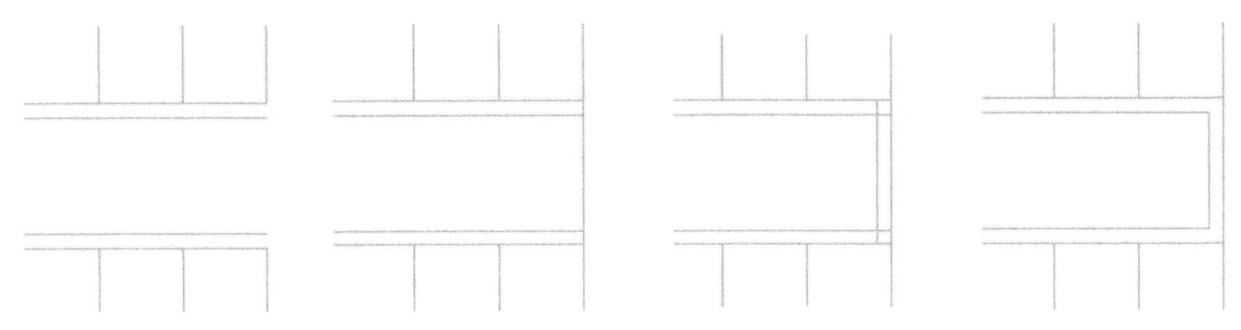

- Create lines connecting the corners of the railing and wall, as shown. Mirror the stair direction arrow and the text. Double click on the text and type STAIR DOWN.

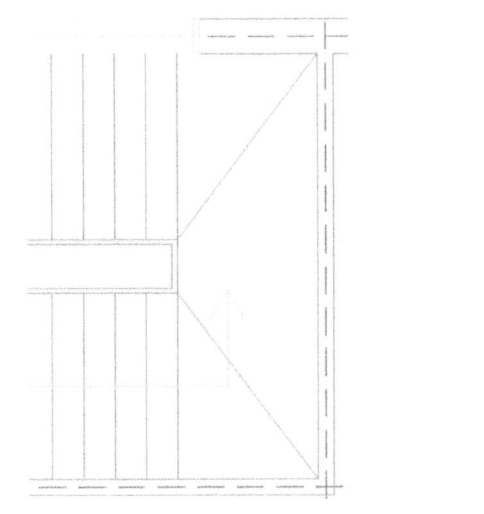

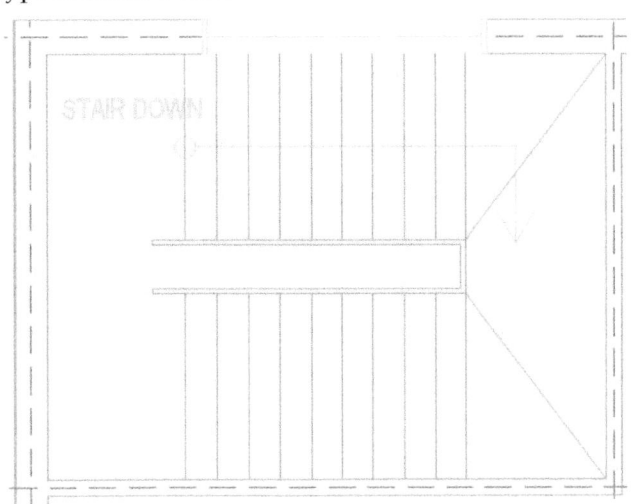

- Delete the left end caps of the railing. Draw a line connecting the upper railing and the horizontal wall. Offset the line up to 50 mm distance right side. Trim the unwanted entities.

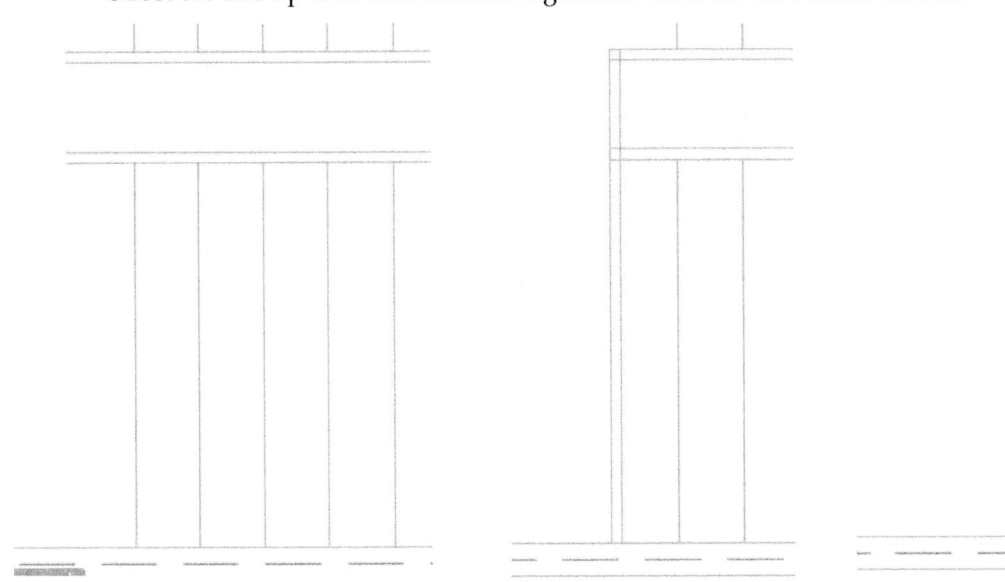

- Insert the Opening block at the left end of the horizontal wall.

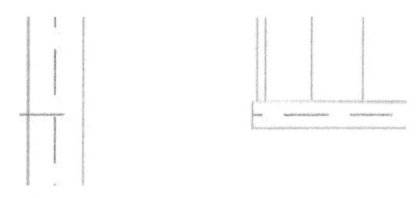

Creating the Sliding Doors

- On the ribbon, click **Home** tab > **Layers** panel > **Layer** drop-down > **A-WALL**. Create two vertical lines of 320 mm length and 1524 apart.

- On the ribbon, click **Home** tab > **Layers** panel > **Layer** drop-down > **A-DOOR**. Activate the **Rectangle** command and select the lower end point of the left vertical line, as shown. Select the **Dimensions** option from the command line. Specify 787 and 50 as length and width of the rectangle, respectively. Move the pointer upward and click to create the rectangle.

- Type **M** in the command line and press Enter. Select the rectangle, and then press Enter. Select its lower left corner point to define the base point. Move the pointer upward and type-in 25 in the command line, and then press Enter.

- On the ribbon, click **Home** > **Modify** > **Explode**, and select the rectangle. Press Enter to explode the rectangle. Activate the **Offset** command and specify 50 as the offset distance. Offset the left and right vertical lines of the rectangle.

- Click the down arrow next to the **Object Snap** icon on the status bar, and make sure that the **Midpoint** option is checked. Activate the **Line** command and select the midpoints of the offset lines. A line connecting the offset lines is created. Press Esc to deactivate the line command.

- Type-in CO in the command line and press Enter. Drag a selection window covering all the elements of the sliding door. Press Enter.

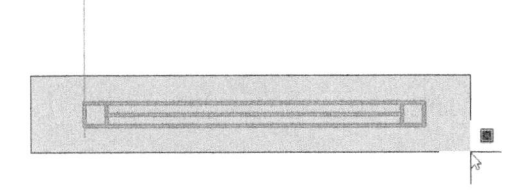

- Select the lower left corner of the sliding door as base point. Move the pointer and select the endpoint of the offset line, as shown. Press **Esc** to deactivate the **Copy** command.

- On the ribbon, click **Home** tab > **Layers** panel > **Layer** drop-down > **WIPEOUT**. Create a rectangle covering all the entities of the sliding door. Activate the **Wipeout** tool and select **Polyline** from the command line. Select the rectangle to convert it into a wipeout. Select the **Yes** from the command line to erase the rectangle. Select the wipeout from the graphics window, right click and select **Draw Order** > **Send To Back**.

- On the ribbon, click **Insert** tab > **Block Definition** panel > **Blocks** drop-down > **Create Block**. On the **Block Definition** dialog, type **Sliding_Door** in the **Name** box. Click the **Select Objects** icon, create a selection window covering all the entities of the sliding door, and press Enter. Click the **Pick point** icon and select the lower end point of the left vertical line. Select the **Delete** option from the **Objects** section. Uncheck the **Open in block editor** option and click **OK**.

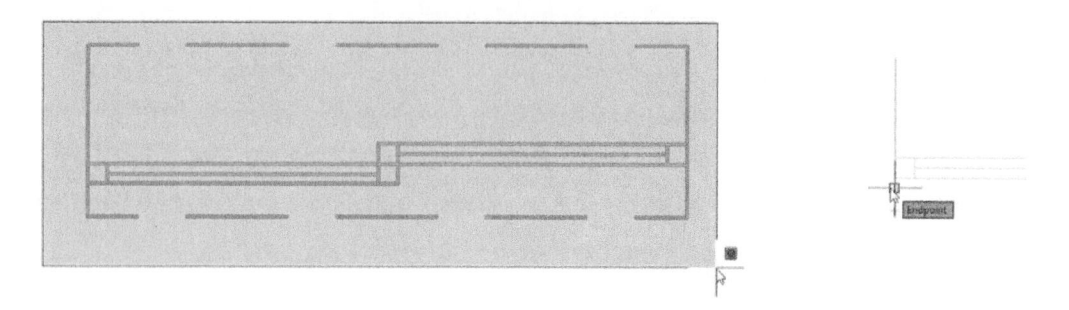

- On the ribbon, click **Insert** tab > **Block** panel > **Insert** gallery > **Sliding _Door**. Select **Rotate** from the command line. Type 90 and press Enter. Press the Shift key and right click. Select **From** from the shortcut menu. Zoom to lower right corner of the first floor plan and select the inner corner point. Move the pointer along the vertical line, type 3870 and press Enter. The block is inserted at the specified distance from the inner corner point.

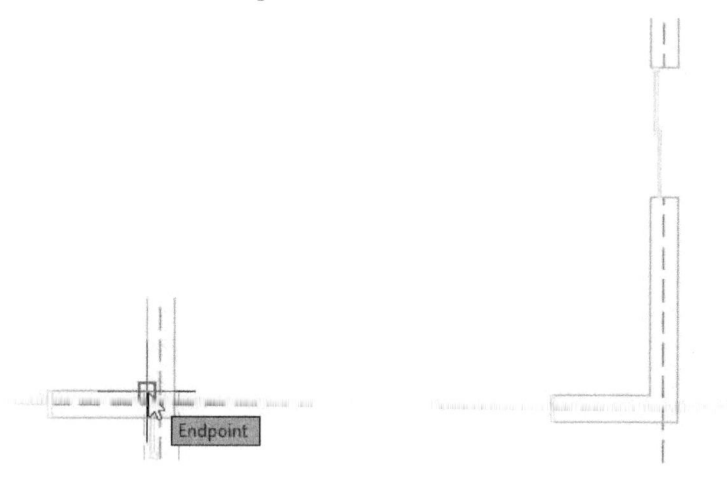

- Likewise, add other slider door to the other bedroom, as shown.

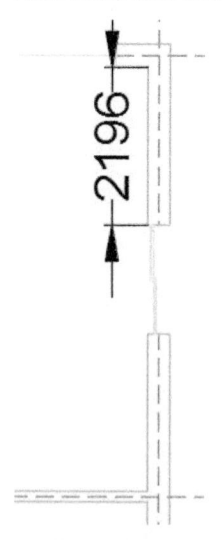

Creating the Balcony

- On the ribbon, click **Home** tab > **Layers** panel > **Layer** drop-down > **A-SLAB**.

47 | AutoCAD 2016 For Architectural Design

- Use the **Polyline** tool to create the balcony, as shown. Offset the polyline by 50 mm and 75 mm inside.

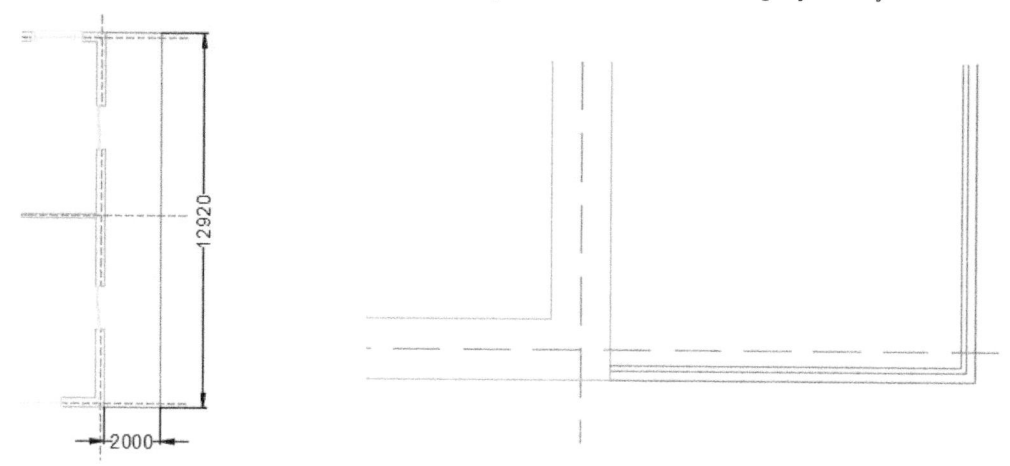

- Select the two offset polylines. On the ribbon, click **Home** tab > **Properties** panel > **Object Color** drop-down > **Index Colors** > 9.

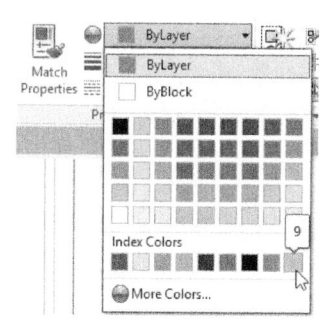

Tutorial 9: Creating Kitchen and Bathroom Fixtures

- On the ribbon, click **Home** tab > **Layers** panel > **Layer** drop-down > **A-KITCHEN**.
- Type O and press Enter. Select **Layer** from the command line, and then select **Current**. Type 660 and press Enter. Zoom to the kitchen area of the ground floor plan. Offset the wall edges, as shown.

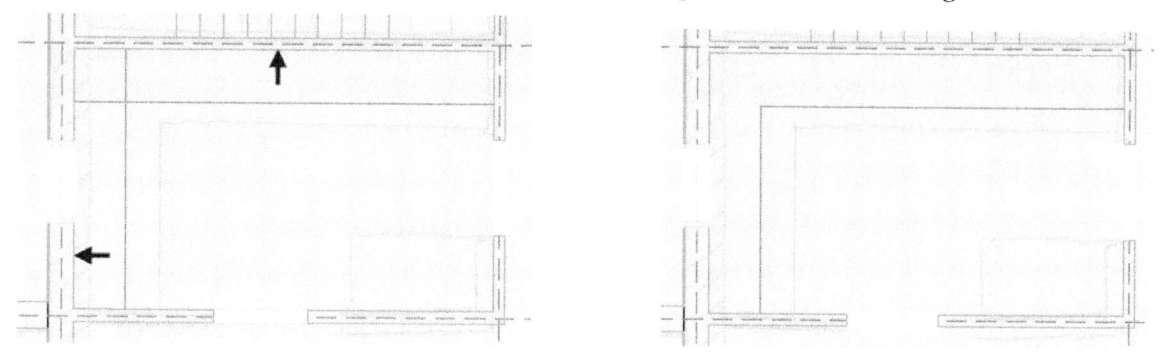

Now you need to create the sink.

- Create offset lines, as shown. Trim the unwanted entities.

48 | AutoCAD 2016 For Architectural Design

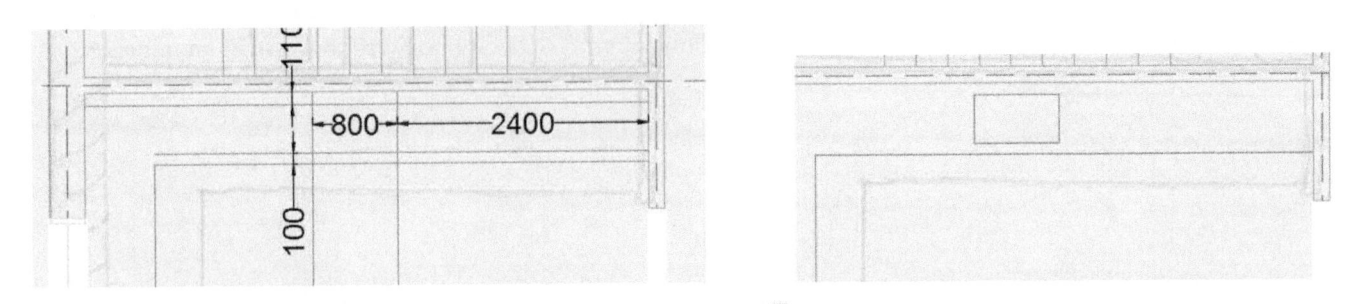

- On the ribbon, click **Home** tab > **Modify** panel > **Fillet**. Select **Radius** from the command line. Type 50 and press Enter. Select **Multiple** from the command line. Select the left vertical line and the horizontal line. A fillet is created at the corner. Likewise, create fillets at the other corners.

- On the **Home** tab of the ribbon, expand the **Modify** panel and click the **Edit Polyline** tool. Select **Multiple** from the command line. Create a selection window covering all the entities of the sink, and press Enter. Select **Yes** to convert the lines and arcs into a polyline. Select **Join** from the command line. Press Enter to accept 0 as the distance between the entities. Press Esc to deactivate the **Edit Polyline** tool.

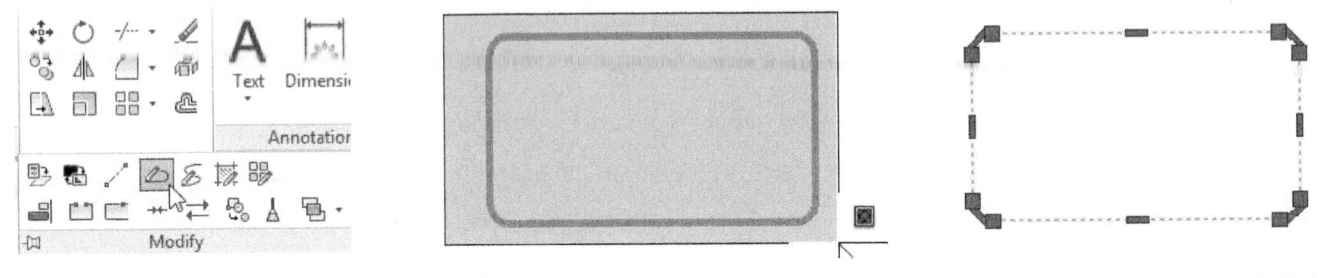

- Type O and press Enter. Type 25 and press Enter to define the offset distance. Select the polyline and click in the area enclosed by it. Press Esc.

- On the ribbon, click **Home** tab > **Draw** panel > **Circle** drop-down > **Center, Diameter**. Select the midpoint of the upper horizontal line. Move the pointer outward, type 75 and press Enter. Draw a vertical line of 125 mm from the center point of the circle.

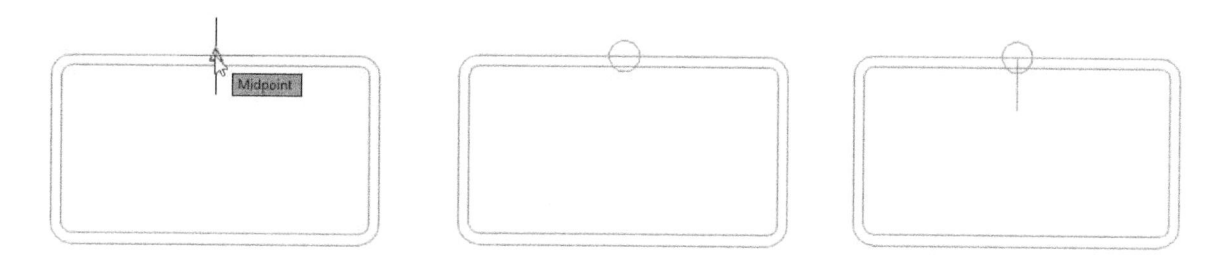

- On the ribbon, click **Home** tab > **Draw** panel > **Circle** drop-down > **Center, Radius**. Select the end point of the vertical line. Move the pointer outward, type 25, and press Enter.

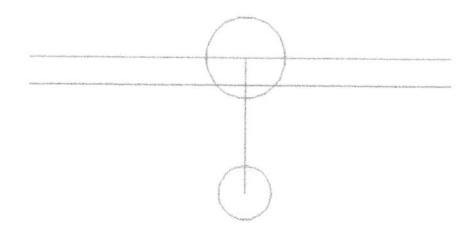

- Type **L** and press Enter. Select the left quadrant point of the small circle. Move the pointer upward and select the left quadrant point of the large circle. Likewise, create another line by selecting the right quadrant points of the two circles.

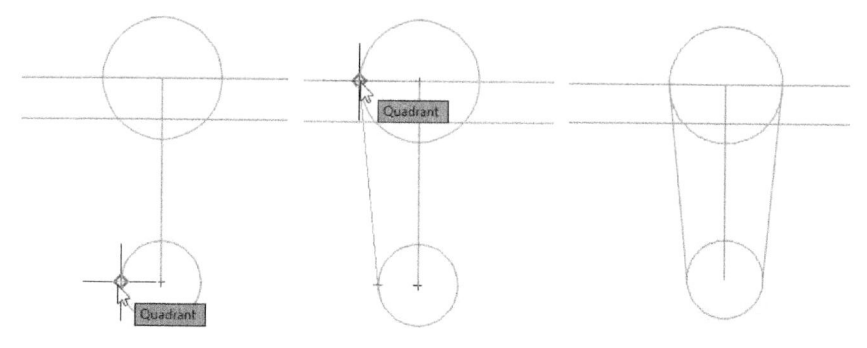

- Delete the vertical line and trim the inner portion of the small circle. Type **M** and press Enter. Create a selection window across circles and inclined lines. Select the center point of the large circle to define the base point. Move the pointer vertically upward, type 55, and press Enter. Trim the horizontal lines between the inclined lines.

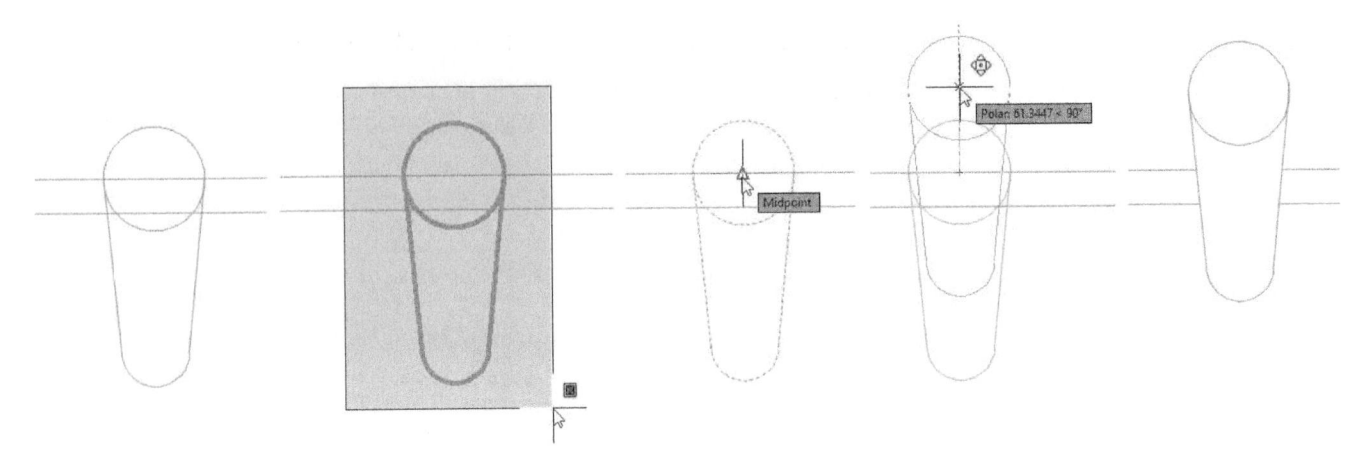

- Type C and press Enter. Place the pointer on the midpoint of the horizontal line. Move the pointer upward. Place the pointer on the midpoint of the vertical line. Move the pointer toward right. Click when the trace lines from the two midpoints intersect. Type 30 as radius, and press Enter to create the circle.

- Press Enter to activate the previous command. Type 20 and press Enter

- Type REC in the command line and press Enter. Select the lower left corner of the kitchen. Select **Dimensions** from the command line. Specify 762 as length and width. Move the pointer up and click to create the rectangle.

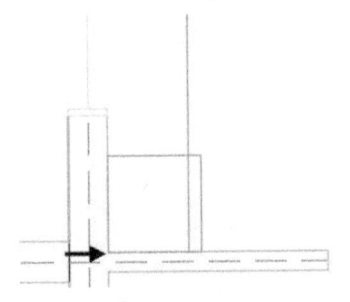

AutoCAD 2016 For Architectural Design

- Select the rectangle and click **Home** tab > **Modify** panel > **Move**. Select the midpoint of the left vertical line of the rectangle. Move the pointer up and select the midpoint of the window. Move the rectangle 10 mm toward right.

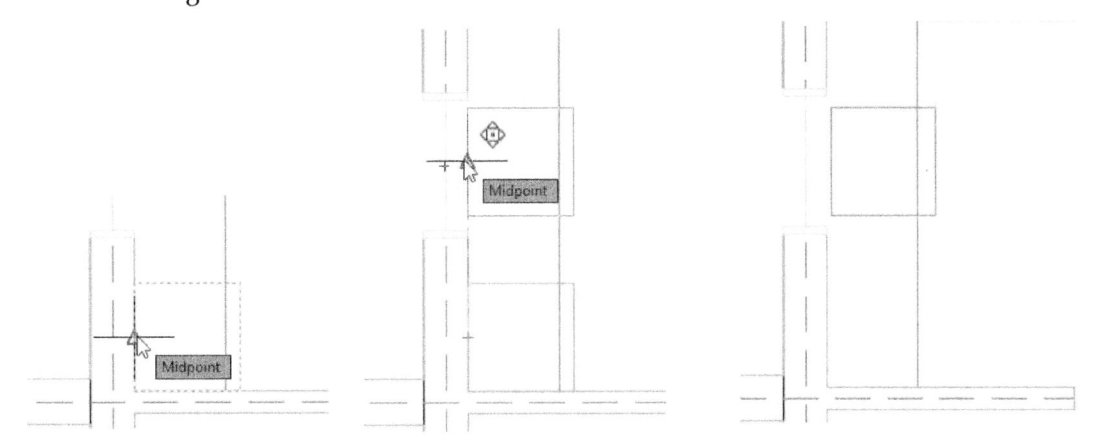

- Create two circles of 250 mm and 200 mm diameters, respectively. Mirror the two circles about the midpoint of the rectangle.

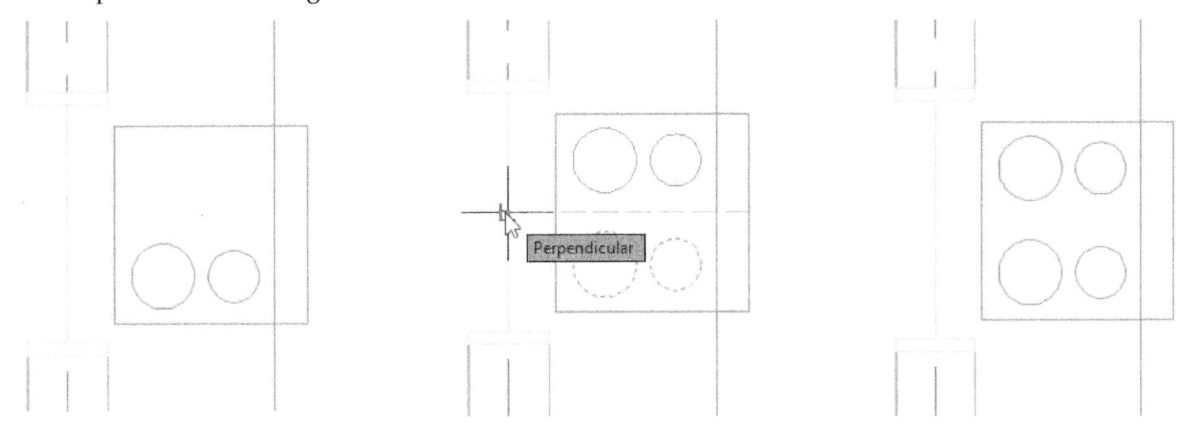

- Create two rectangles as shown. Use the **Move** tool to create gaps between the rectangles and wall. The gap should be 100 mm.

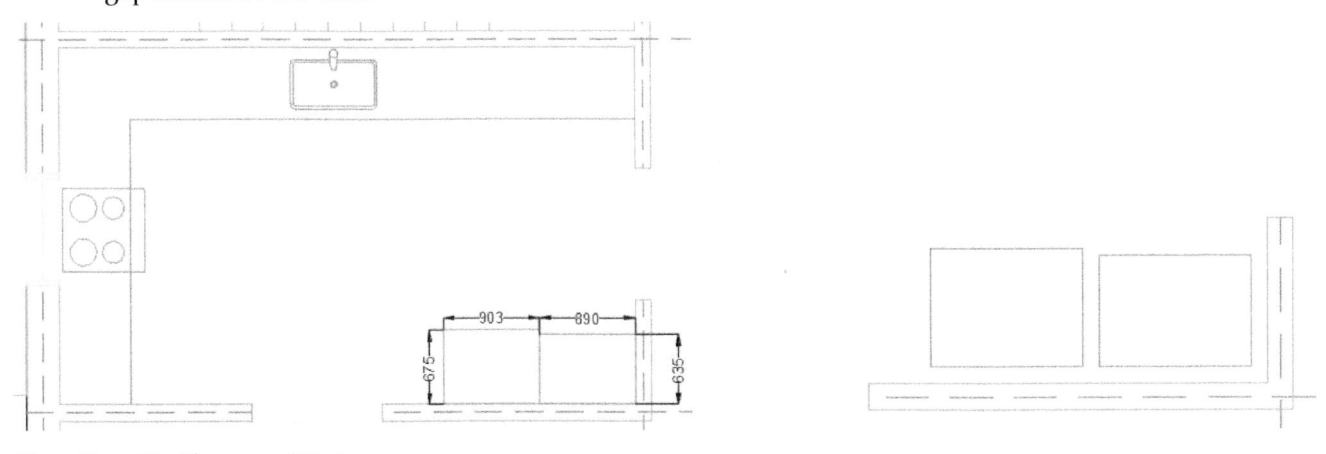

Creating Bathroom Fixtures

- On the ribbon, click **Home** tab > **Layers** panel > **Layer** drop-down > **A-BATHROOM FIXTURES**.

- On the ribbon, click **View** tab > **Palettes** panel > **DesignCenter**. Click on the gear icon on the title bar of the DesignCenter palette and select **Allow Docking**. Again, click on the gear icon and select **Anchor Left <**. Click the **Auto hide** icon on the title bar of the DesignCenter Palette.

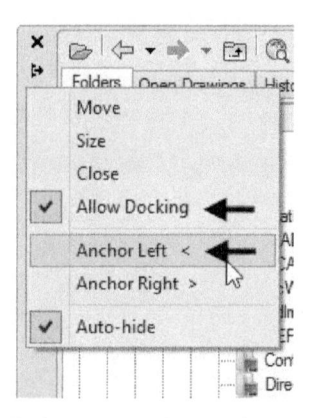

- Click the DesginCenter bar on the left side of the graphics window to expand the **DesignCenter** palette. On the DesignCenter palette, click the **Home** icon. The **Sample** folder is selected in the Folder List. Under the **Sample** node, go to **en-us > DesignCenter** and click the **House Designer.dwg** file. Double click on the Blocks icon. Click and drag the **Toilet-top** block from the DesignCenter palette into the graphics window. Likewise, click and drag the Sink – Oval top block into the graphics window.

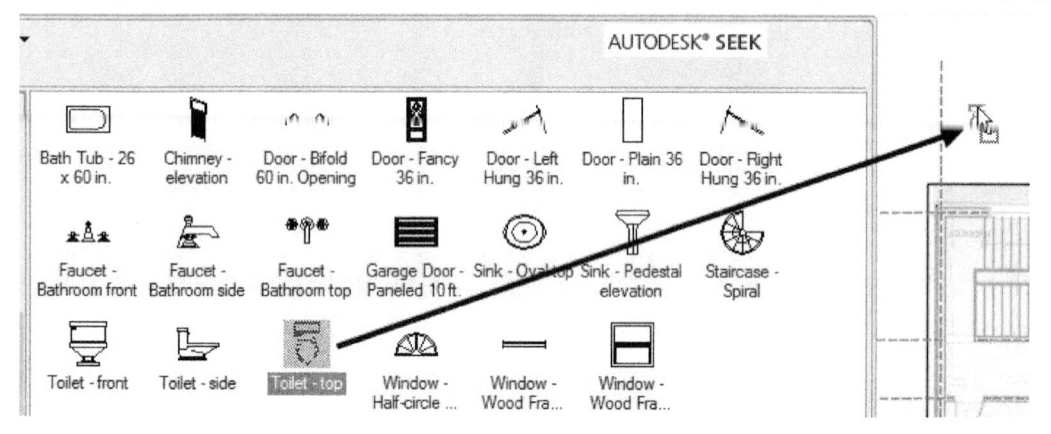

- In the graphics window, click on the Toilet-top block. Right click and select **Copy Selection**. Select the midpoint of the horizontal edge of the block. Zoom to the toilet area of the ground floor plan and select the point, as shown. Press Esc.

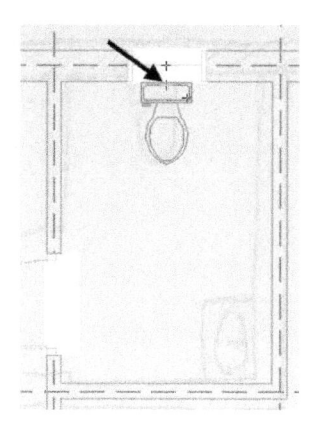

- Select the Sink Oval top block and click **Home** tab > **Modify** panel > **Rotate**. Select the center point of the block to define the base point. Type 90 and press Enter. Copy the Sink Oval top block and place it in the toilet, as shown.

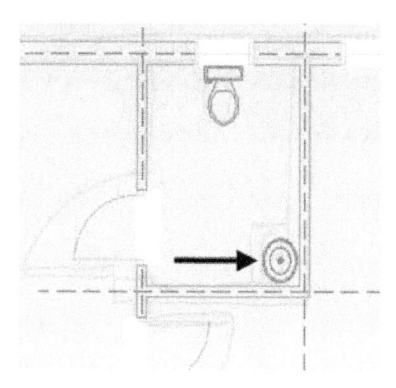

- Likewise, add bathroom fixtures to the first floor plan.

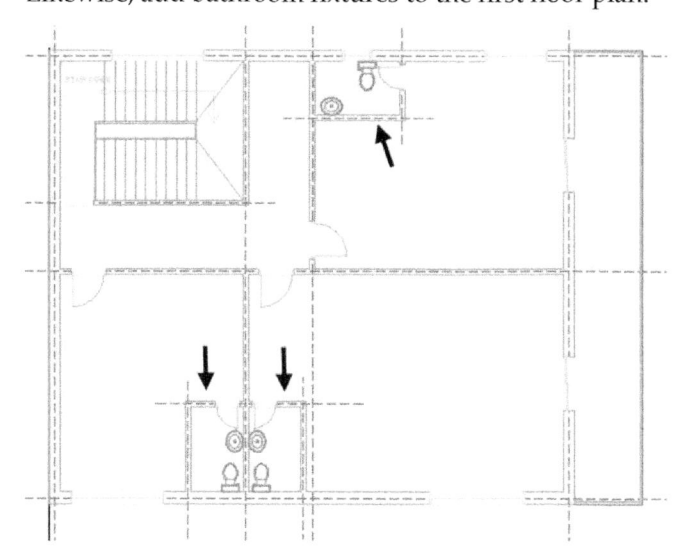

- Go to the following link on the internet and download the bathtub block.

    http://www.cadforum.cz/catalog_en/block.asp?blk=3743

You can download different types of free cad blocks from many websites on the internet. Some of the websites are given below:

http://seek.autodesk.com

http://www.cadforum.cz

http://www.draftsperson.net

http://www.cadcoaching.co.uk

http://www.cad-architect.net

http://www.cadcorner.ca

http://www.bibliocad.com

https://cadaplus.com

- In the Tutorial 1 drawing file, create a circle on the A-BATHROOM FIXTURES layer. Select the circle and press Ctrl+C.
- Open the downloaded drawing file of a Bathtub. Click **NO** on the **AutoCAD** message box. Press Ctrl+V and click to paste the circle in the graphics window. On the ribbon, click **Home** tab > **Properties** panel > **Match Properties**. Select the circle as the source object. Create a selection window across all the entities of the bathtub. Press Enter to match the properties of the circle with the bathtub.

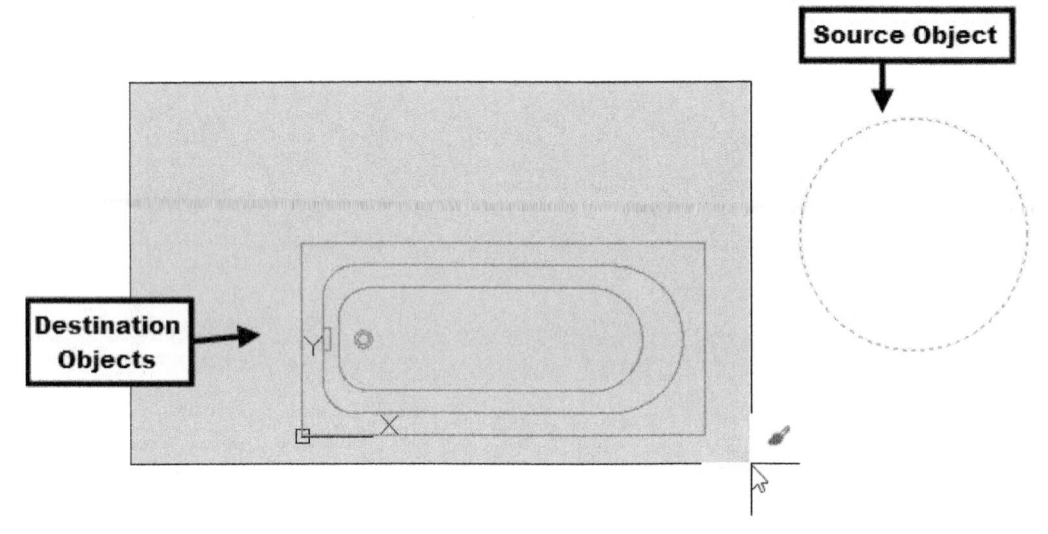

- Type COPYBASE and press Enter. Create a selection window across all the entities of the bathtub. Press Enter. Switch to the Tutorial 1 drawing by clicking the Tutorial 1 tab above the graphics window. Press Ctrl+V and click in the empty space.

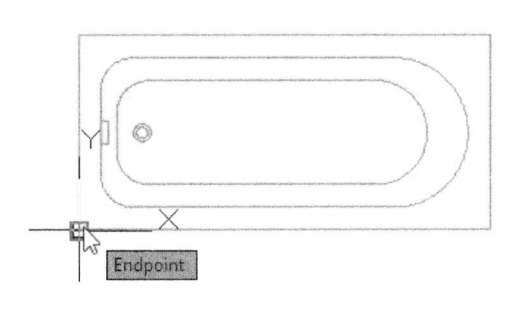

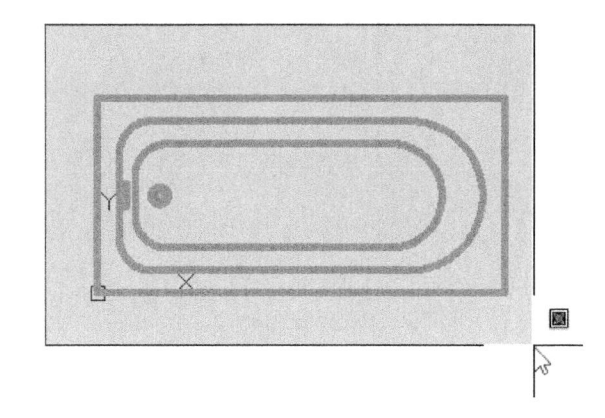

- Select all the entities of the bathtub and rotate them by 90 degrees. Move the bathtub and place it in the left side bathroom in the first floor plan.

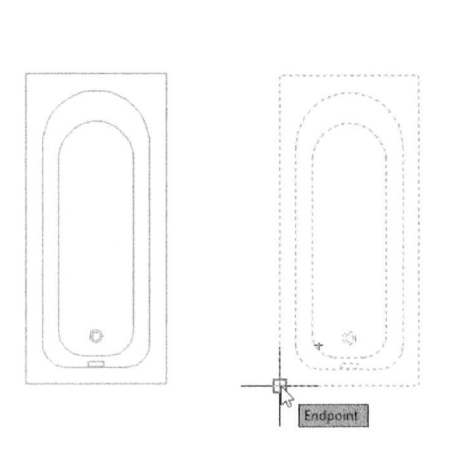

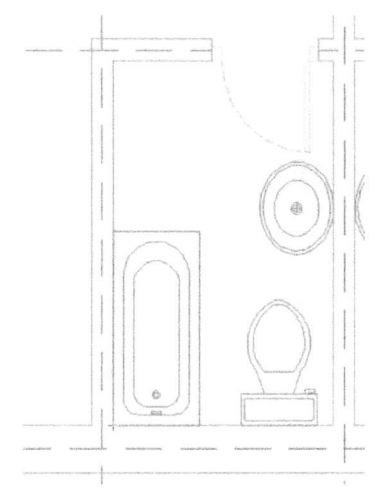

- Zoom to the right side bathroom in the first floor plan. Select the Sink Oval top block, click on the grip, move the block, place it at the corner, as shown. Likewise, move the Toilet-top block, as shown.

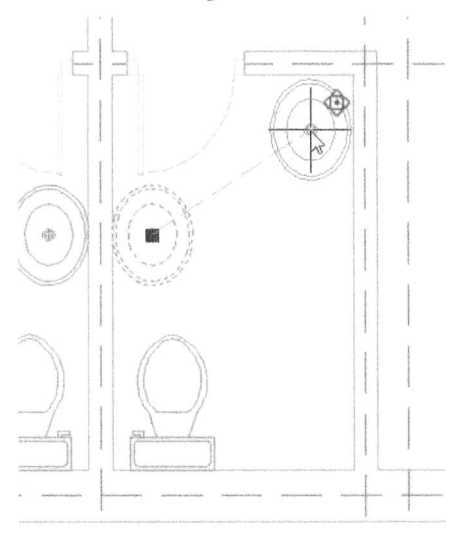

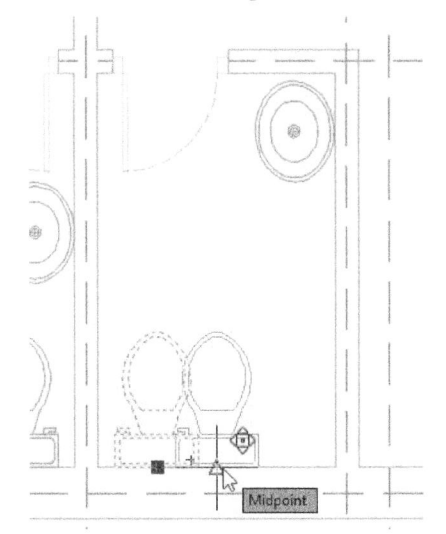

- Add windows to bathrooms. Draw the shower sink in the right side bathroom.

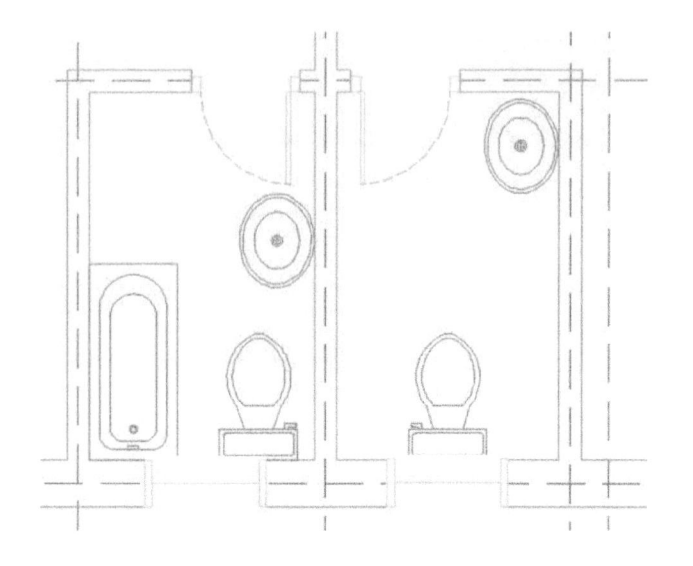

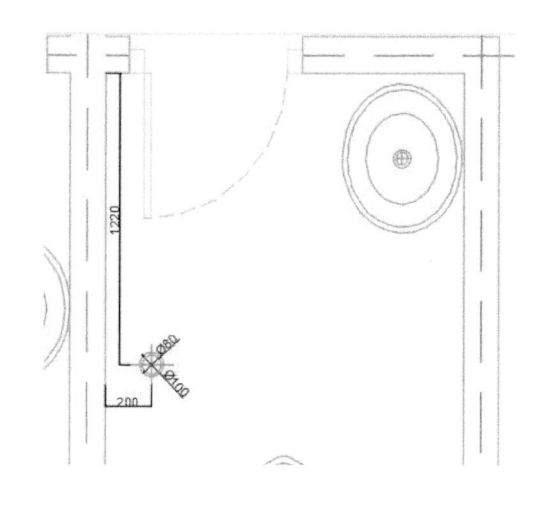

Adding Furniture Blocks

- On the ribbon, click **Home** tab > **Layers** panel > **Layer** drop-down > **A-FURNITURE**.
- Download the Blocks.dwg file from the Companion website. It is a collection of some furniture blocks downloaded from www.cadforum.cz.
- In the Tutorial 1 drawing file, create a circle on the A-FURNITURE layer. Select the circle and press Ctrl+C.
- Open the Blocks.dwg file. Create a selection window across the furniture blocks, and click **Home** tab > **Modify** panel > **Explode**.

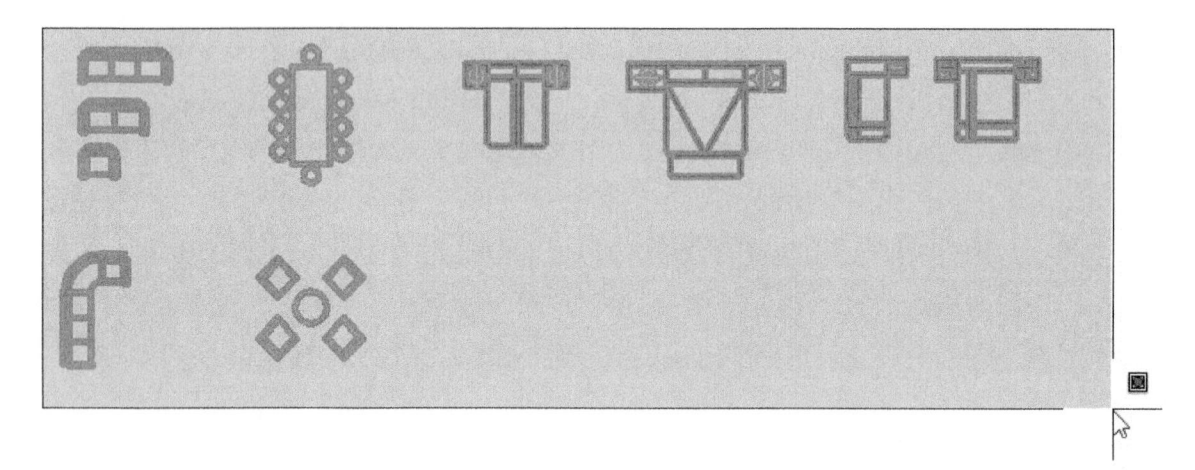

- Press Ctrl+V and click to paste the circle in the graphics window. On the ribbon, click **Home** tab > **Properties** panel > **Match Properties**. Select the circle as the source object. Create a selection window across all the entities of the bathtub. Press Enter to match the properties of the circle with the bathtub.

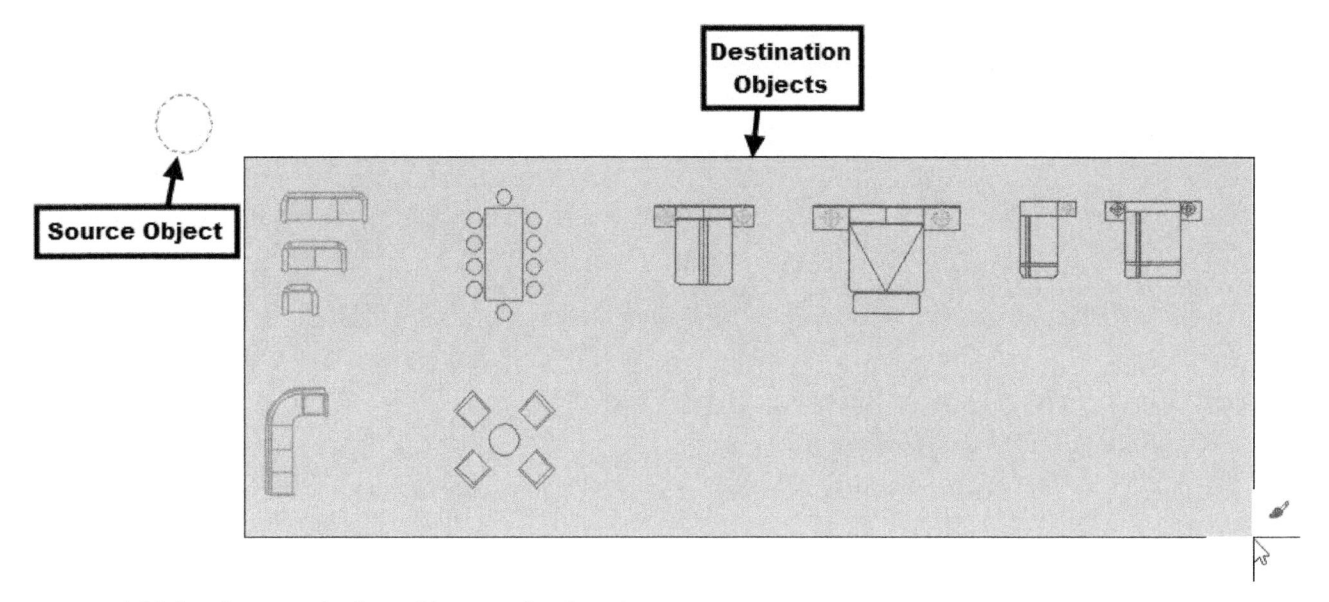

- Add furniture and other objects to the drawing.

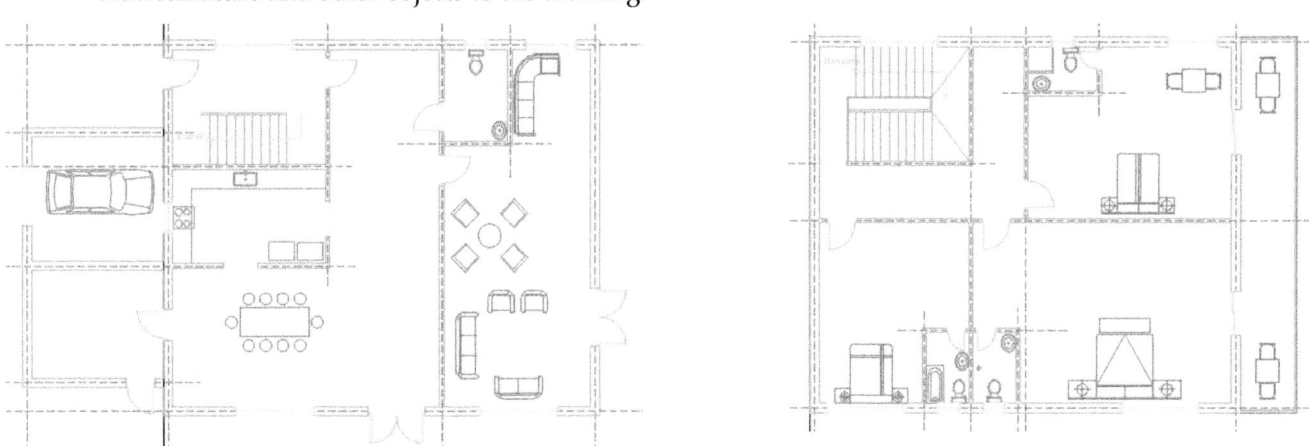

- On the ribbon, click **Home** tab > **Draw** panel > **Ellipse** drop-down > **Center**. Zoom to the sofa set area. Specify the center point, Move the pointer downward and click to specify the major axis. Move the pointer toward right and click to specify the minor axis radius.

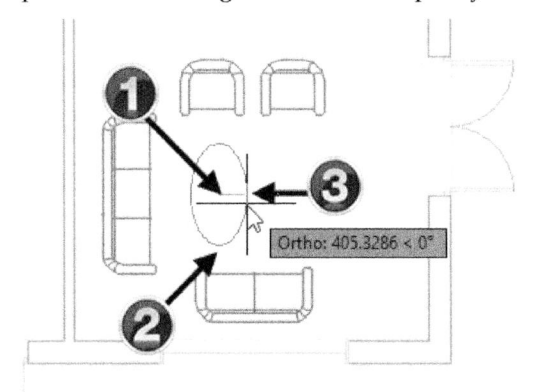

- Draw a rectangle over the sofa set, as shown. Use the **Trim** tool to remove the unwanted portions of the rectangle, as shown.

58 | AutoCAD 2016 For Architectural Design

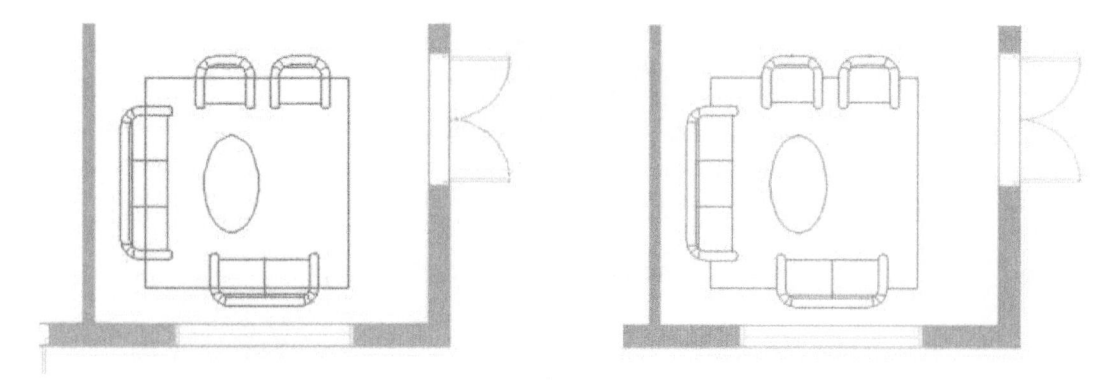

Tutorial 10: Adding Hatch Patterns and Text

- Turn off the **A-GRID**, and **References** layers.

- On the ribbon, click **Home** tab > **Layers** panel > **Layer** drop-down > **A-WALL**.

- On the ribbon, click **Home** tab > **Draw** panel > **Hatch** drop-down > **Hatch**.

- On the **Hatch Creation** tab, select **SOLID** from the **Pattern** gallery. Click in the area enclosed by the wall edges, as shown. Likewise, click in the other areas of the walls. Note that you need to click in the area only when a preview appears.

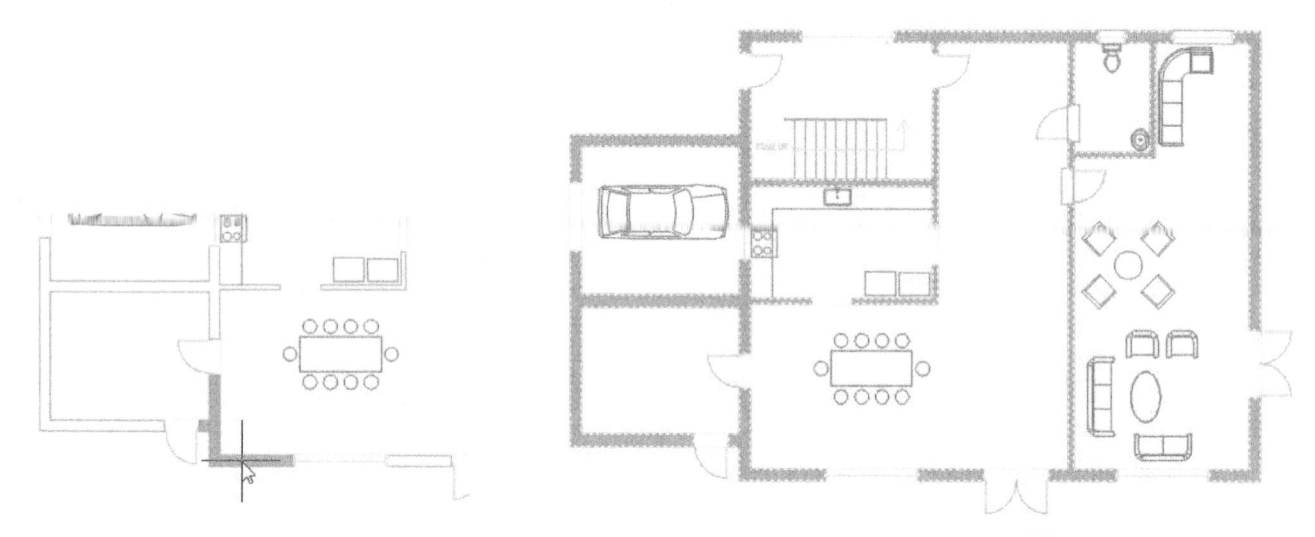

- Add hatch pattern to the walls on the first floor plan. Click **Close Hatch Creation** button on the ribbon.

59 | AutoCAD 2016 For Architectural Design

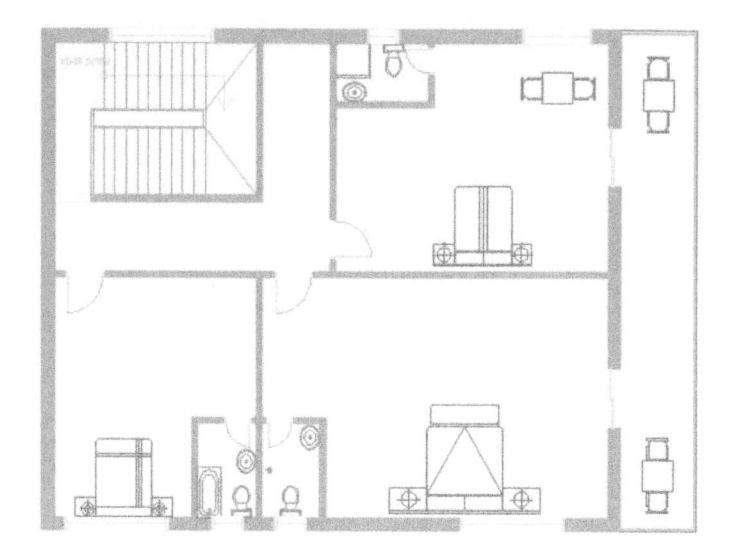

Adding Text Labels

- On the ribbon, click **Home** tab > **Layers** panel > **Layer** drop-down > **A-TEXT**.

- On the **Home** tab of the ribbon, expand the **Annotation** panel and click the **Text Style** icon. On the **Text Style** dialog, click the **New** button. Type **Callout** in the **Style Name** box and click **OK**. Type 500 in the **Height** box and **Width Factor** to 0.75. Click the **Set Current** button, and then close the dialog.

- On the **Home** tab of the ribbon, in the **Annotation** panel, click **Text** drop-down > **Multiline Text**. Click in the lounge area of the ground floor plan to specify the first corner of the multiline text box. Move the pointer and specify the second corner. Type **Lounge** in the text box. Click and drag the ruler to reduce the width of the text box.

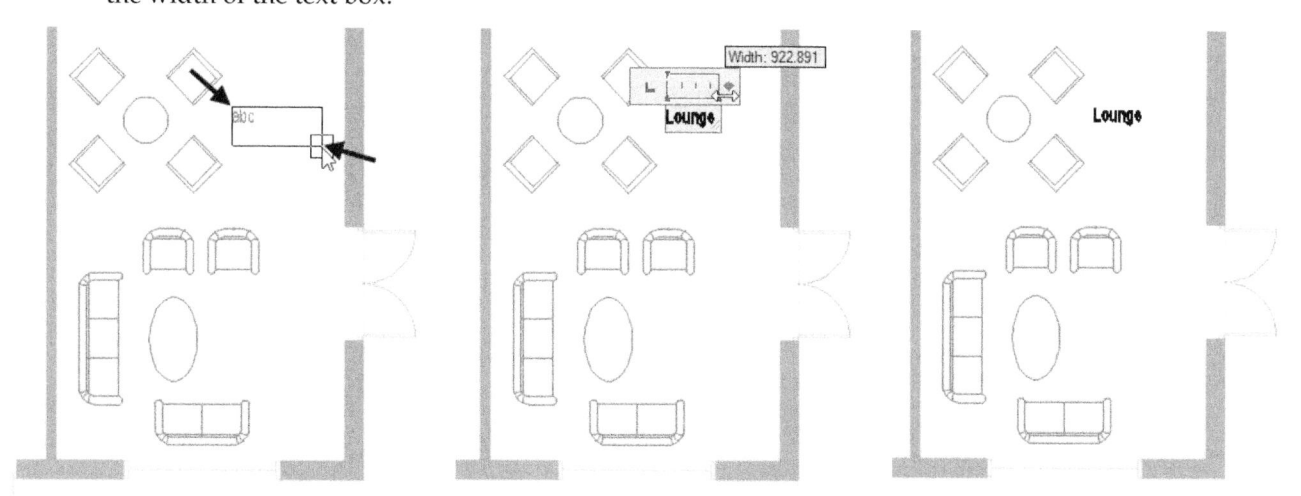

- Likewise, add text labels to ground and first floor plans.

AutoCAD 2016 For Architectural Design

Ground floor plan   First floor plan

- On the DesignCenter palette, click the **Home** icon. The **Sample** folder is selected in the Folder List. Under the **Sample** node, go to **en-us > DesignCenter** and click the **Landscape.dwg** file. Double click on the Blocks icon. Click and drag the **North Arrow** block from the DesignCenter palette into the graphics window.
- Drag the North Arrow block and place it at the bottom right corner of the ground floor plan. Se

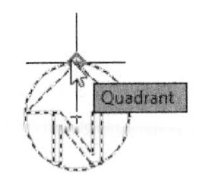

Tutorial 11: Creating Elevations

- Create the layers as shown next.

Layer Name	Color	Linetype
A-ELEV-WALL	cyan	Continuous
A-ELEV-TEXT	Index Color 7	Continuous
A-ELEV-ROOF	green	Continuous
A-ELEV-FOUNDATION	magenta	Continuous
A-ELEV-FLOORING	blue	Continuous
Reference Lines	Index Color 9	Continuous

- Create a selection window across the ground floor plan. Create a copy of the ground floor plan in the empty space, as shown.

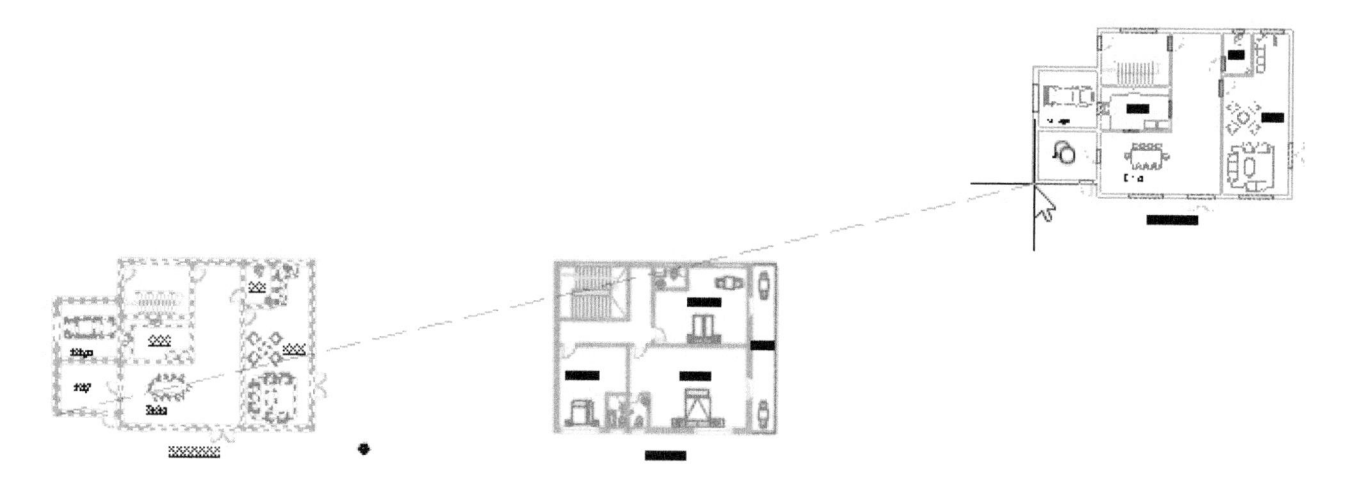

- On the ribbon, click **Home** tab > **Layers** panel > **Layer** drop-down > **A-ELEV-FOUNDATION**. Zoom to the copy of the ground floor plan. Draw a horizontal datum line above the floor plan.

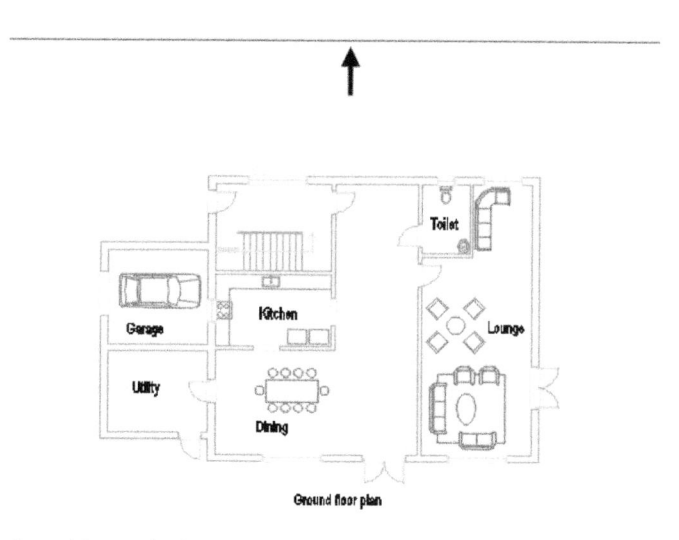

- On the ribbon, click **Home** tab > **Layers** panel > **Layer** drop-down > **A-TEXT**.
- Type PL and press Enter. Select a point on the datum line. Select **Width** from the command line. Type 0 and press Enter to define the starting width. Type 260 and press Enter to define the end width. Move the pointer vertically upward, type 225, and press Enter. Select **Width** from the command line. Type 0 and press Enter twice. Move the pointer horizontally and click.

- Create and place the text above the polyline, as shown.

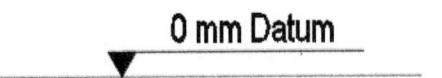

- Offset the datum up to 2490 mm. Copy the floor level annotation and place above the new line.

- Offset the ground floor line up to 200 downward. This defines the floor thickness. Select the two lines defining the floor thickness and click **Home** tab > **Layers** panel > **Layers drop-down** > **A-ELEV-FLOORING**.

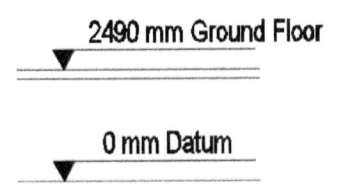

- Create other offset lines, as shown. Select top three horizontal lines and move them to the A-ELEV-ROOF layer.

- On the ribbon, click **Home** tab > **Layers** panel > **Layer** drop-down > **A-ELEV-WALL**. Activate the **Line** tool and select the top left corner of the ground floor plan. Move the pointer upward and click to create a vertical line. Press Esc. Likewise, create other vertical lines, as shown.

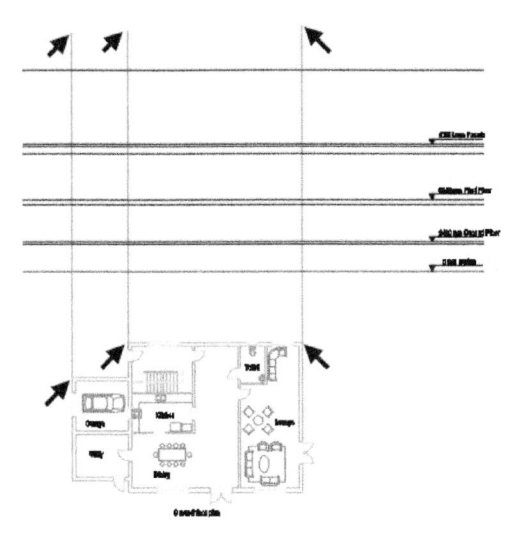

Next, you need to create an overhang for roof.

- Offset the left vertical lines to left side. Likewise, offset the right vertical line to right side. The offset distance is 406 mm.

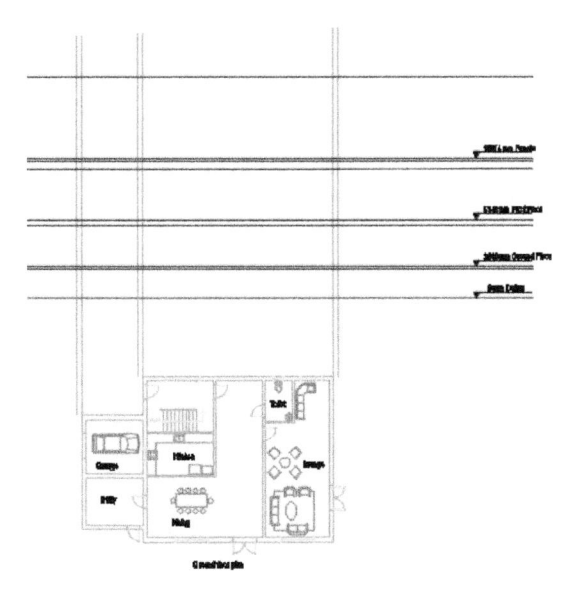

- Type TR and press Enter twice. Create a rectangular selection window across the left portions of the horizontal lines, as shown. Likewise, trim the right side portions of the horizontal lines.

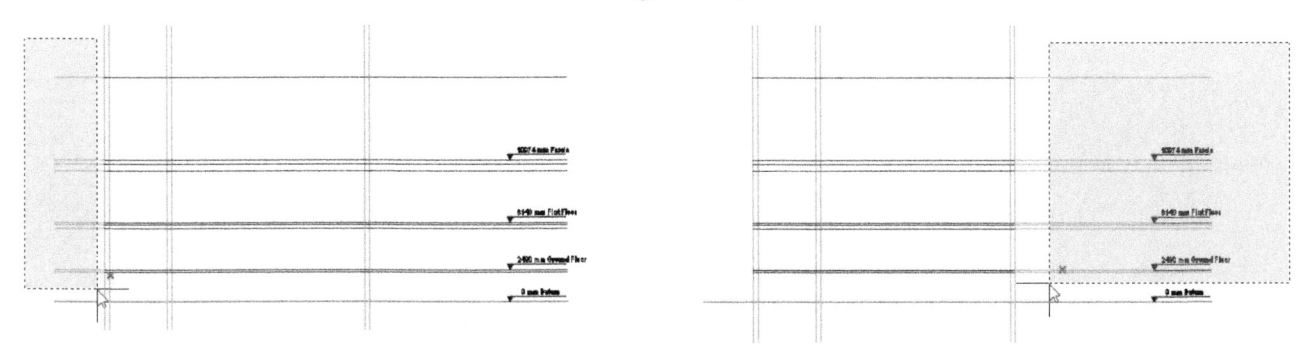

- Trim the upper and lower portions of the vertical lines, as shown.

64 | AutoCAD 2016 For Architectural Design

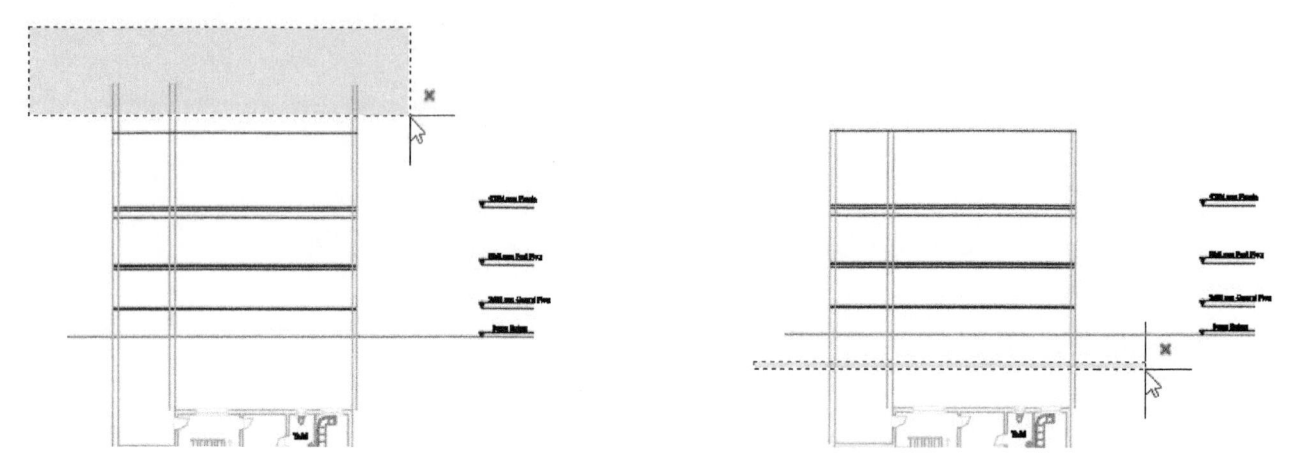

- Trim the other portions of the horizontal lines, as shown. Note that you need to trim from outside towards inward. Also, trim the vertical lines.

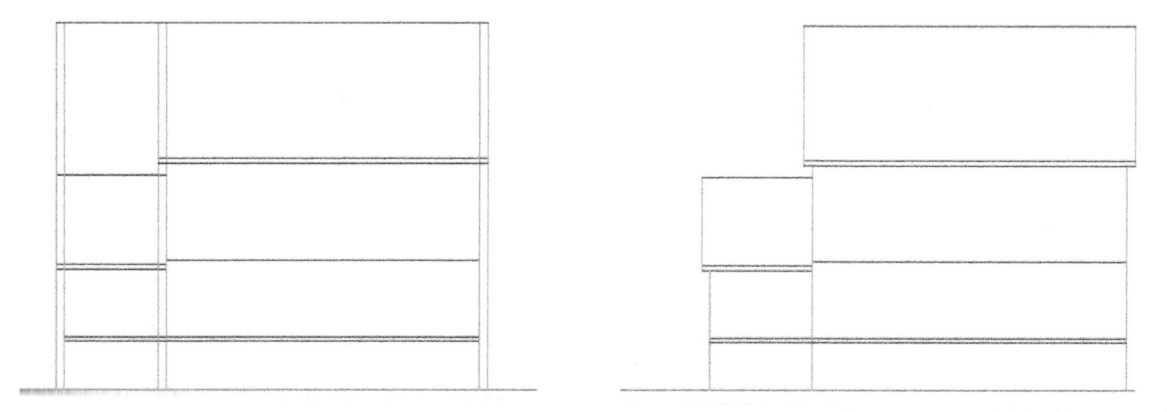

- Draw a vertical line from the top right corner of the ground floor plan, as shown. Copy the first floor plan and place it on the vertical line, as shown. Delete the vertical line.

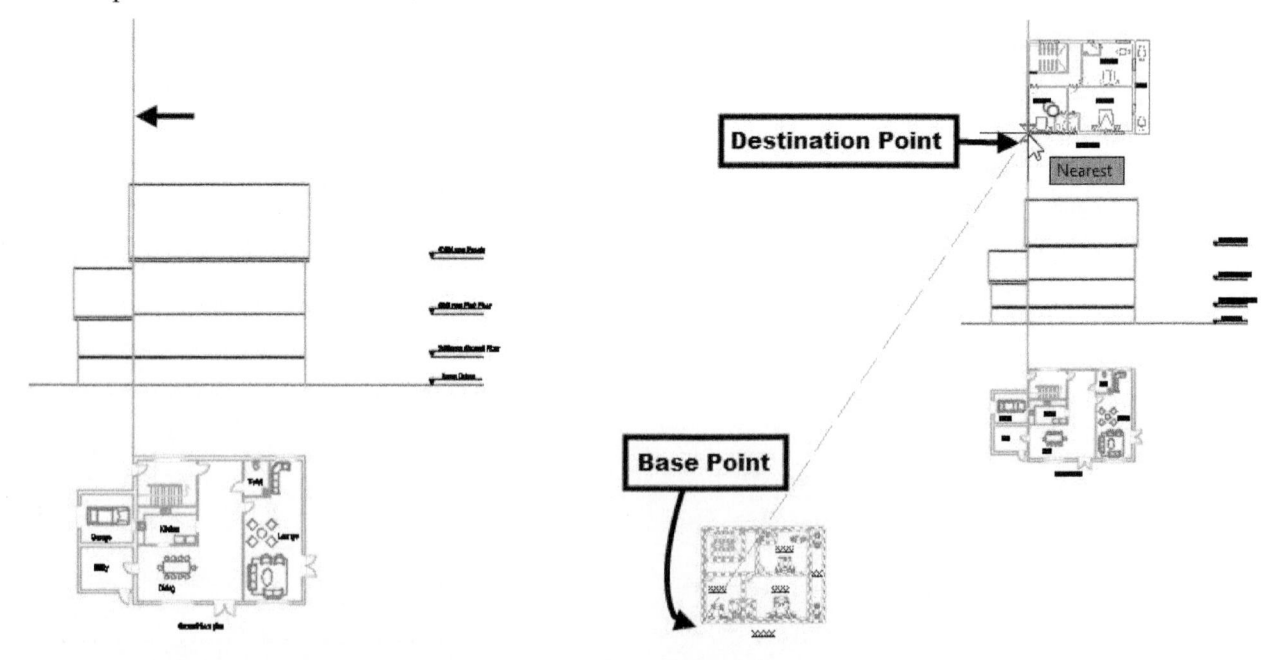

- On the ribbon, click **Home** tab > **Layers** panel > **Layer** drop-down > **Reference Lines**.

- On the **Home** tab of the ribbon, expand the **Draw** panel and click the **Ray** tool. Zoom to the copy of the first floor plan. Make sure that the ORTHOMODE is turned ON. Select the corner point of the balcony, move the pointer downward, and click. Press Esc to deactivate the tool.

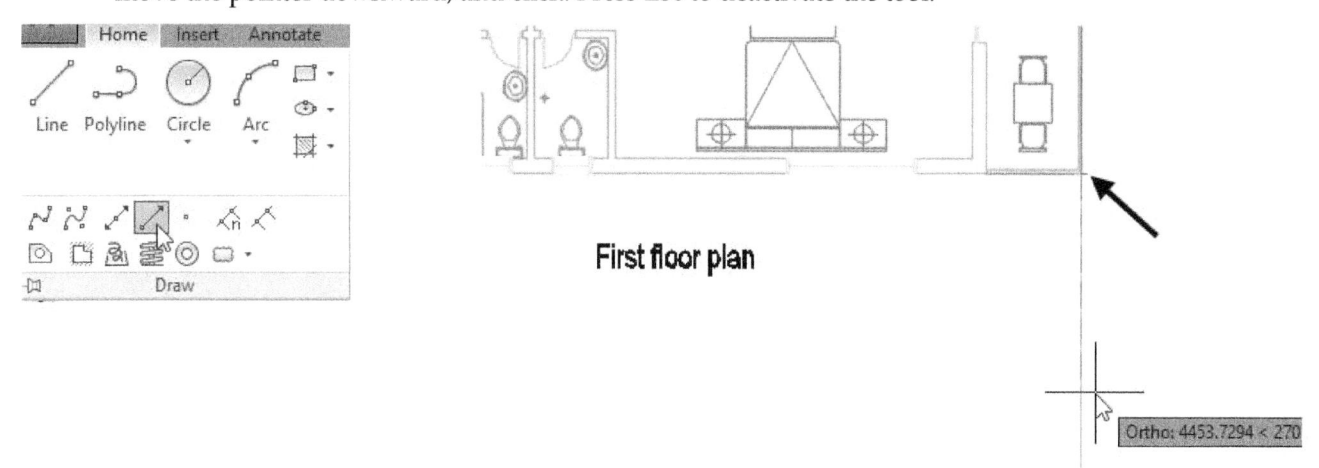

- Likewise, create reference lines from the windows.

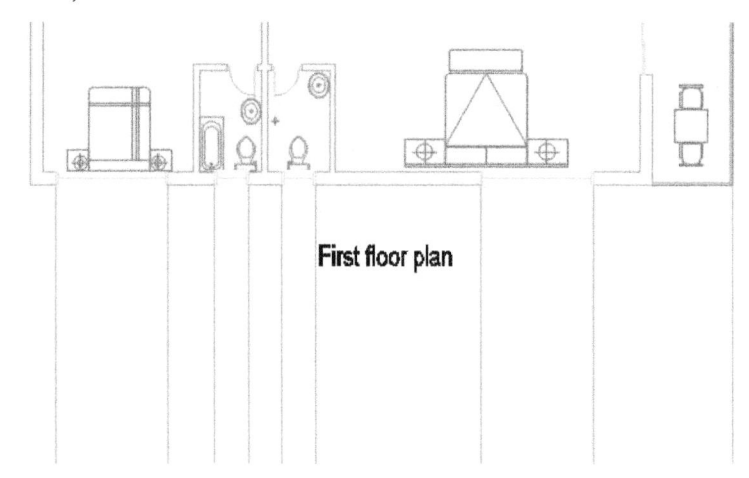

- On the ribbon, click **Home** tab > **Layers** panel > **Layer** drop-down > **A-ELEV-FLOORING**. Create the elements of the balcony using the **Rectangle** tool, as shown.

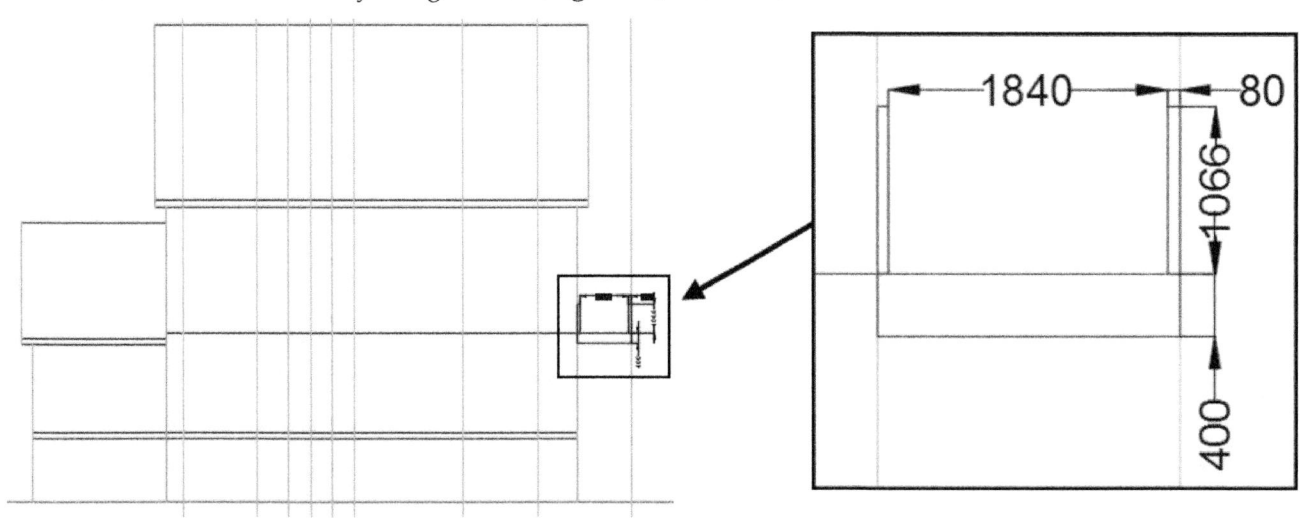

- Use the **Move** tool to move the two rectangles inward by 50 mm.

66 | AutoCAD 2016 For Architectural Design

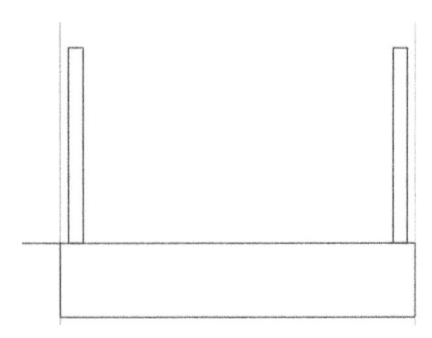

- Type REC and press Enter. Click in the empty space, and select **Dimensions** from the command line. Type 25 and press Enter. Type 65 and press Enter. Move the pointer upward and click to create the rectangle. Select the rectangle, type M, and press Enter. Select the midpoint of the lower horizontal line of the rectangle. Move the pointer and select the midpoint of the balcony post, as shown. Likewise, use the **Copy** tool to copy and place the small rectangle on the other post.

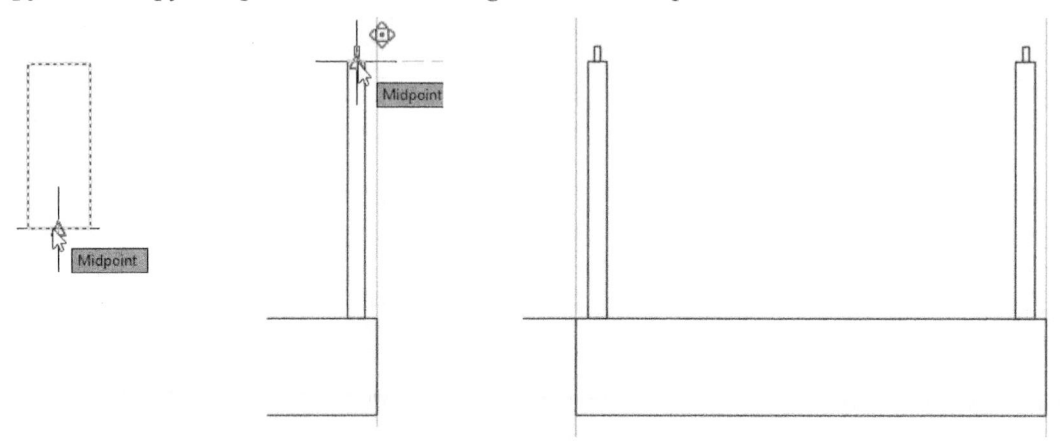

- Create a horizontal line, as shown. Offset the horizontal line by 50 mm.

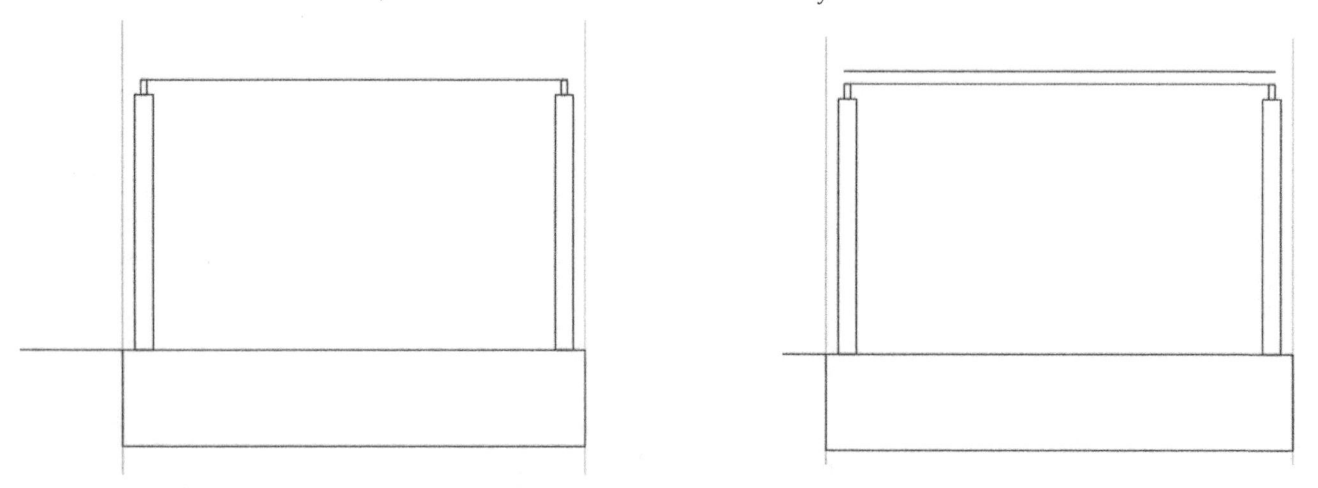

- On the ribbon, click **Home** tab > **Modify** panel > **Trim** drop-down > **Extend**. Press Enter to select all entities as boundary edges. Click on the left end of the horizontal line, as shown; it is extended up to the next entity. Likewise, extend the horizontal lines on both sides, as shown.

67 | AutoCAD 2016 For Architectural Design

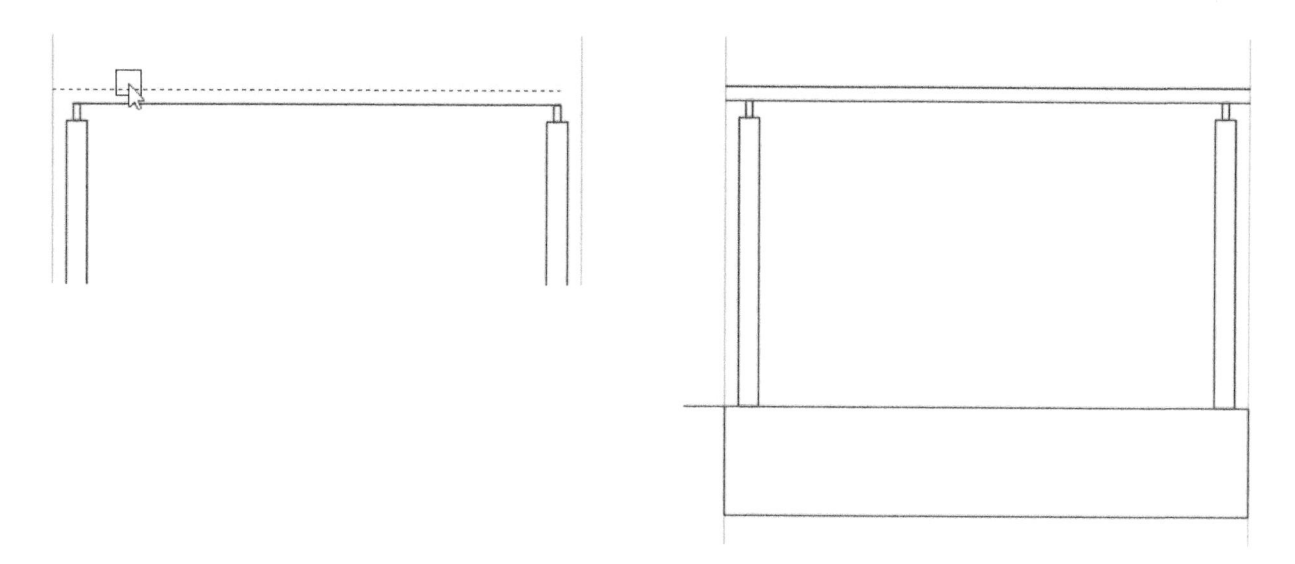

- On the ribbon, click **Home** tab > **Draw** panel > **Arc** drop-down > **Start, End, Direction**. Specify the start and end points of the arc, as shown. Move the pointer horizontally toward right and click.

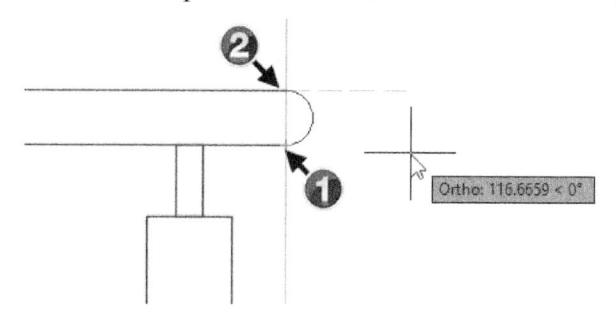

- Create a rectangle by specifying the corner points, as shown. Select the rectangle to display grips on it. Click on the midpoint grip of the lower horizontal line of rectangle, move the pointer upward, type 75, and press Enter. Likewise, move the vertical lines of the rectangle inward by 10 mm.

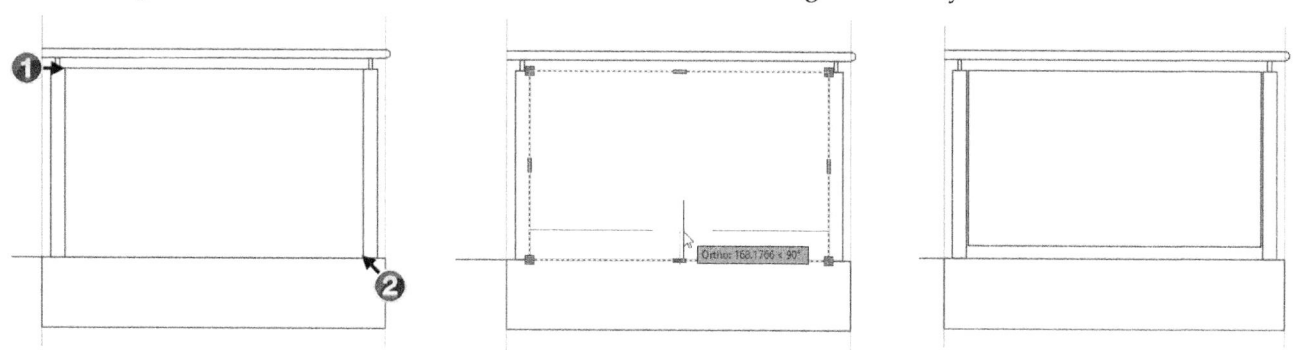

Now, you need to create the sleeve for the glass.

- Type REC and press Enter. Select the top right corner of the left post, as shown. Select **Dimensions** from the command line. Type 40 and press Enter. Type 75 and press Enter. Move the pointer downward and click.

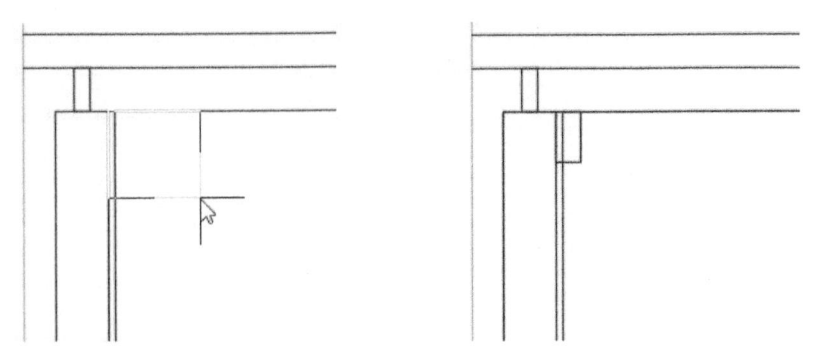

- Select the new rectangle, type **M** and press Enter. Select the top left corner of the rectangle to define the base point. Move the pointer downward, type 100, and press Enter.

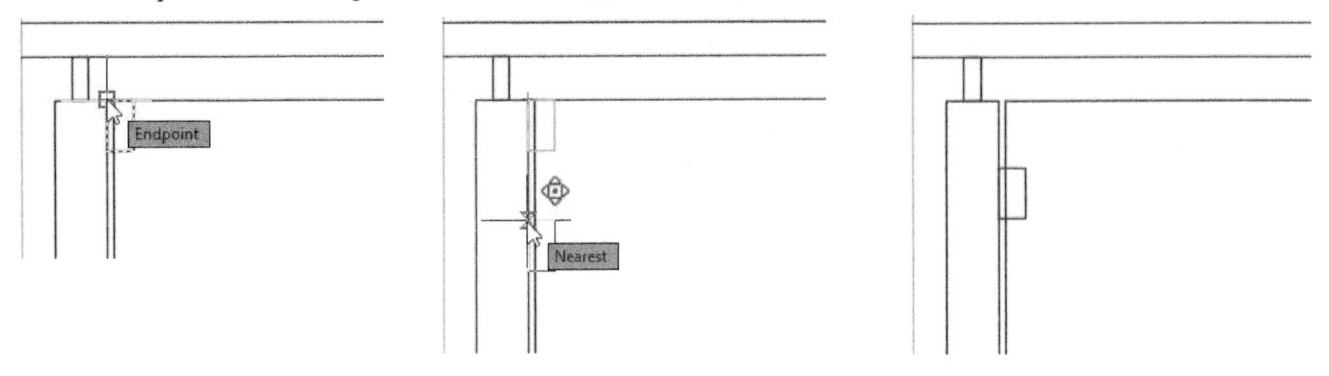

- Activate the **Start, End, Direction** tool. Select the top right and bottom right corners of the new rectangle. Move the pointer horizontally toward right and click. Type TR and press Enter twice. Trim the unwanted portions, as shown.

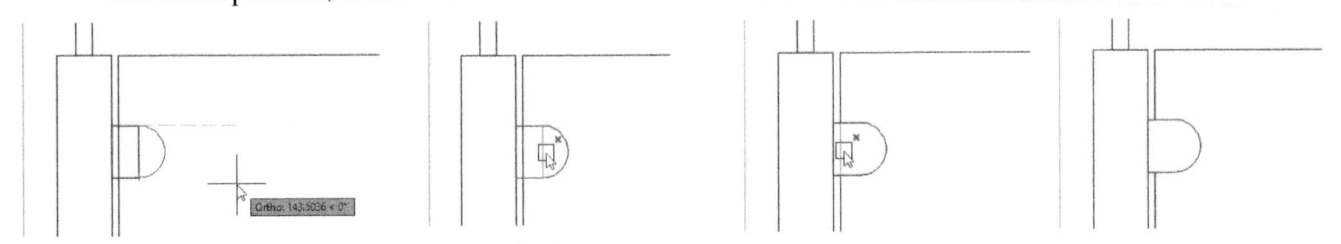

- Select the entities of the sleeve, type MI and press Enter. Select the midpoint of the glass rectangle, move the pointer downward, and click. Select **No** from the command line.

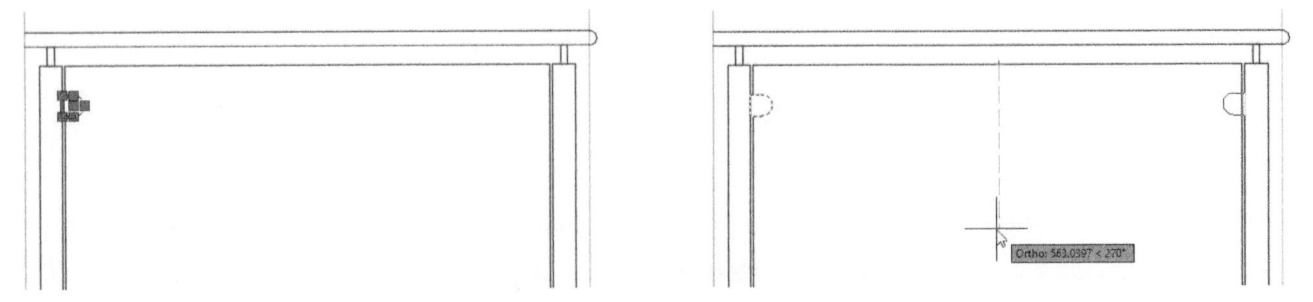

- Select the two sleeves and click **Home** tab > **Modify** panel > **Array** drop-down > **Rectangular Array**. On the **Array Creation** tab of the ribbon, set the **Columns** and **Rows** values to 1 and 2, respectively. Type -716 in the **Between** box on the **Rows** panel. Click **Close Array** on the ribbon.

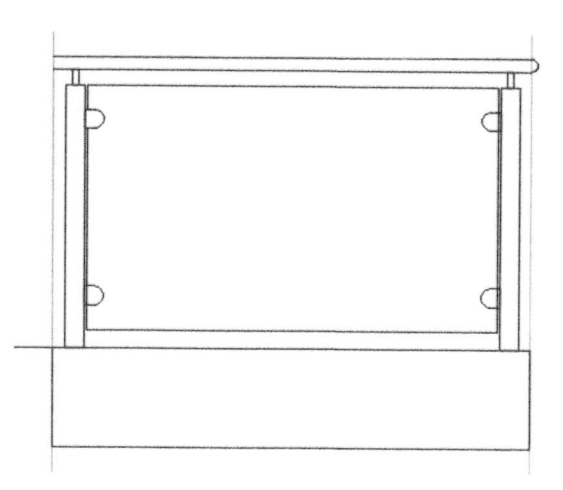

- Trim the unwanted portions of the sleeves, as shown.

- On the Status bar, click the **Polar Tracking** icon. Click the down arrow next to the **Polar Tracking** icon and select 30. Activate the **Line** command and create an inclined line, as shown. Offset the inclined on both sides. The offset distance is 100 mm.

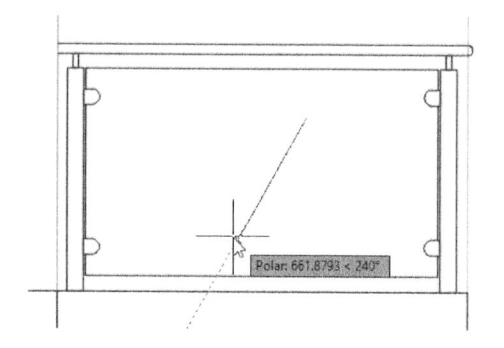

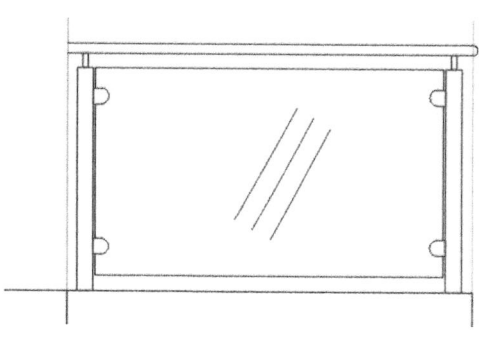

- Select one of the offset lines, type SC, and press Enter. Select midpoint of the offset line, type 0.5, and press Enter. The line is scaled to half of its size. Likewise, scale the other offset line.

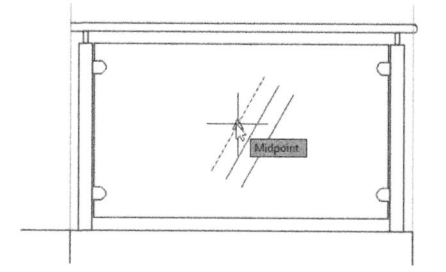

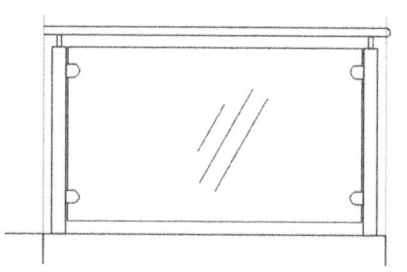

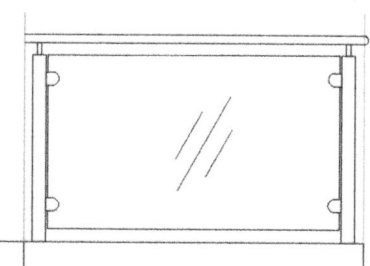

Creating Windows and Doors in the Elevation View

- On the ribbon, click **Home** tab > **Layers** panel > **Layer** drop-down > **A-WINDOW**.
- On the DesignCenter palette, click the **Home** button, and go to **Sample > en-us > Dynamic Blocks**. Expand the **Architectural – Metric.dwg** file and click on the **Blocks** icon. Drag the **Aluminum Window (Elevation Metric)** block and place it in the graphics window.
- Select the window block to display the dynamic block grips. Change the window width and height by using the arrow grips.

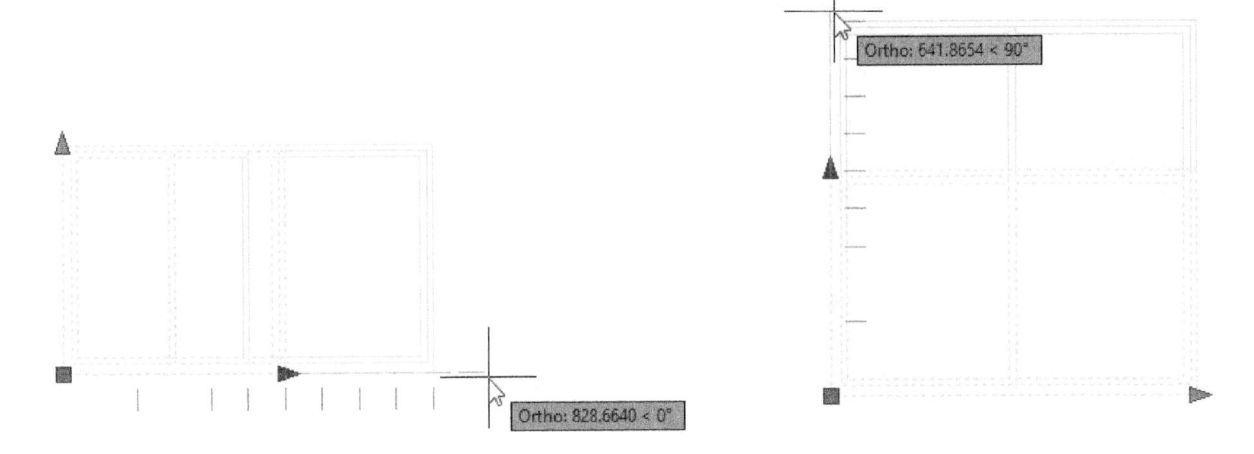

- Copy and place the window block on the elevation view at the locations, as shown.

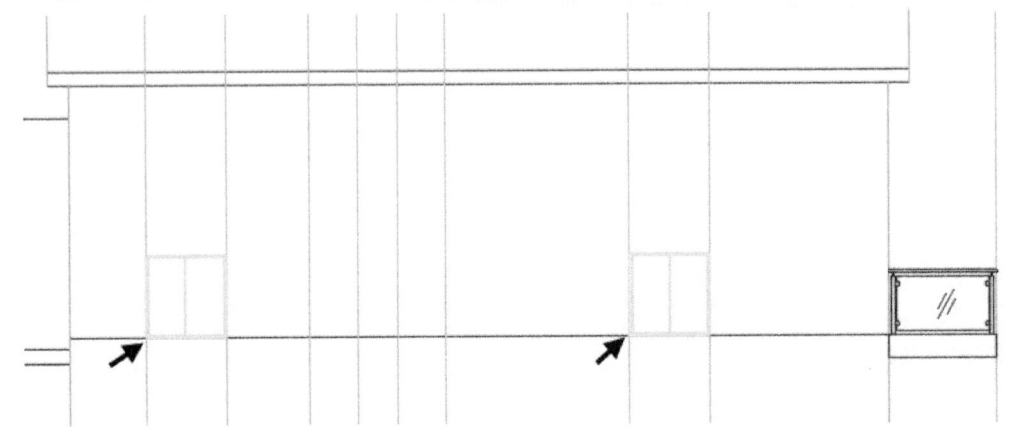

- Turn ON the ORTHOMODE (F8) on the status bar.
- Select the window blocks and click the **Move** tool on the **Modify** panel of the **Home** ribbon tab. Select the lower left corner point of anyone of the selected window blocks. Move the pointer upwards, type 1200 and press Enter.

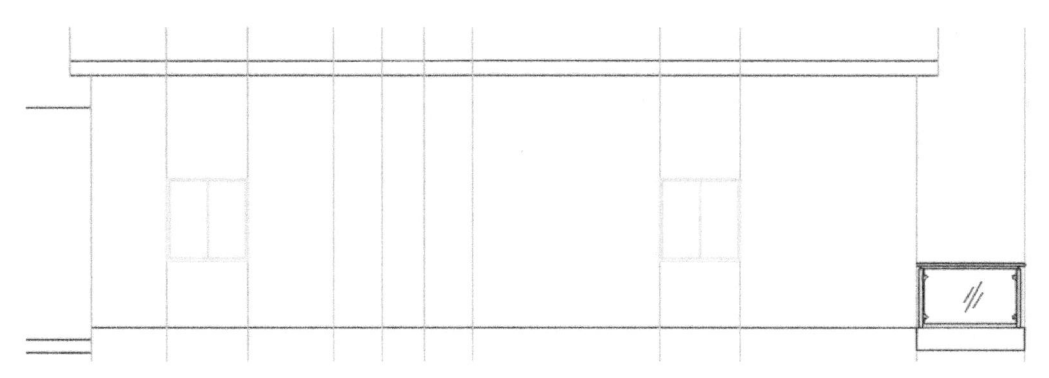

- Create two 900x900 rectangles on the elevation, as shown.

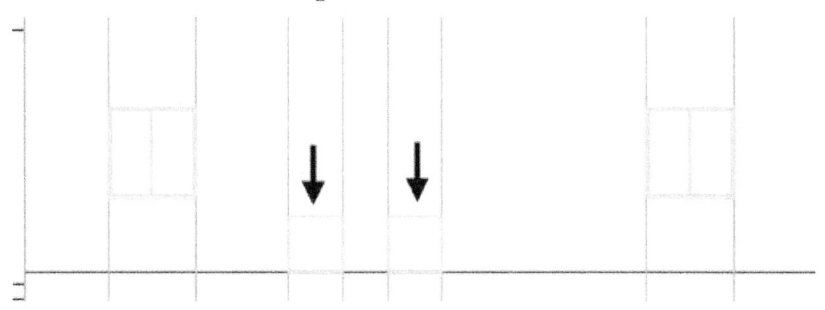

- Move the rectangles upward in the vertical direction up to the distance of 1800 mm. Offset the rectangles by 50 mm inside. Select the reference lines and press Delete.

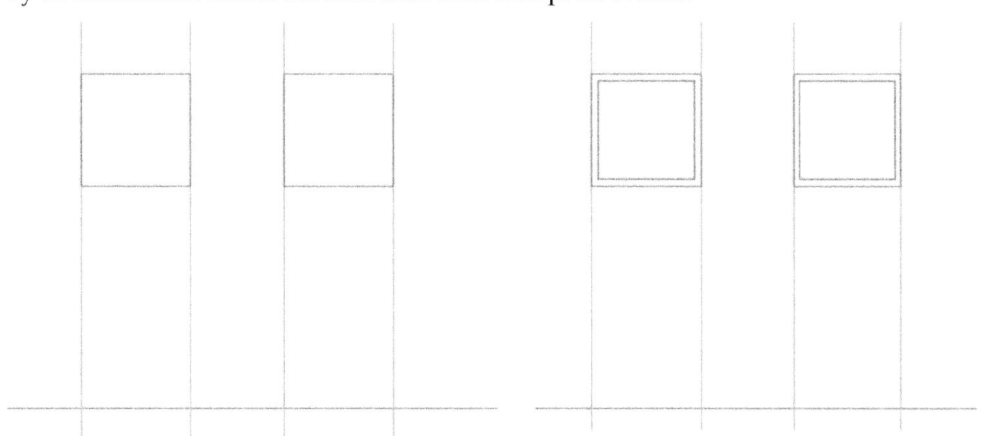

- Select the horizontal line below the ground floor and lengthen it by using the grips.

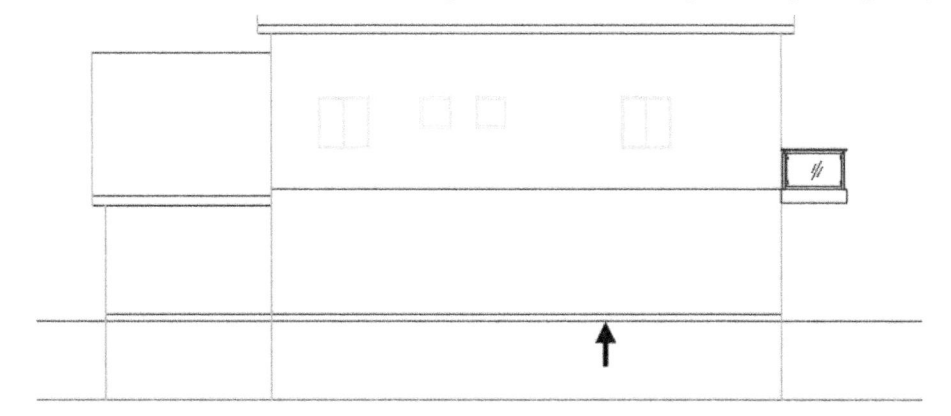

- On the ribbon, click **Home** tab > **Layers** panel > **Layer** drop-down > **Reference Lines**. Create reference

72 | **AutoCAD 2016 For Architectural Design**

lines originating from the door and windows on the ground floor, as shown.

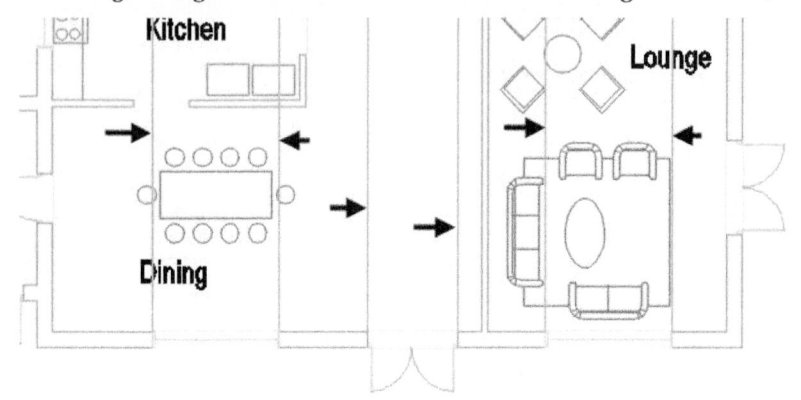

- On the ribbon, click **Home** tab > **Layers** panel > **Layer** drop-down > **A-WINDOWS**. Create a 2750x1500 rectangle on the elevation view, as shown. Move the rectangle vertically up to 1000 mm.

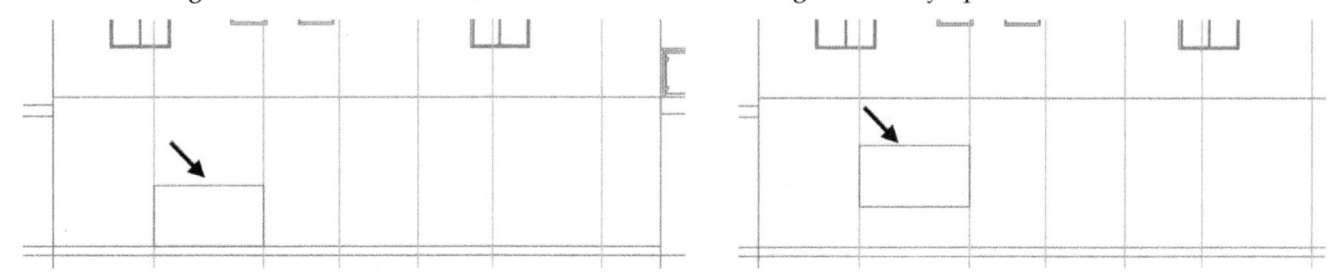

- Offset the rectangle inward by 50 mm. Explode the inner rectangle.

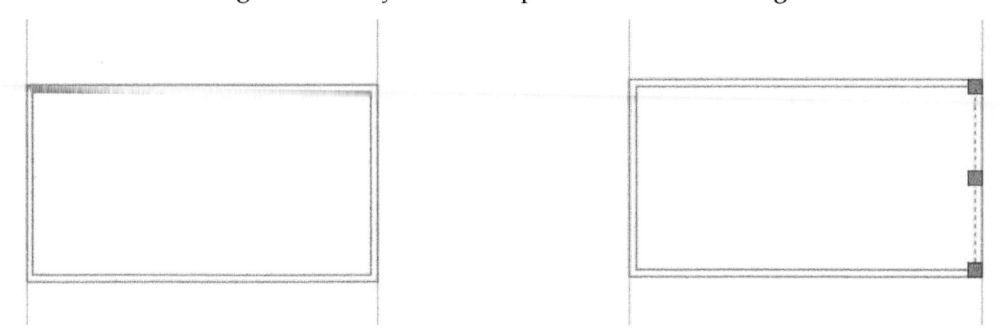

- Offset the inner vertical lines up to 850 mm inside. Again, offset the offset lines up to 50 mm inside.

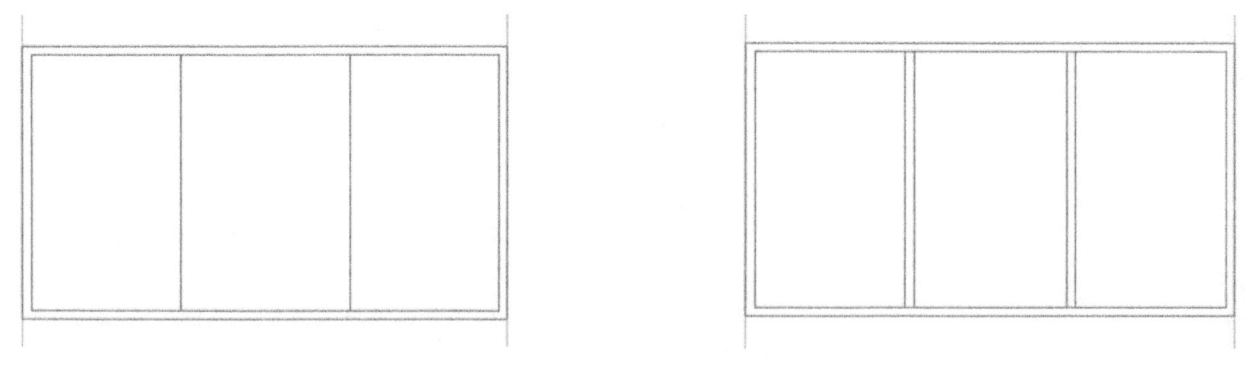

- Create a selection window across all the entities of the window, and click the **Copy** tool on the **Modify** panel of the **Home** ribbon tab. Select the lower left corner of the window to define the base point. Move the pointer toward right and select a point on the reference line, as shown.

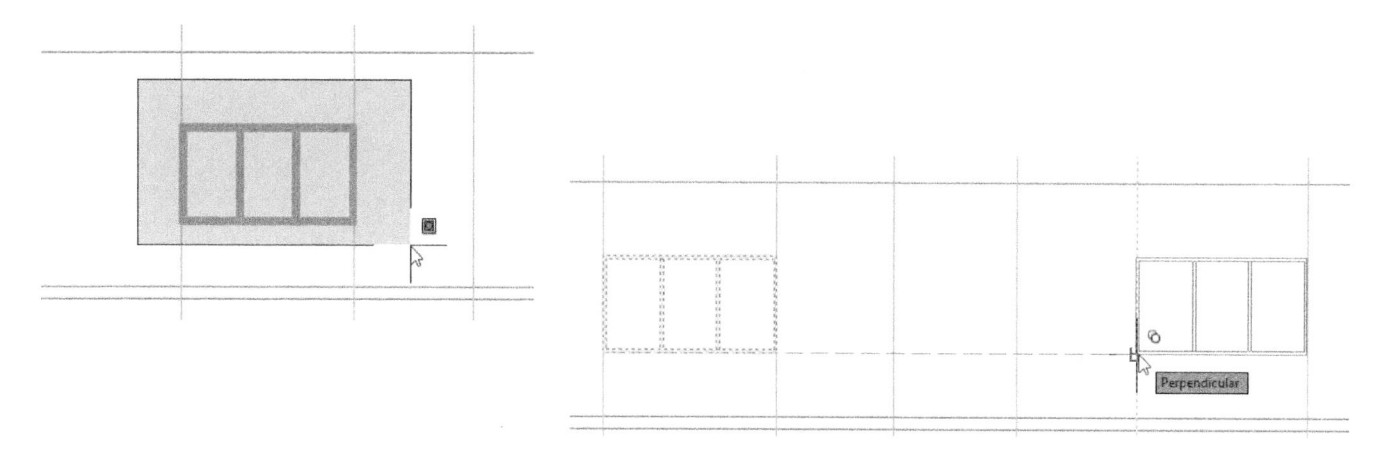

- On the ribbon, click **Home** tab > **Layers** panel > **Layer** drop-down > **A-DOOR**. Type REC and press Enter. Select the intersection point between the reference line and ground floor line, as shown.

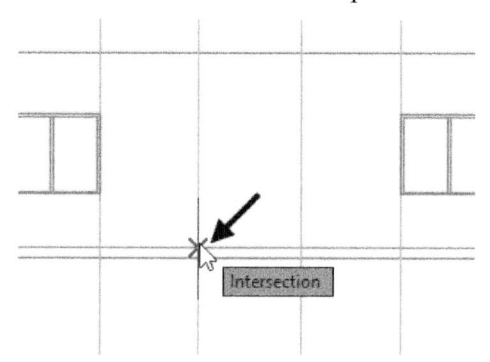

- Select **Dimensions** from the command line. Select the two intersection points on the elevation view, as shown. The distance between the selected points defines the length of the rectangle. Type 2500 and press Enter to define the width of the rectangle. Move the pointer upward and click to create the rectangle.

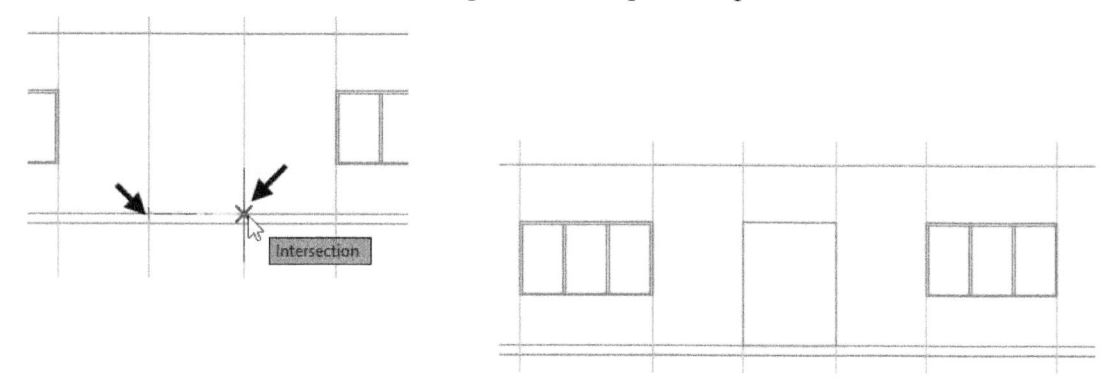

- Offset the rectangle up to 65 mm inside. Select the two rectangles and click the **Explode** tool on the **Modify** panel of the **Home** ribbon tab. Select the lower horizontal line of the inner rectangle and press **Delete**. Type **EX** and press Enter twice. Click on the lower end portions of the inner vertical lines. The selected lines are extended up to the intersecting horizontal line. Press Esc.

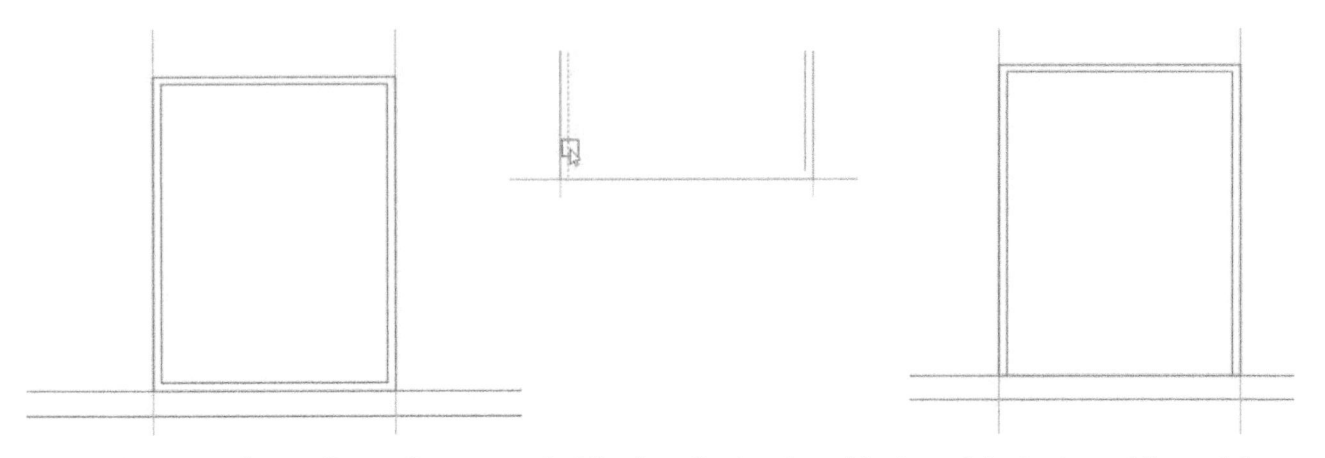

- Type L and press Enter. Create a vertical line by selecting the midpoints of the horizontal lines of the door, as shown. Press Enter twice. Select the upper end point of the new vertical line. Select the midpoint of the left vertical line of the door. Likewise, create other lines by selecting the points, as shown. The inclined lines indicate the hinge direction.

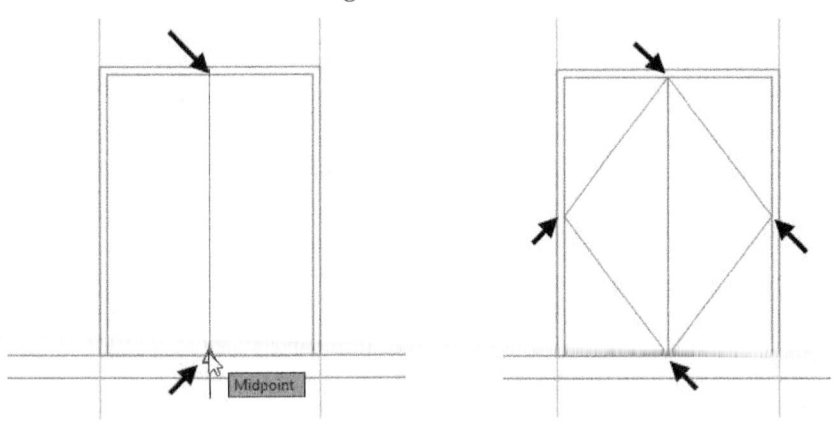

- Select the inclined lines, type PR and press Enter. On the **Properties** palette, change the **Linetype** and **Linetype Scale** to **HIDDEN** and 750, respectively.

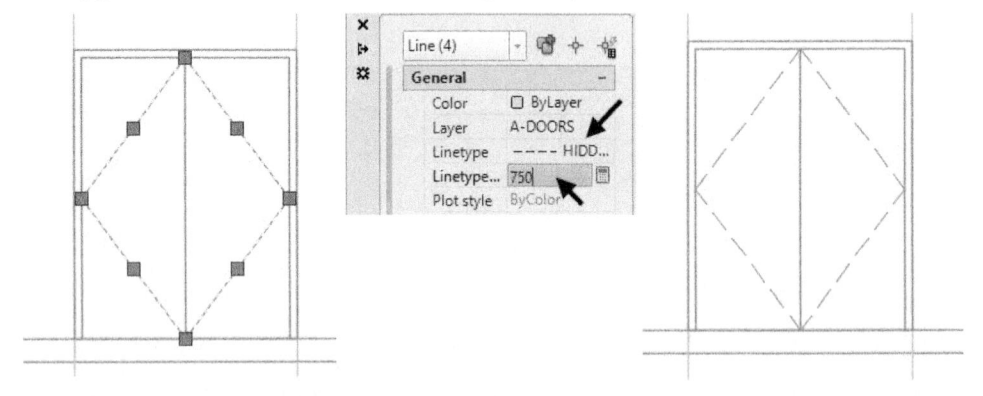

- Likewise, create the utility room door, as shown.

75 | AutoCAD 2016 For Architectural Design

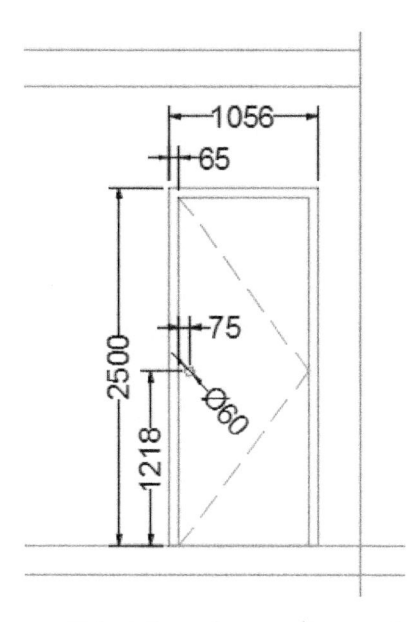

- Select the reference lines and press Delete.

Creating the Opposite Elevation

You can create the elevation opposite to the front elevation by just mirroring it and modifying the internal objects.

- Create a selection window across all the objects of the elevation view. On the ribbon, click **Home tab > Modify panel > Move**. Select any point on the elevation view, move the pointer downward, and place the elevation view below the ground floor plan.

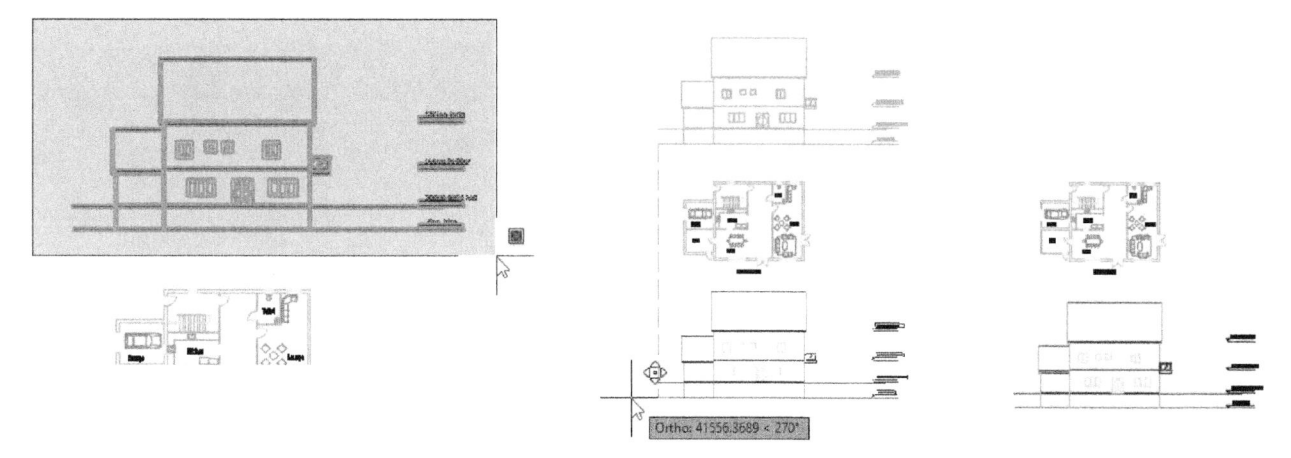

- Create a selection window across the elevation view, type MI, and press Enter. Select the midpoint of a vertical line on the ground floor elevation. Move the pointer horizontally toward right and click to mirror the elevation view. Select **No** from the command line.

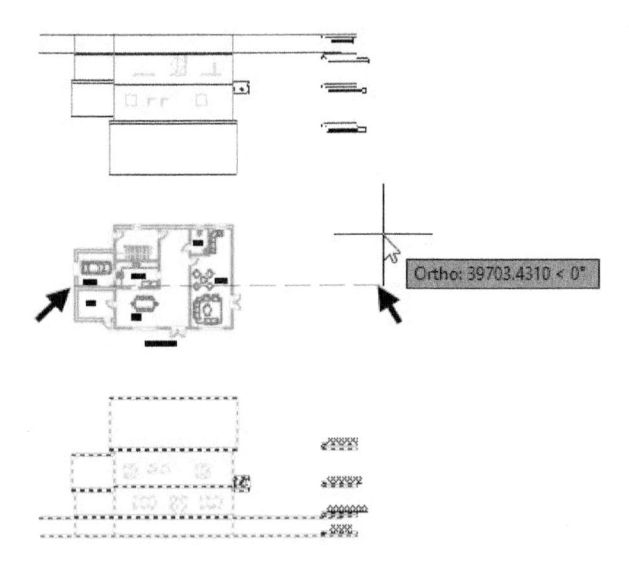

Now, you need to change the orientation of the UCS (User Coordinate System) to match the mirrored elevation view.

- Type UCS and press Enter. Select **Z** from the command line. Type 180 and press Enter. The UCS is rotated about the Z-axis by 180 degrees.

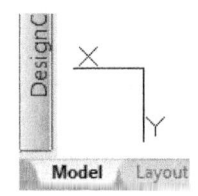

- Type **PLAN** and press Enter. Select **Current ucs** from the command line to orient the drawing with UCS.
- Type **Z** and press Enter. Select **Center** from the command line. Type 0 and press Enter to specify the zoom center. Type 150000 and press Enter to specify the magnification height. Press and hold the middle mouse button and drag the pointer to bring the elevation view to the center. Scroll the mouse wheel to magnify the elevation view.

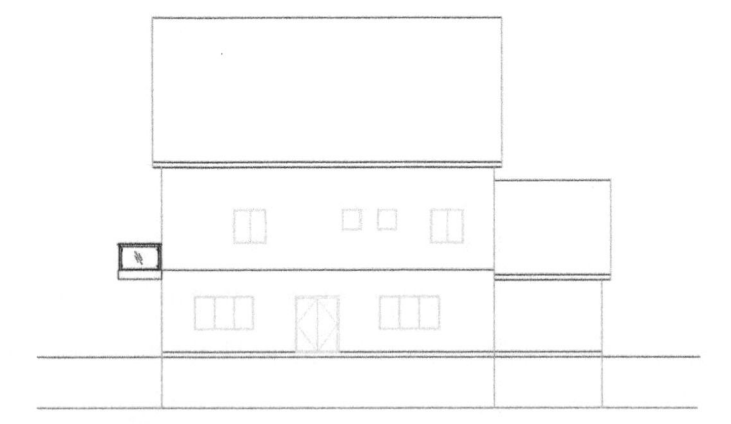

- Select the doors and windows on the elevation view and press **Delete**.
- On the ribbon, click **Home** tab > **Layers** panel > **Layer** drop-down > **Reference Lines**. Create reference

lines from the rare windows of the ground floor plan.

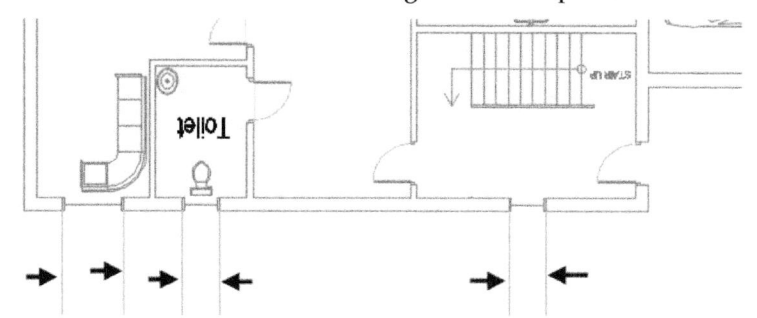

- On the ribbon, click **Home** tab > **Layers** panel > **Layer** drop-down > **A-WINDOWS**.
- On the ribbon, click **Insert** tab > **Block** panel > **Insert** gallery > **Aluminum Window (Elevation) – Metric**. Select the intersection point between the ground floor line and the reference line from the left-side window, as shown. Select the window block, and then select its base point. Move the pointer along the reference line, type 1200 and press Enter.

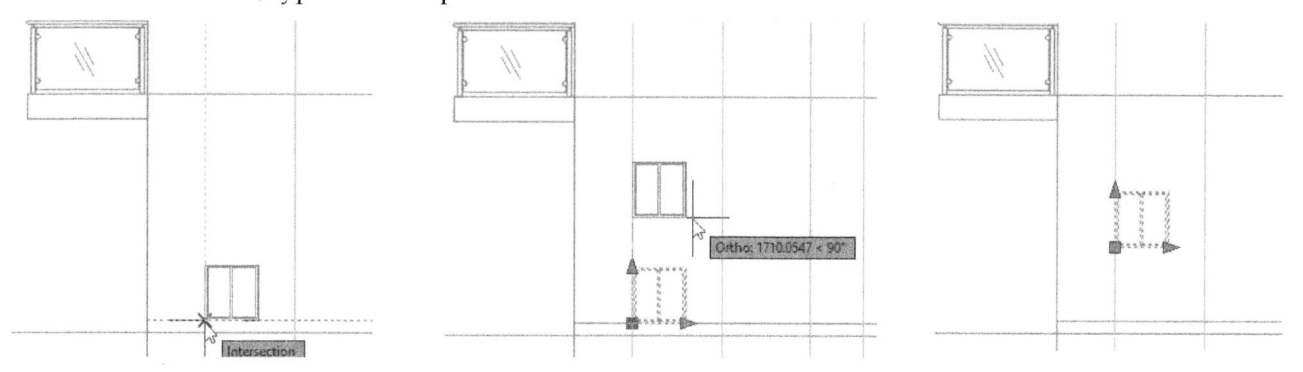

- Use the arrow grips of the window block to set its width and height.

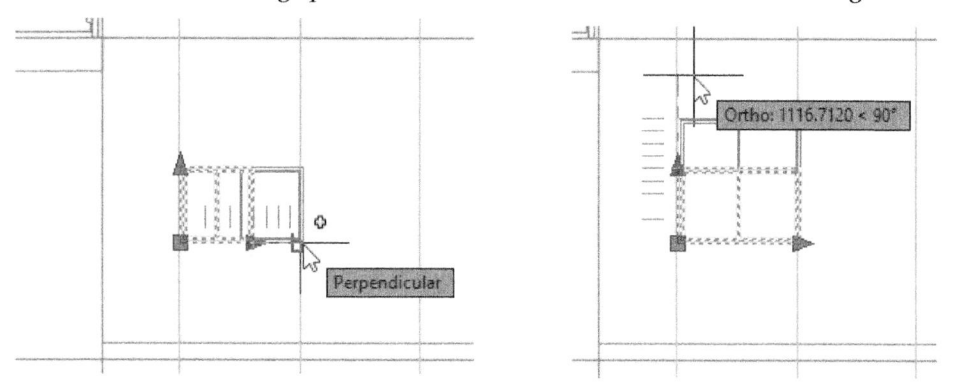

- Create the bathroom window using the **Rectangle** tool, as shown.

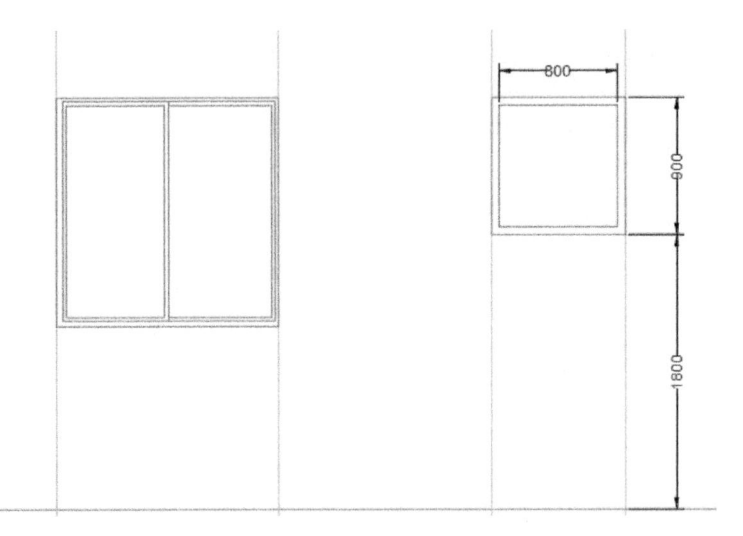

- Create the stair window **Rectangle**, **Explode**, and **Offset** tools, as shown. Select the reference lines and press Delete.

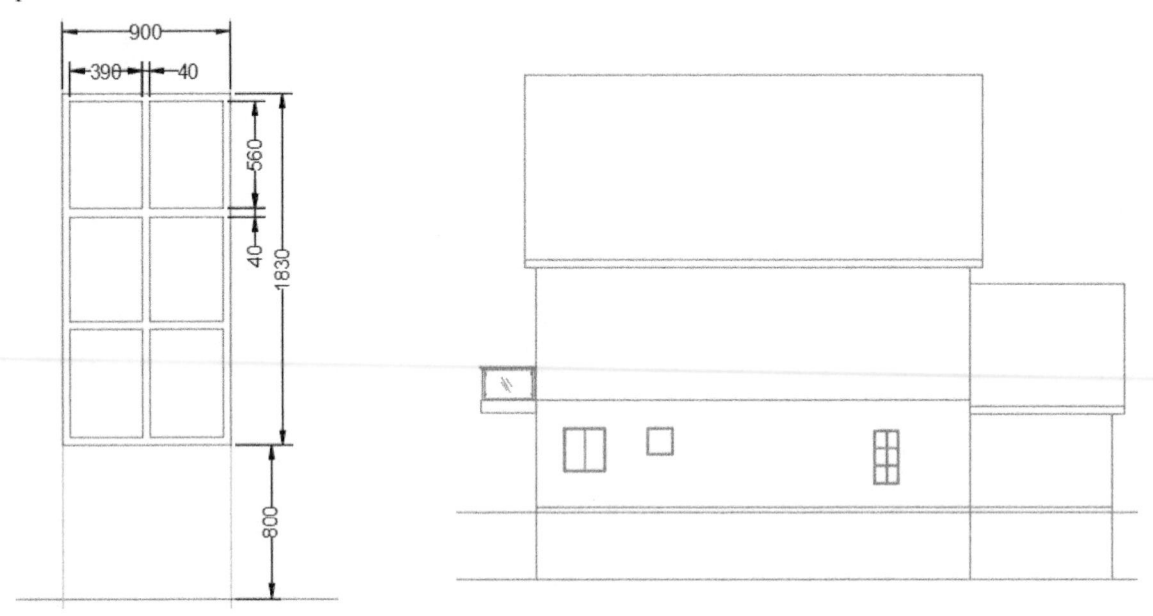

- Switch to the **Reference Lines** layer and create the rays from the windows of rear side of the first floor plan.

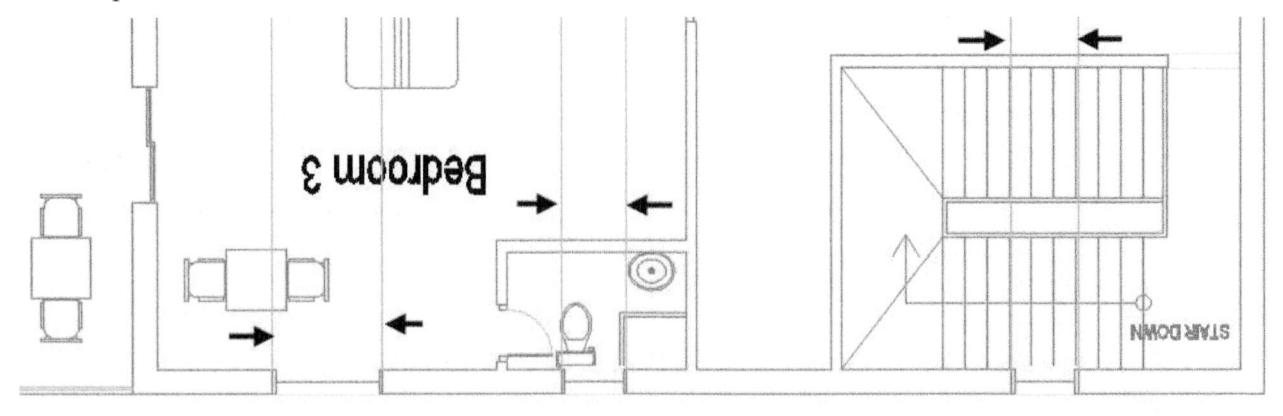

79 | **AutoCAD 2016 For Architectural Design**

- Copy the existing windows one-by-one and place them at the locations, as shown.

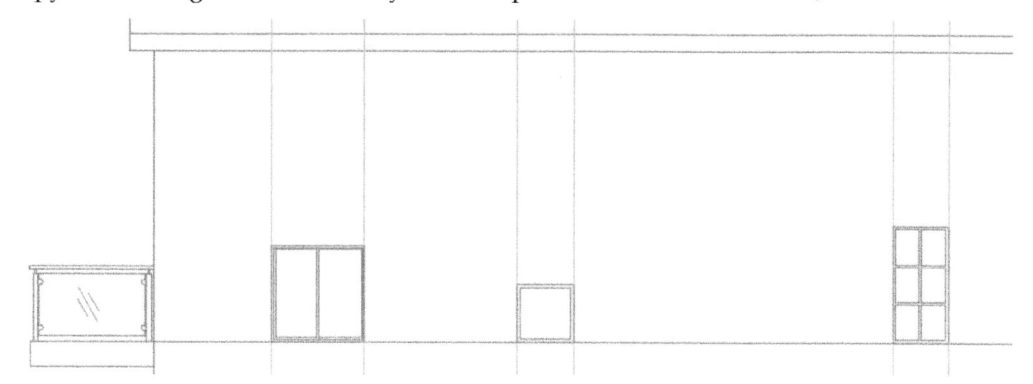

- Move the windows up to the distances, as shown. Delete the reference lines.

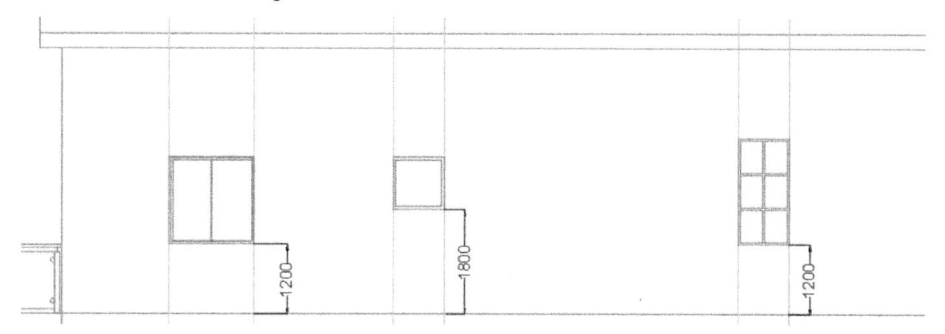

- On the **View** tab of the ribbon, click the right mouse button on anyone of the panels and select **Show Panels > Coordinates**. The **Coordinates** panel appears on the **View** tab of the ribbon.

- On the **Coordinates** panel, click the **UCS, Named UCS** tool.

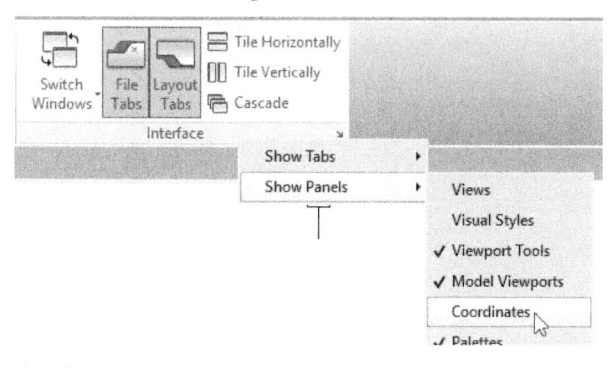

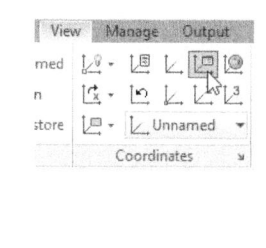

- On the **UCS** dialog, click the **Named UCS** tab. Right click on the **Unamed** ucs and select **Rename**. Type **North Elev**. Click **OK**.

- On the **View** tab of the ribbon, right click on anyone of the panels and select **Show Panels > Views**. The **Views** panel appears on the ribbon. On the **Views** panel, click the **View Manager** tool to open the **View Manager** dialog. Click the **New** button on the **View Manager** dialog to open the **New View/Shot Properties** dialog. Type **North Elev** in the **View name** box.

- Select the **Define window** option and create a window enclosing the elevation view. Press Enter to accept. Make sure that **North Elev** is selected in the **UCS** drop-down and click **OK**. The **Views** list in the **View Manager** dialog displays the **North Elev** view.

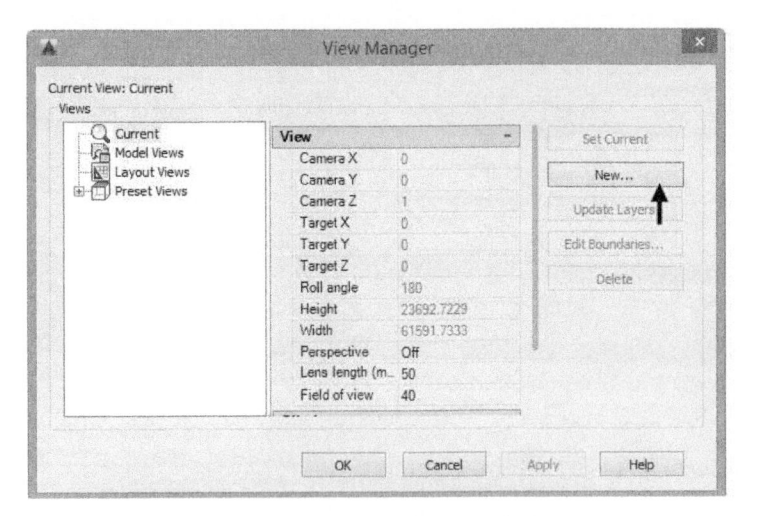

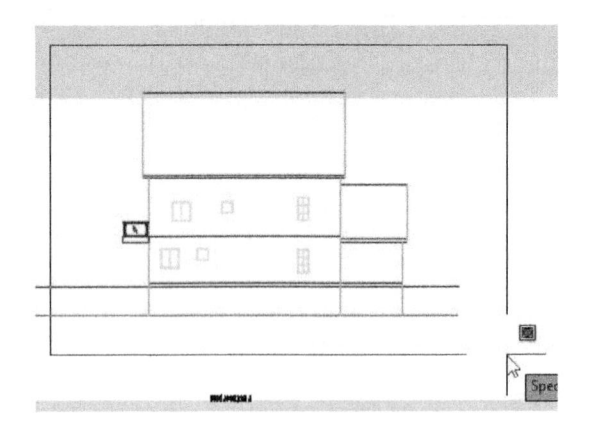

- Click **OK** on the **View Manager** dialog.

Now, you need switch back to the default view orientation.

- On the **View** tab of the ribbon, in the **Views** panel, select **Top** from the **Preset View** gallery. The default orientation of the drawing is displayed.

- Type **Z** and press Enter. Select **Center** from the command line. Type 0 and press Enter to specify the zoom center. Type 150000 and press Enter to specify the magnification height. Press and hold the middle mouse button and drag the pointer to bring the elevation view to the center.

- Select all the annotations showing the floor levels and mirror them about the midpoint of the elevation.

Creating the Front and Rear Elevations

- On the ribbon, click **Home > Layers > Layer** drop-down **> Reference Lines** to make it current.
- Create a 45-degree from the lower right corner point of the ground floor plan. You can use the polar tracking to create the inclined line.

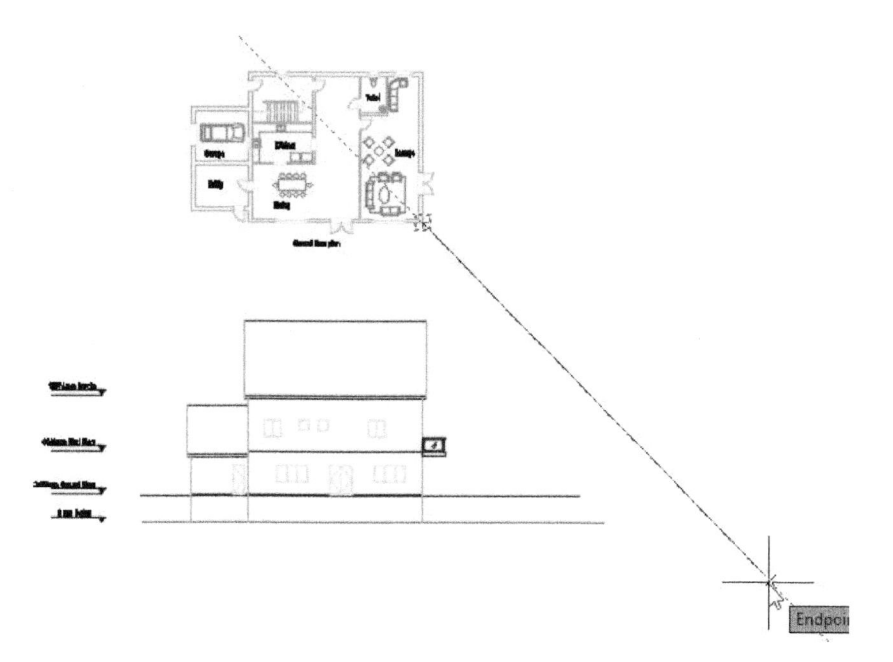

- On the **Home** tab of the ribbon, expand the **Draw** panel and click **Construction Line** tool. Select **Hor** from the command line. Select the top corner pointe of the South Elevation, as shown. A horizontal construction line is created passing through the selected point.

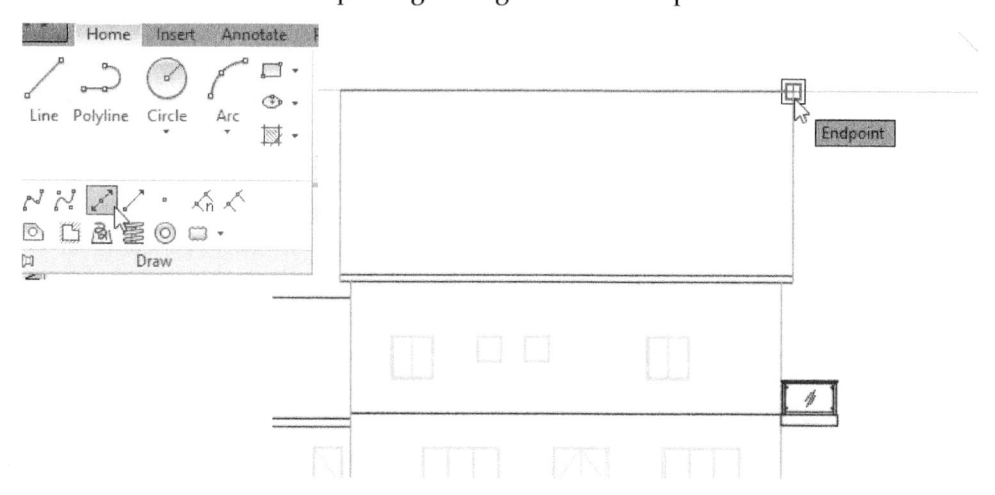

- Likewise, create other construction lines, as shown. Press Esc.

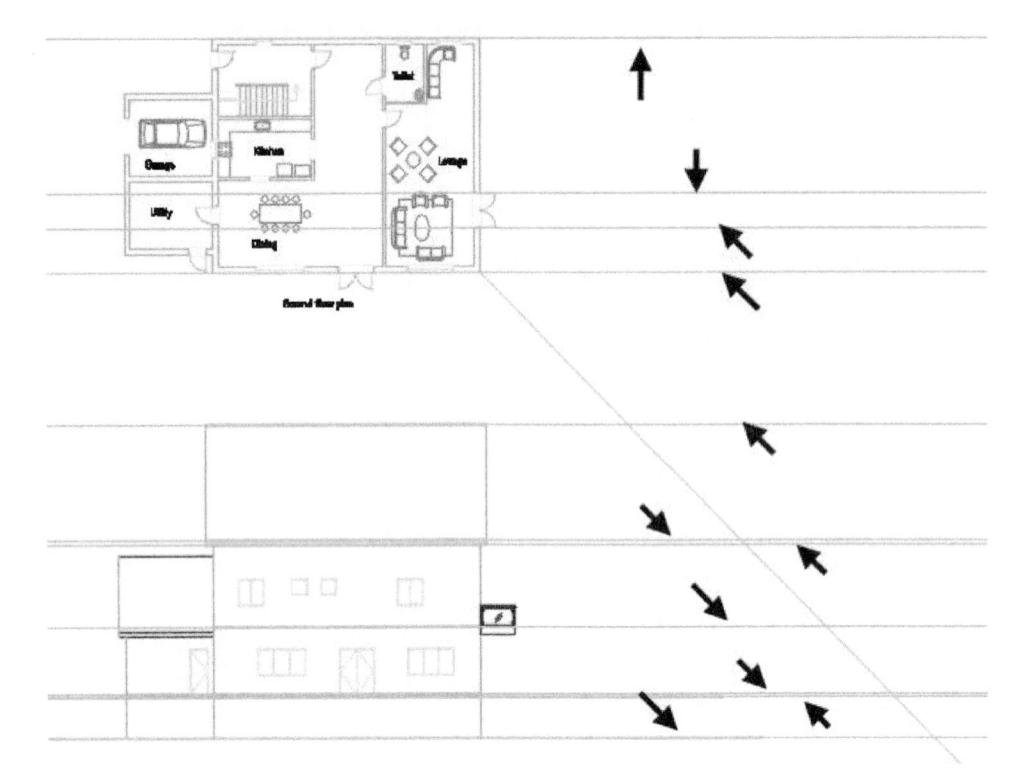

- Type **XL** and press Enter. Select **Ver** from the command line. Select the intersection point between the horizontal construction line and the inclined, as shown. Likewise, select the intersection points between the inclined and other horizontal construction lines.

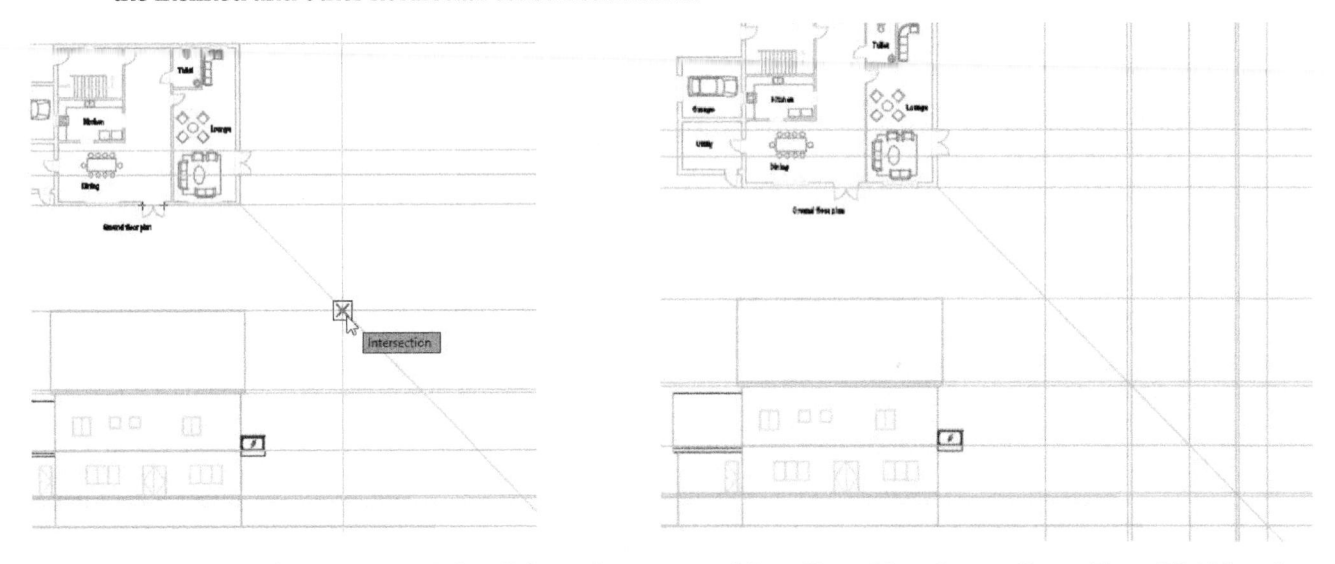

- Type **UCS** and press Enter. Select Z from the command line. Type 90 and press Enter. Type PLAN and press Enter. The UCS is rotated by 90 degrees about the Z-axis. Zoom to the area below the ground floor plan, as shown.
- Create a construction line passing through the center of the ground floor plan, as shown.

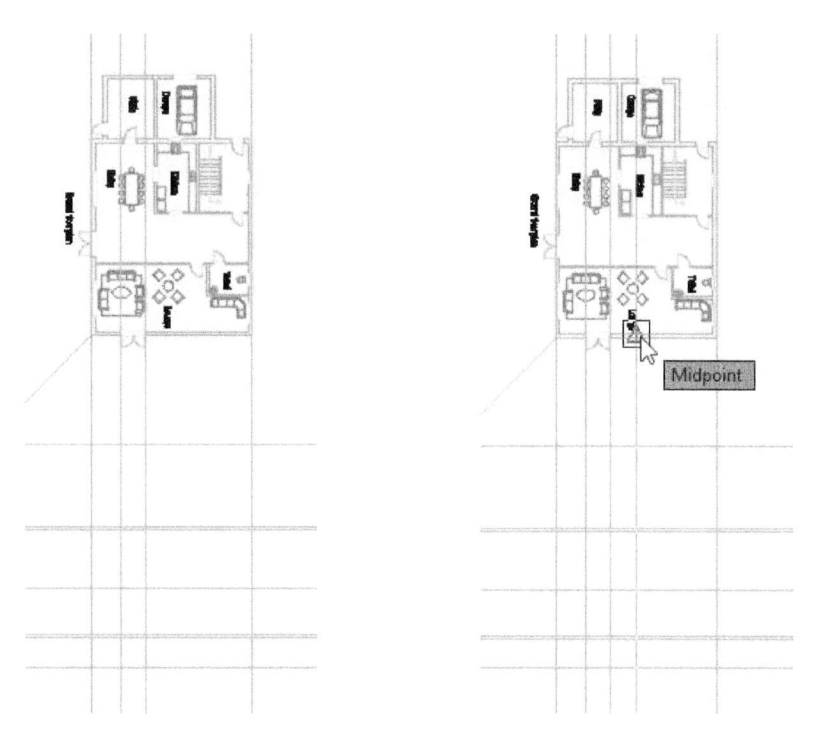

- Create two construction lines at the 406 mm distance from the exterior walls, as shown. These lines will help you to draw the roof overhang.

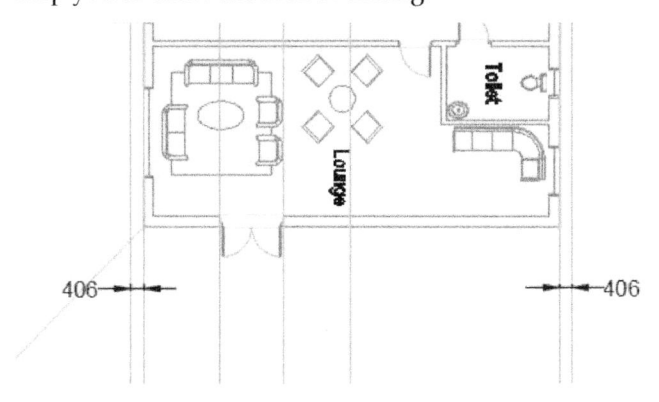

- Create the foundation, floors, and walls on A-ELEV-FOUNDATION, A-ELEV-FLOORING, and A-ELEV-WALL layers, respectively.

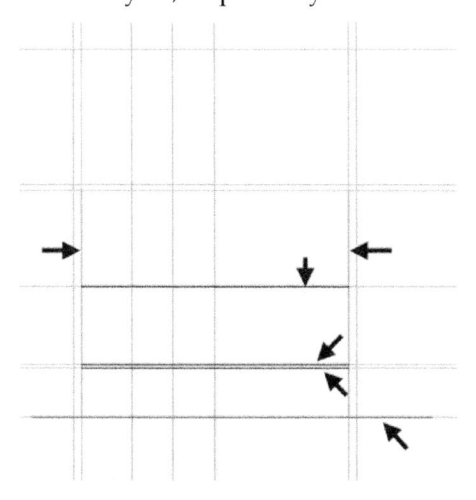

84 | AutoCAD 2016 For Architectural Design

- On the ribbon, click **Home** tab > **Layers** panel > **Layer** drop-down > **A-ELEV-ROOF**. Type REC and press Enter. Select the intersection point between the construction lines, as shown. Select **Dimension** from the command line. Type 1100 and press Enter to define the length. Type 254 and press Enter to define the width. Move the pointer toward right and click.

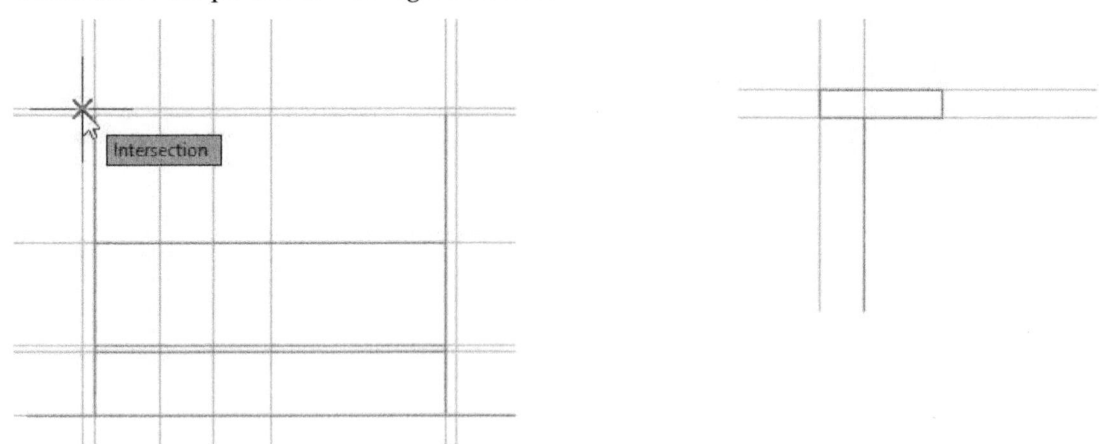

- On the ribbon, click **Home** tab > **Modify** panel > **Fillet** drop-down > **Chamfer**. Select **Angle** from the command line. Select the two intersection points to define the chamfer length on the first line, as shown. Type 15 and press Enter to define the chamfer angle. Select the lower horizontal and left vertical line of the rectangle.

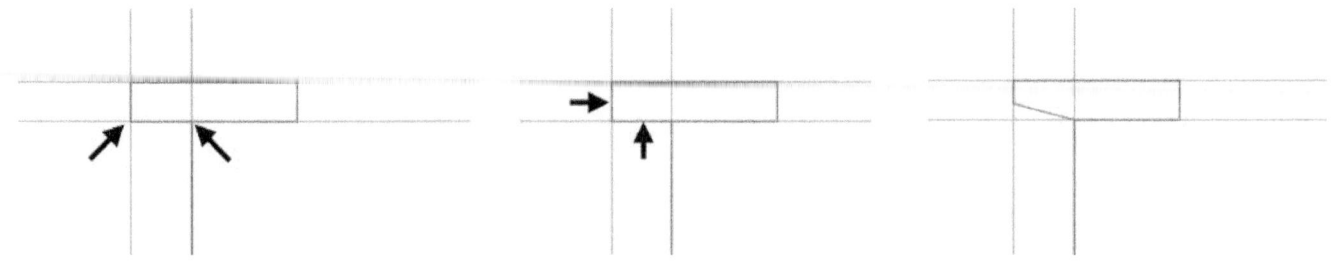

- Type L and press Enter. Select the intersection points between the construction lines, as shown. Press Esc.

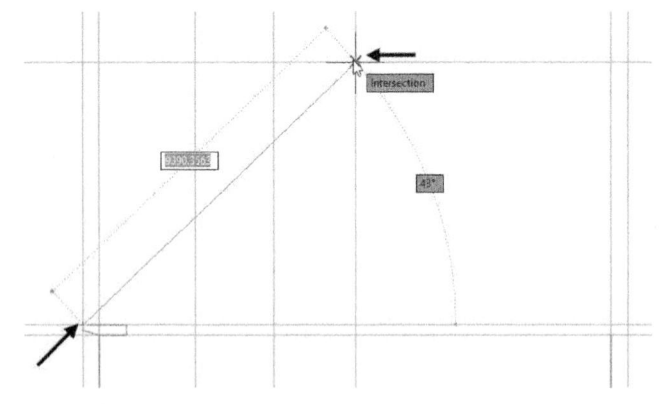

- Type O and press Enter. Type 100 and press Enter. Select the newly created inclined line. Move the pointer downwards and click. The intersecting portion between the offset line and the rectangle, as shown.

85 | AutoCAD 2016 For Architectural Design

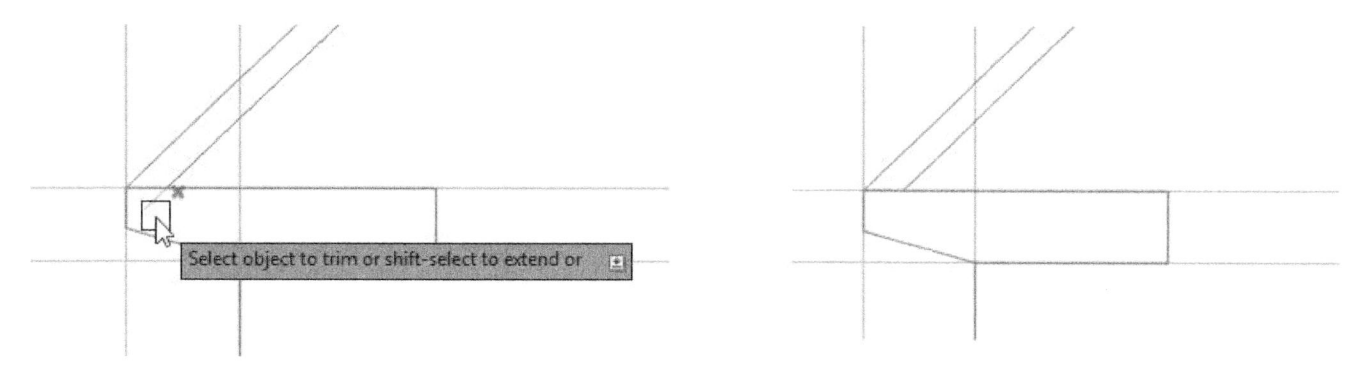

- Select the two inclined lines and the rectangle. Type MI and press Enter. Select the top end point of the inclined line, move the pointer vertically downward, and click. Select **No** from the command line to retain the source objects.

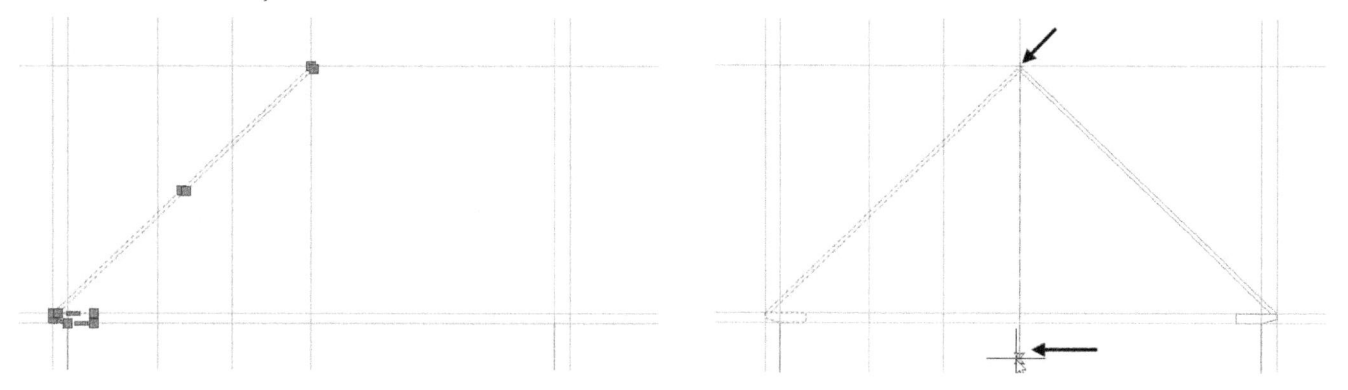

- Zoom to the top portion of the roof and trim the unwanted portions, as shown.

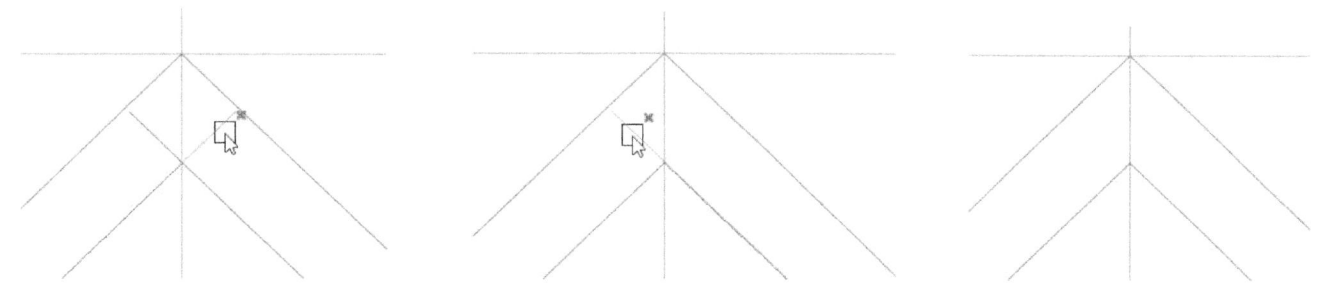

- Deactivate the ORTHOMODE (F8) icon on the status bar.
- Zoom to the South elevation. Create a selection across all the elements of the balcony. Type **CO** and press Enter. Select the point on the balcony, as shown. Move the pointer diagonally toward the Front elevation, and select the endpoint of the first floor, as shown. Press Esc.

86 | AutoCAD 2016 For Architectural Design

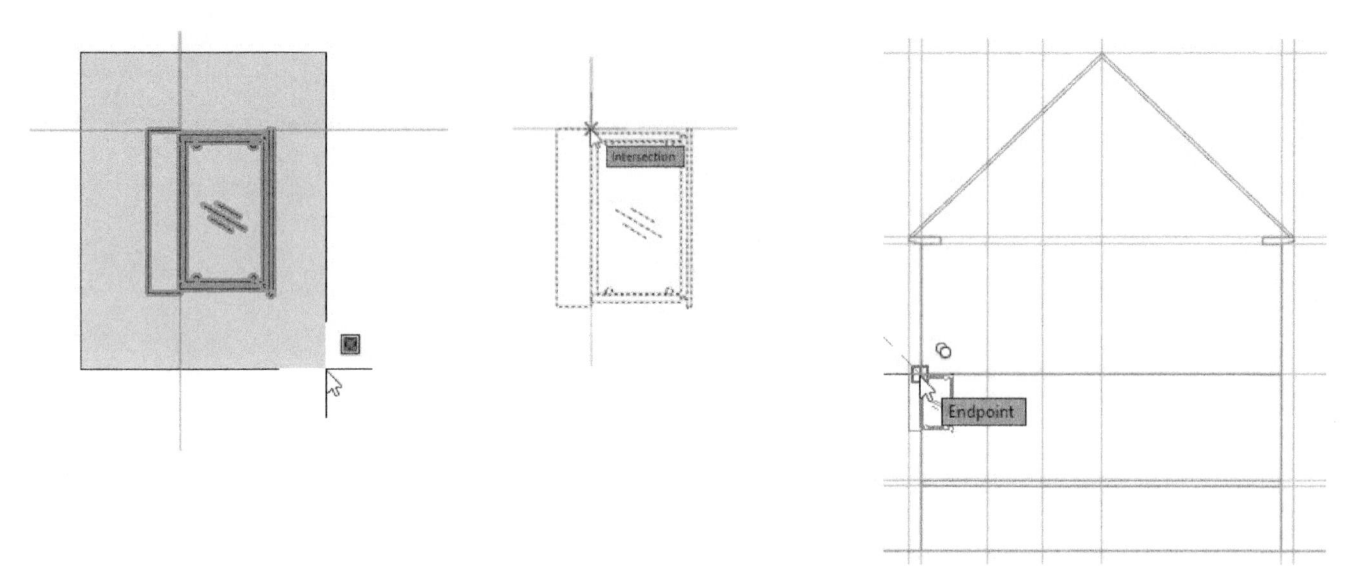

- Activate the ORTHOMOD (F8) icon on the status bar. Create a selection window across the copied balcony. Type RO and press Enter. Select the base point, as shown. Move the pointer vertically upward and click.

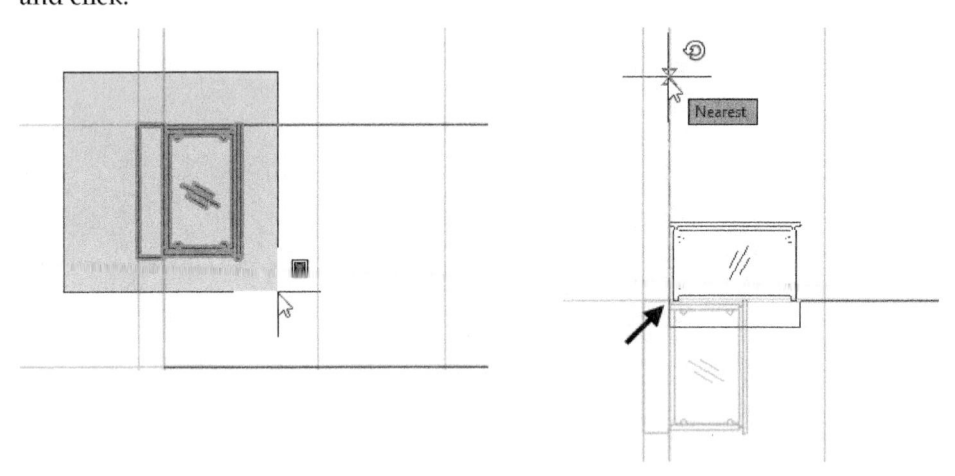

- Select the rectangle of the balcony and click on the midpoint grip of its right vertical line. Move the pointer horizontally toward right and select a point on the line, as shown.

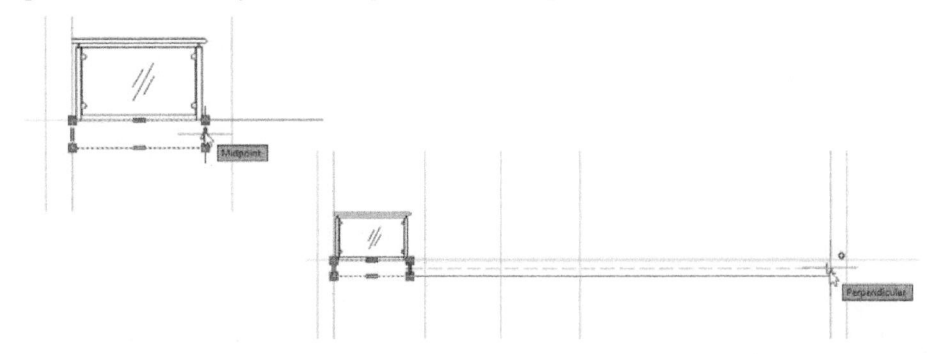

- Select the two rectangles of the balcony, as shown. On the ribbon, click **Home** tab > **Modify** panel > **Array** drop-down > **Rectangular Array**. On the **Array Creation** tab of the ribbon, type 7 and 1 in the **Columns** and **Rows** boxes, respectively. Type **1820** in the **Between** box on the **Columns** panel. Click **Close Array**.

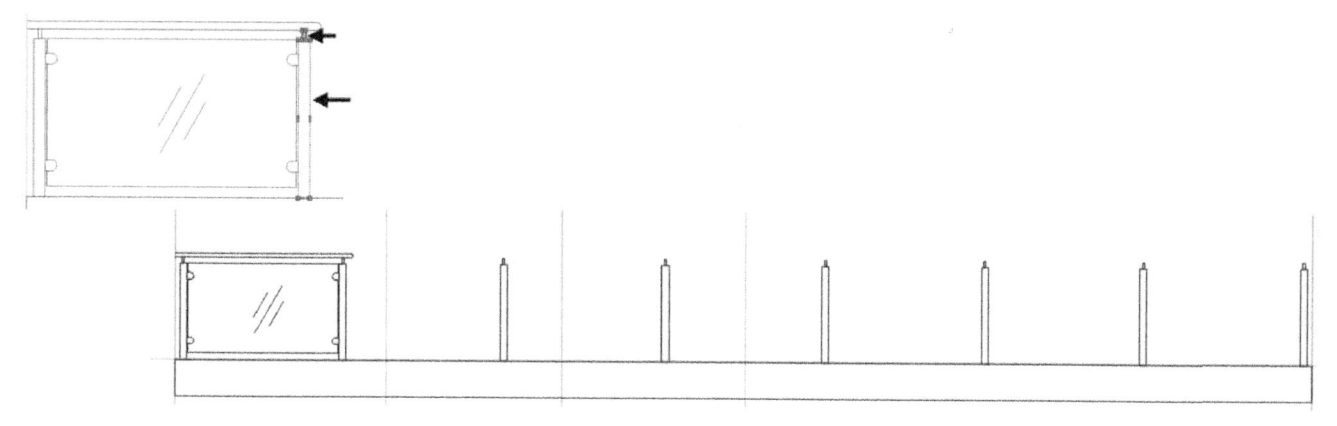

- Select the glass and sleeves, as shown. Type **CO** and press Enter. Select the corner point of the rectangle as shown.

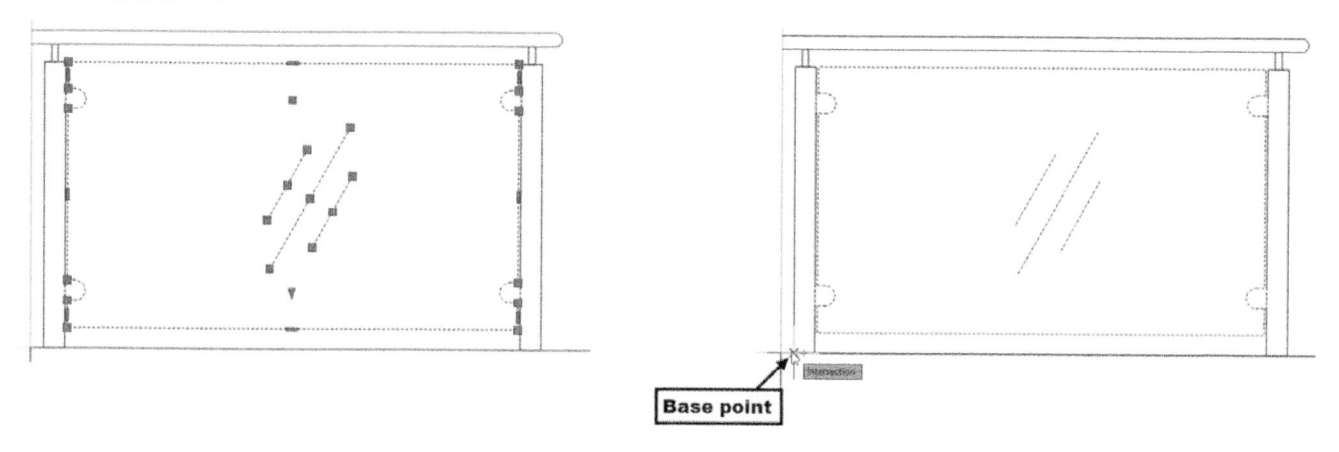

- Move the pointer horizontally and select the corner point of the rectangle, as shown. Likewise, place the glass and sleeve copies, as shown.

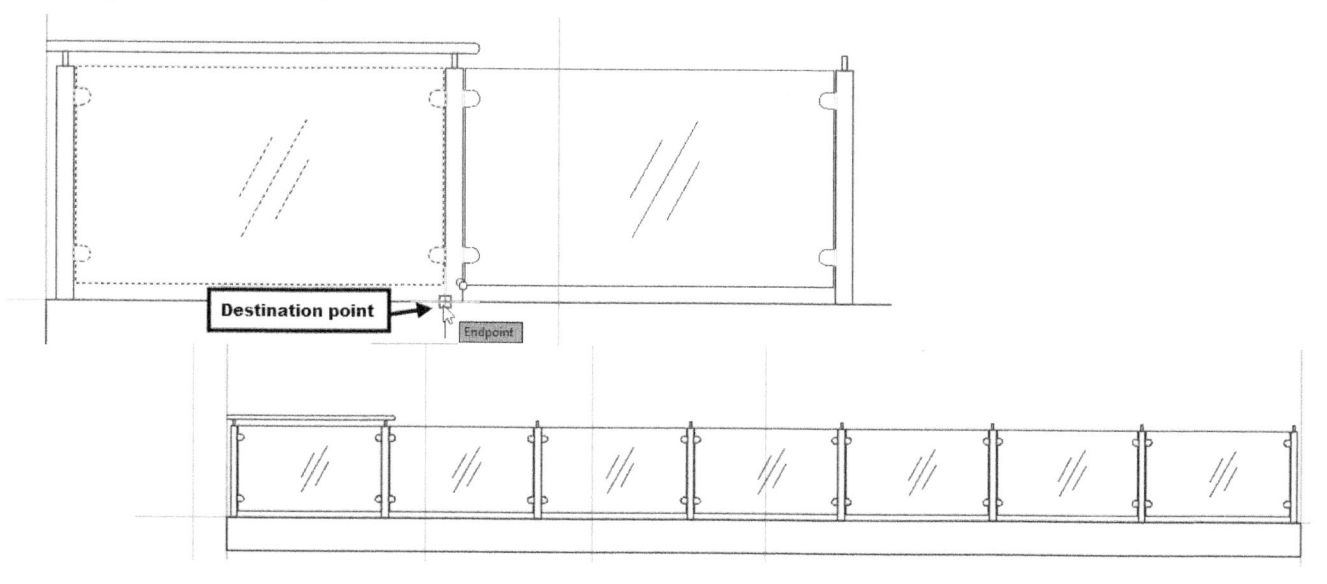

- Delete the arc on the railing, extend the railing up to the wall edge.

88 | AutoCAD 2016 For Architectural Design

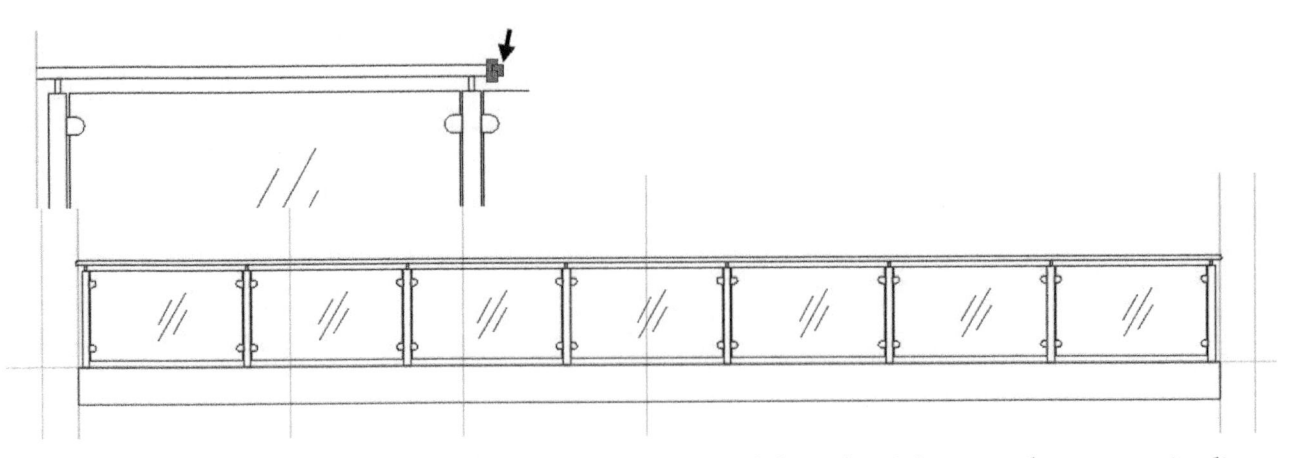

- Copy the double door from the South elevation, rotate it, and then place it between the construction lines, as shown. Likewise, copy the bathroom window, rotate it, and place it and location, as shown. Delete the construction lines, as shown.

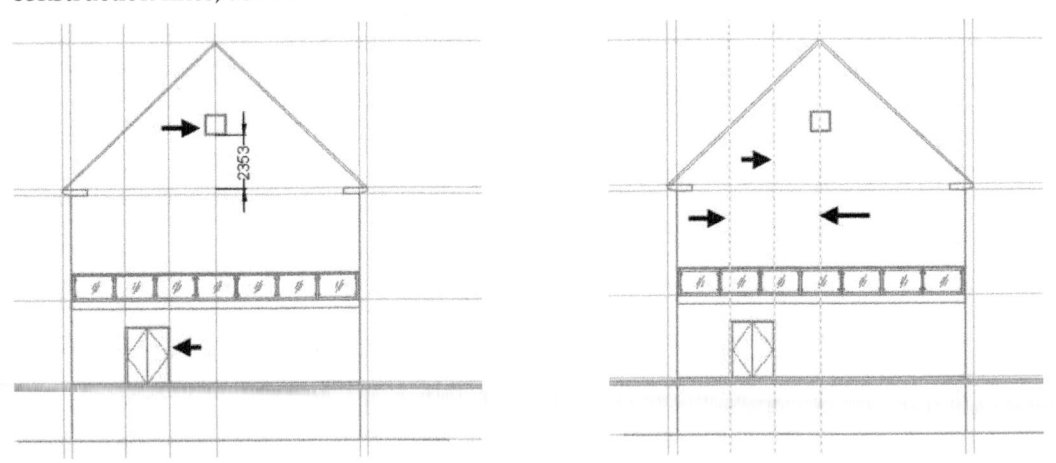

- Create construction lines passing through the sliding doors on the first floor plan, as shown.

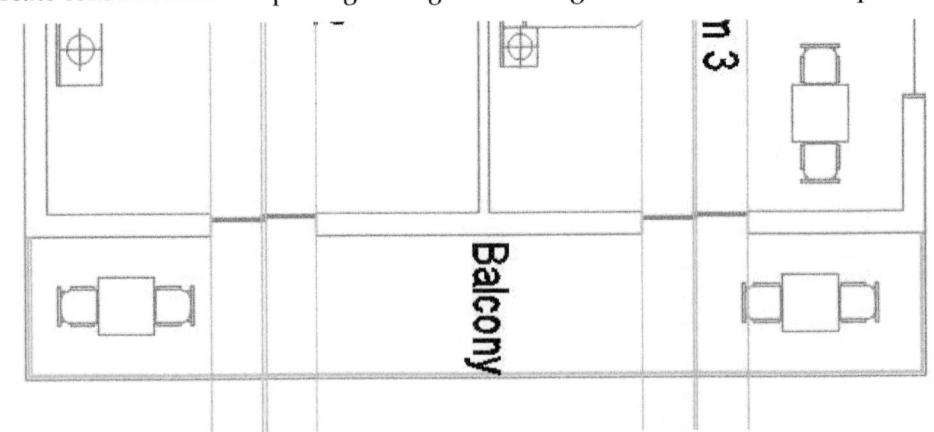

- Select the construction line and click the **Move** tool on the **Modify** panel of the **Home** ribbon tab. Select the base point on the first floor plan, as shown. Move the pointer and select the destination point on the ground floor plan, as shown.

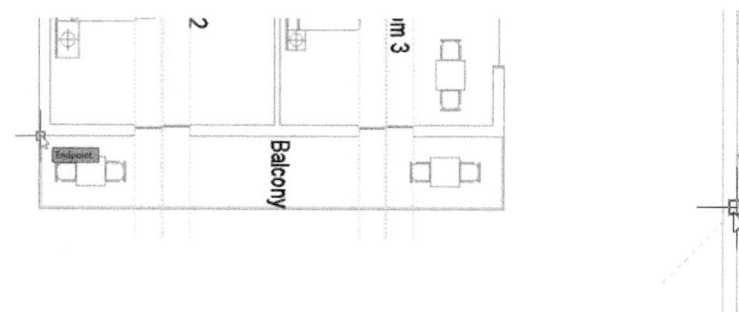

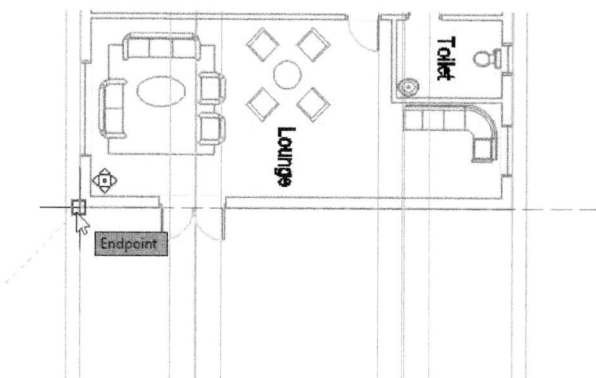

- Create the sliding doors on the Front elevation, as shown.

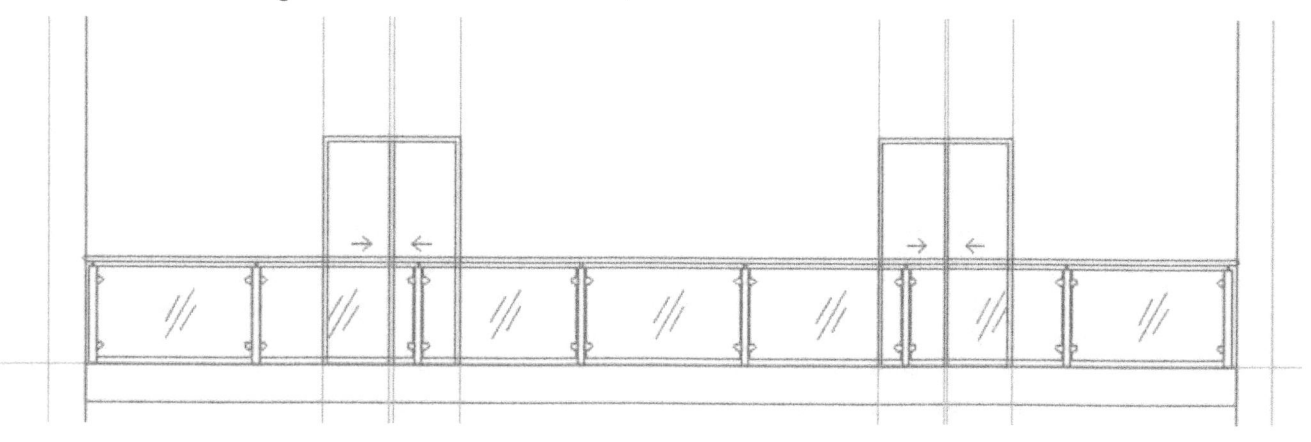

- Type UCSMAN and press Enter. On the UCS dialog, right click on the **Unamed** ucs and select **Rename**. Type **Front-Elev** and click **OK**.

- On the ribbon, click **View** tab > **Views** panel > **View Manager**. Click the **New** button on the **View Manager** and create a new view with the name Front-Elev.

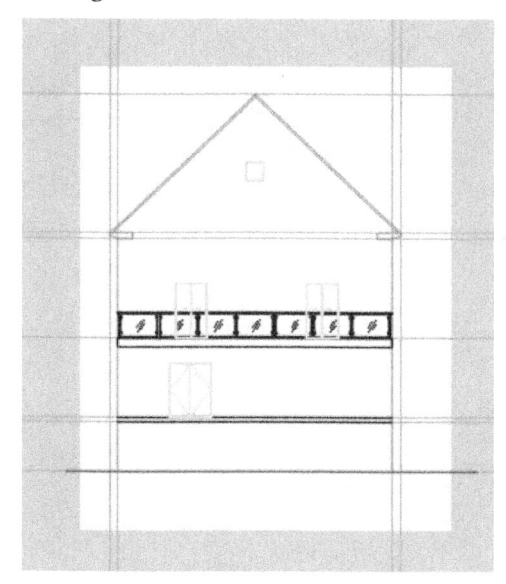

- In the top left corner of the graphics window, click **Front-Elev** and select **Top** from the menu. Zoom to the elevation views.

90 | AutoCAD 2016 For Architectural Design

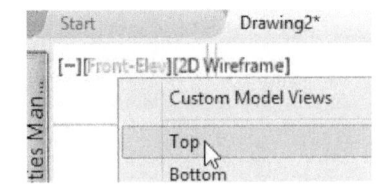

- Mirror the Front elevation about the approximate center of the ground floor plan.

- Type UCS and press Enter. Select Z from the command line. Type 270 and press Enter. Type PLAN and press Enter. The UCS is rotated by 270 degrees about the Z-axis. Zoom to the elevation views.

- Delete the doors and balcony on the elevation view.

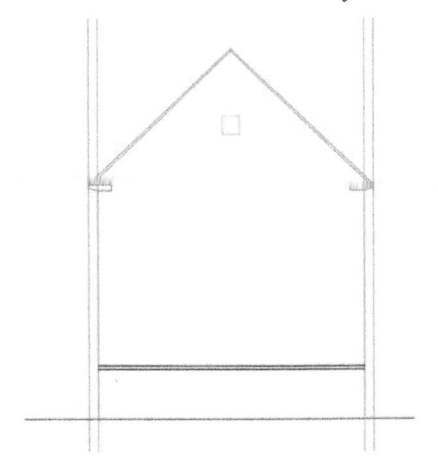

- Activate the **Reference Lines** layer. Create the construction lines projecting from the garage, and rear entrance. Also, create a construction line from the center of the garage.

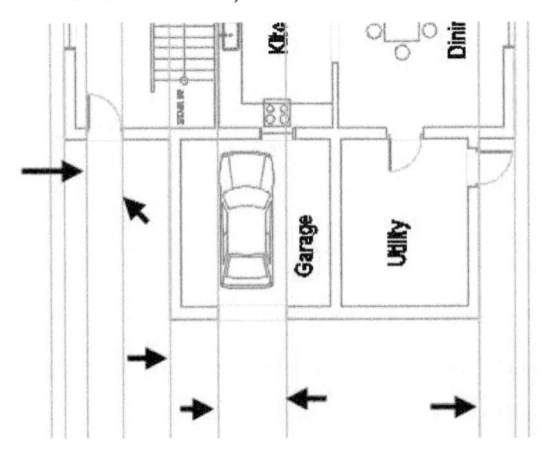

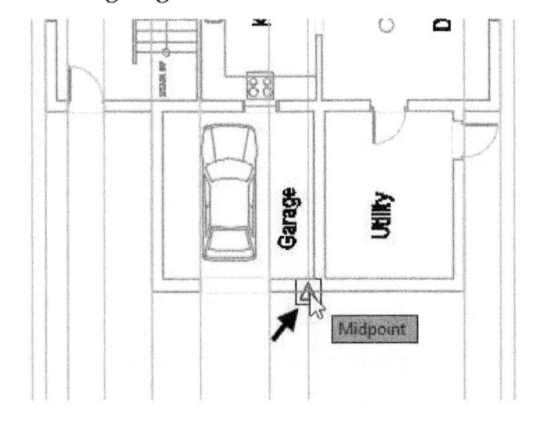

91 | AutoCAD 2016 For Architectural Design

- Create two construction lines at the 406 mm distance from the exterior walls, as shown. These lines will help you to draw the roof overhang.

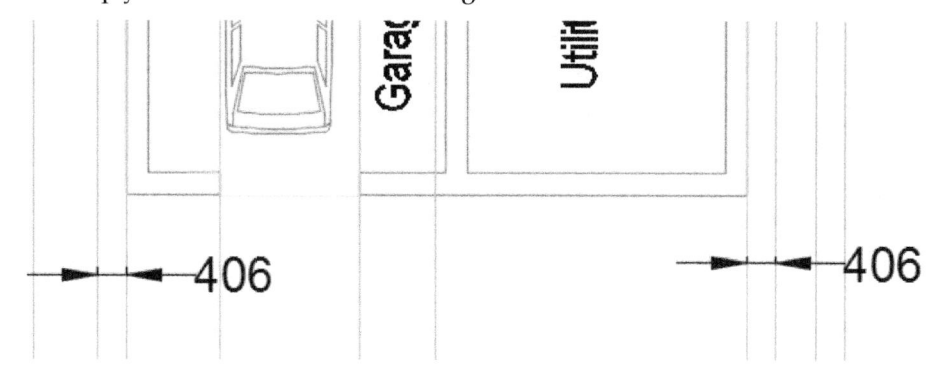

- Type XL and press Enter. Select **Offset** from the command line. Type 3204 and press Enter. Select the ground level line, move the pointer up, and click to create a construction line. Use the **Offset** tool to create other construction lines, as shown.

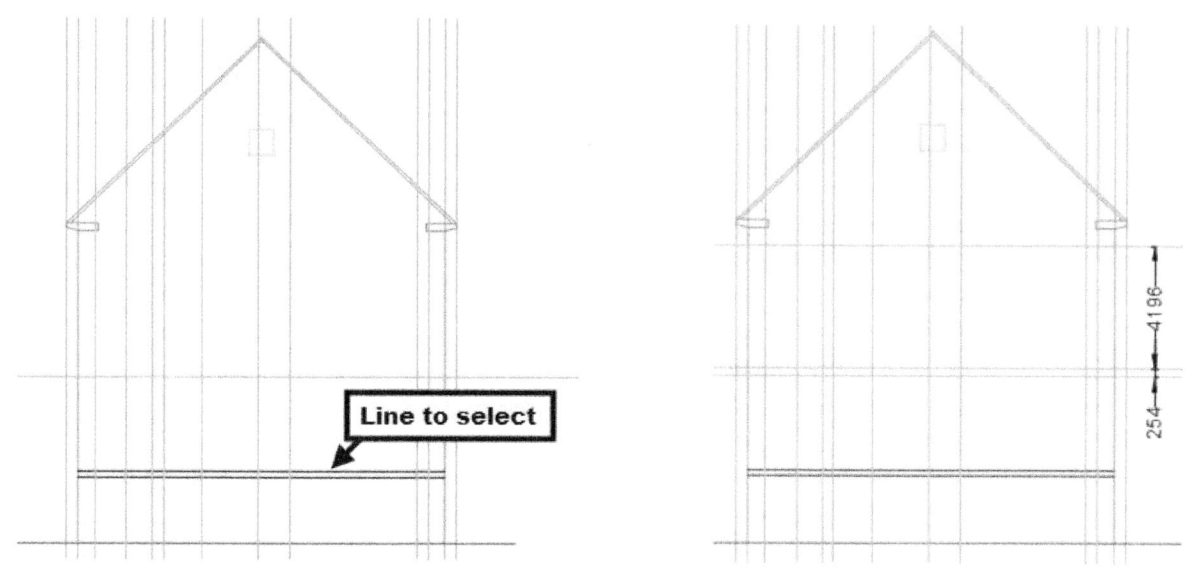

- Create the walls, door, roof, window, and opening on the Rear elevation, as shown.

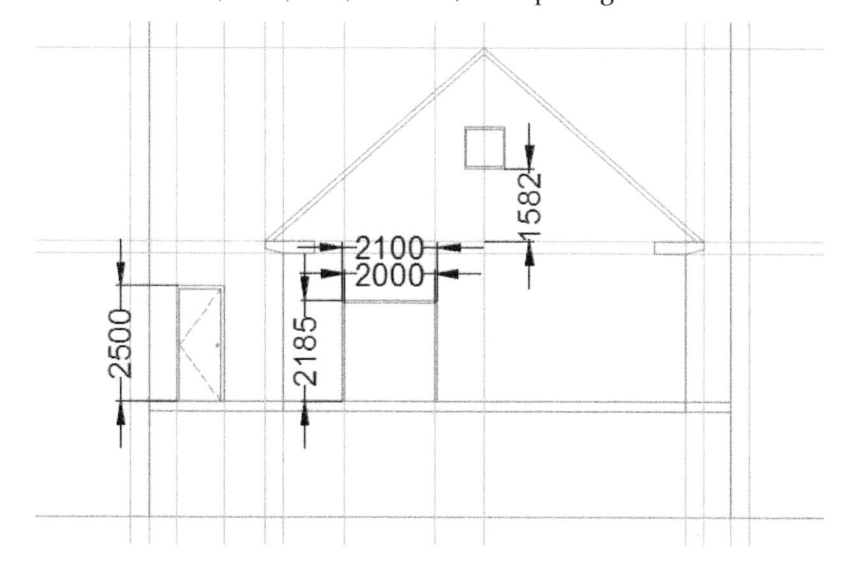

92 | AutoCAD 2016 For Architectural Design

- Save the view as Rear-Elev and switch to the default orientation of the UCS.

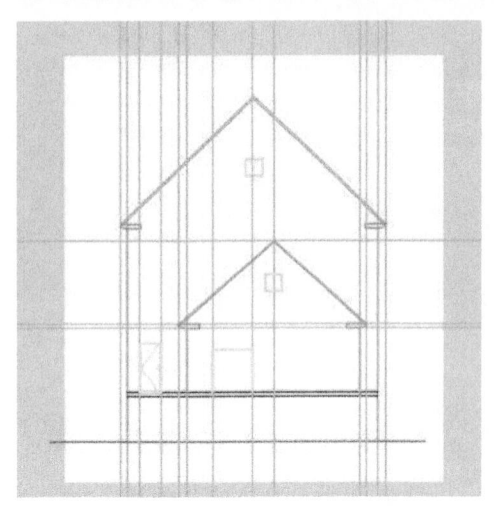

- Freeze the **Reference lines** layer by clicking the sun icon next to **Reference Lines** on the **Layer** drop-down.

Hatching the Elevation Views

- Create the following layers:

Layer Name	Color	Linetype
A-ELEV-WALL-PATT	cyan	Continuous
A-ELEV-ROOF-PATT	green	Continuous
A-ELEV-FOUNDATION-PATT	Index Color 8	Continuous

- Activate the A-ELEV-ROOF-PATT layer. On the ribbon, click **Home** tab > **Draw** panel > **Pattern** drop-down > **Hatch**.
- On the **Hatch Creation** tab of the ribbon, on the **Pattern** panel, expand the gallery and select the **AR-RSHKE** pattern. Zoom to the South elevation and click in the roof area.

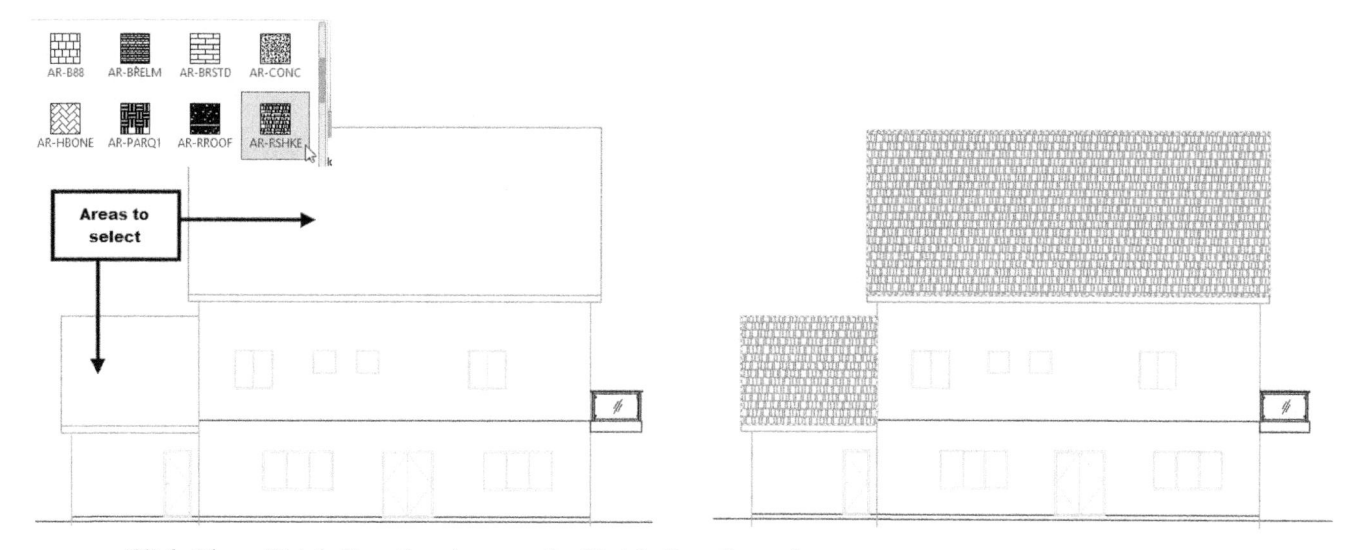

- Click **Close Hatch Creation** icon on the **Hatch Creation** tab.
- Select the roof hatch pattern and notice that a single hatch pattern is created in two areas. On the **Hatch Creation** tab of the ribbon, expand the **Options** panel and click the **Separate Hatches** tool. The hatches are separated.

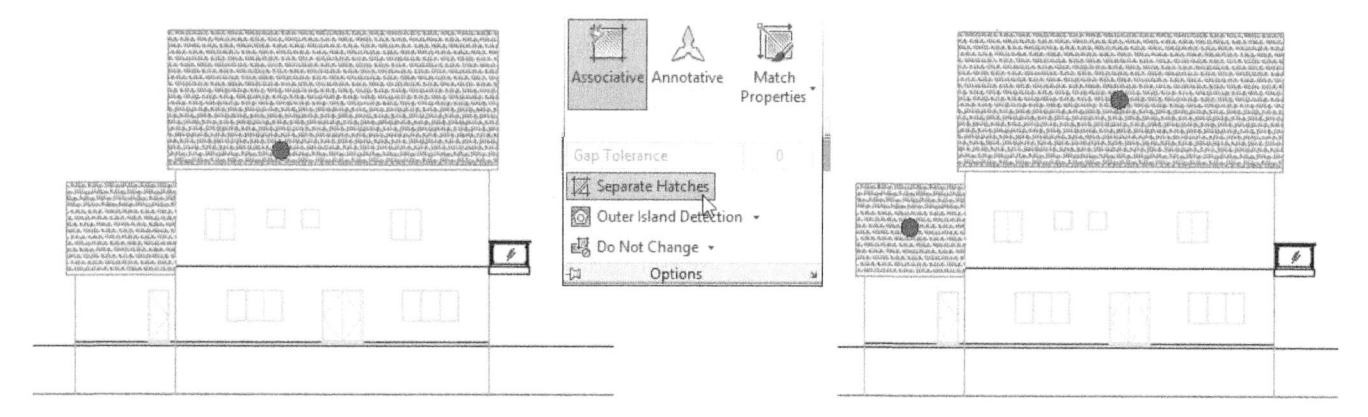

- On the ribbon, click **Home** tab > **Layers** panel > **Layer** drop-down > **A-ELEV-WALL-PATT**.
- Type **Hatch** and press Enter. On the **Hatch Creation** tab of the ribbon, on the **Pattern** panel, expand the gallery and select the **AR-B816C** pattern. On the **Hatch Creation** tab of the ribbon, expand the **Options** panel and click the **Separate Hatches** tool. Pick a point in the areas, as shown. Click **Close Hatch Creation**.

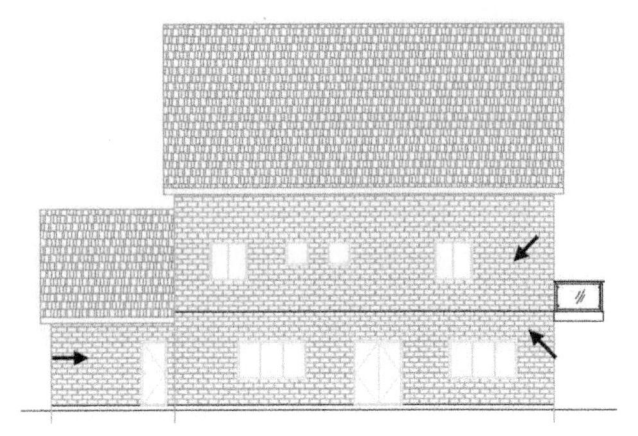

- Activate the A-ELEV-FOUNDATION-PATT layer and fill the AR-CONC hatch, as shown.

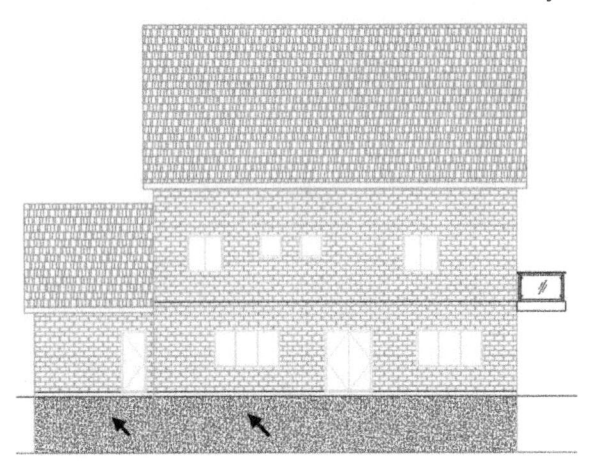

Tutorial 12: Adding Dimensions

- On the ribbon, click **Home > Layers > Layer drop-down > A-DIM** to make it current.
- Type **D** in the command line and press Enter. On the **Dimension Style Manager** dialog, select the **Standard** dimension style and click the **New** button. Type-in Architectural in the **New Style Name** box and click **Continue**.
- Click the **Primary Units** tab and select **Unit format > Decimal**.
- Set **Precision** to **0.0.**
- Click the **Symbol and Arrows** tab.
- Under the **Arrowhead** section, select **First > Architectural tick**. The second arrowhead is automatically changed to **Architectural tick**.
- Select **Leader > Closed Filled** and enter 150 in the **Arrow Size** box.
- Click the **Lines** tab and set **Extend beyond dim lines** and **Offset from origin** to 75 and 25, respectively.
- Click the **Text** tab and **Text height** to 150.
- In the **Text placement** section, set the following settings.

95 | AutoCAD 2016 For Architectural Design

Vertical-Centered

Horizontal-Centered

View Direction-Left-to-Right

- In the **Text alignment** section, select the **Aligned with dimension line** option.
- Click the **Fit** tab, and select **Either text or arrows (best fit)** option from the **Fit Options** section.
- In the **Text placement** section, select the **Over dimension line, without Leader** option.
- Click **OK** and click **Set Current** on the **Dimension Style Manager**. Click **Close**.
- On the ribbon, click **Annotate > Dimensions > Dimension**.
- Select the points on the vertical grid lines, as shown below.
- Move the pointer and click to locate the dimension.

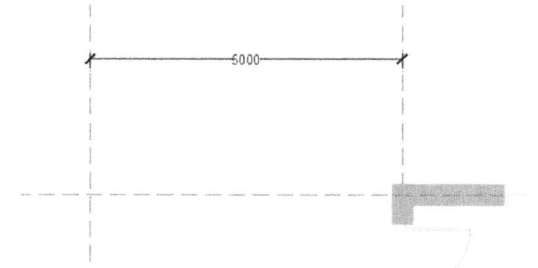

- On the ribbon, click **Annotate > Dimensions > Continue**. You will notice that a dimension is attached to the pointer.
- Move the pointer and click on the next grid line.
- Likewise, move the pointer and click on the next grid line.
- Activate the **Dimension** command create the overall horizontal dimension.

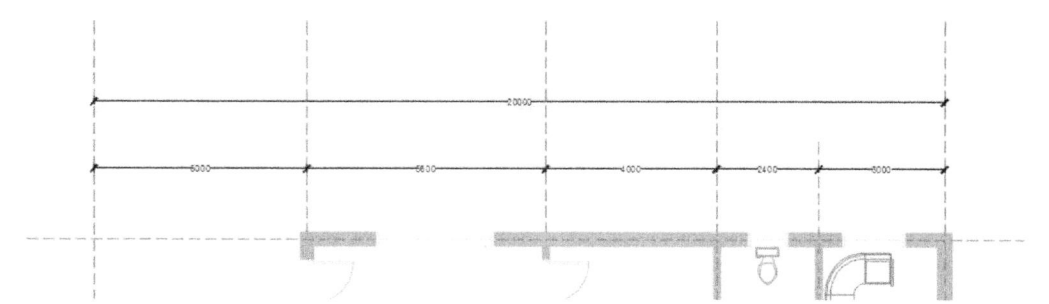

- Likewise, add vertical dimensions to the grid lines.

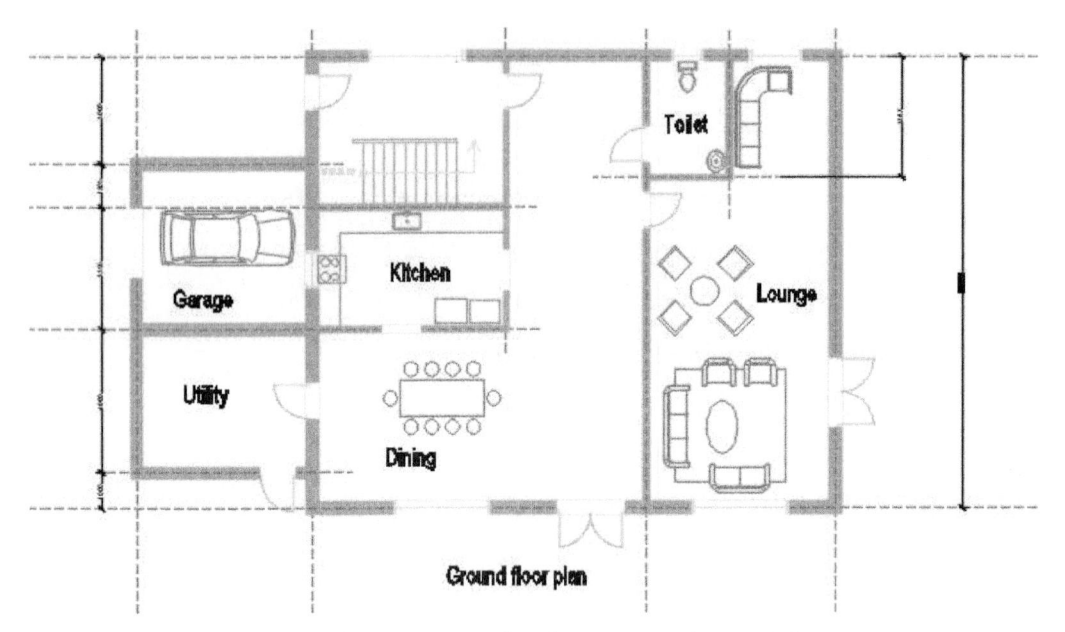

- Complete adding dimensions to the drawing, as shown below.

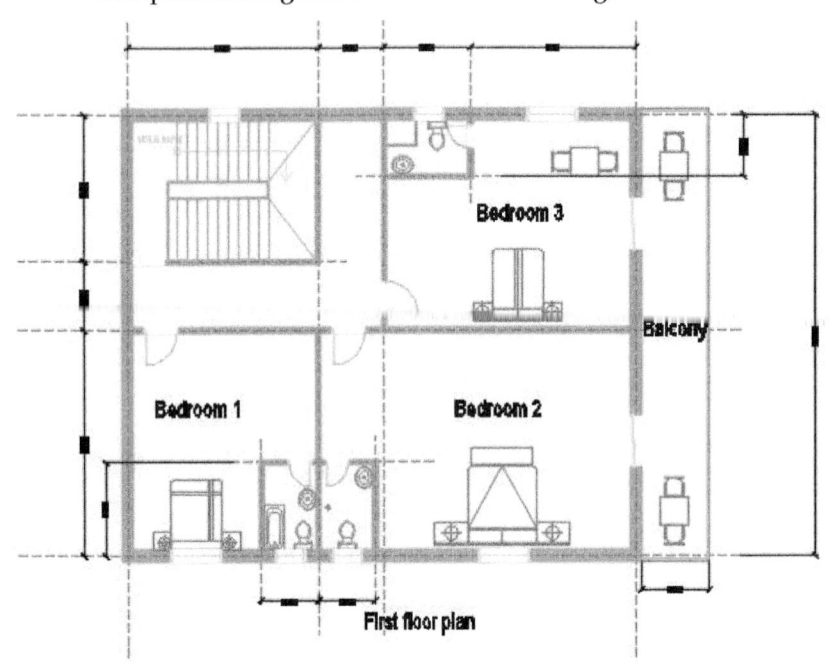

Tutorial 13: Creating Grid Bubbles
- Create the **A-GRIDBUBBLE** layer and activate it. Create a circle of 12 diameter.
- On the ribbon, click **Insert > Block Definition > Define Attributes**.

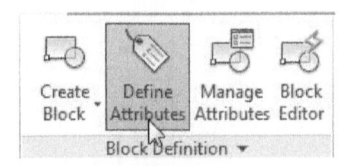

- On the **Attribute Definition** dialog, type-in GRIDBUBBLE in the **Tag** box and select **Justification > Middle center**. Select **Text Style > Standard**. Type-in 150 in the **Text height** box and click **OK**. Select the center point of the circle. The attribute text will be place at it center.

AutoCAD 2016 For Architectural Design

GRIDBUBBLE

- On the ribbon, click **Insert > Block Definition > Create Block**. Type-in Grid bubble in the **Name** box and click the **Select objects** button. Draw a crossing window to select the circle and attribute. Press Enter to accept the selection.
- Click the **Pick point** option under the **Base point** section. Select the lower quadrant point of the circle to define the base point of the block. Uncheck the **Open in block editor** option. Select **Delete** from the **Objects** section and click **OK**.
- On the ribbon, click **Insert > Block > Insert > Grid bubble**.
- Select the top endpoint of the first vertical grid line; the **Edit Attributes** dialog pops up. Type-in **A** in the GRIDBUBBLE box and click **OK**.

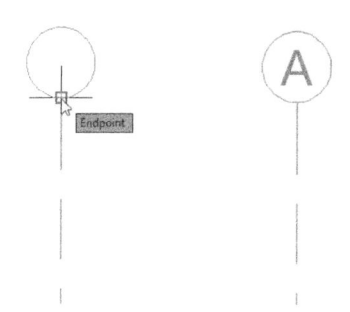

- Likewise, add other grid bubbles to the vertical grid lines.

- Create another block with name Vertical Grid bubble. Make sure that you select the right quadrant point of the circle as the base point.

VERTICALGRIDBUBBLE

- Insert the vertical grid bubbles, as shown below.

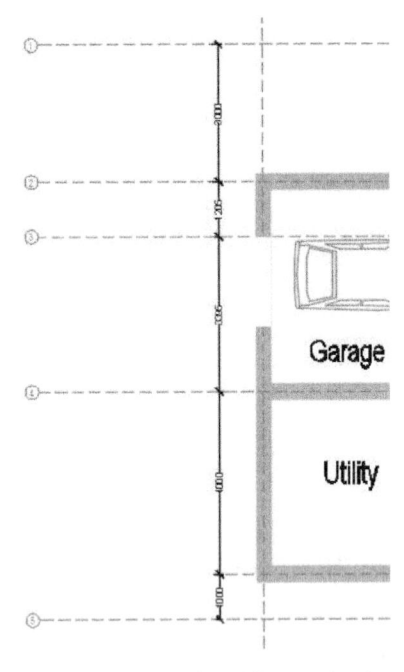

- Likewise, add grid bubbles to the first floor plan.

Tutorial 14: Layouts and Title Block
- Click the **Layout 1** tab at the bottom of the graphics window.

You will notice that a white paper is displayed with viewport created, automatically. The components of a layout are shown in figure below.

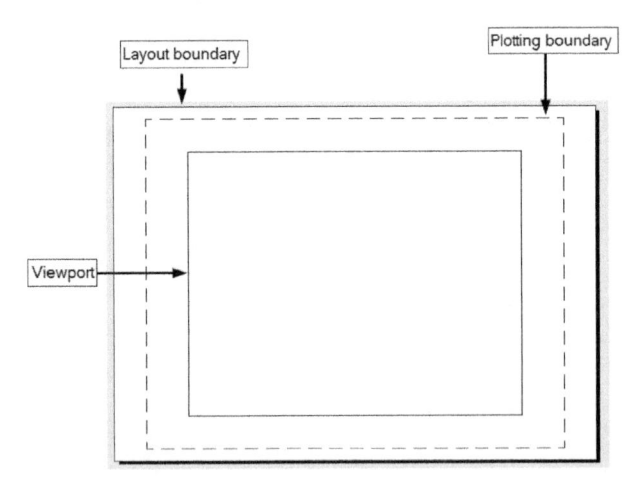

- Click **Output > Plot > Page Setup Manager** on the ribbon; the **Page Setup Manager** dialog appears. On the **Page Setup Manager** dialog, click the **Modify** button; the **Page Setup –Layout1** dialog appears.

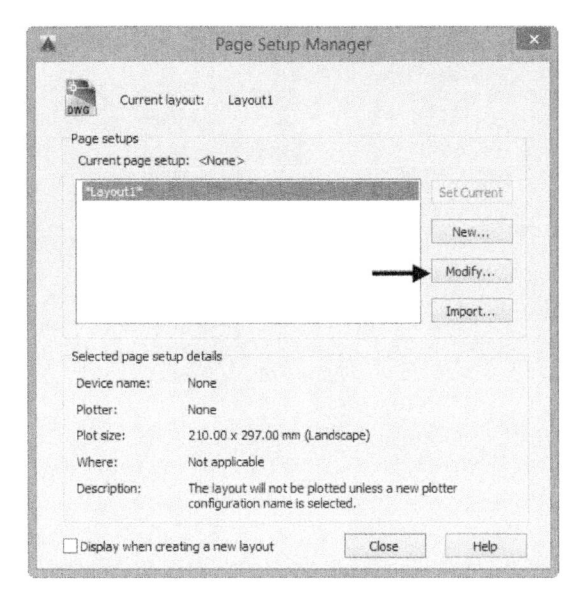

- On the **Page Setup** dialog, select **DWG to PDF.pc3** from the **Name** drop-down under the **Printer/Plotter** group. Set the **Plot Style table** to **acad.ctb**. Set the **Paper size** to ISO A1 (841.00 x 594.00 MM). Set the **Plot scale** to **1:1**. Click **OK**, and then click **Close** on the **Page Setup Manager** dialog.
- Double-click on the **Layout1** tab and enter **ISO A1**; the **Layout1** is renamed.
- Similarly, rename the **Layout2** to **ISO A2**.

Creating the Title Block on the Layout

You can draw objects on layouts to create a title block, borders and viewports. However, it is not recommended to draw the actual drawing on layouts. You can also create dimensions on layouts.

- Click the **ISO A1** layout tab.
- Create the **Title Block** layer and make it current. Select the viewport on the layout and press Delete.
- Create the border and title block, as shown. Insert text inside the title block, as shown.

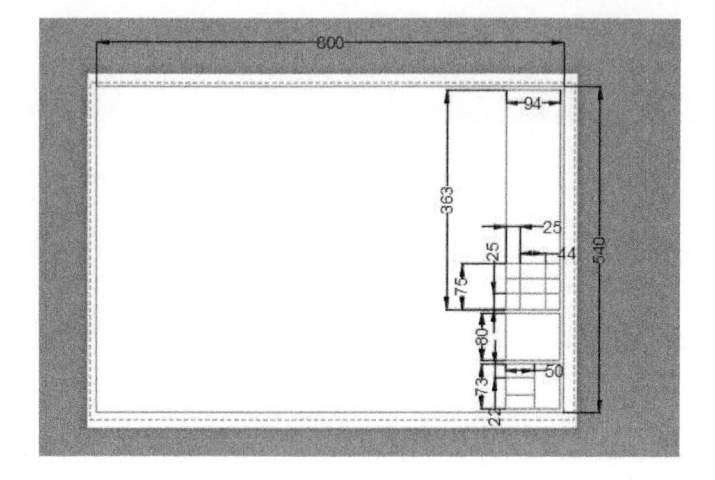

- Use the **Create Block** tool and convert it into a block. Use the **Insert** tool and insert the block on the layout.

Creating Viewports in the Paper space

The viewports that exist in the paper space are called floating viewports. This is because you can position them anywhere in the layout and modify their shape size with respect to the layout.

- Open the ISO A1 layout, if not already open.
- Click **Layout > Layout Viewports > Rectangular** on the ribbon.

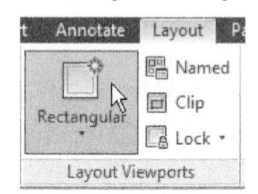

- Create the rectangular viewport by picking the first and second corner points, as shown in figure.

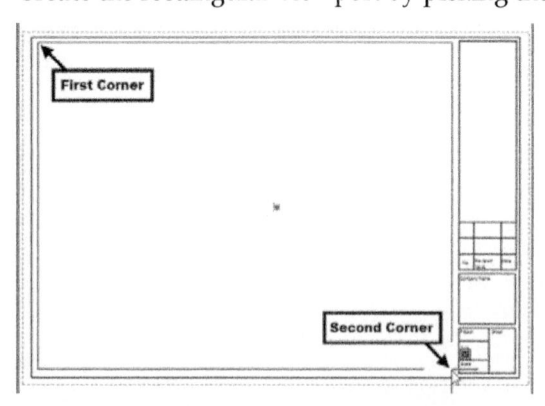

- Click the **Model** tab at the bottom left corner of the window.

101 | Creating Architectural Drawings

- On the ribbon, click **View > Views > View Manager**. Create two named views of ground and first floor plans. Also, create another named view of the South Elevation.

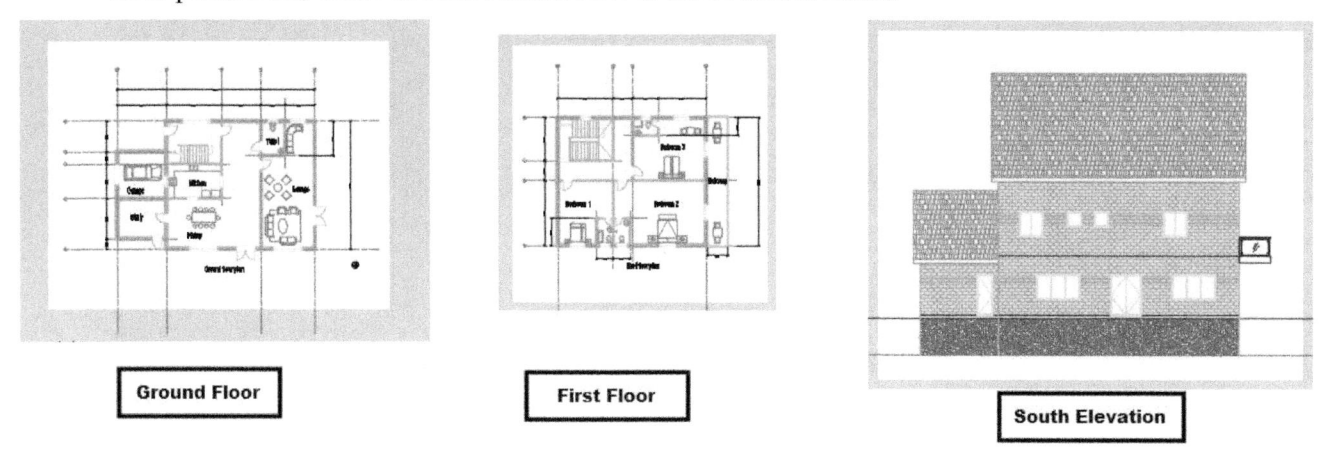

Ground Floor

First Floor

South Elevation

- Click the **PAPER** button on the status bar; the model space inside the viewport will be activated. In addition, the viewport frame will become thicker when you are in model space.

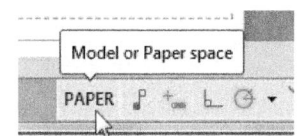

- On the ribbon, click **View** tab > **Views** panel > **Views** gallery > **Ground Floor**.

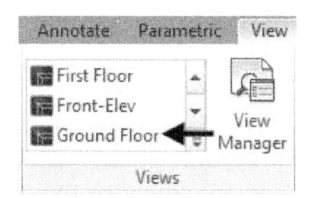

- Click the **Viewport Scale** button and select **1:50** from the menu; the drawing is zoomed out.

- After fitting the drawing inside the viewport, you can lock the viewport position by clicking the **Lock/Unlock Viewport** button on the status bar.

After locking the viewport, you cannot change the scale or position of the drawing.

- Click the **MODEL** button on the status bar to switch back to paper space.

102 | Creating Architectural Drawings

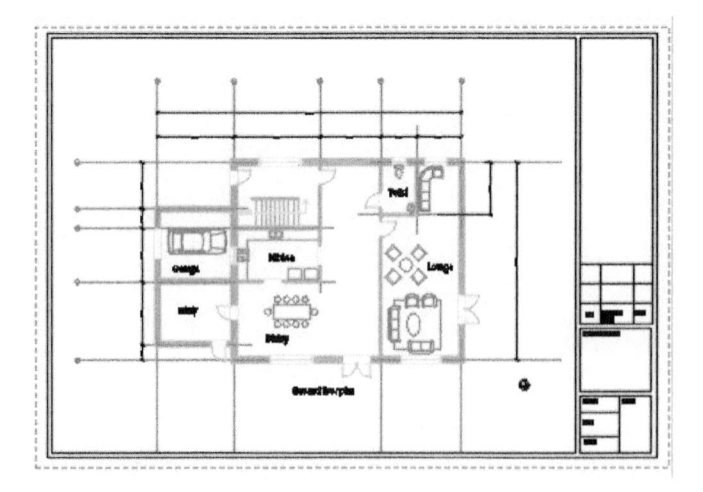

To hide viewport frames while plotting a drawing, follow the steps given below.

- Type **LA** in the command line to open the **Layer Properties Manager**.
- In the **Layer Properties Manager**, create a new layer called **Hide Viewports** and make it current.
- Deactivate the plotter symbol under the **Plot** column of the **Hide Viewports** layer; the object on this layer will not be plotted. Close the **Layer Properties Manager**.
- Click the **Home** tab on the ribbon and expand the **Layers** panel. Click the **Change to Current Layer** button on the **Layers** panel.

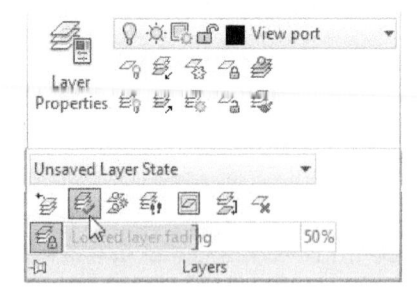

- Select the viewport in the **ISO A1** layout and press ENTER; the viewport frames will become unplottable. To check this, click the **Preview** button on the **Plot** panel of the **Output** ribbon tab; the plot preview will be displayed as shown below.

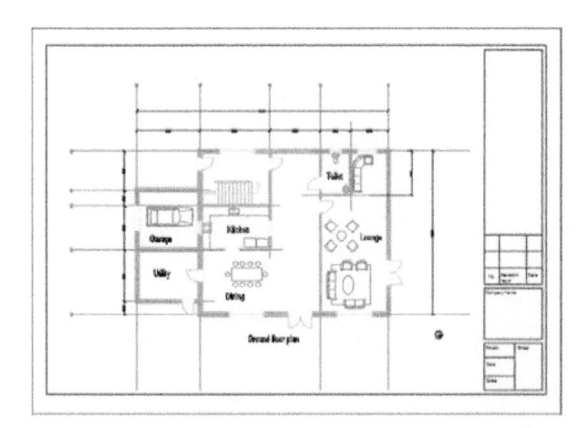

103 | Creating Architectural Drawings

- Close the preview window.

Creating layouts for the other views

- Right click on the Layout2 and select Delete.
- Click the right mouse button on the **ISO A1** layout and select **Move or Copy**. Select (move to end) from the **Move or Copy** dialog. Check the **Create a copy** option and click **OK**.
- Likewise, create five more copies of the **ISO A1** layout.

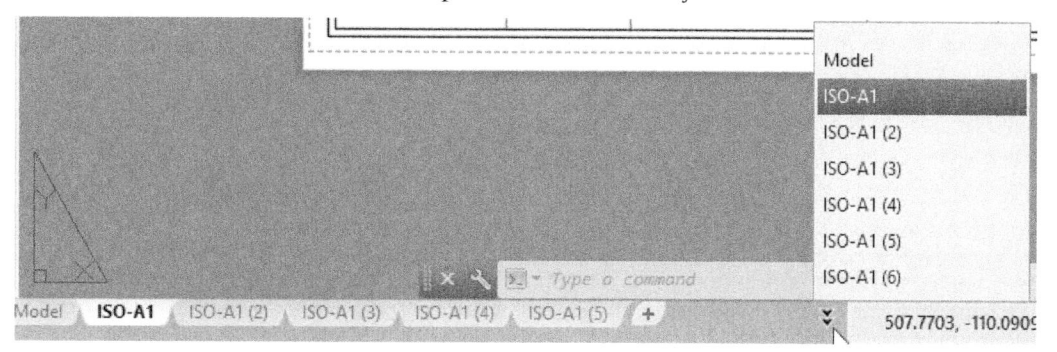

- Rename the layouts, as shown.

- Select the **First Floor Plan** layout tab. Double click in the viewport, and then click the **Lock** icon on the status bar; the viewport is unlocked. On the ribbon, click **View** tab > **Views** panel > **Views** gallery > **First Floor**. Click the **Viewport Scale** button and select **1:50** from the menu. Click the **Lock/Unlock Viewport** button on the status bar.
- Likewise, compose the **South Elevation**, **North Elevation**, **Front Elevation**, and **Rear Elevation** layouts.

Changing the Layer Properties in Viewports

The layer properties in viewports are not related to the layer properties in model space. You can change the layer properties in viewports without any effect in the model space.

- Select the **Front Elevation** layout tab. In the **Layer Properties Manager**, click the icon in the **VP Freeze** column of the **Reference Lines** layer; the reference lines will disappear in the viewport, as shown below.

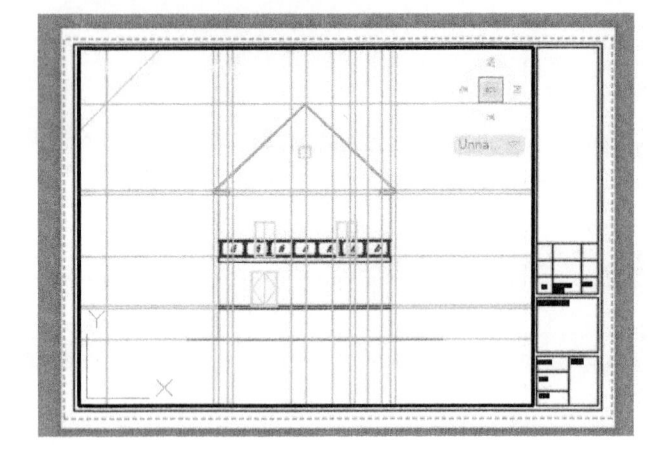

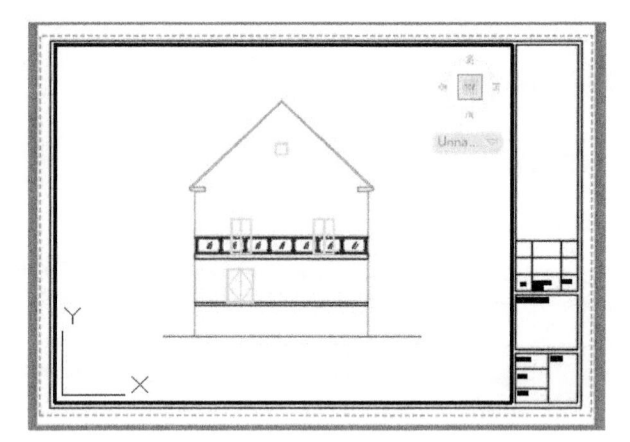

- Double-click outside the viewport to switch to paper space.
- Click the **Model** tab below the graphics window.
- Save the drawing file.

Tutorial 15: Printing

- On the Application Menu, click **Print > Manage Plot Styles**. Double click on the **acad** icon.

- Click the **Form View** tab on the **Plot Style Table Editor** dialog. Select the **Color 1** from the **Plot Styles** list. In the **Properties** section, set the Lineweight to 0.1. Likewise, change the lineweights of the other colors, as shown.

Color	Lineweight
Color 1	0.1 mm
Color 2	0.2 mm
Color 3	0.4 mm
Color 4	0.5 mm
Color 5	0.7 mm
Color 6	1.0 mm

Creating Architectural Drawings

Color 8	0.09 mm
Color 9	0.05 mm

- Press and hold the Shift key and select Color 1 and Color 9. Set **Color to Black** in the **Properties** section. Click **Save & Close**.

- Click the **Ground Floor Plan** layout tab at the bottom on the window.

- On the ribbon, click **Output** tab > **Plot** panel > **Preview** ; the print preview of the drawing appears. Notice that the linetype scale of the dashed lines is changed. You need to change the PSLTSCALE variable value to 0 in order to retain the original linetype scale of the lines.

- Click **Close Preview Window** on the top right corner.

- Type PSLTSCALE and press Enter. Type 0 and press Enter.

- On the ribbon, click **Output** tab > **Plot** panel > **Print** . On the **Plot** dialog, select **Layout** from the **Plot area** section. Set the **Scale** and **Drawing orientation** to **1:1** and to **Landscape**, respectively. Click **OK** to print the drawing. Likewise, print other layouts.

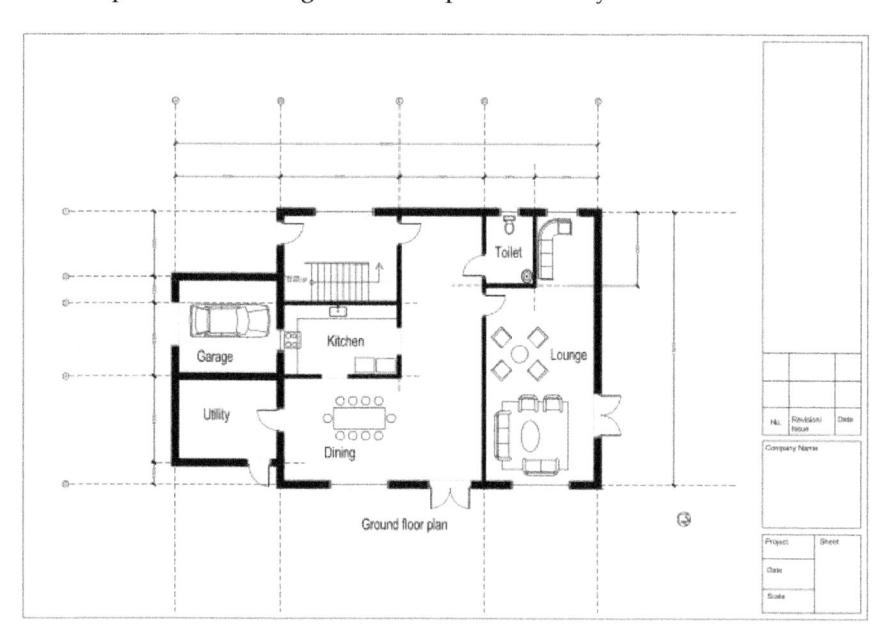

- Save and close the drawing.

Part 2: Creating 3D Architectural Model

In this chapter, you will learn to do the following:

- **Work with Visual Styles**
- **Create Doors and Window openings**
- **Create the Ceiling**
- **Create Doors and Windows**

- Create Stairs
- Create Balcony
- Create Railing
- Create Roof
- Create Terrain surface

Tutorial 1: Importing 2D Drawings

- Download the 2D-Drawings.dwg file from the companion website.
- Start a new drawing file using the **acadiso** template.
- On the ribbon, click **Home** tab > **Block** panel > **Insert**. On the **Insert** dialog, click the **Browse** button. Go to the location of the 2D-Drawings.dwg, select it and click **Open**. On the **Insert** dialog, uncheck the **Specify On-screen** option under the **Insertion point** section, and then click **OK**. Type Z and press Enter. Type A and press Enter. The entire drawing is visible in the graphics window.
- Select the block reference and click **Home** tab > **Modify** panel > **Explode** on the ribbon. The block reference is exploded and the individual entities of the drawing are selectable.

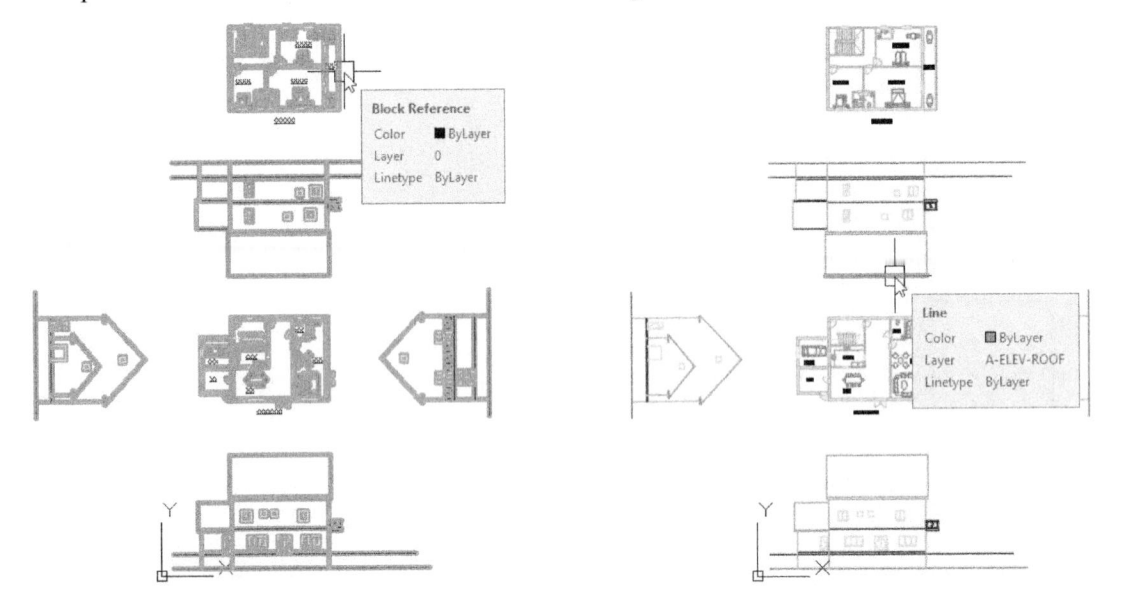

After inserting the 2D drawings into the graphics window, you need to remove the entities of the drawing that are not used to create the 3D model. For example, the texts and annotations are not used to create the 3D model. You can delete the unwanted entities by deleting the entire layer associated with it. However, AutoCAD will not allow you to delete a layer, which has objects on it. There is a special tool to delete all the objects on a layer, and then purge the layer.

- On the **Home** tab of the ribbon, expand the **Layer** panel and select the **Delete** tool. Select the text and the stair callout, and then press Enter. Select **Yes** from the command line.

Creating Architectural Drawings

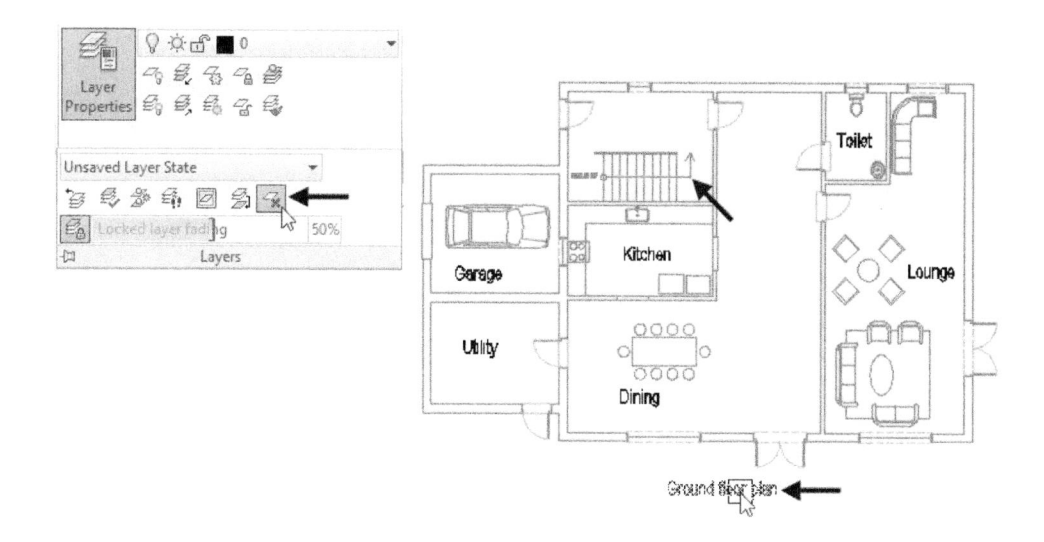

- Type **WIPEOUT** and press Enter. Select **Frames** from the command line. Select **OFF** to turn off the wipeout frames of the drawing.
- On the ribbon, click **Home** tab > **Layers** panel > **Off**. Select the car block, kitchen fixtures, and bathroom fixtures. Press Esc.

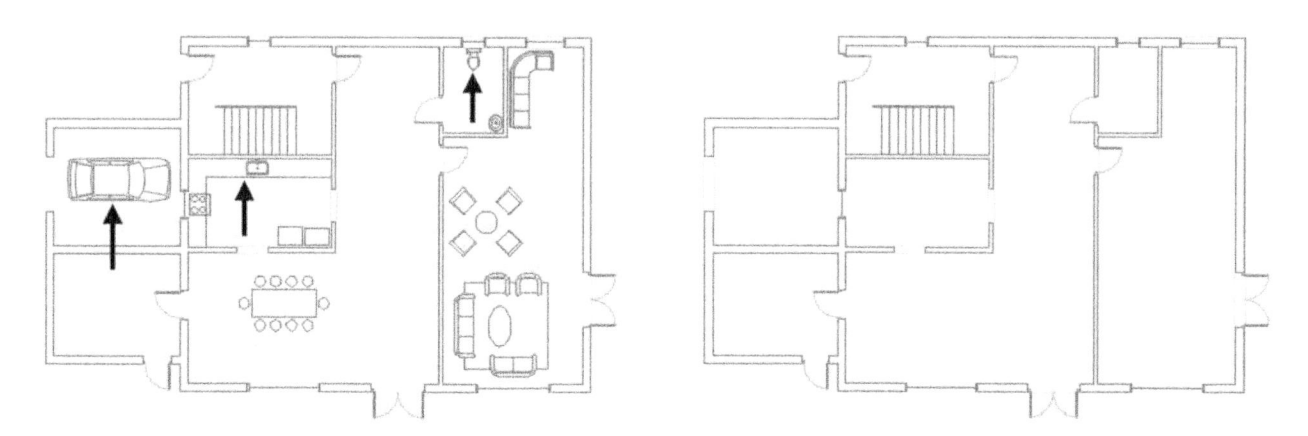

Tutorial 2: Creating 3D Walls

- Create a new layer with name **3D-Walls** and set its color to Index color 8. Activate the new layer.
- On the status bar, activate the **Object Snap** icon and click the down-arrow next to it. Make sure that the **Endpoint** option is checked.
- On the ribbon, click **Home** tab > **Draw** panel > **Polyline**. Create a closed polyline by selecting the corner points of the ground floor plan, as shown.

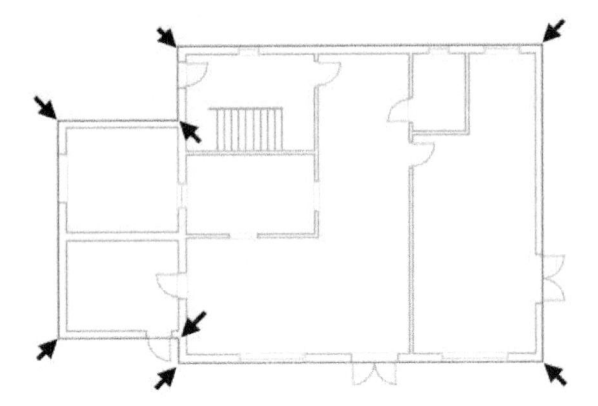

- Activate the **Rectangle** tool and create rectangles by selecting the corners, as shown. Activate the **Polyline** tool and create the other loops, as shown.

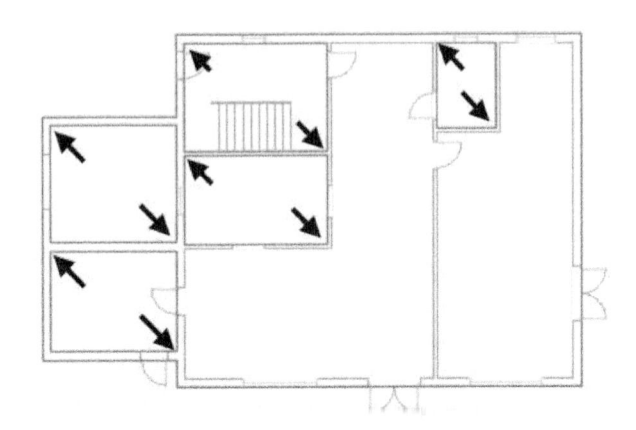

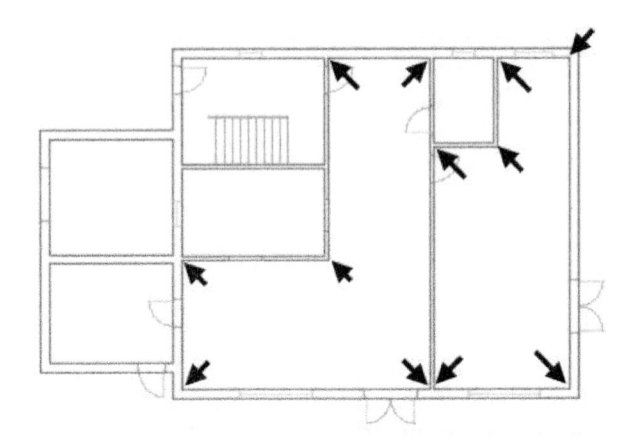

- Change the Workspace to **3D Modeling** by using the **Workspace** drop-down on the **Quick Access Toolbar** or **Workspace Switching** menu on the status bar.

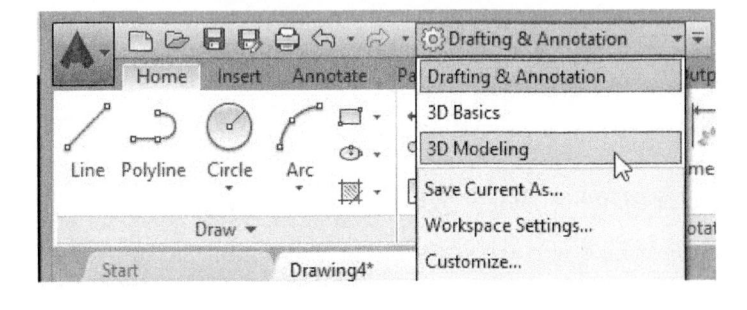

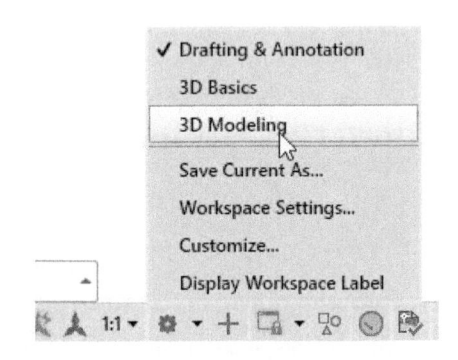

- On the ribbon, click **Home** tab > **Groups** panel > **Group**. Create a selection window covering all the entities of the South elevation. Press Enter to group the selected entities. Likewise, create groups of the other elevations.

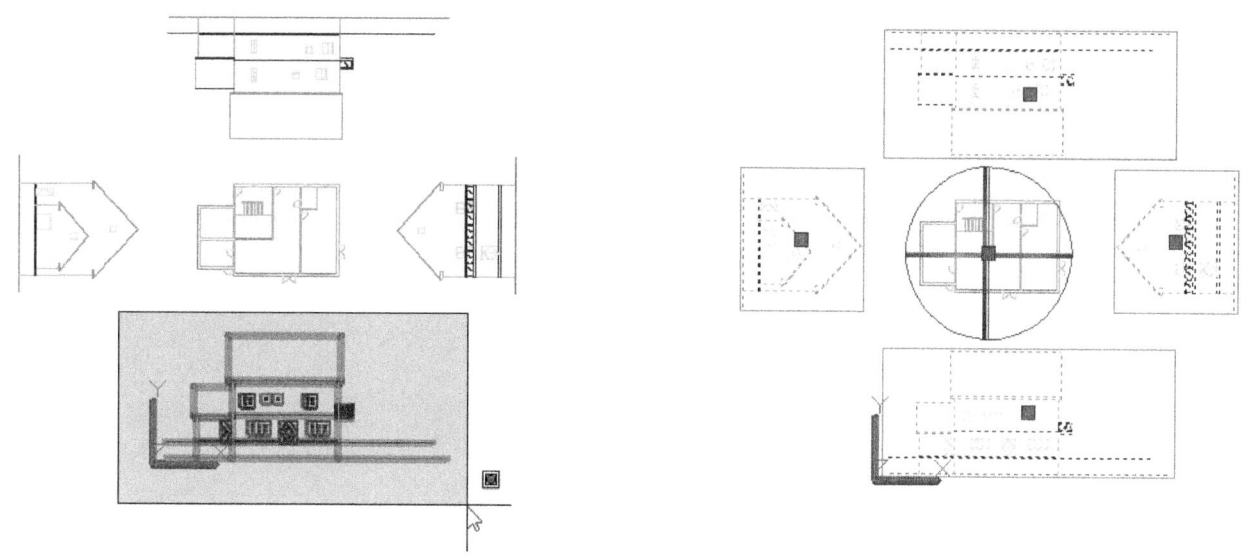

Now, you need to change the orientation of the drawing using the ViewCube located at the top right corner of the graphics window.

- On the ViewCube, click the lower right corner. The orientation of the drawing changes along with the ViewCube.

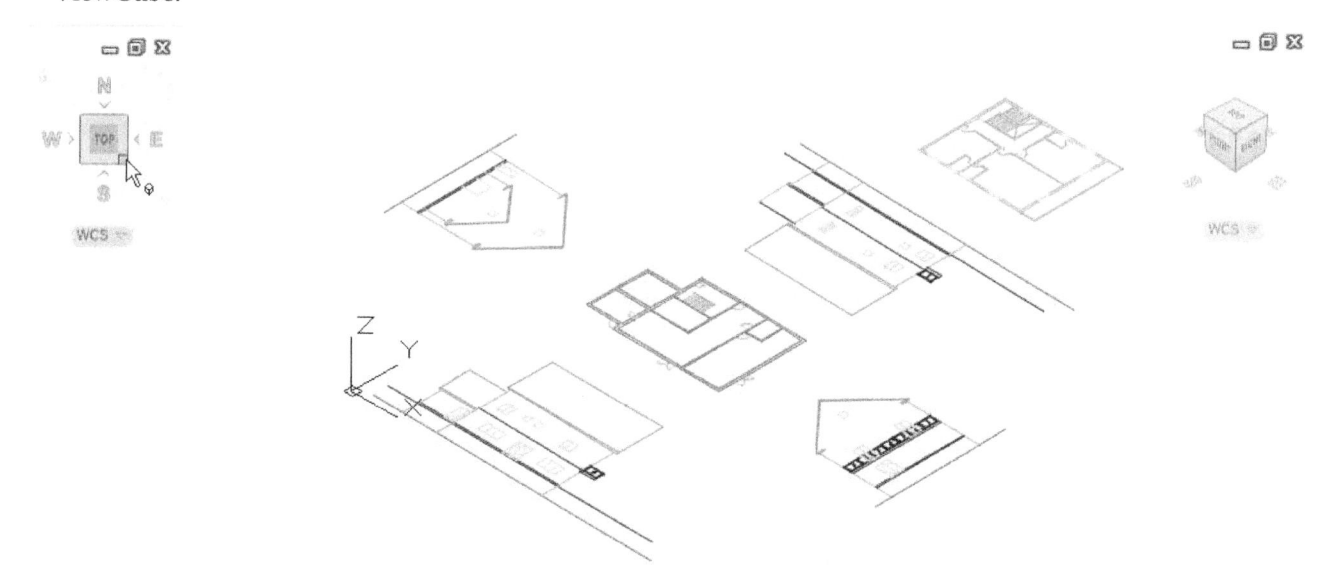

Now, you need to rotate the elevation views by 90 degrees using the Rotate Gizmo. By default, the Move Gizmo appears when you select any entity in the drawing.

- Select the South Elevation group from the drawing and notice the Move Gizmo. On the ribbon, click **Home** tab > **Selection** panel > **Gizmo** drop-down > **Rotate Gizmo**. The Rotate Gizmo appears on the select group.
- Select the origin point of the group, move the pointer and select the endpoint of the ground level line, as shown.

110 | Creating Architectural Drawings

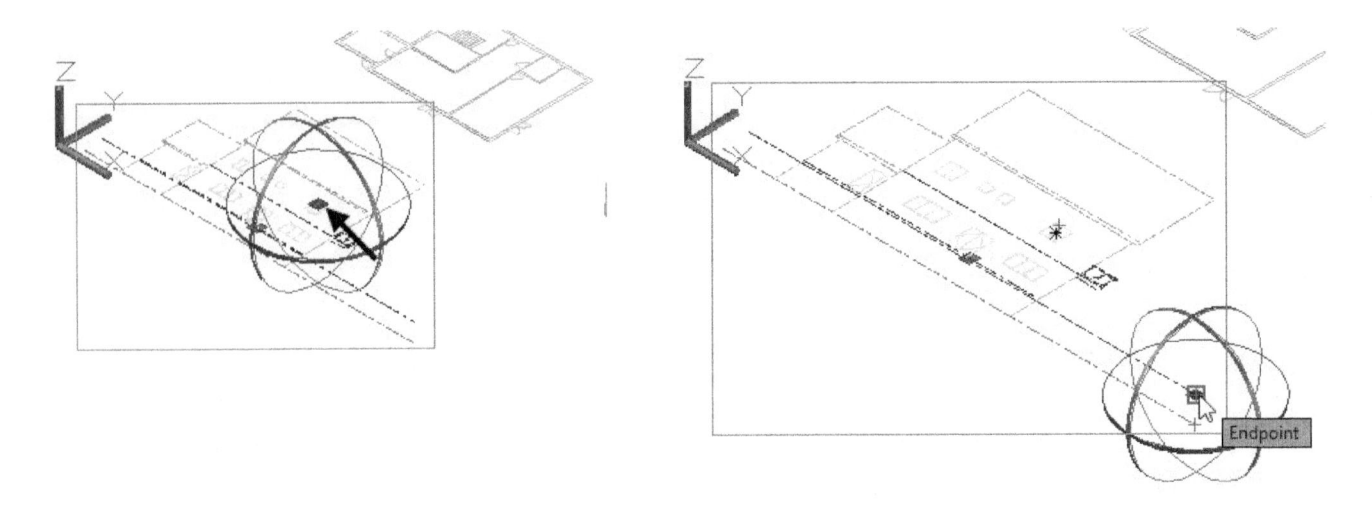

- Click on the red ring of the Rotate Gizmo, move the pointer upward, and click to rotate the elevation view by 90 degrees.

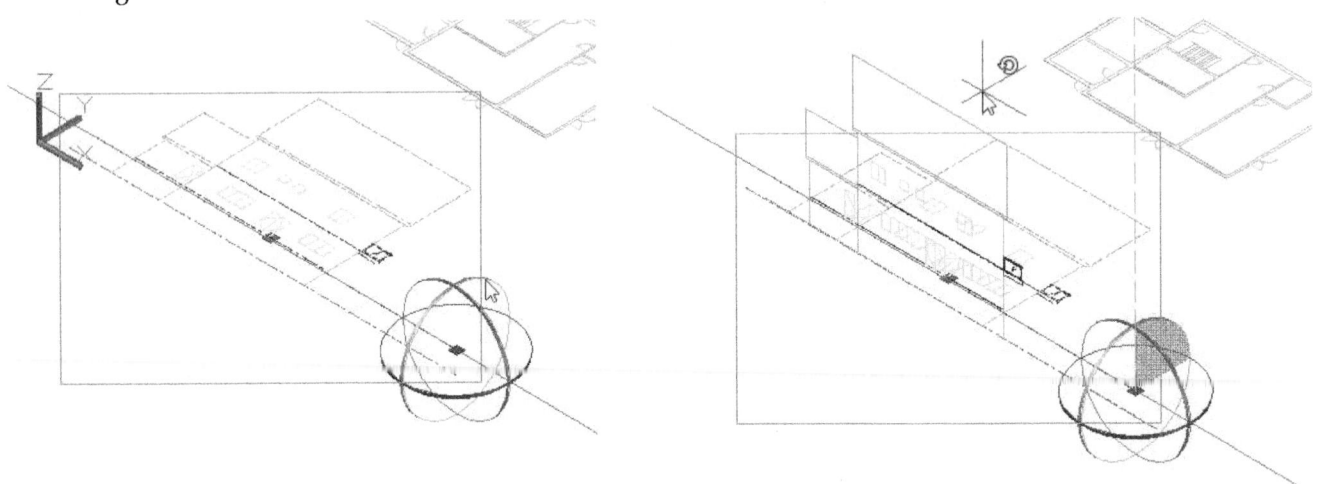

- Click the Front face of the ViewCube. The elevation view becomes parallel to the screen. Notice that the ground level coincides with the X-axis of the UCS. Click the top right corner of the ViewCube to switch back to previous orientation.

- Rotate the other elevations about the ground level lines.

111 | Creating Architectural Drawings

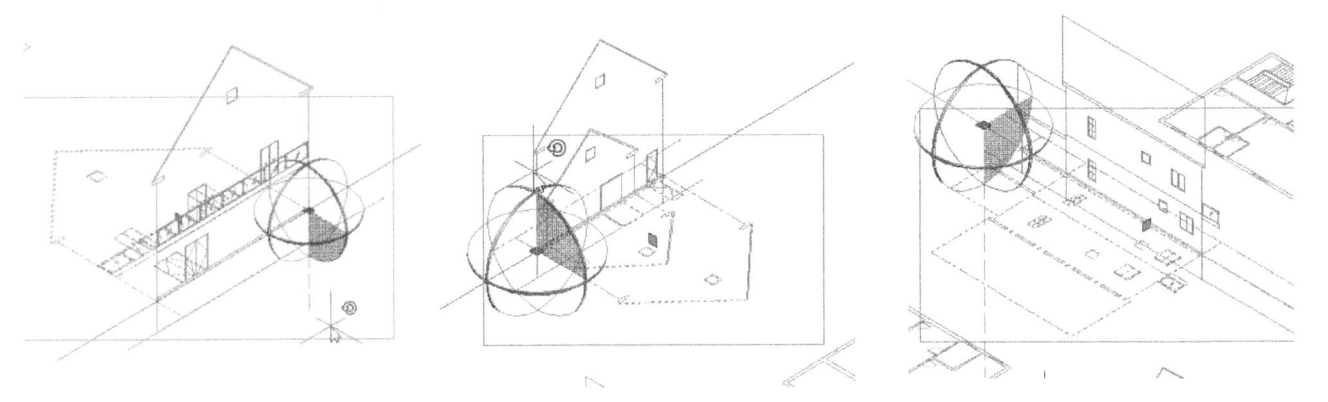

- Open the **Layers Properties Manager** and turn off the A-WALL, A-WINDOWS, A-DOORS, A-SLAB, WIPEOUT, and DOOR_SWING layers.

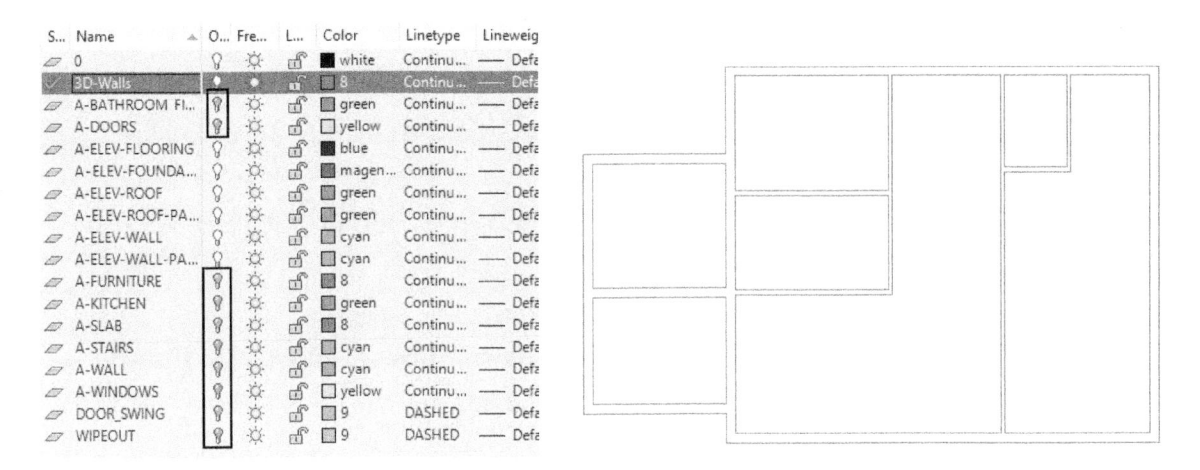

- In the top left corner of the graphics window, click **Wireframe** and select **Shades of Grey** from the Menu.

- On the ribbon, click **Home** tab > **Modeling** panel > **Presspull**.

- Zoom to the ground floor plan and click in area enclosed by the polyline. Zoom-out of the floor plane and select a point on the first floor level on the South elevation. The 3D walls are created up to the first floor level.

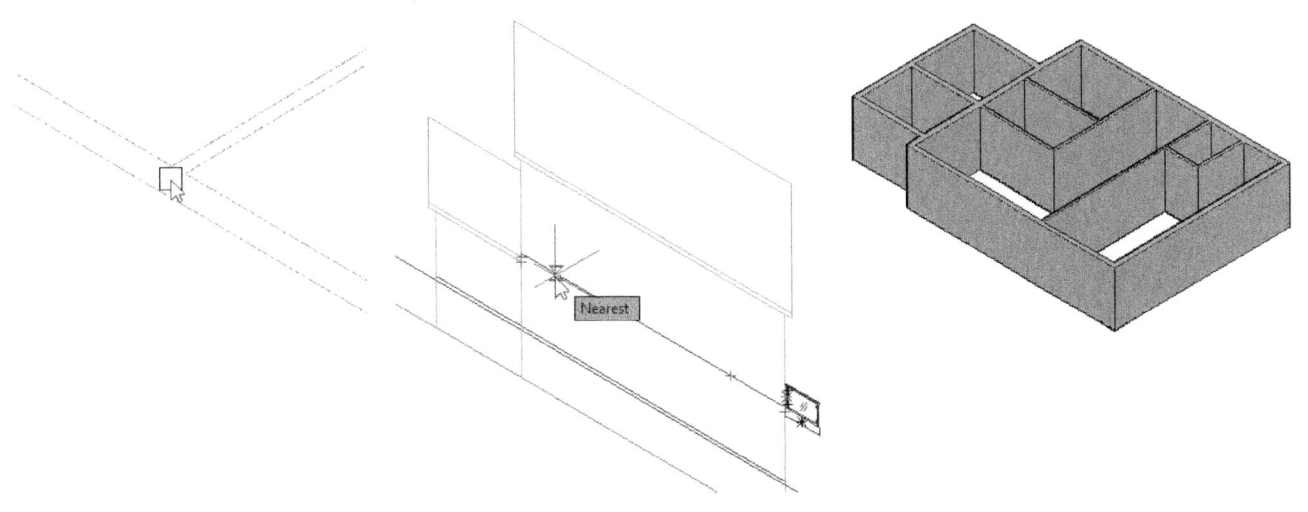

- On the ribbon, click **Home** tab > **Layers** panel > **Layer Properties Manager**. On the Layer Properties Manager,

Creating Architectural Drawings

turn ON the light bulb icons of A-WINDOWS, A-DOORS, DOOR_SWING layers.

- On the ribbon, click **Home** tab > **View** panel > **View Styles** drop-down > **Wireframe**.

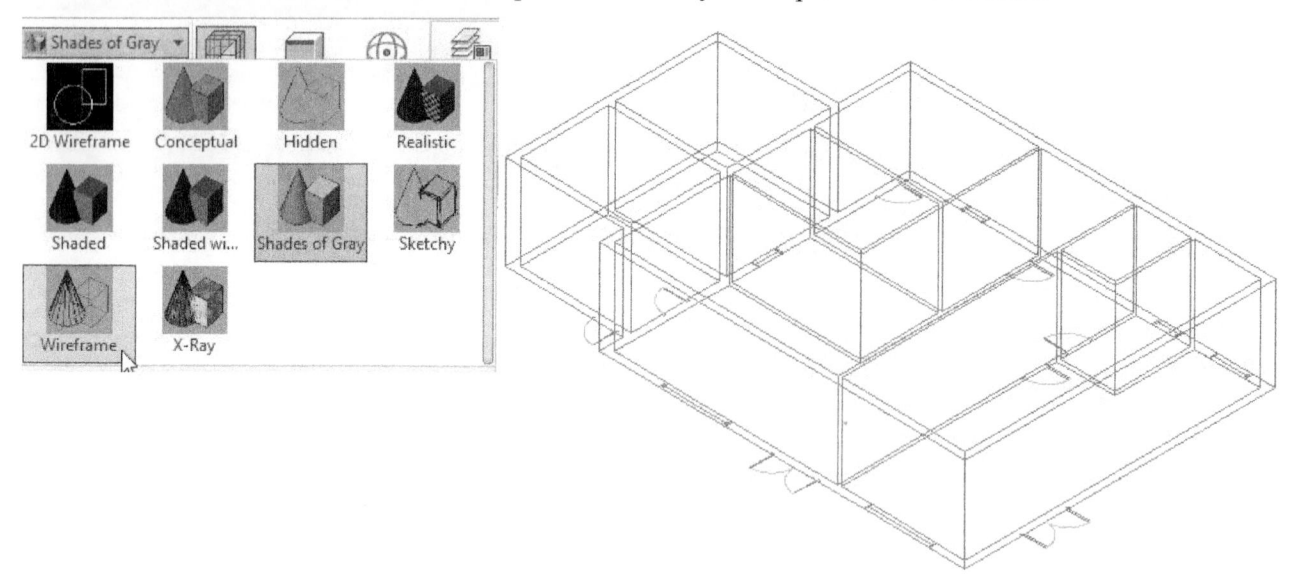

- Deactivate the **Dynamic UCS** icon on the status bar. Click the down-arrow next to the **Object Snap** icon and make sure that the **Apparent Intersection** option is checked.

- On the ribbon, click **Home** tab > **Modeling** panel > **Primitive** drop-down > **Box** . Specify the first and second corners of the box, as shown. Zoom to the South elevation and select the corner point of the double-door, as shown. The box is created.

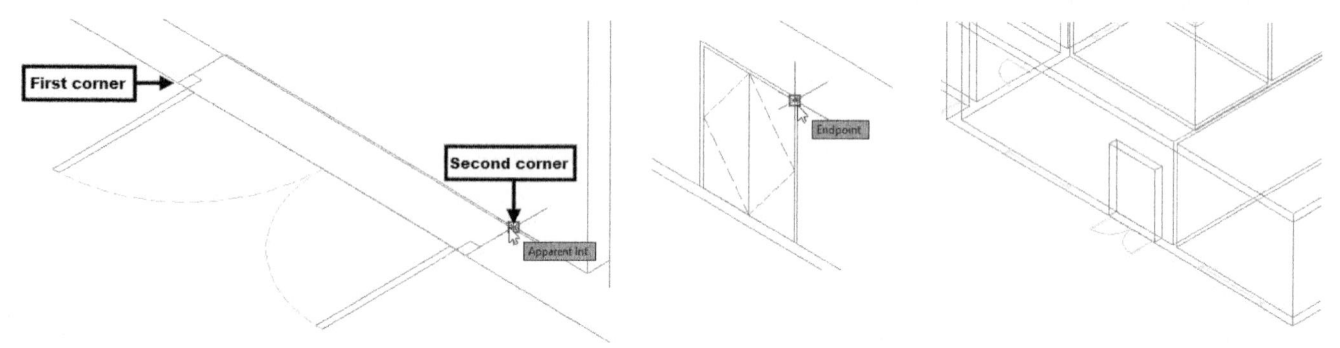

Now, you will use the **3D Align** tool to copy the box and place it on the other double-door location.

- On the ribbon, click **Home** tab > **Modify** panel > **3D Align** . Select the box from the graphics window, and press Enter. Select **Copy** from the command line.
- Select the base, second, and third points on the box, as shown. Zoom to the other double-door location on the floor plan. Select the first, second, and third destination points, as shown.

Creating Architectural Drawings

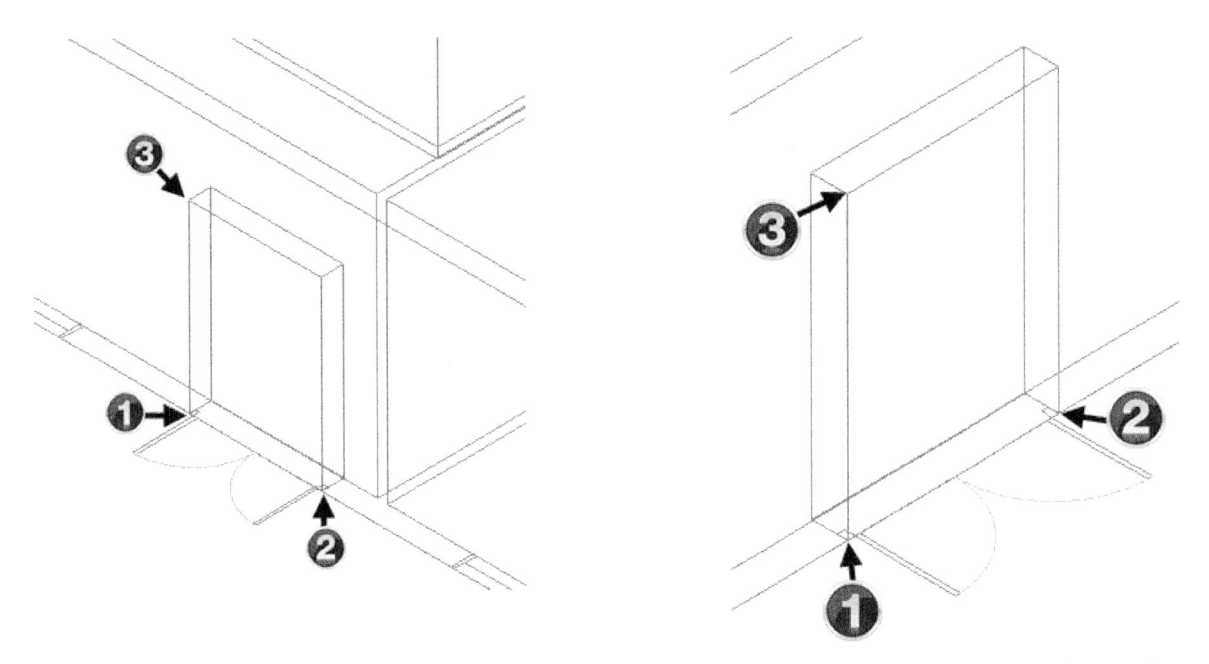

- On the Navigation Bar, click **Zoom** drop-down > **Zoom Window**. Specify the first and second corners of the Zoom window, as shown. Type **BOX** and press Enter. Select the first and second corners of the box. Zoom to the South elevation and select the top right corner of the single door, as shown.

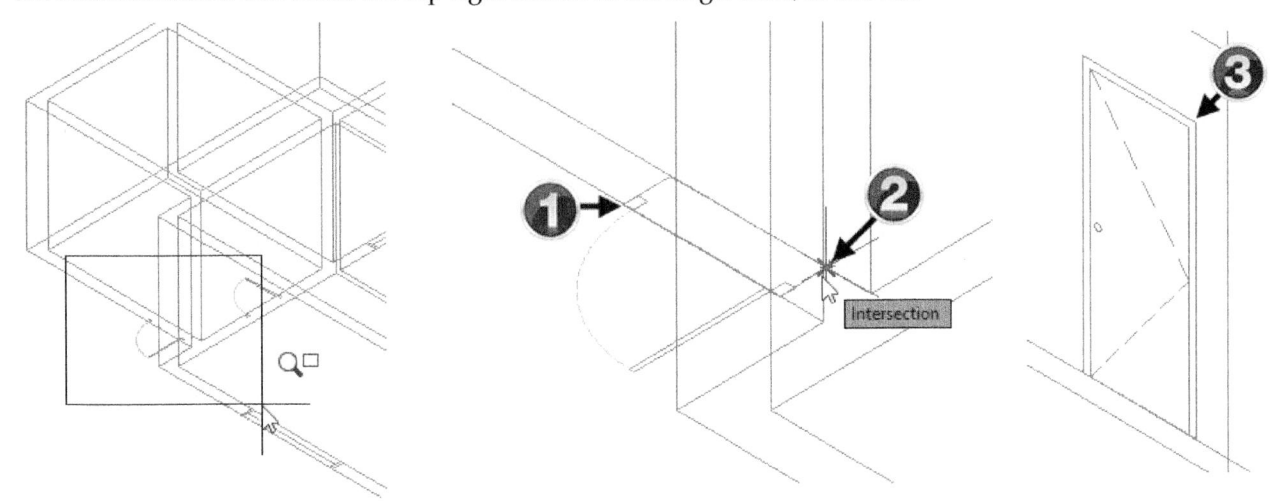

- Zoom to the utility room by using the **Zoom Window** tool. Activate the **Box** tool and specify the first and second corners of the box. Move the pointer upward and select the top right corner of the box created in the last step.

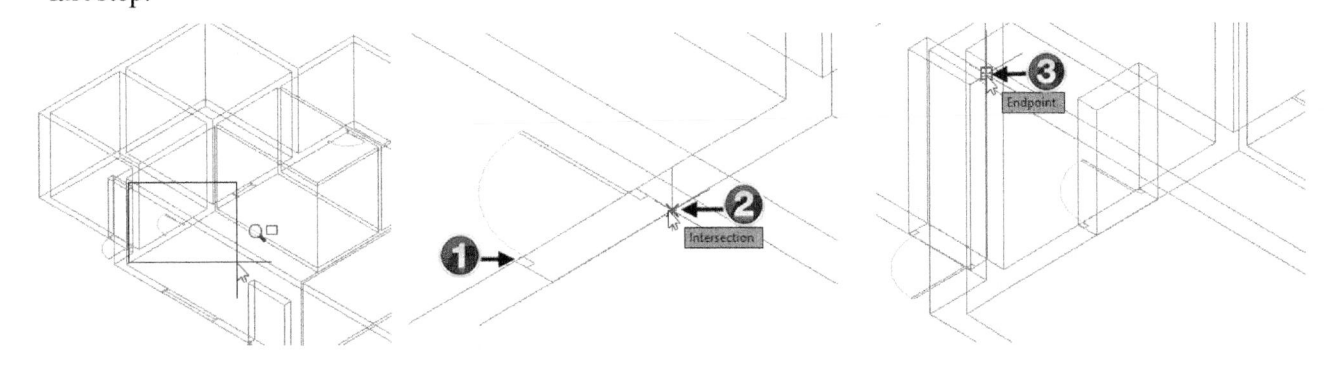

114 | Creating Architectural Drawings

- Likewise, create other boxes at the other single door locations, as shown.

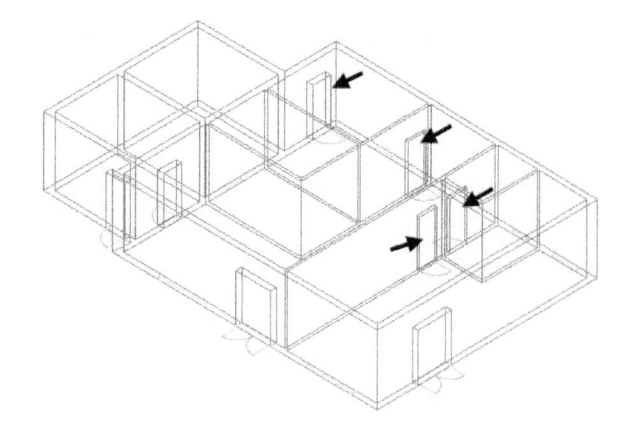

- Turn ON the A-WALL layer. Create two boxes at the kitchen openings.

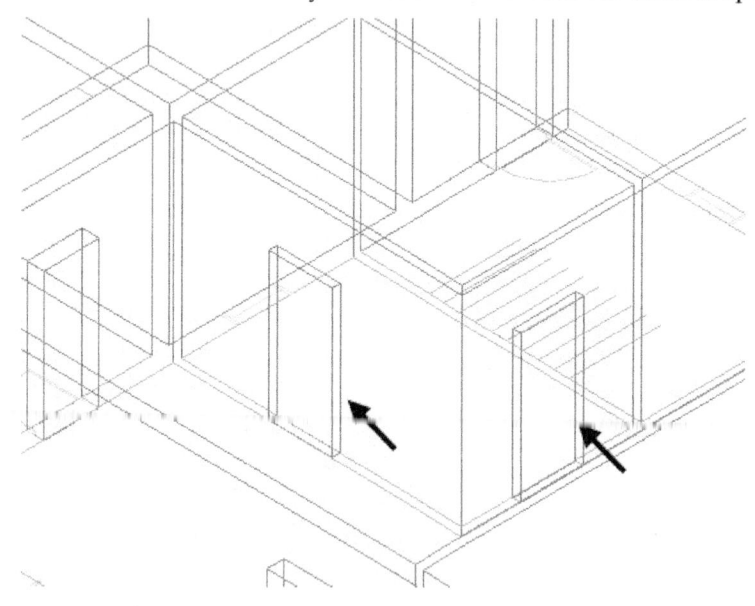

- Zoom to the garage area and create a box on the garage opening. Use the garage opening on the Rear elevation to define the box height.

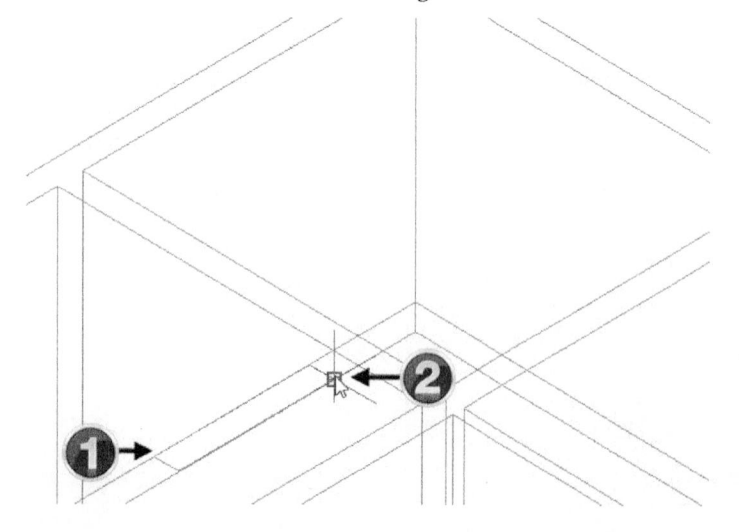

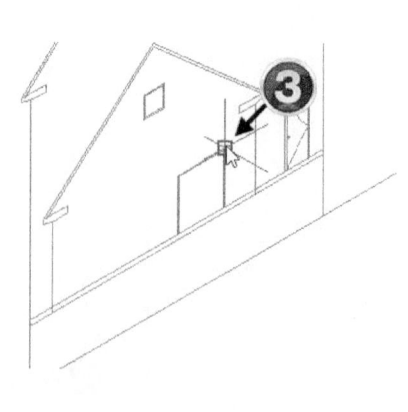

- On the ribbon, click **Home** tab > **Solid Editing** panel > **Solid, Subtract**. Select the 3D walls and press Enter. Select all the boxes created at the doors and opening locations. Press Enter to subtract the boxes from the walls.

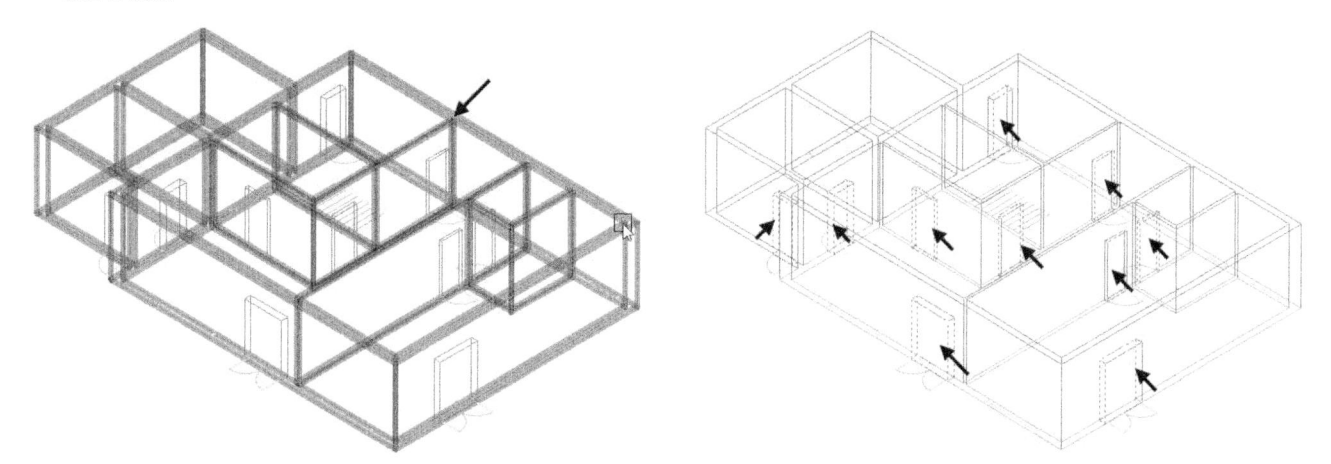

- In the top left corner of the graphics window, click **Wireframe** from the In-canvas tools, and select **Shades of Gray** from the menu.

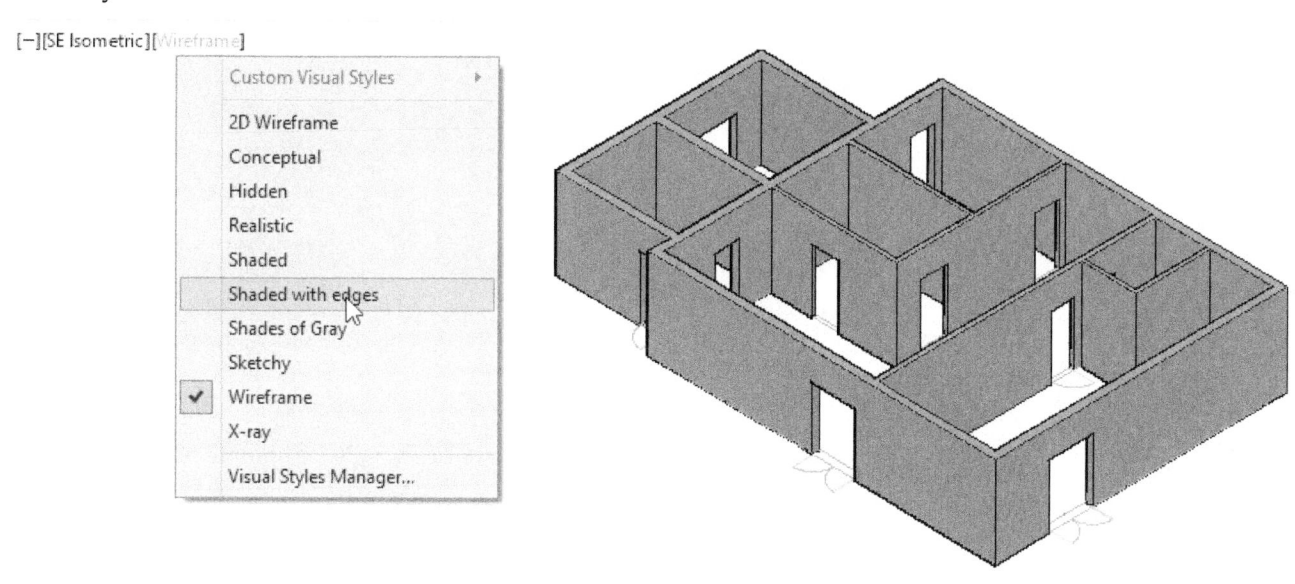

- On the ribbon, click **Home** tab > **Modeling** panel > **Presspull**. Zoom to the right side window on the South elevation. Select the outer rectangle of the window. Move the pointer toward the walls and select the corner point, as shown.

116 | Creating Architectural Drawings

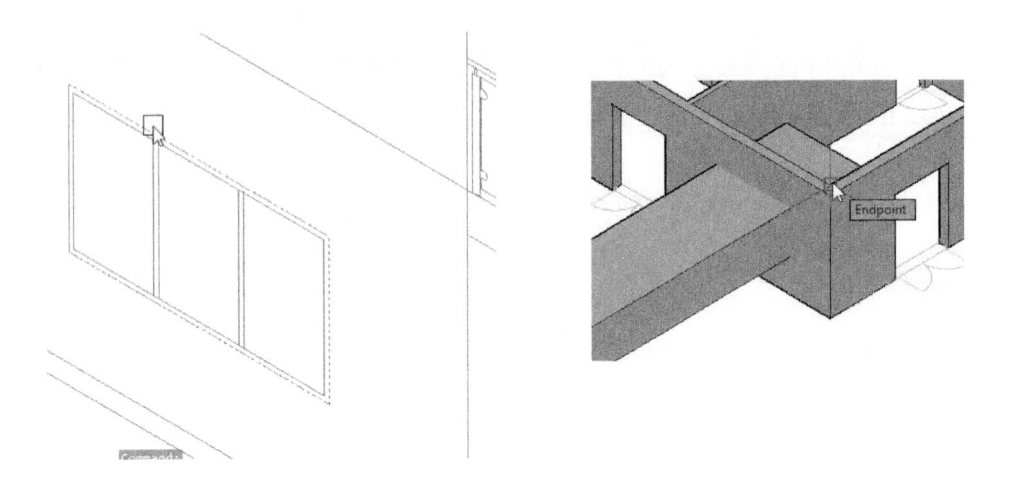

- Zoom to the left side window of the South elevation and select the outer rectangle. Move the pointer towards the walls and select the corner point, as shown.

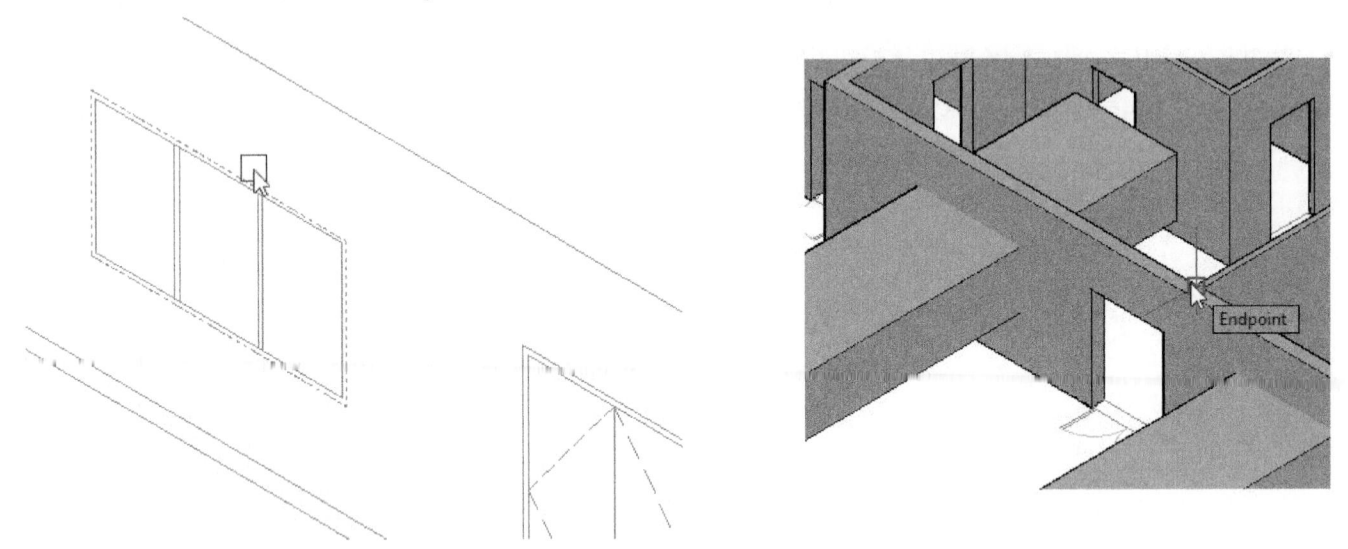

- Zoom to the left side window of the North elevation and select the outer rectangle, as shown. Move the pointer towards the walls and select the corner point, as shown.

117 | **Creating Architectural Drawings**

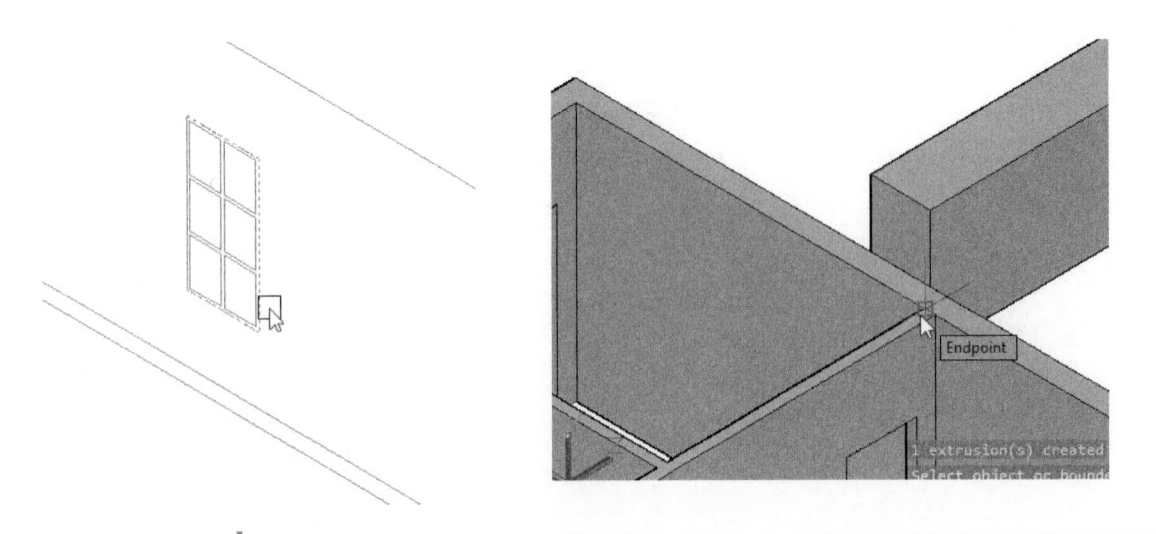

- Zoom to the middle window of the North elevation and select the outer rectangle, as shown. Move the pointer towards the walls and select the corner point, as shown.

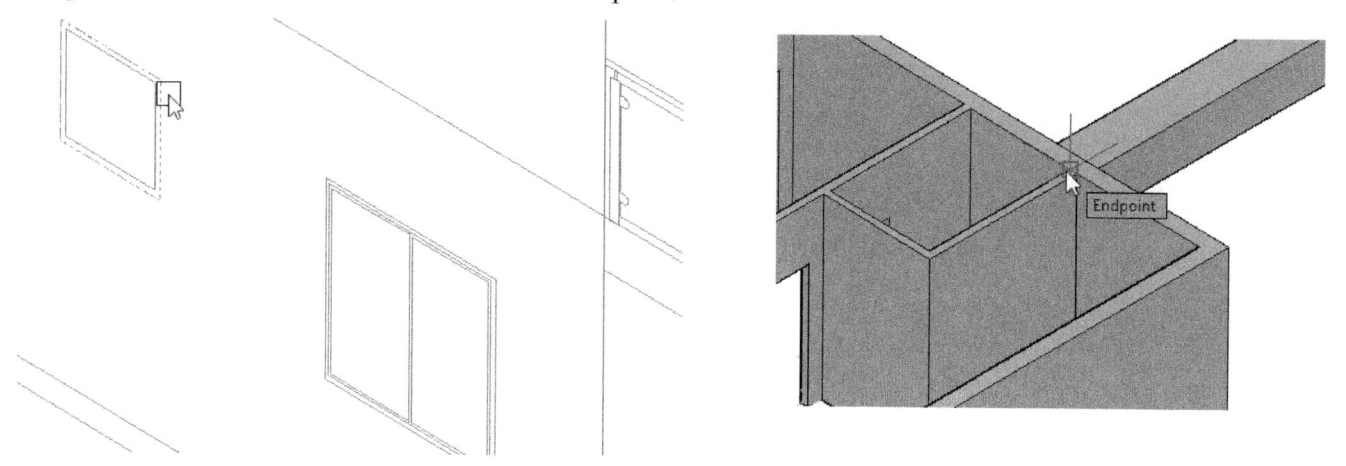

- On the ribbon, click **Home** tab > **Coordinates** panel > **UCS**. Zoom to the extreme right window of North elevation, and select the top left corner of the window. Make sure that the ORTHOMODE(F8) is active. Move the pointer downward and select the lower left corner of the window. Move the pointer toward right and select the top right corner of the window. The UCS is positioned, as shown.

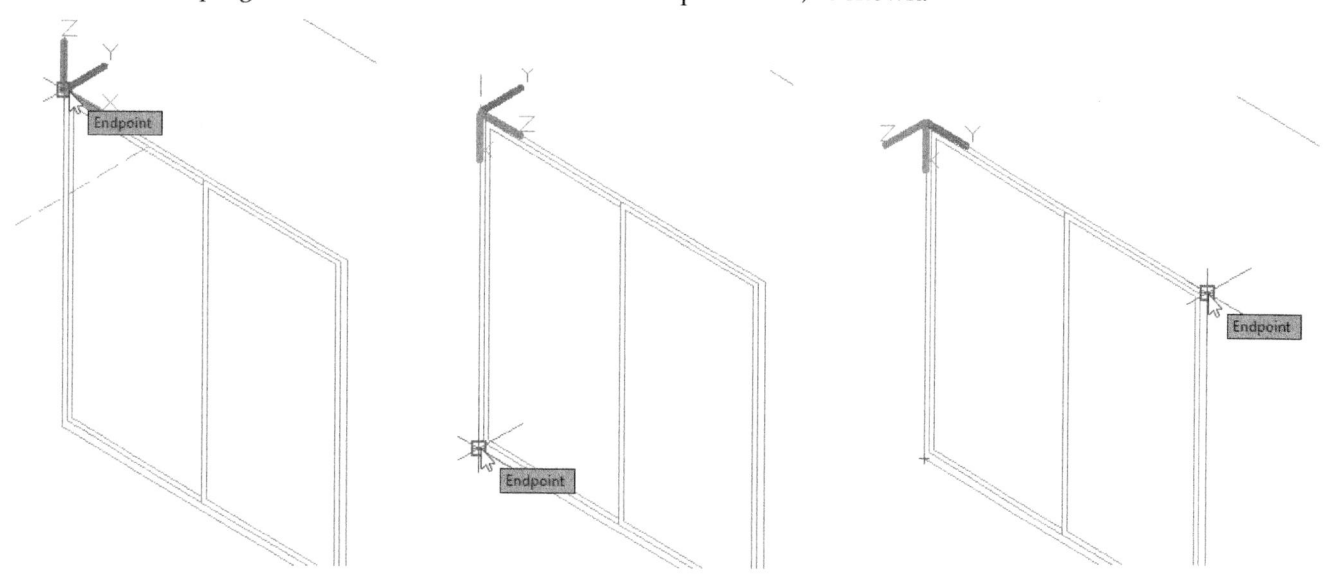

- Create a box by specifying the first, second, third corner, as shown.

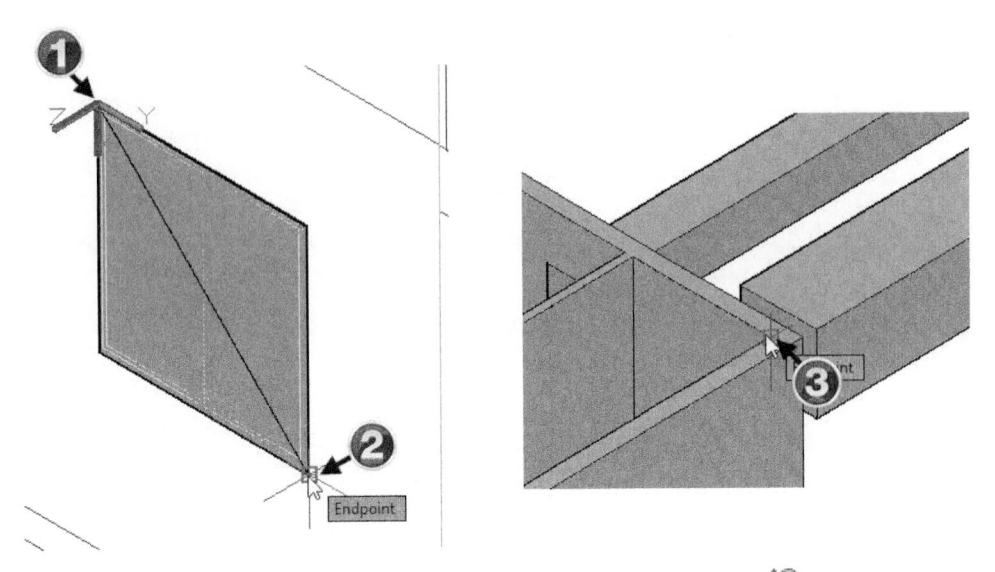

- On the ribbon, click **Home** tab > **Coordinates** panel > **UCS, World**. The UCS is brought to its default position and orientation.

- On the ribbon, click **Home** tab > **Solid Editing** panel > **Solid, Subtract**. Select the 3D walls and press Enter. Select all the boxes created using the **Presspull** and **Box** tools. Press Enter to create the window openings.

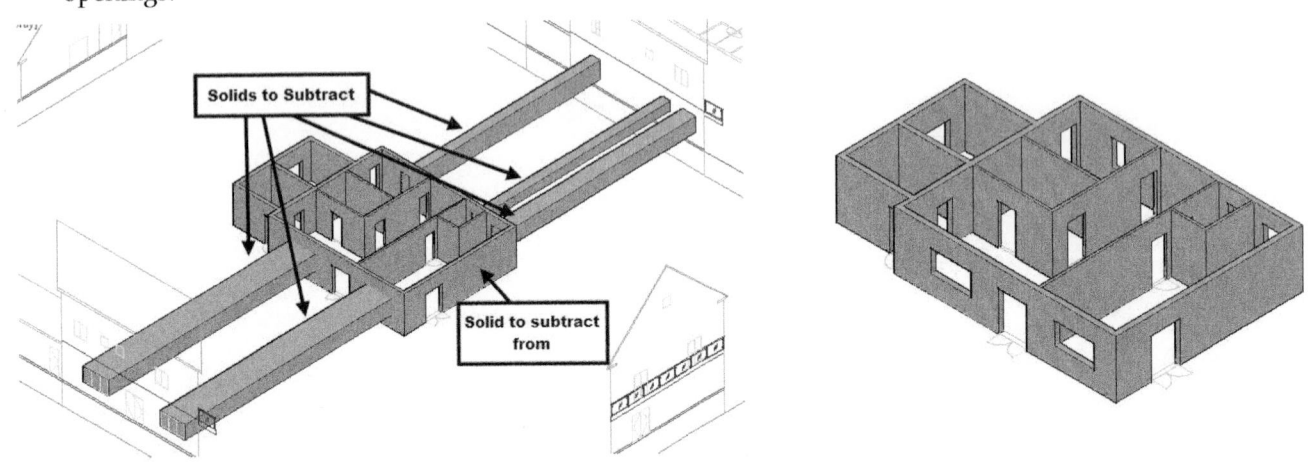

- On the ribbon, click **Visualize** tab > **Visual Styles** panel > **Visual Styles** drop-down > **Wireframe**.
- Zoom to the kitchen area. Activate the **Box** tool and specify the first and second corners, as shown. Select **2Point** from the command line. Select two points to define the height of the box, as shown.

119 | **Creating Architectural Drawings**

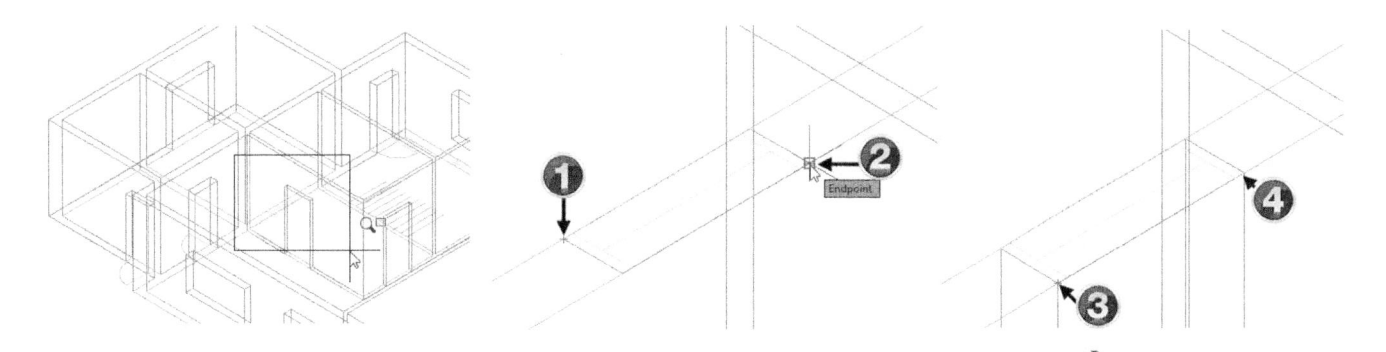

- On the ribbon, click **Home** tab > **Selection** panel > **Gizmo** drop-down > **Move Gizmo**. Select the box created in the last step. Select the origin of the **Move Gizmo**, move the pointer, and select the lower left corner of the box. Select the Z-axis (blue vertical arrow) of the Move Gizmo, move the pointer upward, type 1800, and press Enter.

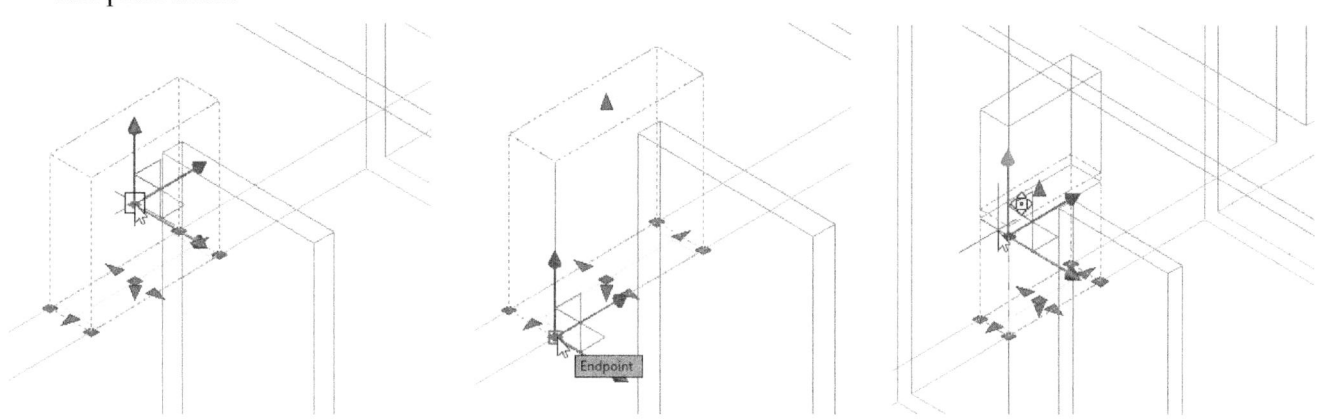

- Type SU and press Enter. Select the 3D walls and press Enter. Select the box created in the last step, and press Enter. The window opening is created.

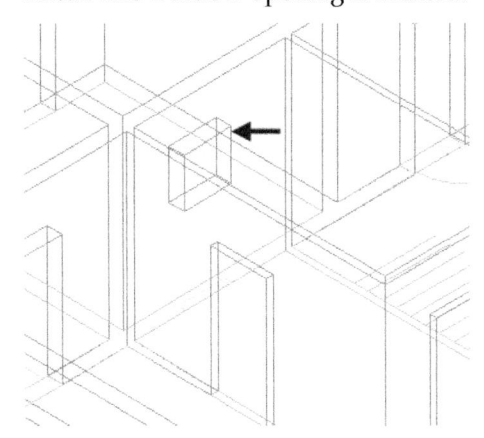

Tutorial 3: Create the Ceiling

- Create a new layer with the name 3D-Floor. The layer color should be Yellow. Make the 3D-Floor as current.
- On the ribbon, click **Home** tab > **View** panel > **3D Navigation** drop-down > **Top**. The view orientation is changed to Top.
- On the ribbon, click **Home** tab > **Draw** panel > **Polyline**. Activate the **Dynamic UCS** icon on the

120 | Creating Architectural Drawings

Status bar. Place the pointer on the top face of the 3D walls. Move the pointer and select the lower left corner point, as shown. Likewise, select the other corner points, as shown. Select **Close** from the command line.

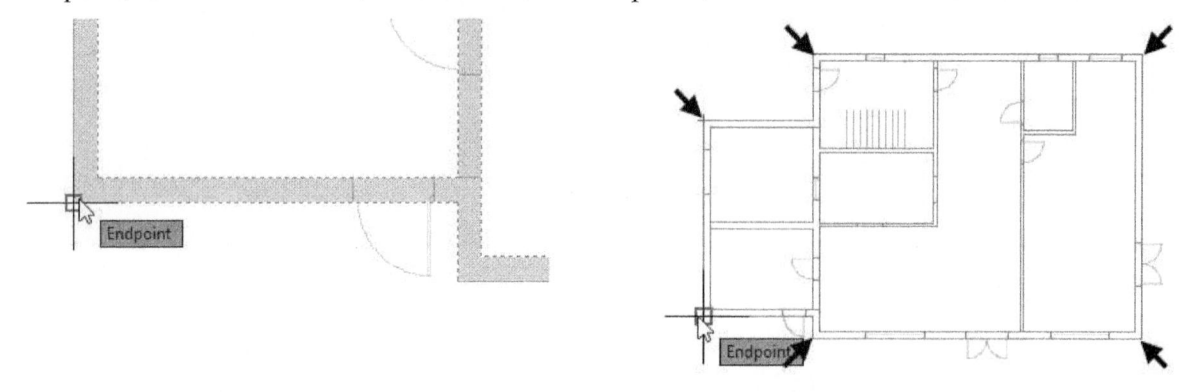

- Type O and press Enter. Type 320 and press Enter to define the offset distance. Select the polyline and click inside to specify the offset side. Press Esc to deactivate the tool.

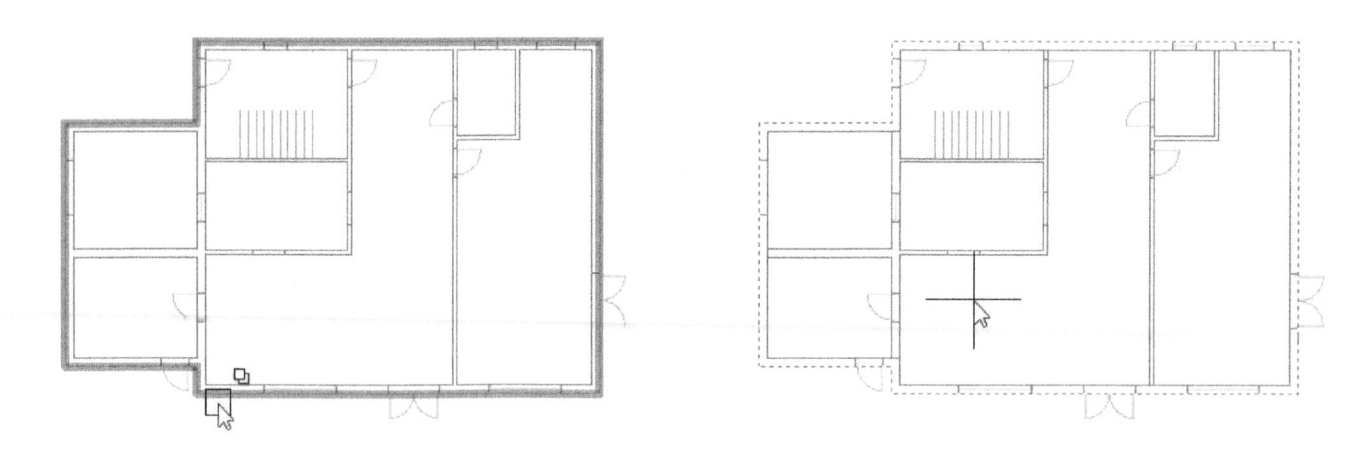

- On the ribbon, click **Home** tab > **Madeling** panel > **Extrude** . Select the offset line and press Enter. Type -200 and press Enter. On the ribbon, click **Home** tab > **View** panel > **3D Navigation** drop-down > **SE Isometric** . The view orientation is changed to SE Isometric. Change the **View Style** to **Shades of Gray**.

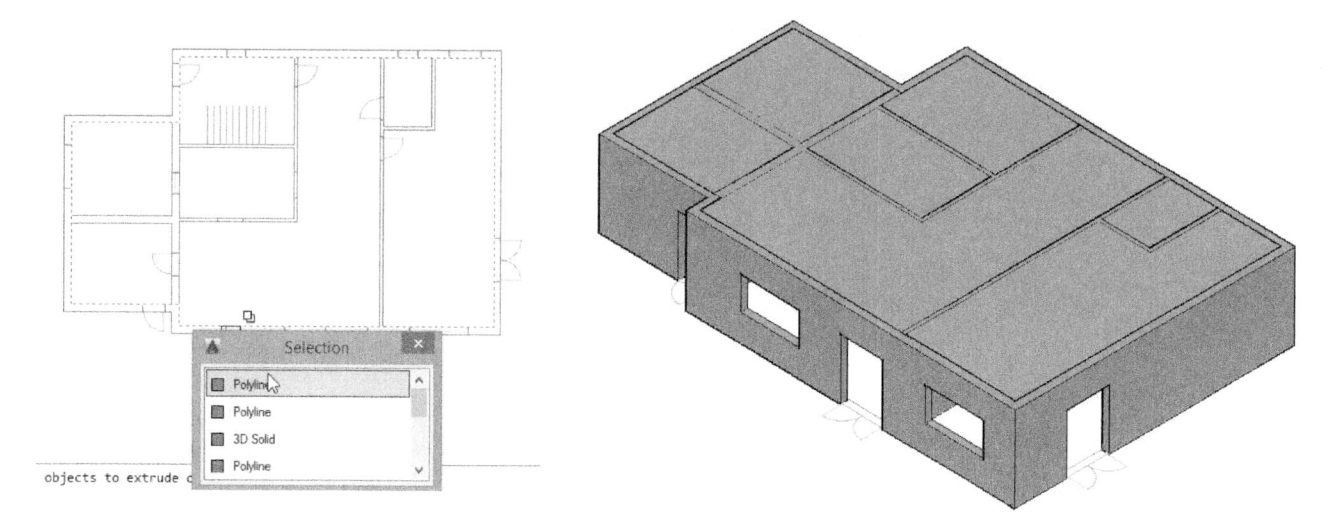

- Select the extruded solid and notice the Move Gizmo attached to it. Click on the Z-axis (blue arrow) o the Move Gizmo, and then select **Copy** from the command line. Move the pointer upward and click to create a copy of the extruded solid. Select **eXit** from the command line. Press Esc to deselect the extruded solid.

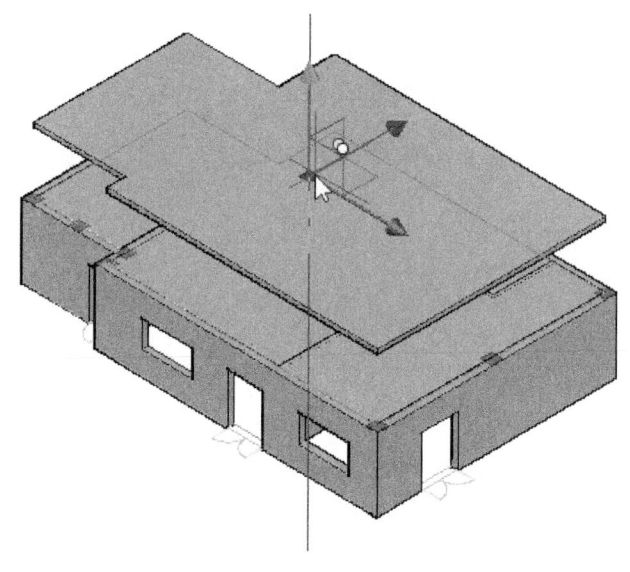

- On the ribbon, click **Home** tab > **Solid Editing** panel > **Solid, Subtract**. Select the 3D walls and press Enter. Select the extruded solid and press Enter.

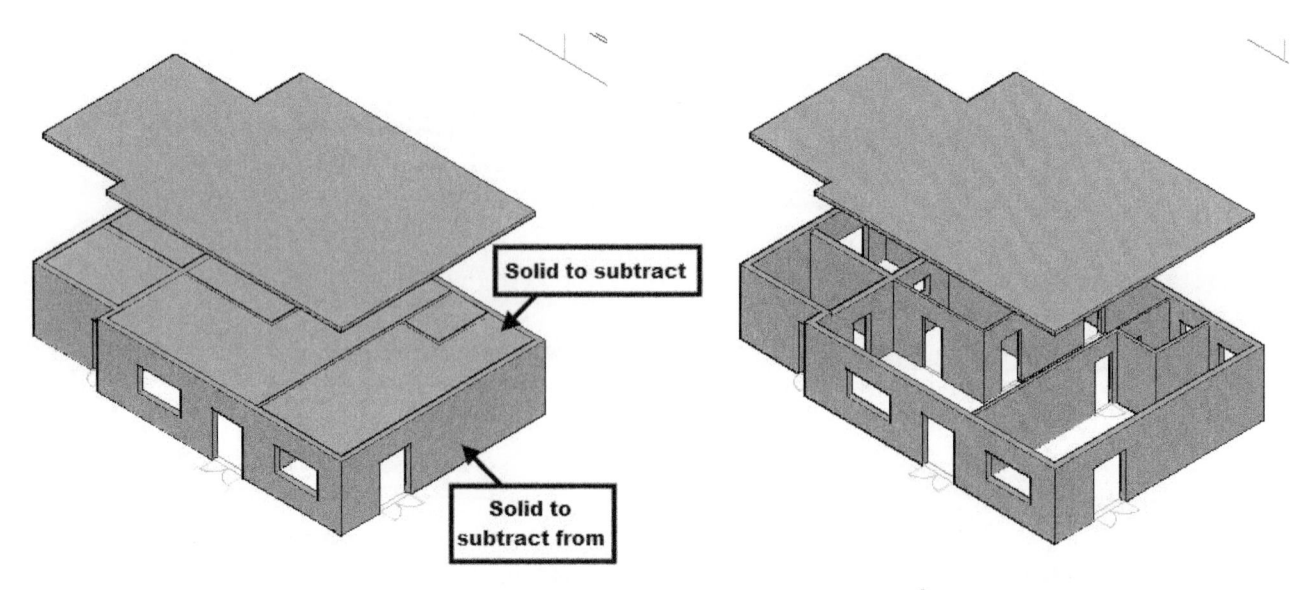

- Select the copied extruded solid and click **Home** tab > **Modify** panel > **Move**. Select the base point and destination point, as shown. The extruded solid is positioned above the walls.

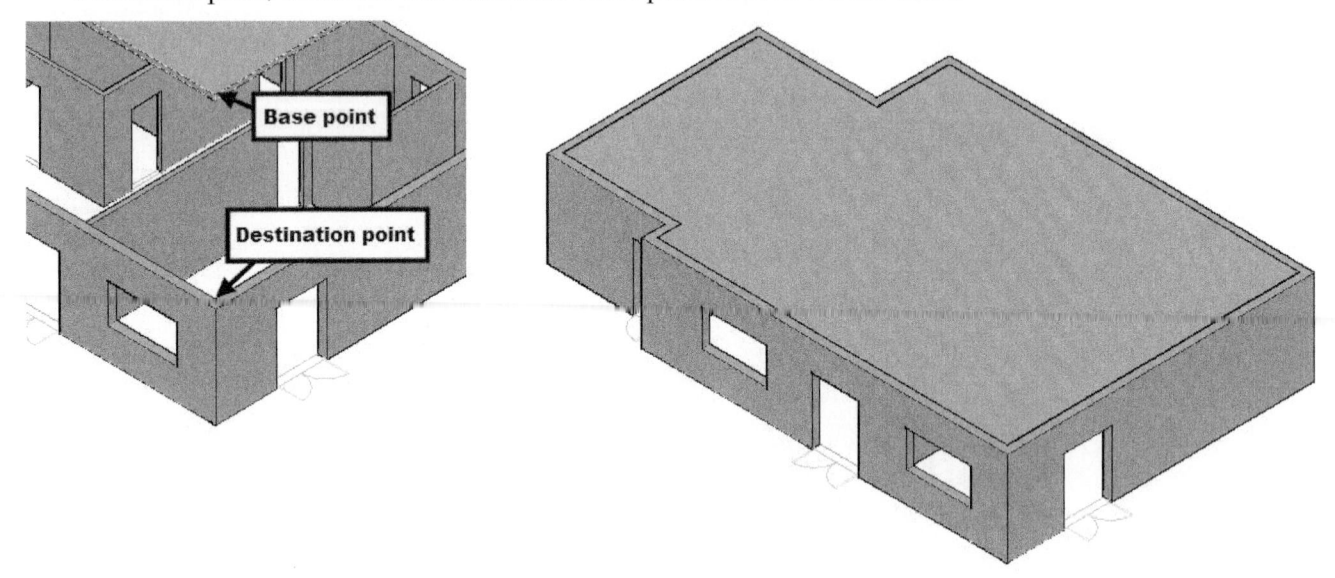

Now, you need to create the slab.

- Type EXT and press Enter. Select the polyline created on the top face of the 3D walls. Type 200 and press Enter.

Creating Architectural Drawings

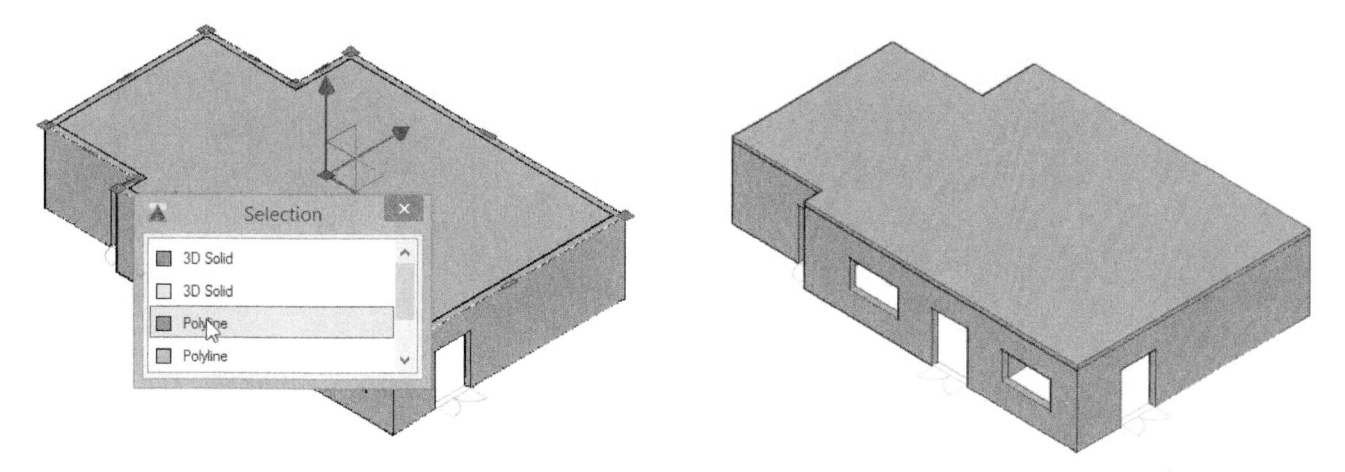

- Select the newly created extruded solid. On the ribbon, click **Home** tab > **Modify** panel > **Copy**. Select the base point and destination point, as shown.

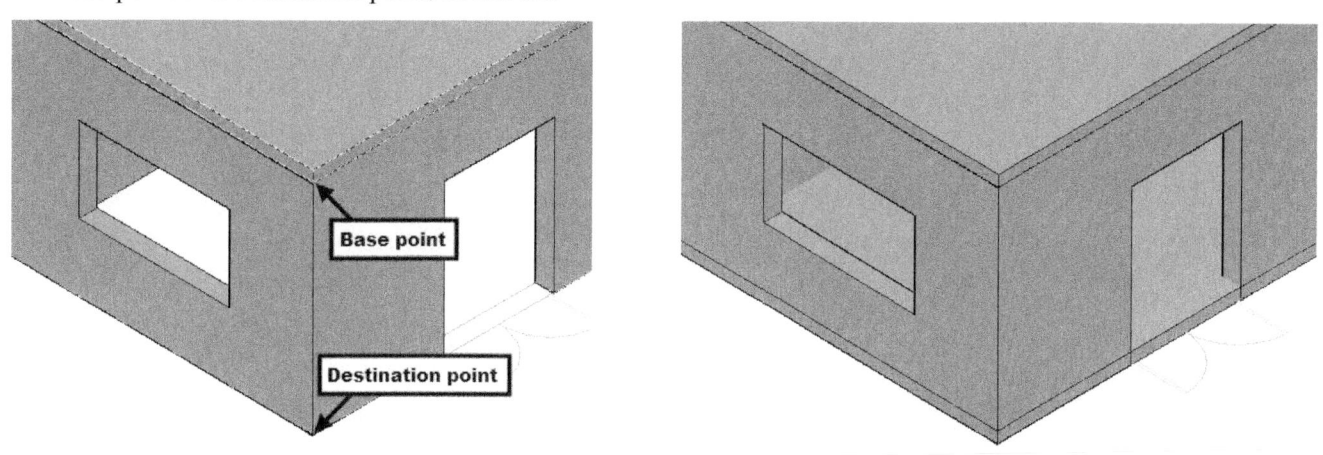

- On the ribbon, click **Home** tab > **Solid Editing** panel > **Solid, Subtract**. Select the 3D walls and press Enter. Select the extruded solid at the bottom of the 3D walls, and press Enter.

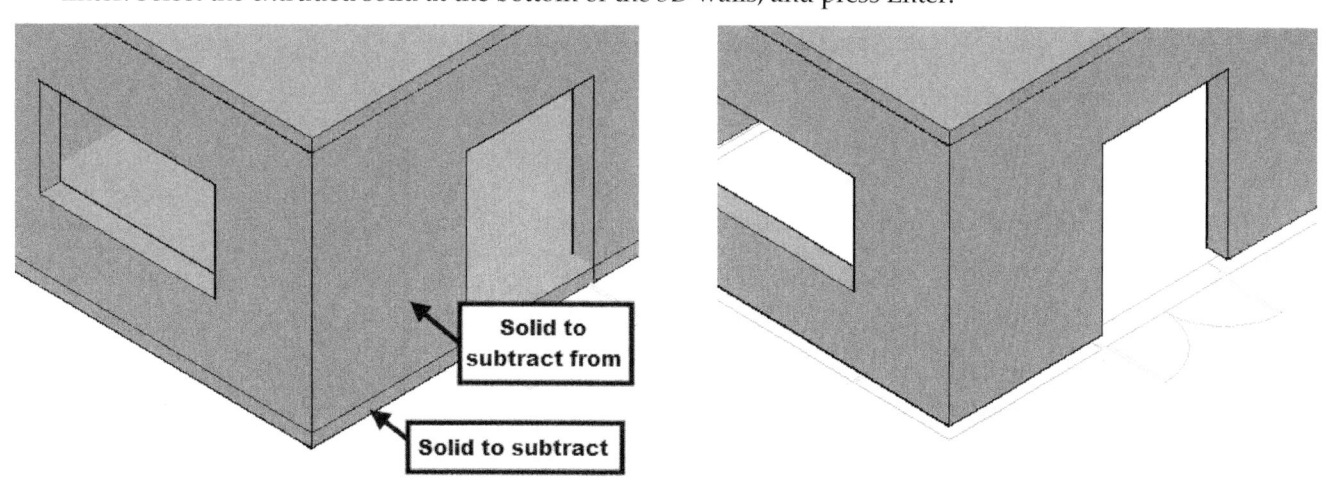

- Select the copied extruded solid and click **Home** tab > **Modify** panel > **Move**. Select the base point and destination point, as shown. The extruded solid is positioned below the walls.

Creating Architectural Drawings

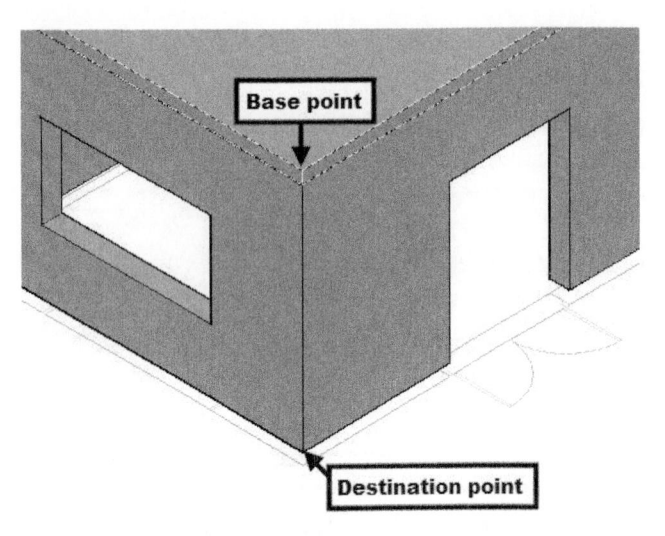

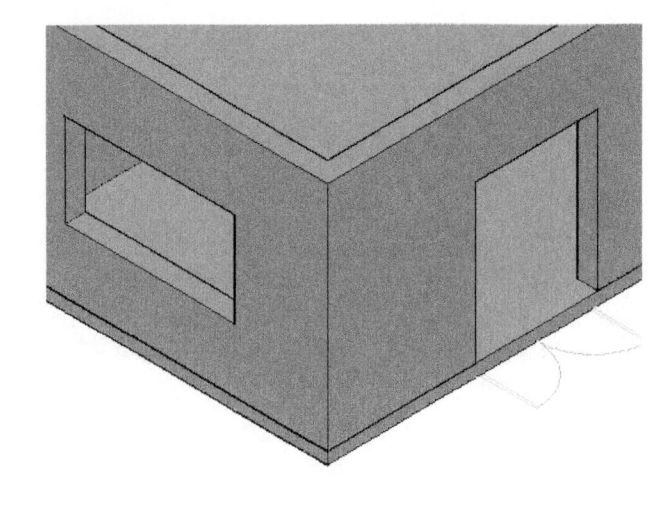

Tutorial 4: Creating Doors on the Ground Floor

- Create two layers "3D-Door" and "3D-Doorframe". Set the colors to Index color 30 and 22, respectively. Set the 3D-Doorframe layer as current.

- On the ribbon, click **Home** tab > **Layers** panel > **Off**. Select anyone of the floors to turn off its layer.

- Type PL and press Enter. Make sure that the **Dynamic UCS** icon is turned ON on the Status bar. Zoom to the double-door location and place the pointer on the outer face of the wall. Move the pointer on the highlighted face and select the lower left corner of the door opening.

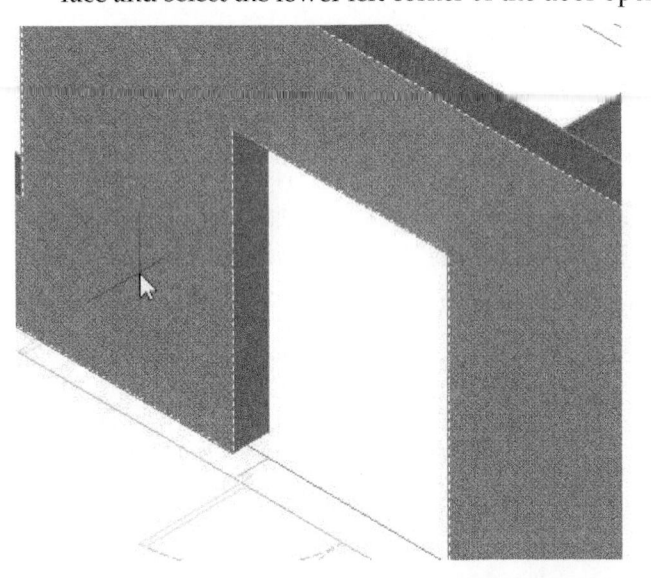

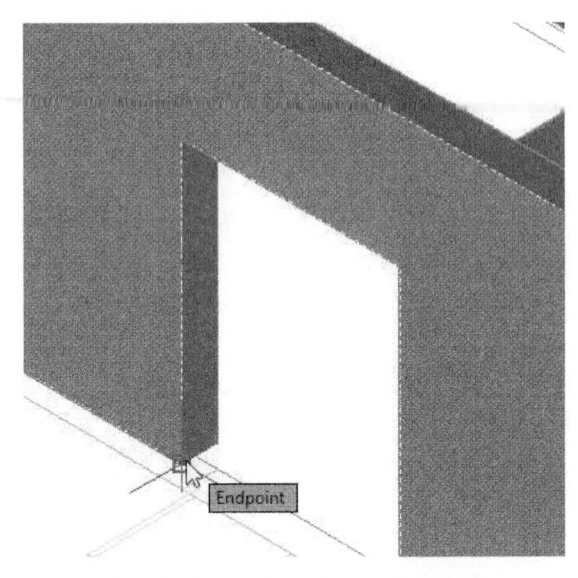

- Select the other corners of the door opening in the clockwise direction. Press Esc to deactivate the tool.

- On the **Home** tab of the ribbon, expand the **Modify** panel and click the **Explode** tool. Select the 2D door block and press Enter. The block is exploded into individual entities.

Creating Architectural Drawings

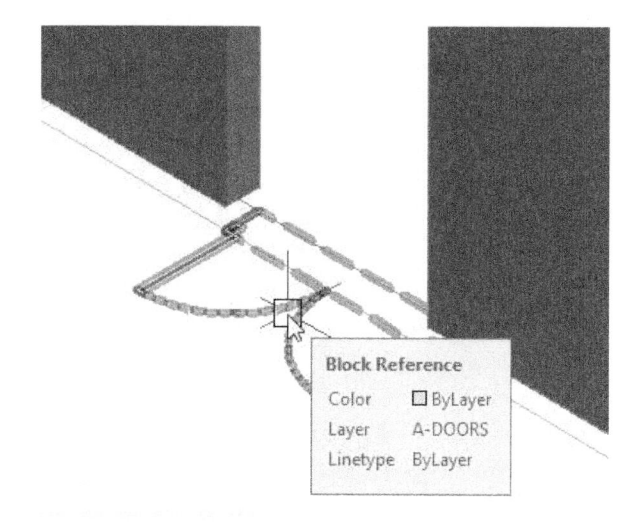

- On the ribbon, click **Home** tab > **Modeling** panel > **Extrude** drop-down > **Sweep**. Select the rectangle of the 2D door and press Enter. Select **Base point** from the command line and select the corner point of the rectangle, as shown.

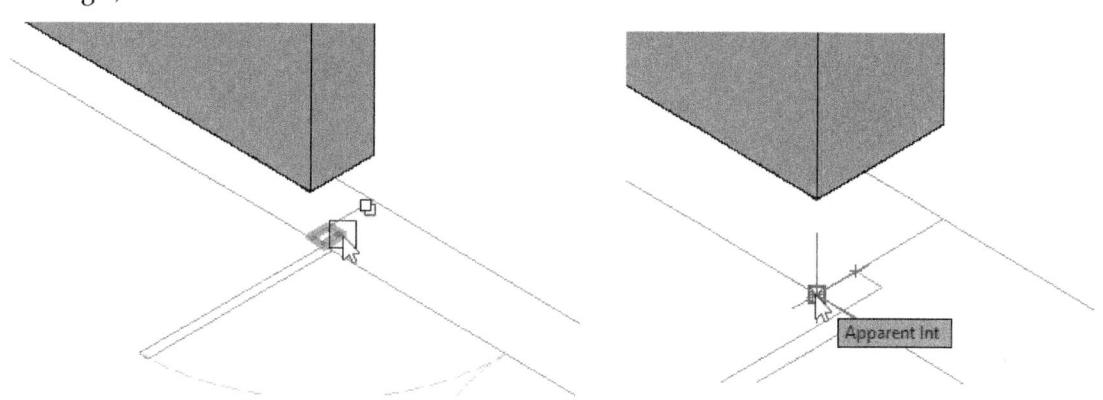

- Select the polyline created on the door opening edge, and press Enter. The door frame is created, as shown.

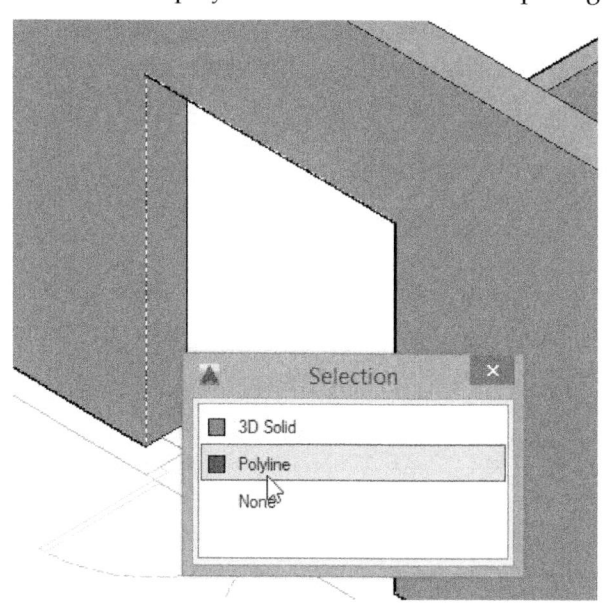

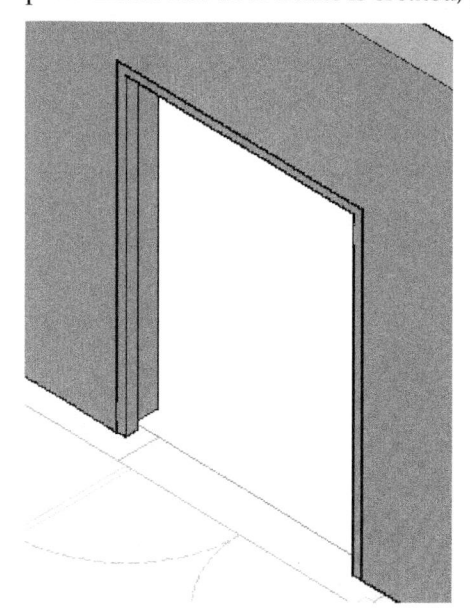

- On Navigation Bar, click the Orbit tool. Press and hold the left mouse button and drag the mouse toward right; the model is rotated toward right. Place the pointer on the single door opening of the utility room, move forward the mouse wheel.

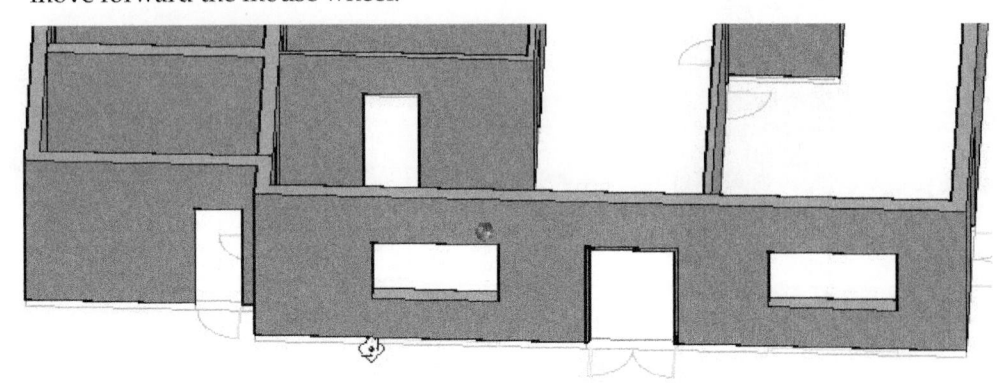

- Create the door frame using the **Sweep** tool.

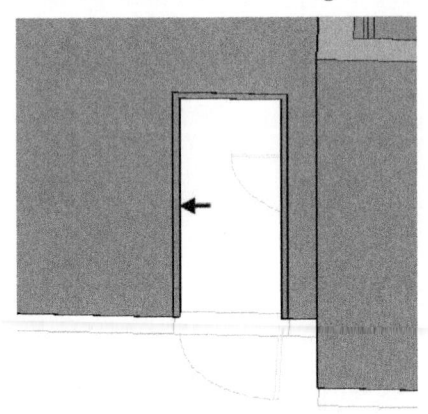

- On the ribbon, click **Home** tab > **View** panel > **3D Navigation** drop-down > **SE Isometric**.
- On the ribbon, click **Home** tab > **Layers** panel > **Layer** drop-down > **3D-Door**. Type **BOX** and press Enter. Place the pointer on the front face of the double-door frame. Move the pointer on the highlighted face and select the lower left corner point, as shown. On the status bar, click the down arrow next to the **Object Snap** icon and make sure that the **Midpoint** option is selected. Move the pointer upward and select the midpoint of the horizontal portion of the door frame. Type 45 and press Enter to create the door.

127 | Creating Architectural Drawings

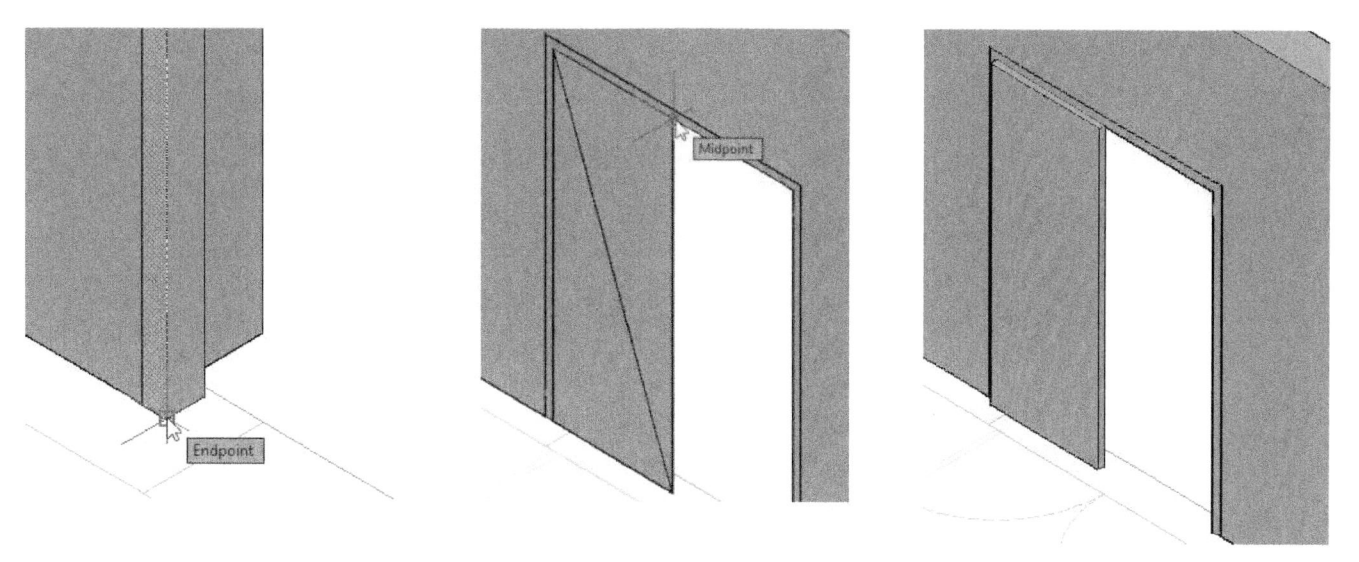

- Select the door and click the **Move** tool on the **Modify** panel of the **Home** ribbon tab. Select the corner point of the door, as shown. Move the pointer inwards, type 100, and press Enter.

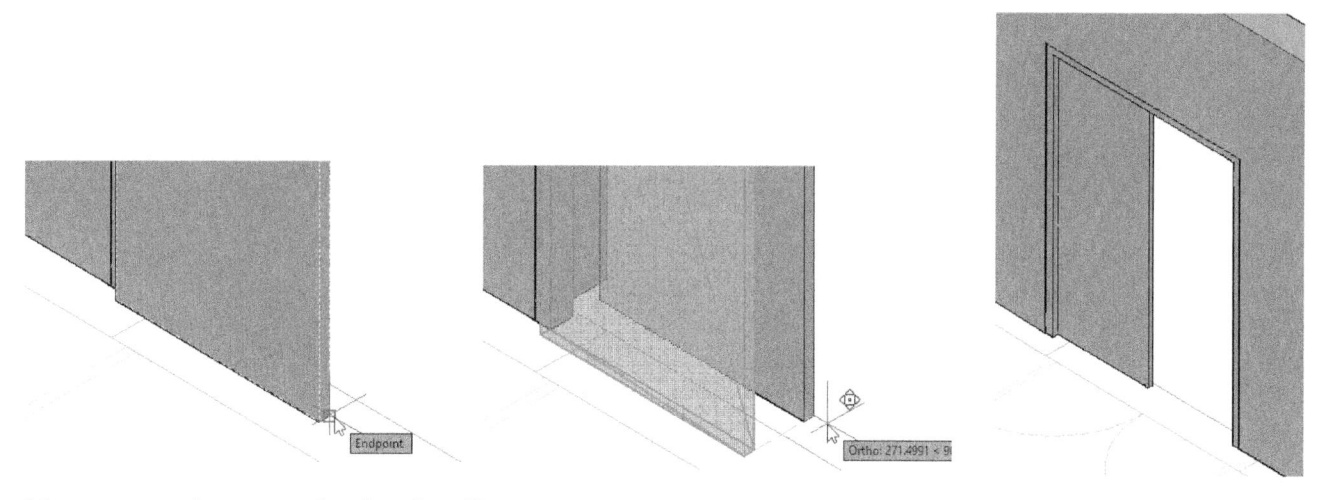

Now, you need to create the door handle.

- On the ribbon, click **Home** tab > **Modeling** panel > **Primitives** drop-down > **Sphere**. Select the lower right corner of the door to specify the center of the sphere. Move the pointer outward, type 40 and press Enter.

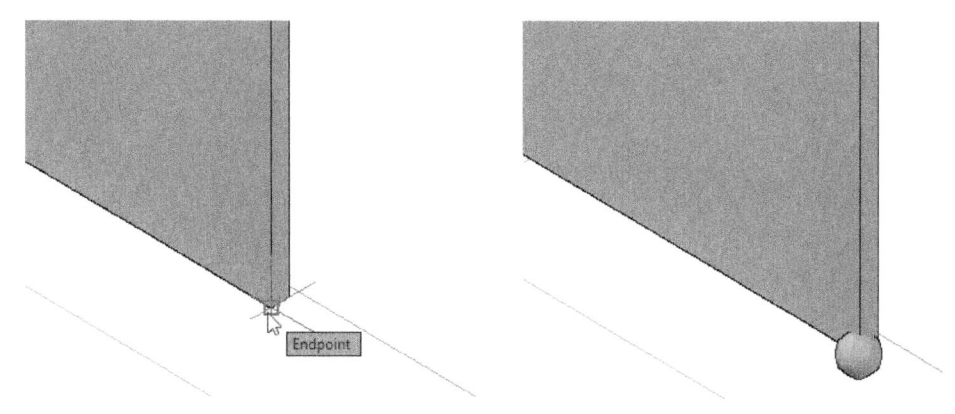

128 | Creating Architectural Drawings

- Select the sphere and click the **Move** tool on the **Modify** panel of the **Home** ribbon tab. Select the corner point of the door, as shown. Move the pointer upwards and select the midpoint of the door edge.

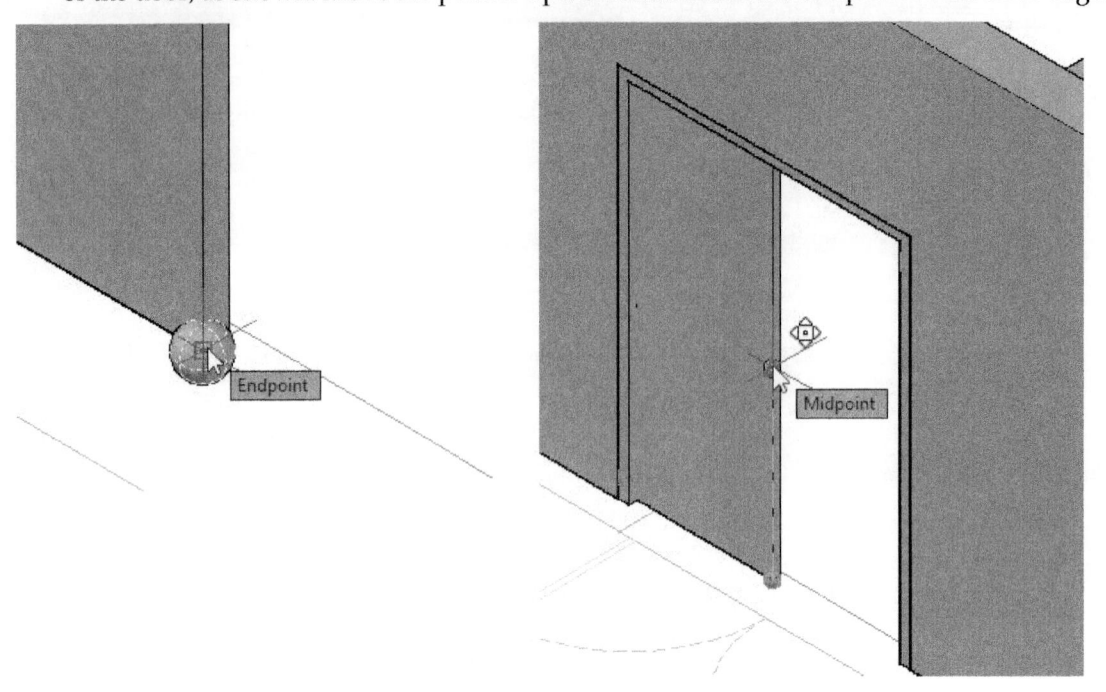

- Select the sphere and click on the X-axis (red arrow) of the Move Gizmo. Move the pointer toward left, type 90, and press Enter.

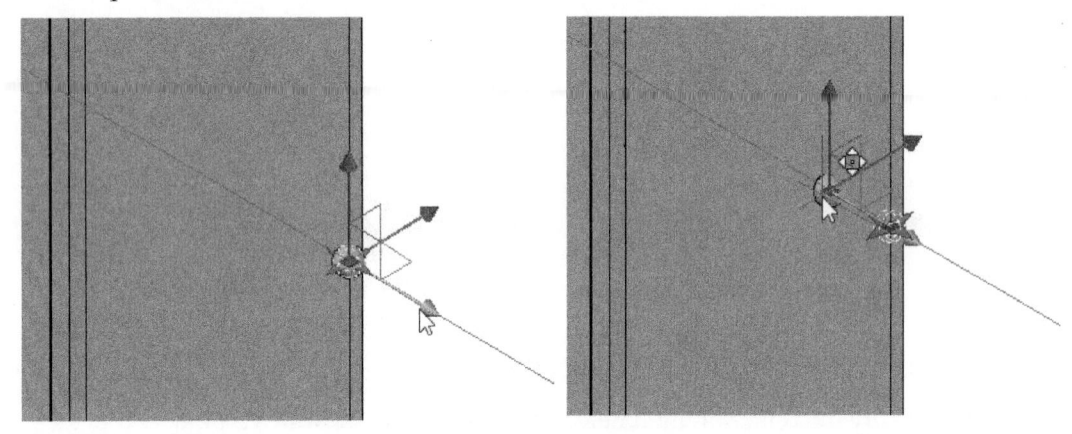

- Select the Y-axis (green arrow) of the Move Gizmo and move the sphere forward. Type 25 and press Enter. Press Esc to deselect the sphere.

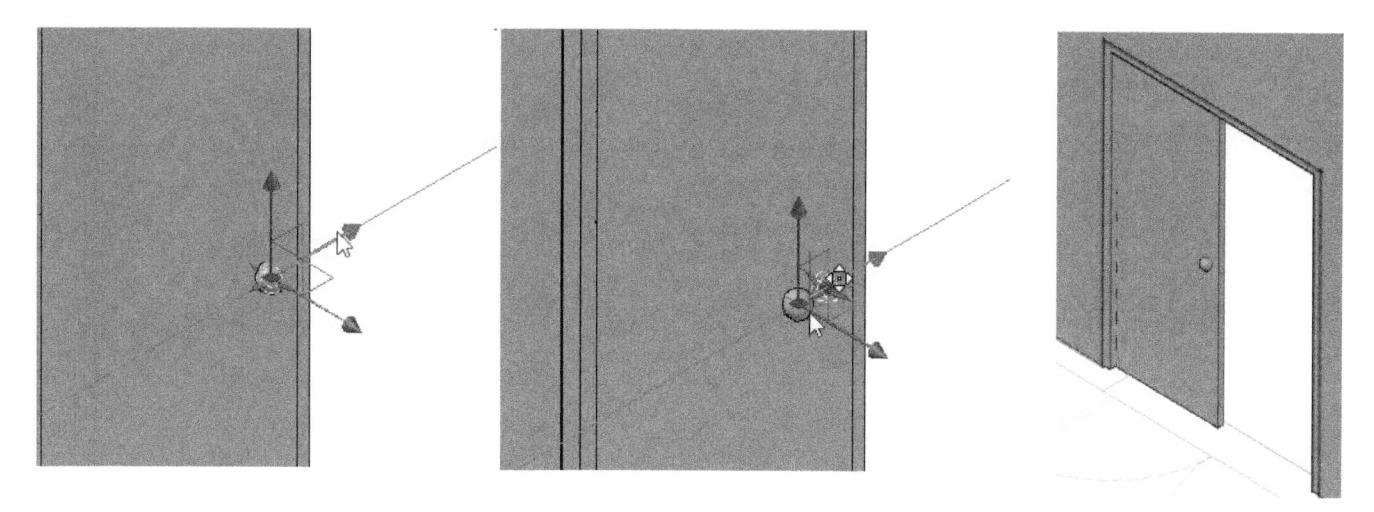

- On the ribbon, click **Solid** tab > **Solid Editing** panel > **Offset Edge**. Select the front face of the door. Select **Distance** from the command line. Type 180 and press Enter. Click on the door to offset the edges. Again, select the front face of the door. Select **Distance** from the command line. Type 200 and press Enter. Click on the door to create another offset edge. Press Esc to deactivate the tool.

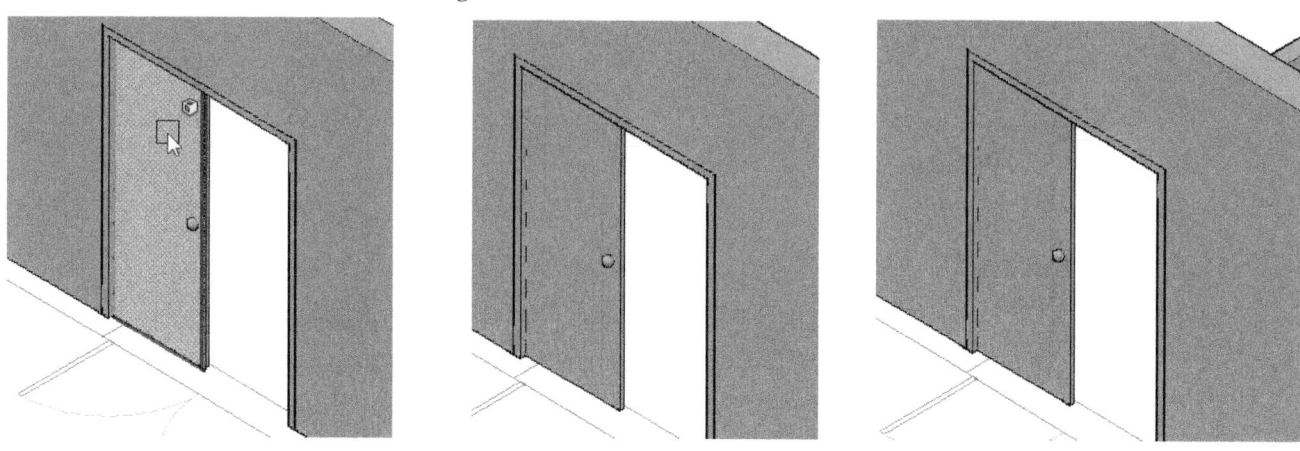

- On the ribbon, click **Solid** tab > **Solid Editing** panel > **Imprint**. Select the door, and then select anyone of the offset polylines. Select **Yes** from the command line; the selected polyline is imprinted onto the front face of the door. Select the other offset polyline, and then select **Yes** from the command line.

- On the ribbon, click **Home** tab > **Solid Editing** panel > **Union**. Select the door and sphere, and then press Enter; both the solids are combined together.

- Select the door, type MI, and press Enter. Place the pointer on the front face of the door frame and select the midpoint of its horizontal edge. Move the pointer downward and click to mirror the door. Select **No** from the command line to retain the source object.

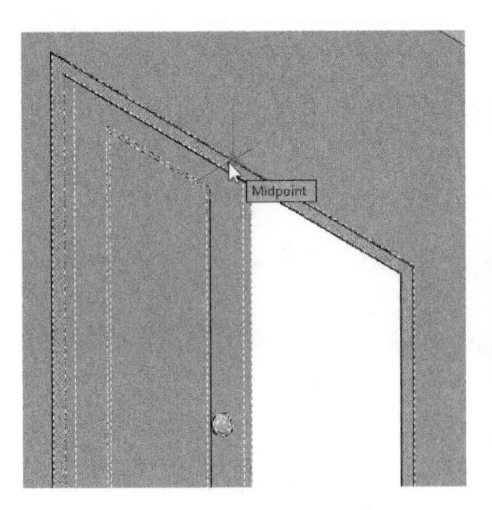

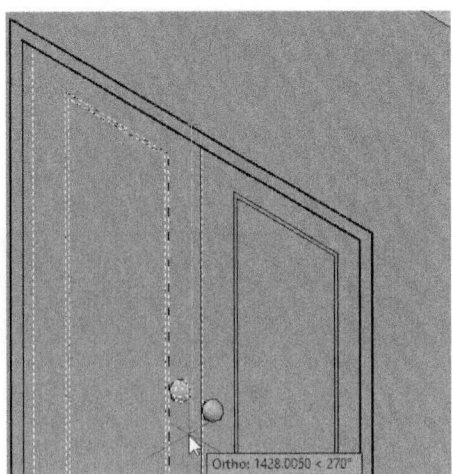

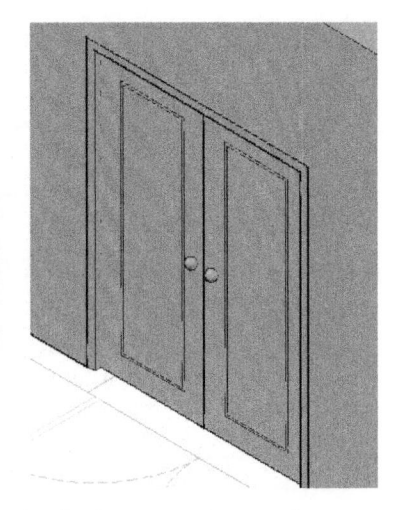

- On the Navigation Bar, click the **Orbit** tool and rotate the model such that the single door opening on the utility room appears.
- Select the mirrored door, type CO, and press Enter. Select lower left corner of the door as the base point. Move the pointer toward left and select the lower left corner of the door frame, as shown.

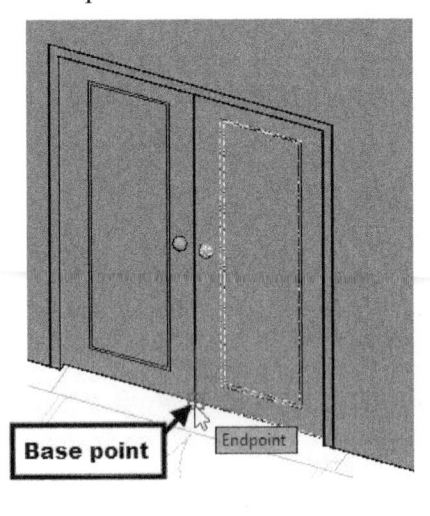

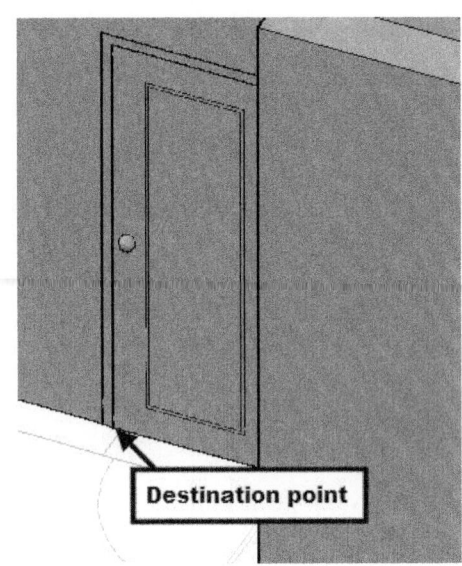

- Select the single door of the utility room. Click on the Y-axis (green arrow) of the Move gizmo, move the pointer inside the wall. Type 55 and press Enter.

131 | Creating Architectural Drawings

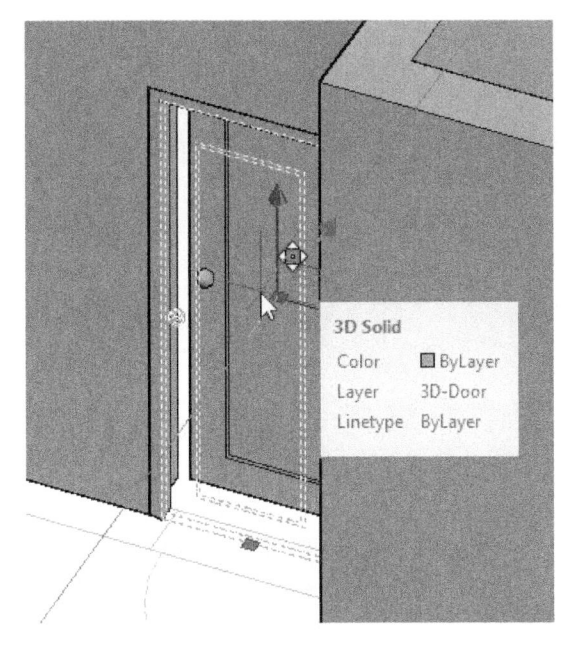

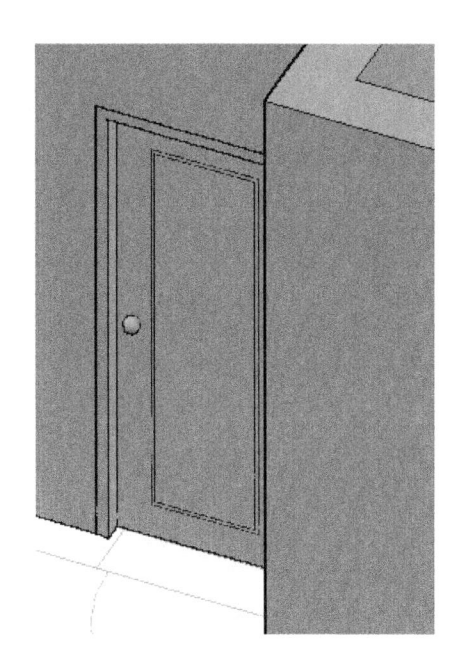

- Zoom to the double-door and select the doors and door frame. On the ribbon, click **Home** tab > **Groups** panel > **Group**. The three solids are grouped together.

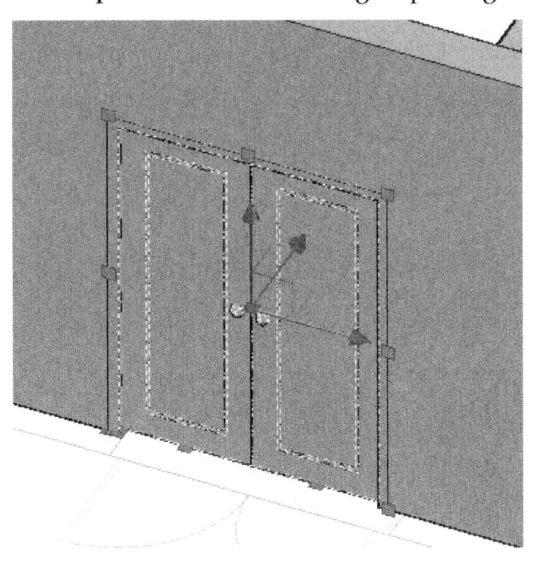

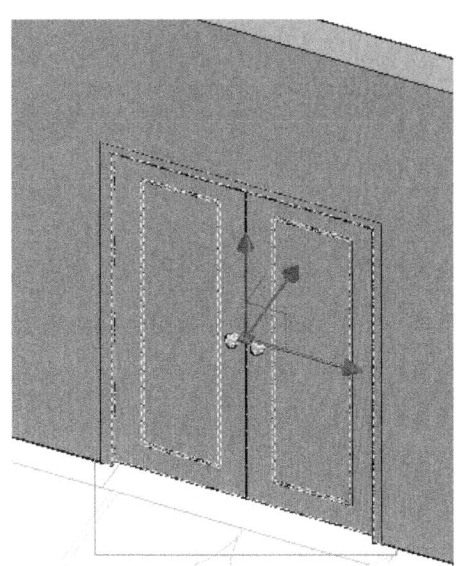

- On the ribbon, click **Home** tab > **Modify** panel > **3D Align**. Select the double-door group and press Enter. Select **Copy** from the command line. Select the first, second, and third base points, as shown. On the Navigation Bar, click the **Orbit** tool and rotate the model such that the double-door opening on the front elevation side is visible. Right click and select **Exit** to deactivate the **Orbit** tool. Select the first, second, and third destination points, as shown.

132 | Creating Architectural Drawings

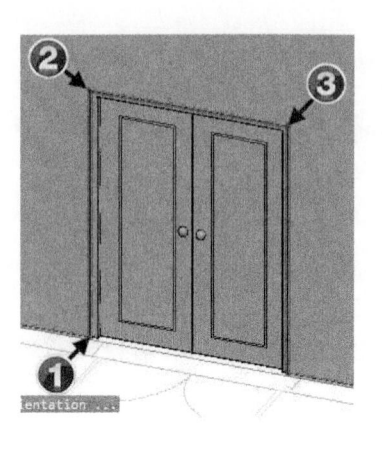

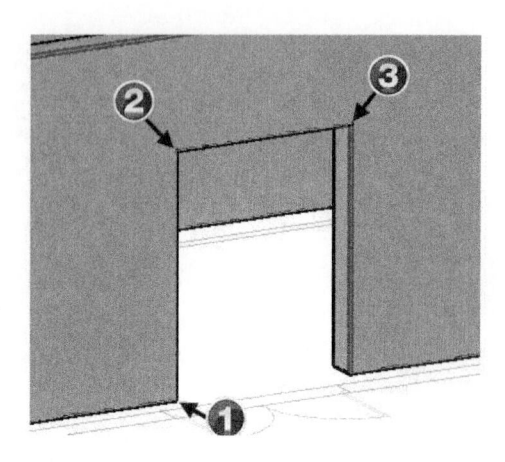

- On the ribbon, click **Home** tab > **View** panel > **3D Navigation** drop-down > **SW Isometric**.

- On the ribbon, click **Insert** tab > **Block Definition** panel > **Create Block**. Type 3D-Single door in the **Name** box. Click the **Select Objects** icon on the dialog, and then select the single door and its door frame. Press Enter to display the dialog. Click the **Pick point** icon. Zoom to the single door and select the top left corner of the door frame. Select **Retain** from the **Objects** section on the dialog. Uncheck the **Open in block editor** option and click **OK**.

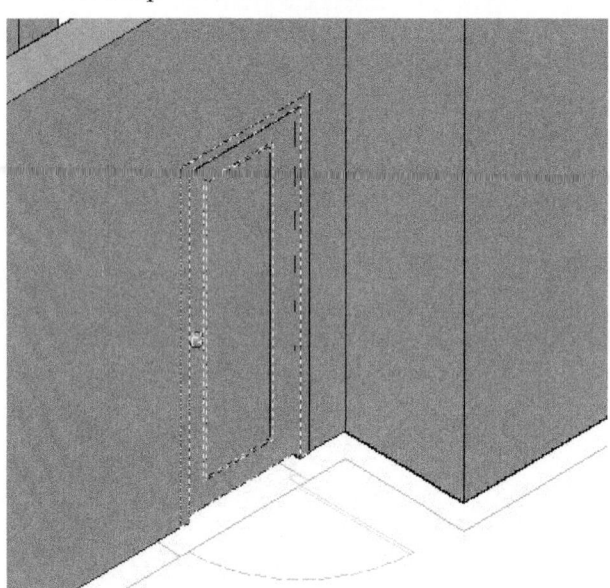

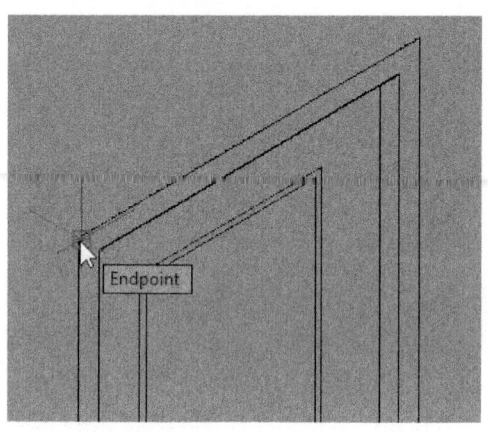

- On the ribbon, click **Insert** tab > **Block** panel > **Insert** gallery > **3D-Single door**. Click in the empty space to position the block. Select the block, type RO, and press Enter. Select the top left corner of the block to define the base point. Move the pointer toward left and click to rotate the block by 90 degrees.

Creating Architectural Drawings

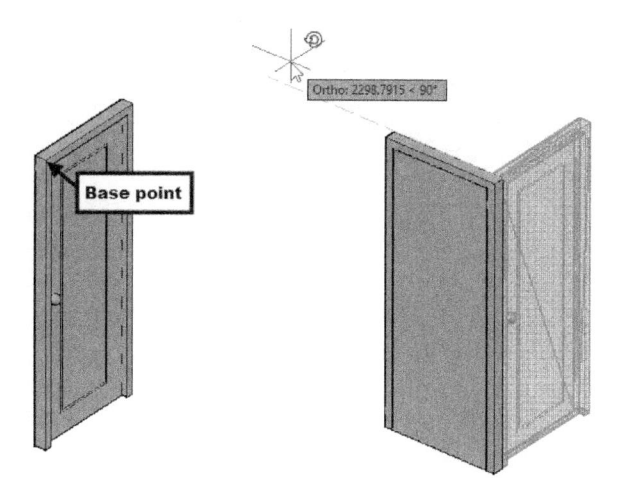

- Select the block, type M, and press Enter. Select the top right corner as the base point, as shown. Use the **Orbit** tool to rotate the model such that the door opening of the utility room appears. Right click and select **Exit** to deactivate the orbit mode. Select the top right corner of the door opening, as shown.

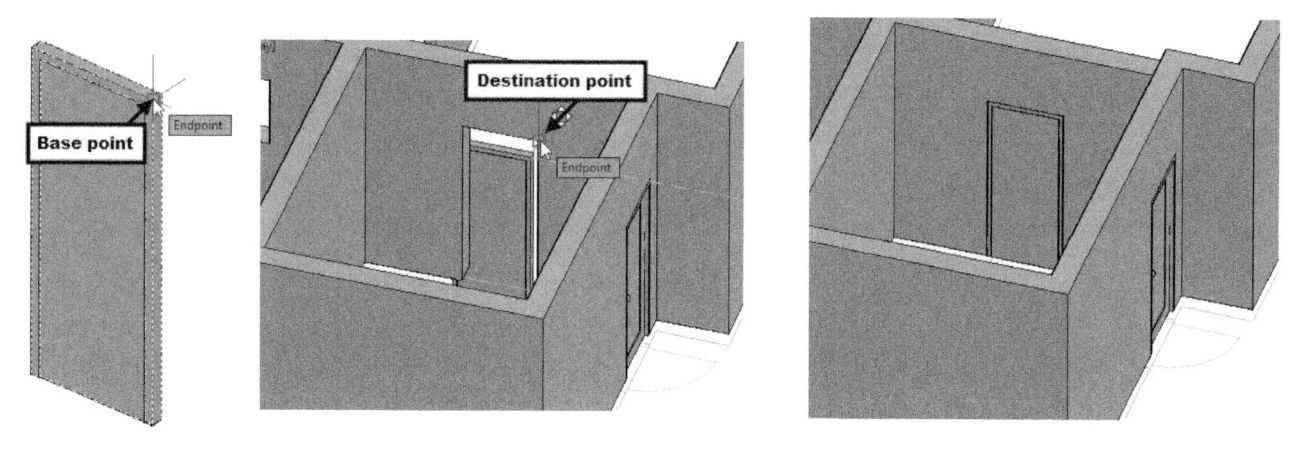

- Insert another instance of the 3D-Single door block. Select the block, type MI, and press Enter. Select the top left corner of the door frame, move the pointer forward, and then click to mirror the door block. Select **Yes** to delete the source object.

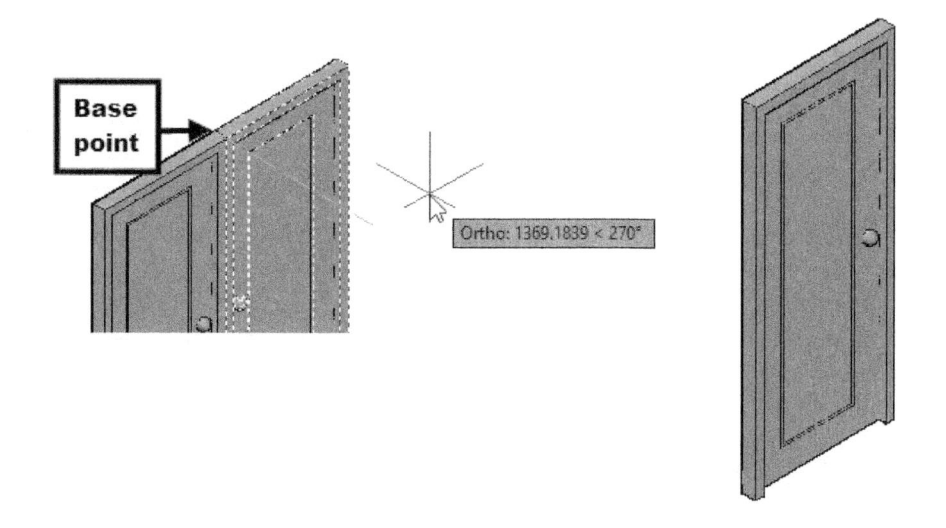

134 | Creating Architectural Drawings

- Rotate the door by 270 degrees. Copy the door block and place it at the door opening on the rear elevation, as shown.

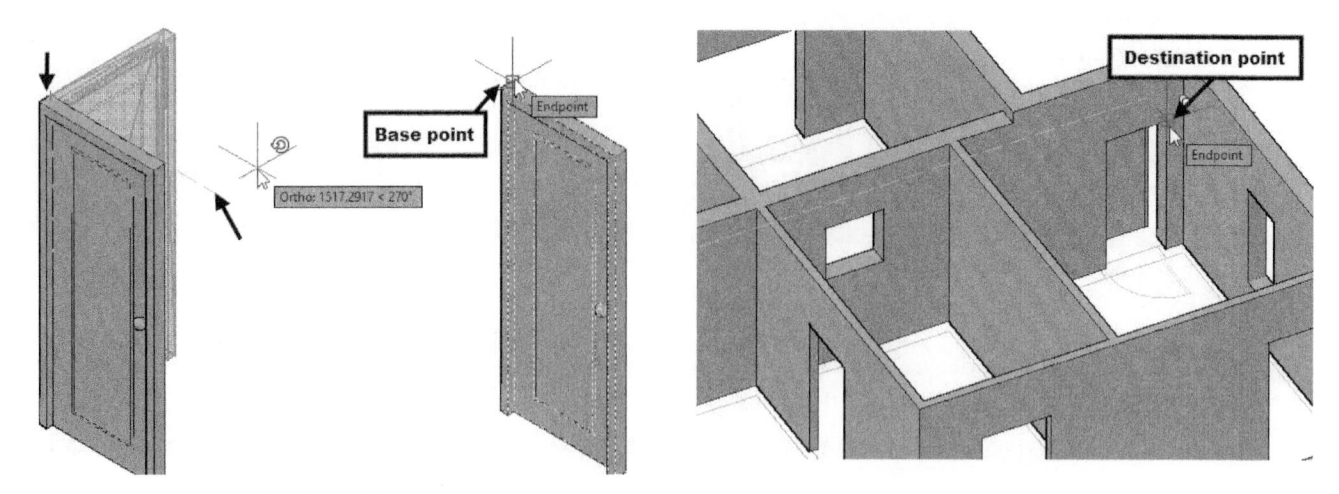

- Place the copy of the door block at other openings, as shown.

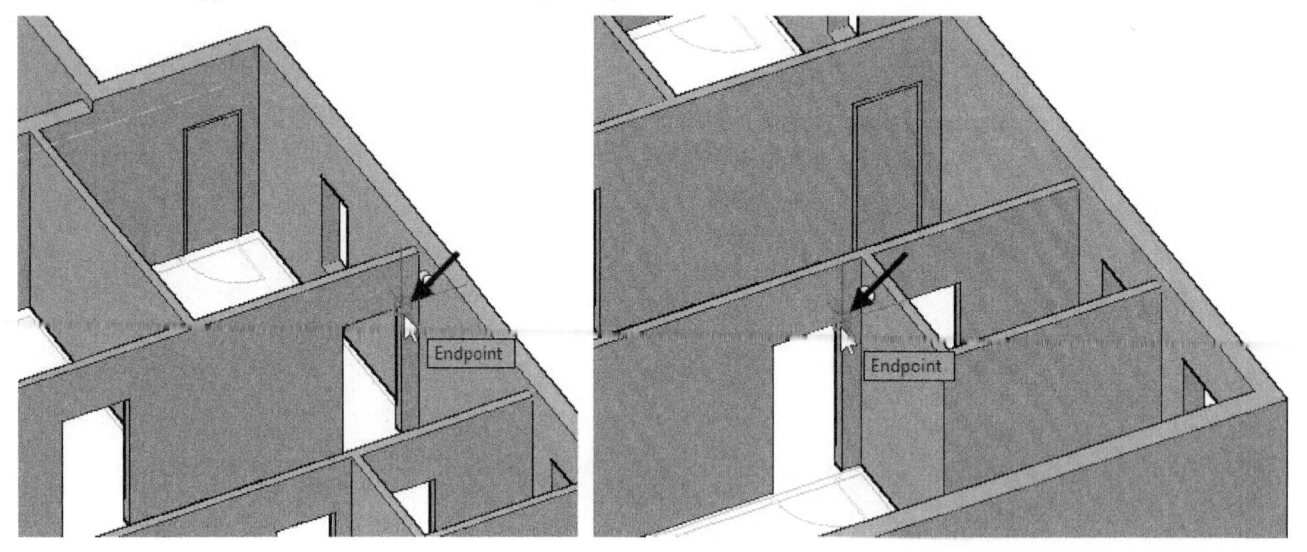

- Change the view orientation to SW Isometric. Mirror the door block, as shown. Move the door block and place it on the bathroom door opening.

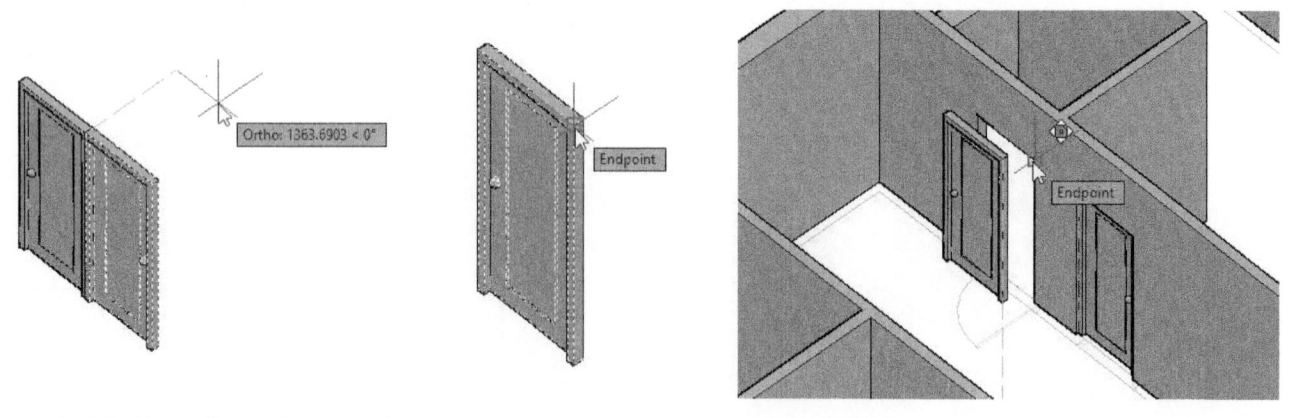

Tutorial 5: Creating 3D Windows

- Create a new layer "3D-Windows". Set the layer color to yellow, and then activate the layer.

135 | **Creating Architectural Drawings**

- Change the view orientation to SE Isometric.
- Zoom to the South elevation and create a selection window over the 2D-window. Type CO and press Enter. Select the top right corner of the window, move the pointer toward the 3D walls, and then select the top right corner of the window opening.

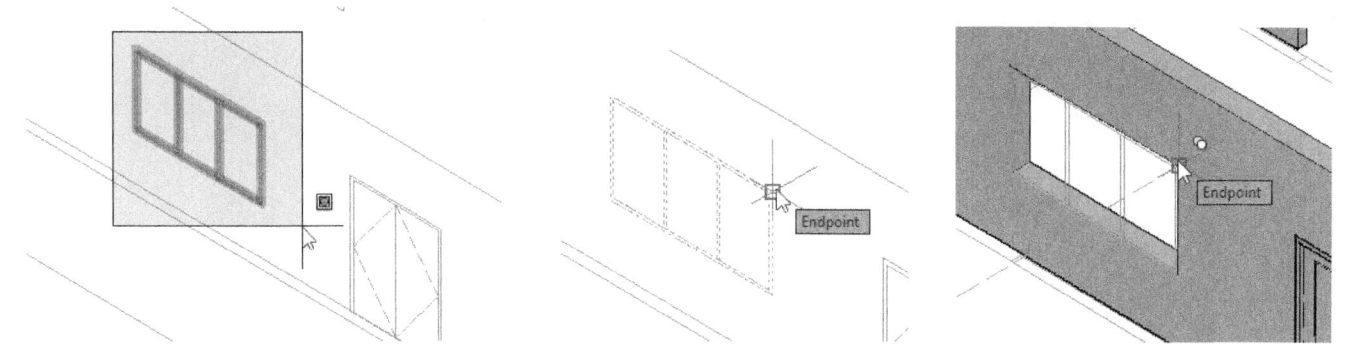

- Type EXT and press Enter. Select the outer polyline of the window, as shown. Type -50 and press Enter to extrude the polyline.

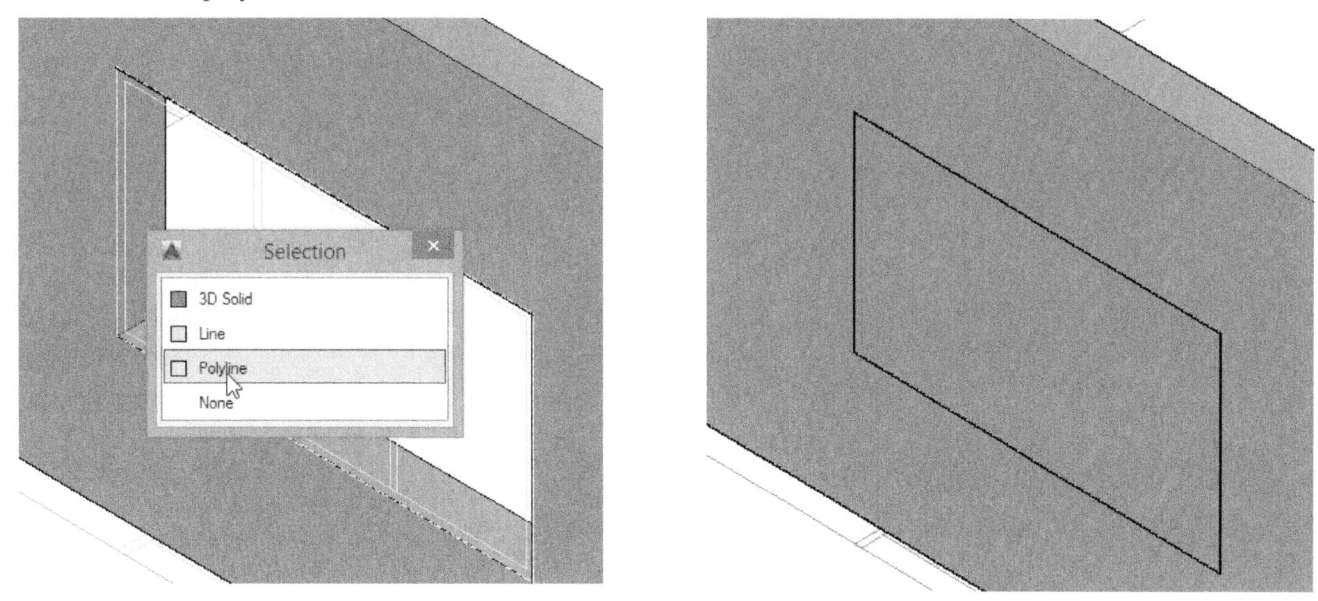

- Turn off the 3D-Walls layer. On the ribbon, click **Home** tab > **Modeling** panel > **Presspull**. Click in the region enclosed by the rectangle, as shown. Move the pointer, type -10. Likewise, presspull the other two regions, as shown.

136 | Creating Architectural Drawings

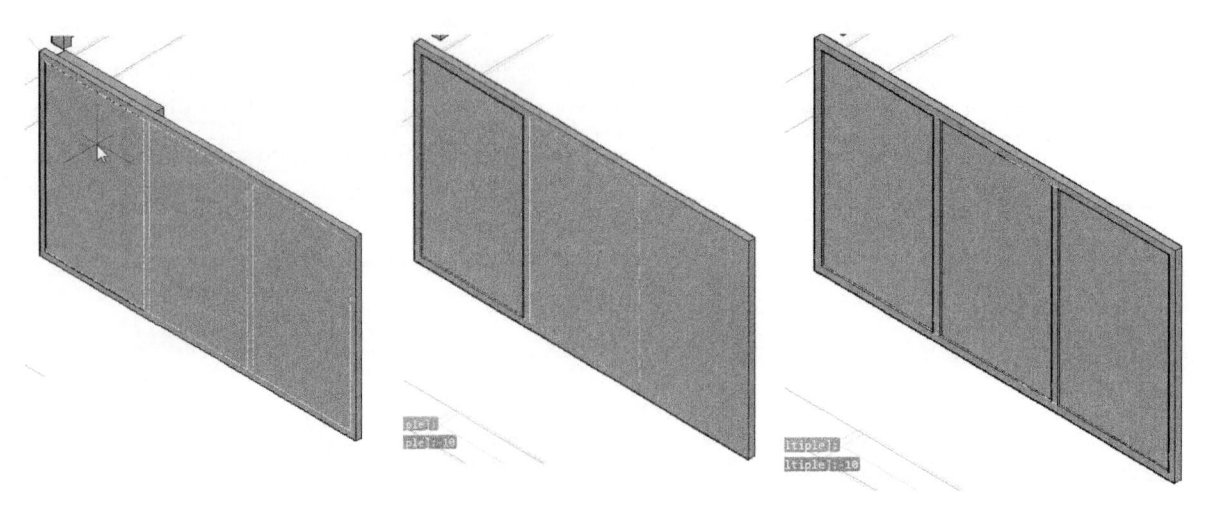

- On the ribbon, click **Solid** tab > **Solid Editing** panel > **Offset Edge**. Select a press-pulled face. Select **Distance** from the command line. Type 25 and press Enter. Click on the selected face to offset the face edges.

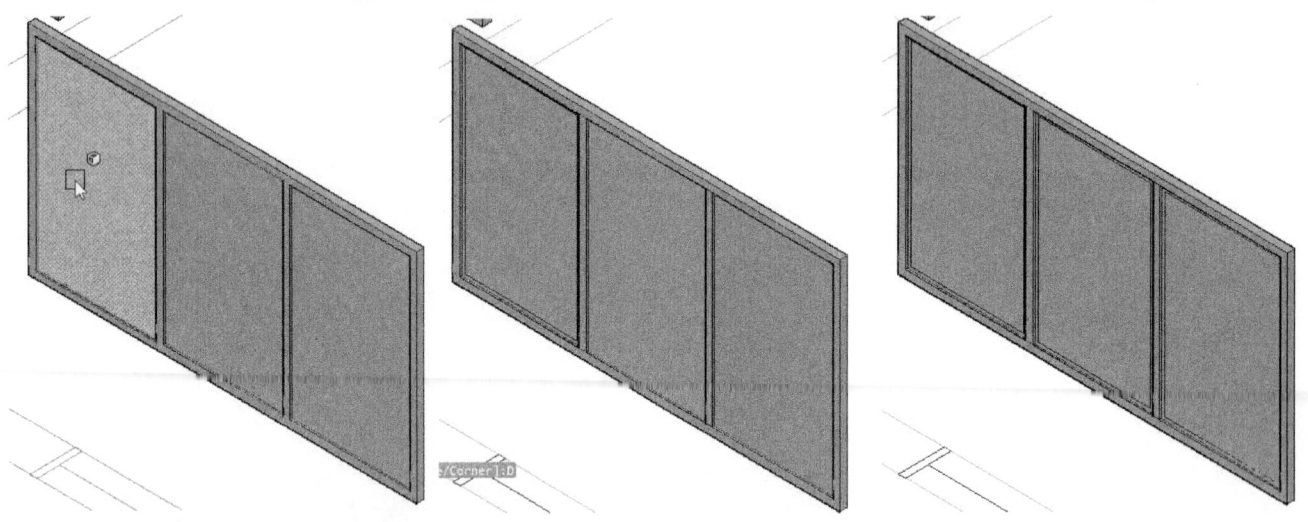

- On the ribbon, click **Solid** tab > **Solid** panel > **Presspull**. Select a press-pulled face and move the pointer. Type 38 and press Enter. Likewise, press-pull the other faces, as shown.

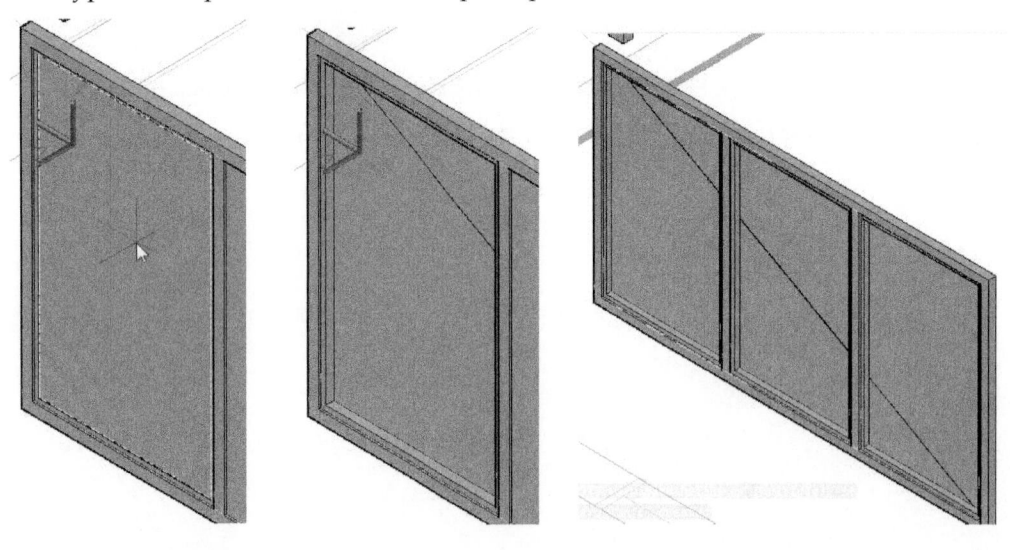

Creating Architectural Drawings

- On the ribbon, click **Home** tab > **Selection** panel > **Filter** drop-down > **Face**. Select the faces, as shown. Right click and select **Properties**. On the **Properties** palette, select **Blue** from the **Color** drop-down. The color of the selected faces is changed to blue. You can notice the difference when you set the **View Style** to **Shaded with Edges**. Press Esc.

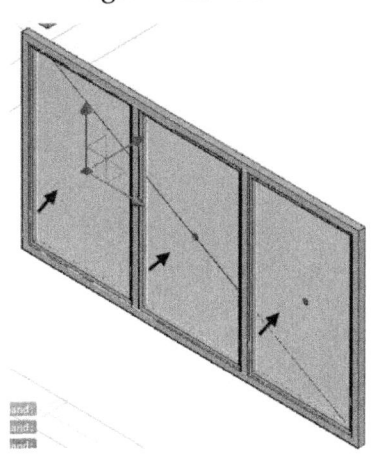

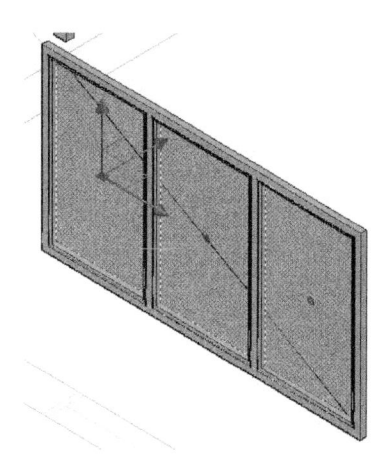

- On the ribbon, click **Home** tab > **Selection** panel > **Filter** drop-down > **No Filter**. Select the window, type MI, and press Enter. Zoom to the top right corner of the window. Place the pointer on the side face of the window, move the pointer and select the corner point, as shown. Move the pointer downward and click to mirror the window. Select the **No** option from the command line.

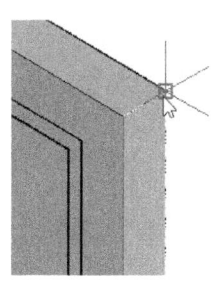

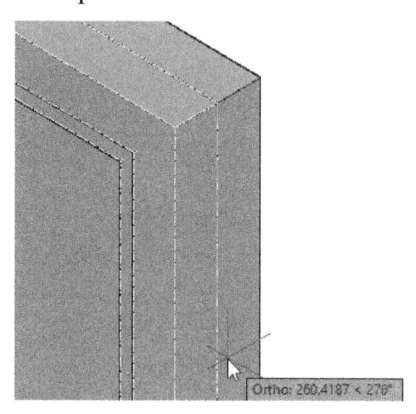

- Type **UNI** and press Enter. Select two window pieces and press Enter. The selected solids are united together.

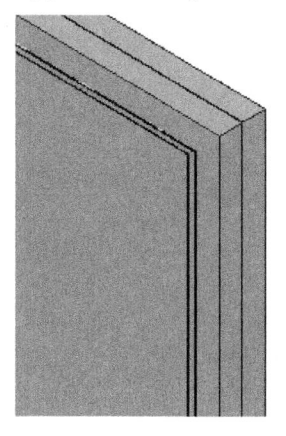

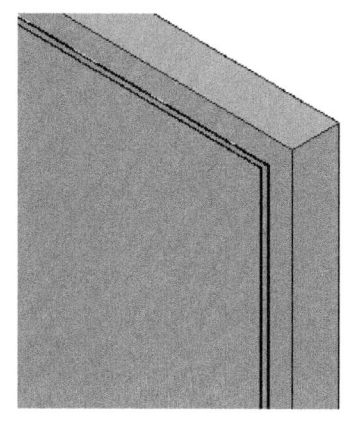

138 | Creating Architectural Drawings

- Turn on the 3D-Wall layer. Select the window, click on the Y-axis (green arrow) of the Move gizmo, and move the pointer inside the 3D wall. Type 150 and press Enter. Select the lines and polyline placed on the window opening and press **Delete**.

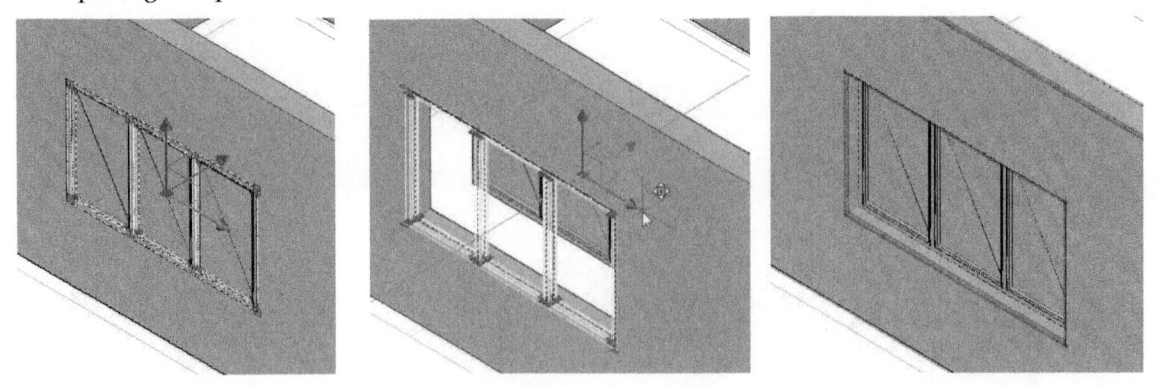

- Select the window, type CO, and press Enter. Select the lower left corner of the window opening to define the base point. Move the pointer toward the right side window opening, and then select its lower left corner point. Press Esc.

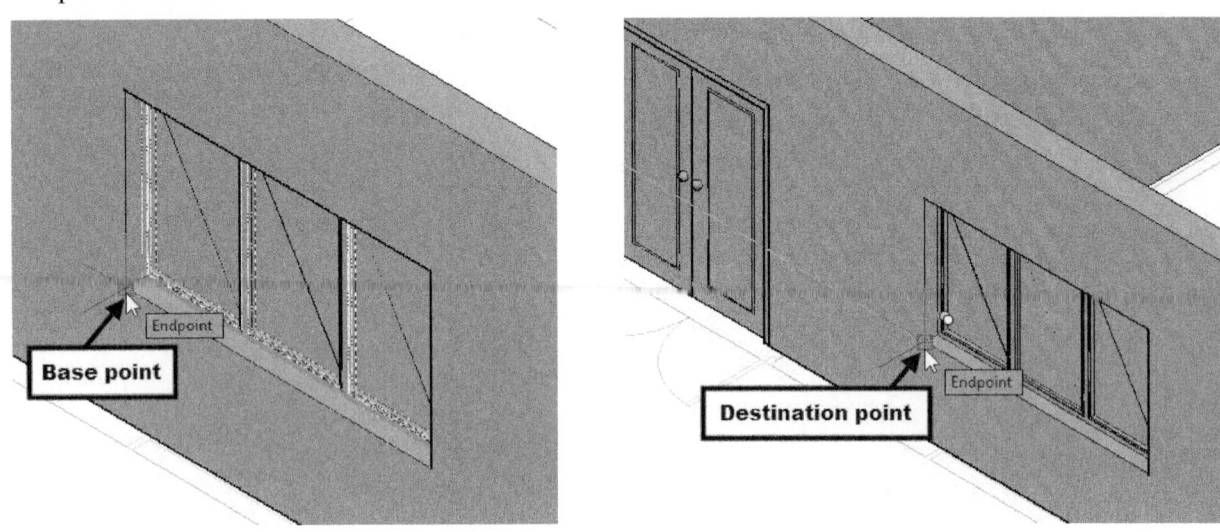

- Change the view orientation to NW Isometric. Select the 2D windows on the North elevation view by creating selection windows over them. Type **CO** and press Enter. Zoom to the extreme left window and select its lower left point. Move the pointer toward the 3D walls and select the lower left corner point of the extreme left window opening.

139 | **Creating Architectural Drawings**

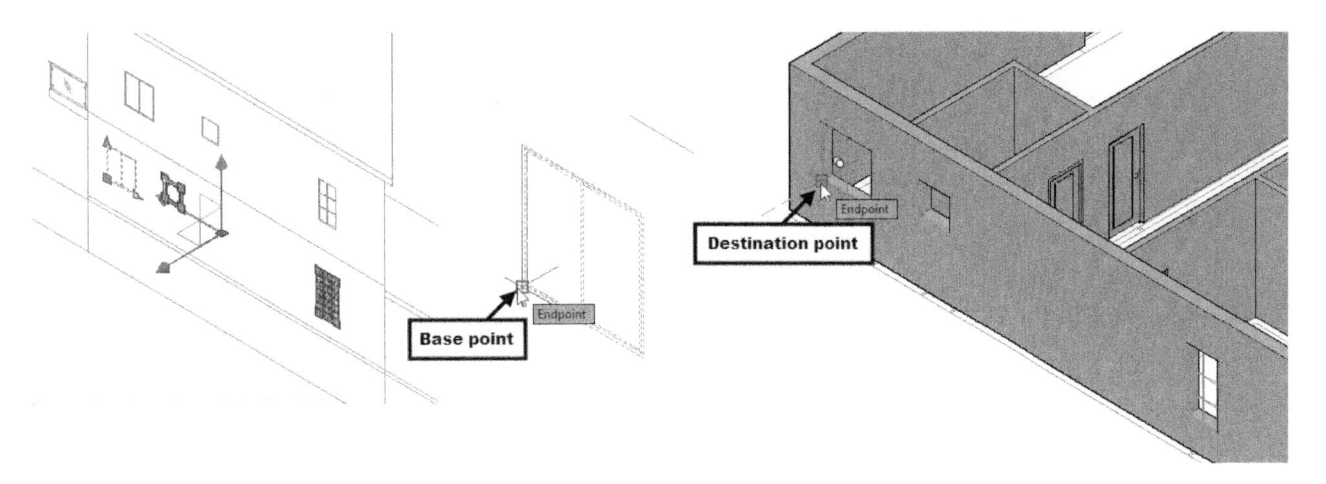

- Select the copy of the extreme left 2D-window. On the **Home** tab of the ribbon, expand the **Modify** panel and click the **Explode** tool; the block is exploded.

- On the ribbon, click **Home** tab > **Modeling** panel > **Polysolid**. Select the **Height** option from the command line. Type 100 and press Enter. Select the **Width** option from the command line, and the enter 38. Select **Justify** from the command line, and then select **Right**. Select **Object** from the command line. Select the outer rectangle of the window, as shown.

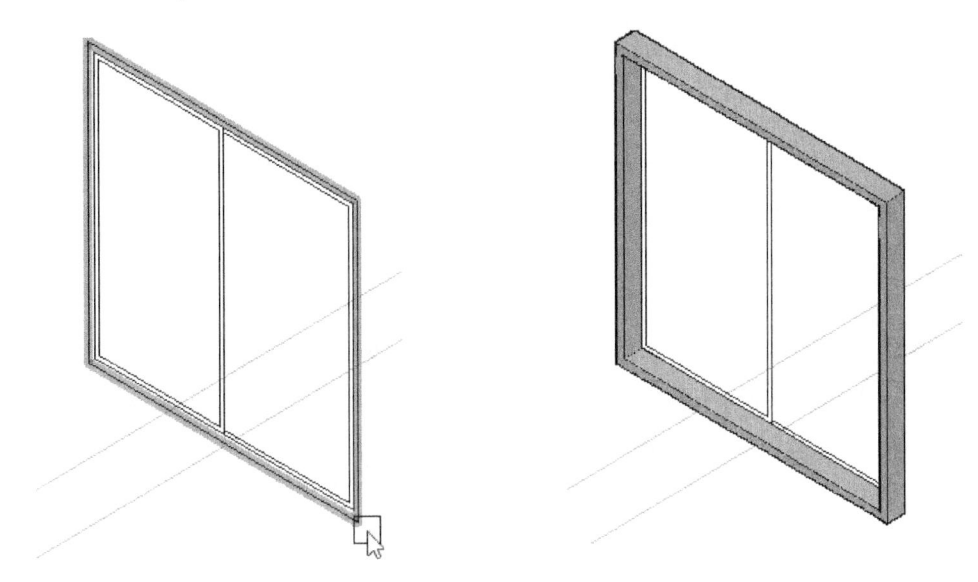

- On the ribbon, click **Home** tab > **Modeling** panel > **Box**. Specify the first and second corners of the box, as shown. Type -50 and press Enter create the box.

140 | Creating Architectural Drawings

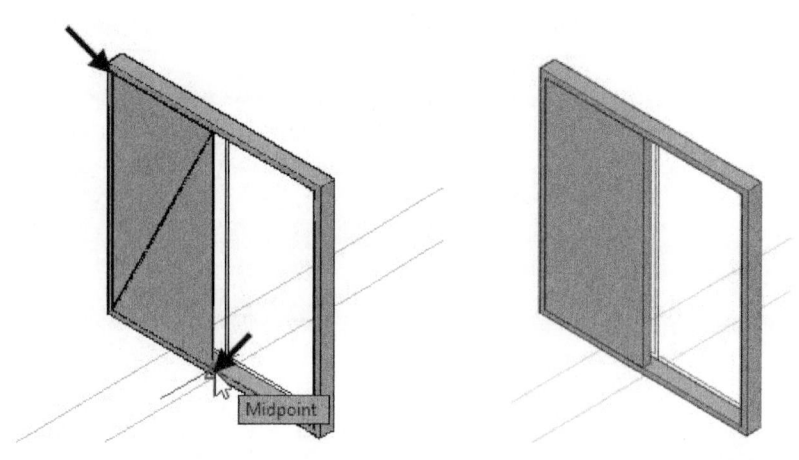

- On the ribbon, click **Solid** tab > **Solid Editing** panel > **Offset Edge**. Select the front face of the box. Select **Distance**, and then enter 25. Click on the front face of the box to offset the edges of the selected face.
- Activate the **Presspull** tool and click in the area enclosed by the offset edge. Move the pointer inside the box and click to remove material.

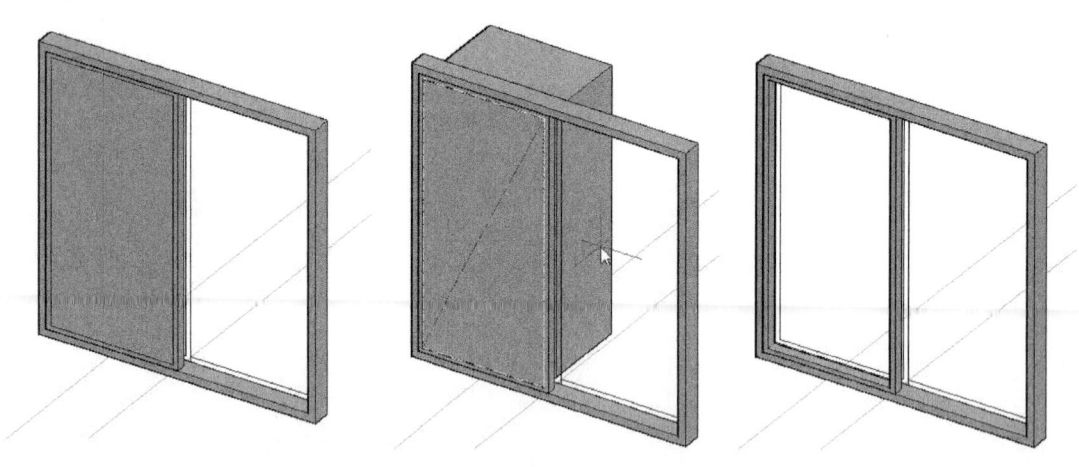

- On the ribbon, click **Home** tab > **Modeling** panel > **Box**. Specify the first and second corners of the box, as shown. Type 4 and press Enter create the box. Select the window, click on the Y-axis (green arrow) of the Move gizmo, and move the pointer inside the 3D wall. Type 27 and press Enter.

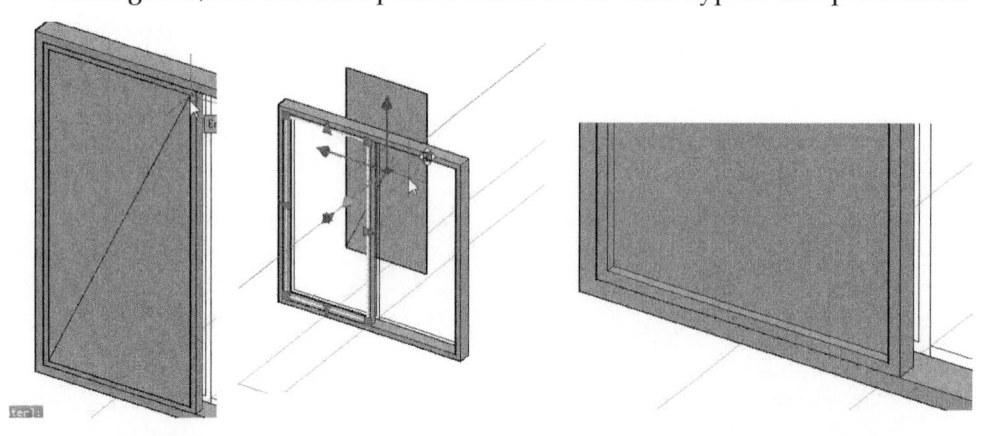

- Select the box, right click and select **Properties**. On the **Properties** palette, select **Blue** from the **Color** drop-down.

141 | **Creating Architectural Drawings**

- Type **UNI** and press Enter. Select the box created in the last step and the press-pulled solid. Press Enter to unite them.
- Select the combined solid, type CO, and press Enter. Select the lower left corner point of the combined solid. Select the lower right corner point on the other back side. Press Esc.

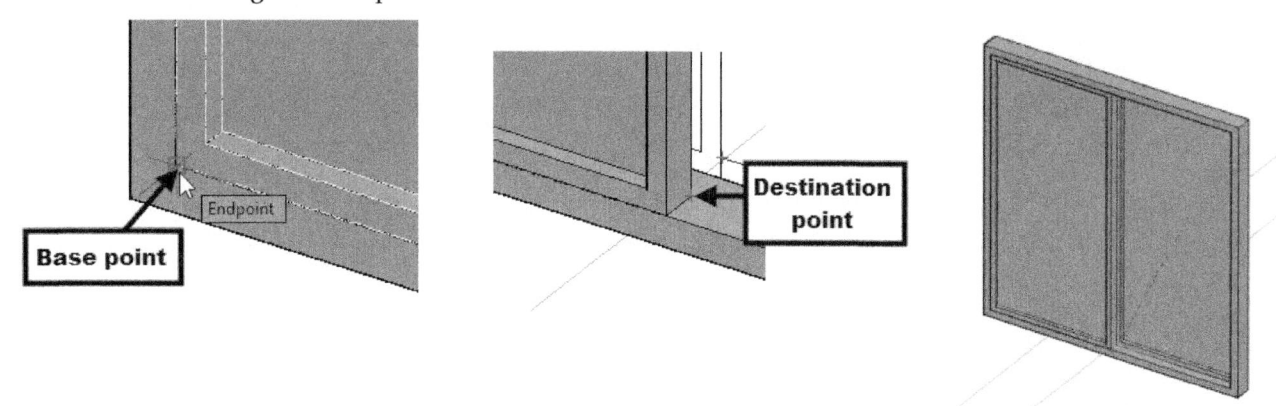

- Create a selection window over the window. On the ribbon, click **Home** tab > **Groups** panel > **Group**.
- Select the window group, type **M**, and press Enter. Select the top left corner point of the window group. Move the pointer inside the wall, type 250 and press Enter.

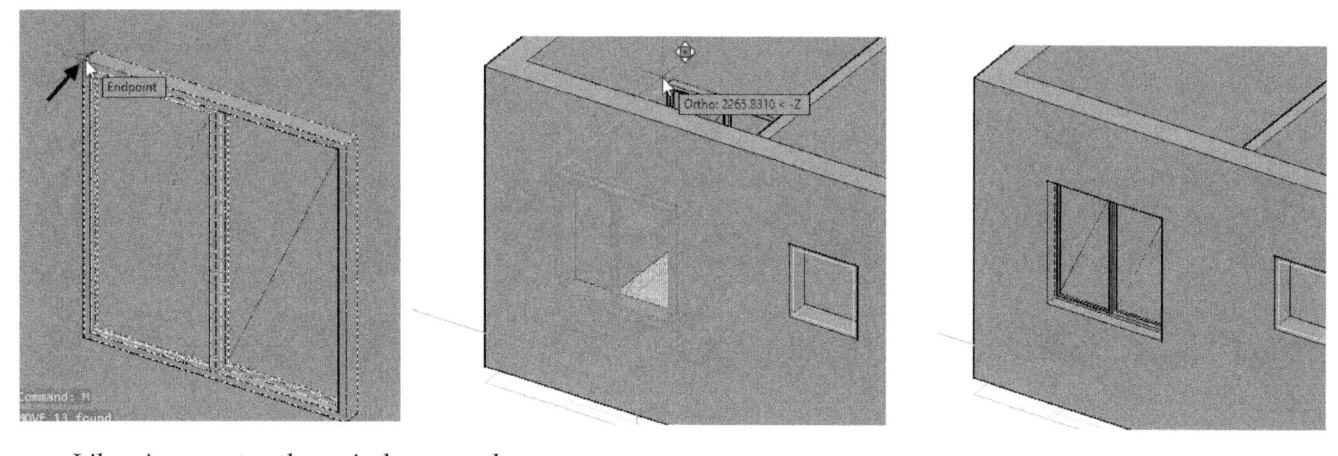

- Likewise, create other windows, as shown.

142 | Creating Architectural Drawings

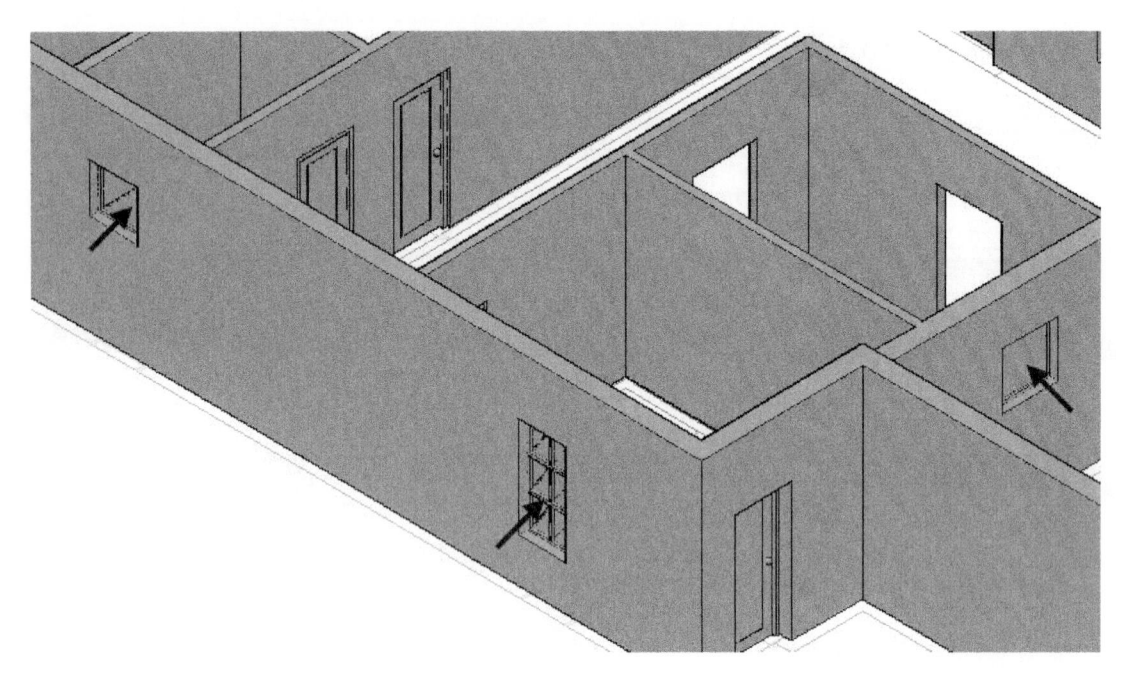

Tutorial 6: Creating 3D Stairs

- Create a layer "3D-Stair" and set the color to Index color 150. Set the 3D-Stair layer as current.
- On the ribbon, click **Home** tab > **Modeling** panel > **Primitive** drop-down > **Box**. Zoom to stairs area. Make sure that the Dynamic UCS icon is activated on the status bar. Place the pointer on the top face of the inner walls and select the corner point, as shown. Select the diagonally opposite corner, as shown.

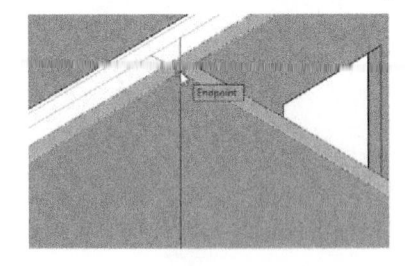

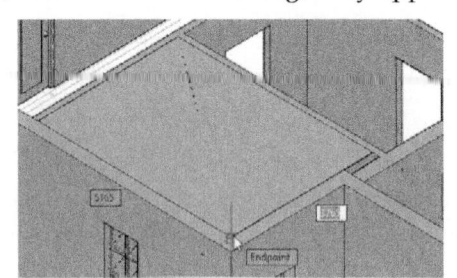

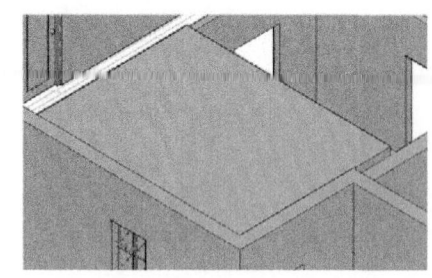

- Turn on the 3D-Floor layer. Type SU and press Enter. Select the first floor and press Enter. Select the box created in the last step and press Enter.

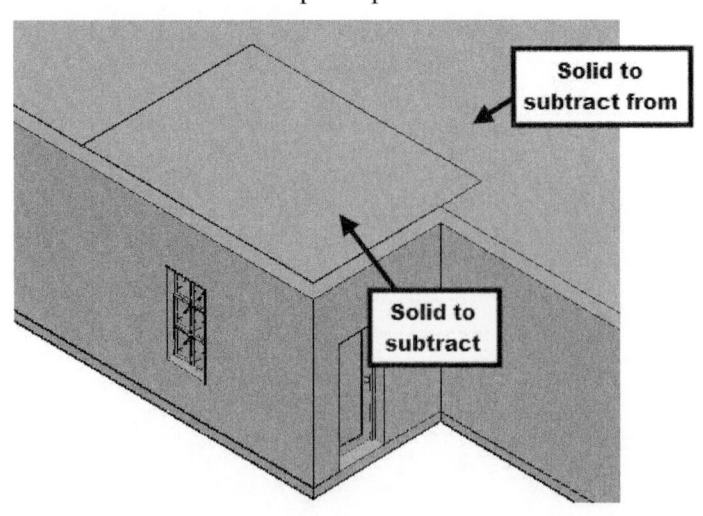

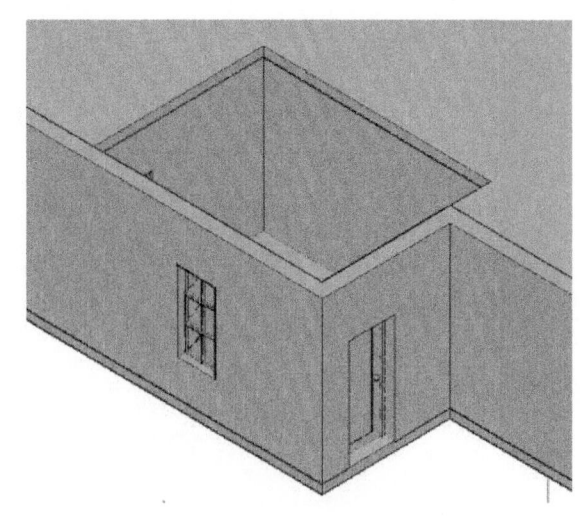

143 | Creating Architectural Drawings

- Type 3DO and press Enter. Rotate the model, as shown. Press Esc.

- On the ribbon, click **Home** tab > **Modeling** panel > **Primitive** drop-down > **Wedge**. Place the pointer on the ground floor, and then select the corner point, as shown. Make sure that the **Dynamic Input** icon is activated on the status bar. Move the pointer toward right. Type 4360 and press Tab. Type 1732 and press Enter. Move the pointer upward, type 3658, and press Enter.

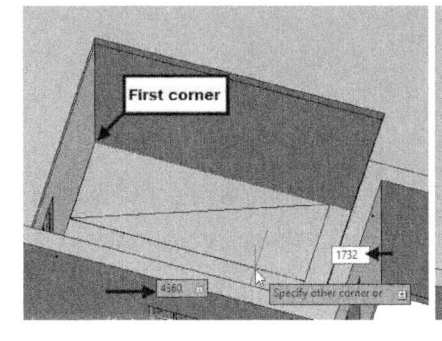

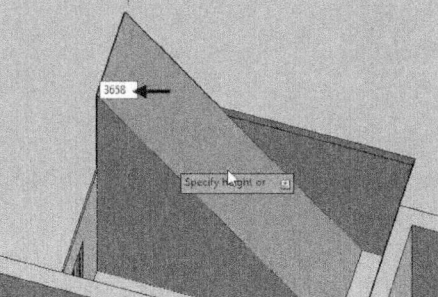

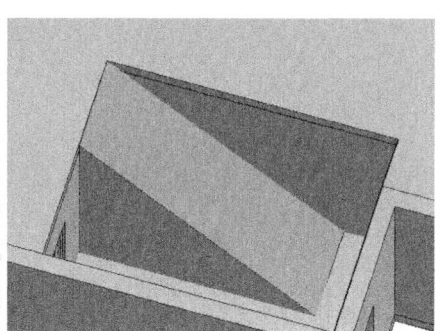

- On the ribbon, click **Home** tab > **Solid Editing** panel > **Edges** drop-down > **Extract Edges**. Select the wedge and press Enter.
- Type **UCS** and press Enter. Select **Face** from the command line. Select the side face of the wedge, and then select accept from the command line. The UCS is positioned on the selected face.

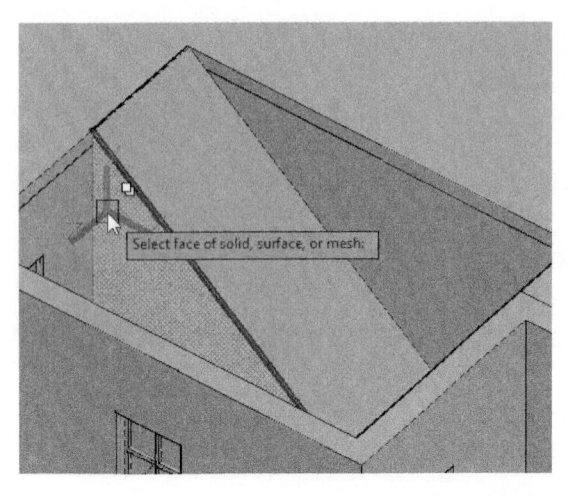

- Type **O** and press Enter. Type 450 and press Enter. Select the inclined extracted edge. Move the pointer downward and click to offset the line. Press Esc.

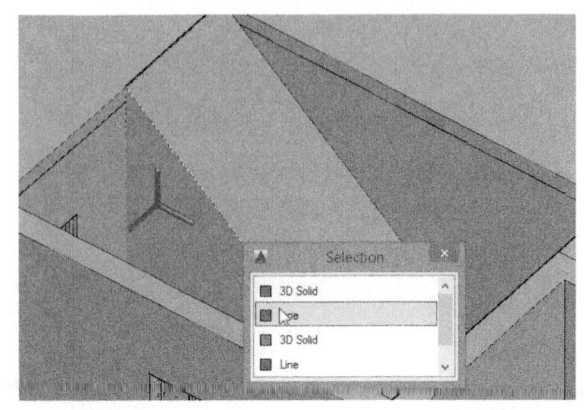

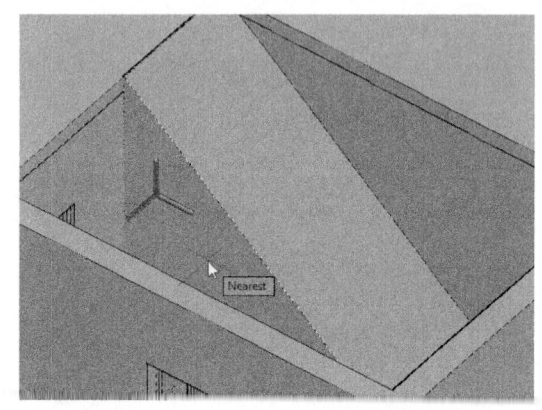

- On the ribbon, click **Home** tab > **Coordinates** panel > **UCS, World**. The UCS is restored to its default position.
- On the ribbon, click **Home** tab > **Modeling** panel > **Presspull**. Click on the side of the wedge in the region below the offset edge, as shown. Move the pointer into the wedge, type 1732, and press Enter. Press Esc.

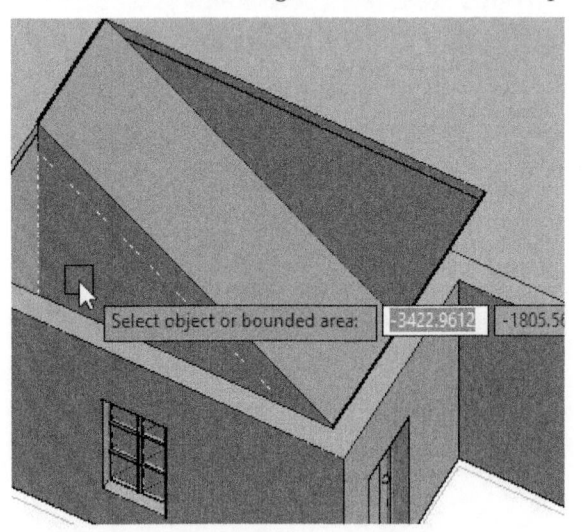

- Activate the **Box** tool and place the pointer on the top face of the first floor. Move the pointer and select the corner point, as shown. Move the pointer forward. Specify the length and width as 1732 and 218, respectively,

145 | **Creating Architectural Drawings**

and then press Enter. Move the pointer downward, type 183, and press Enter.

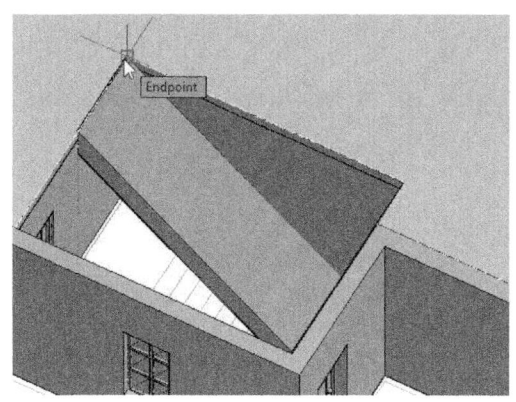

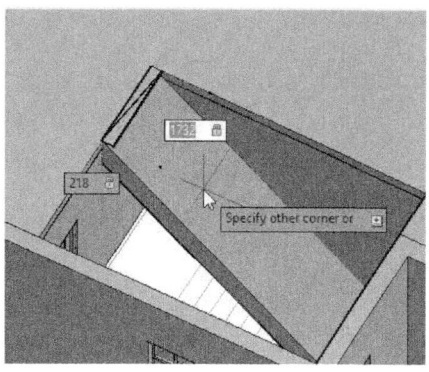

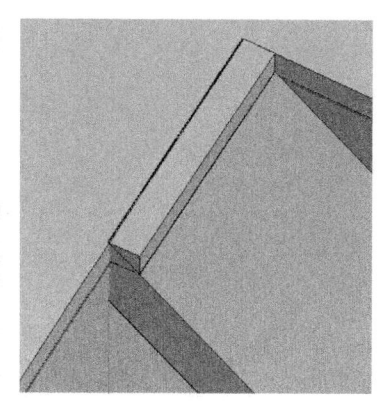

- On the ribbon, click **Home** tab > **Modify** panel > **Array** drop-down > **Polar Array**. Select the box and press Enter. Select the extracted inclined line. On the **Array Creation** tab, on the **Properties** panel, click **Measure Method** drop-down > **Divide**. On the **Items** panel, change the **Items** value to **21**. Click **Close Array** on the **Array Creation** ribbon tab.

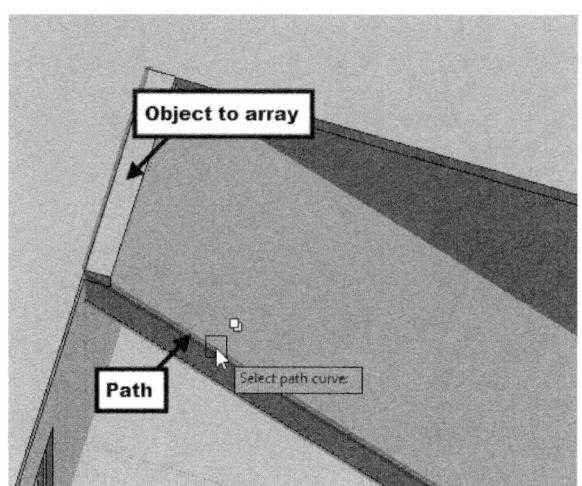

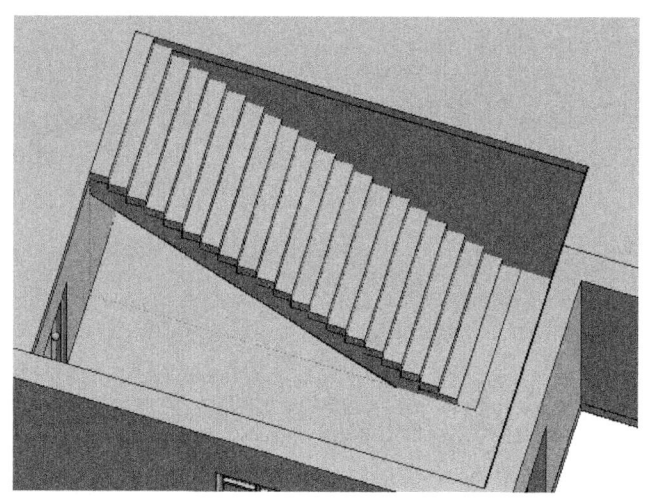

- On the **Home** tab of the ribbon, expand the **Modify** panel and click the **Explode** tool. Select the polar array and press Enter; the array is exploded into individual objects.
- Select the bottom most stair and press **Delete**.

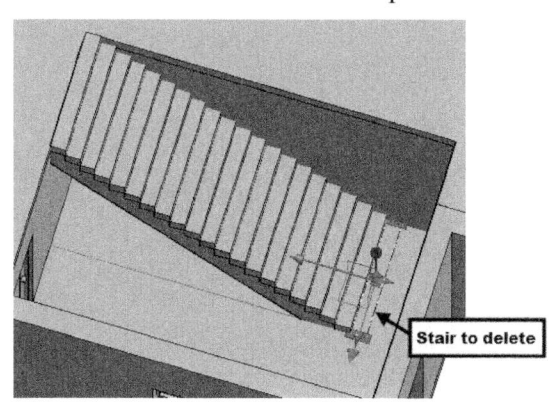

146 | Creating Architectural Drawings

- On the ribbon, click **Home** tab > **Layers** panel > **Isolate**. Select anyone of the stair and press Enter; all the layers except the layer of the selected object are hidden.
- Select anyone of the extracted edges. Right click and select **Select Similar**; all the extracted edges are selected. Press **Delete** to delete all the selected edges.

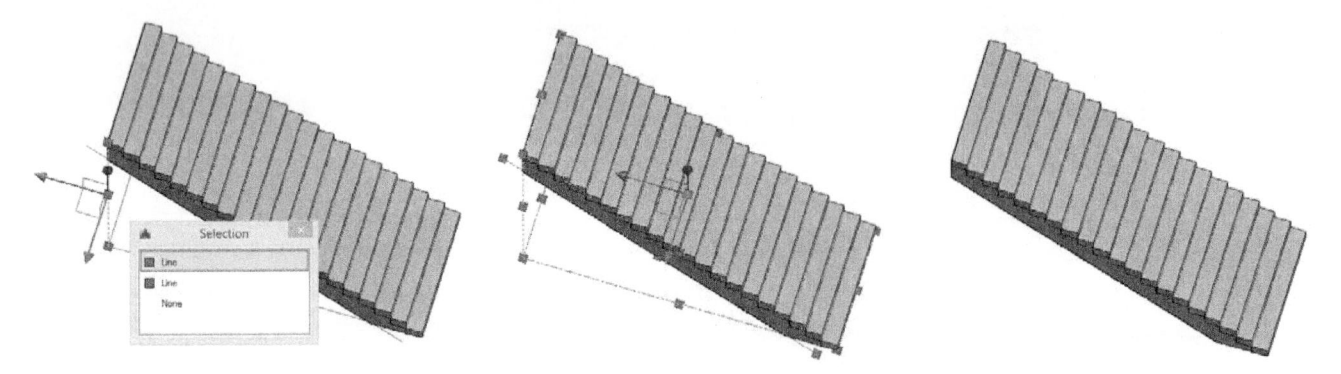

- Type **UNI** and press Enter. Create a selection window over all the objects of the staircase and press Enter.

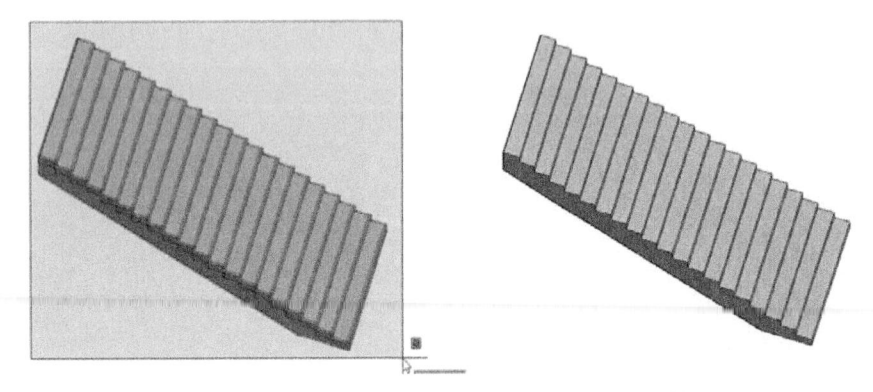

- On the ribbon, click **Home** tab > **Layers** panel > **Unisolate**. All the layers are turned on.

Tutorial 7: Modeling the First Floor
- On the ribbon, click **Home** tab > **View** panel > **3D Navigation** drop-down > **Top**.
- On the ribbon, click **Home** tab > **Layers** panel > **Off**. Zoom to the first floor plan and select the objects, as shown.

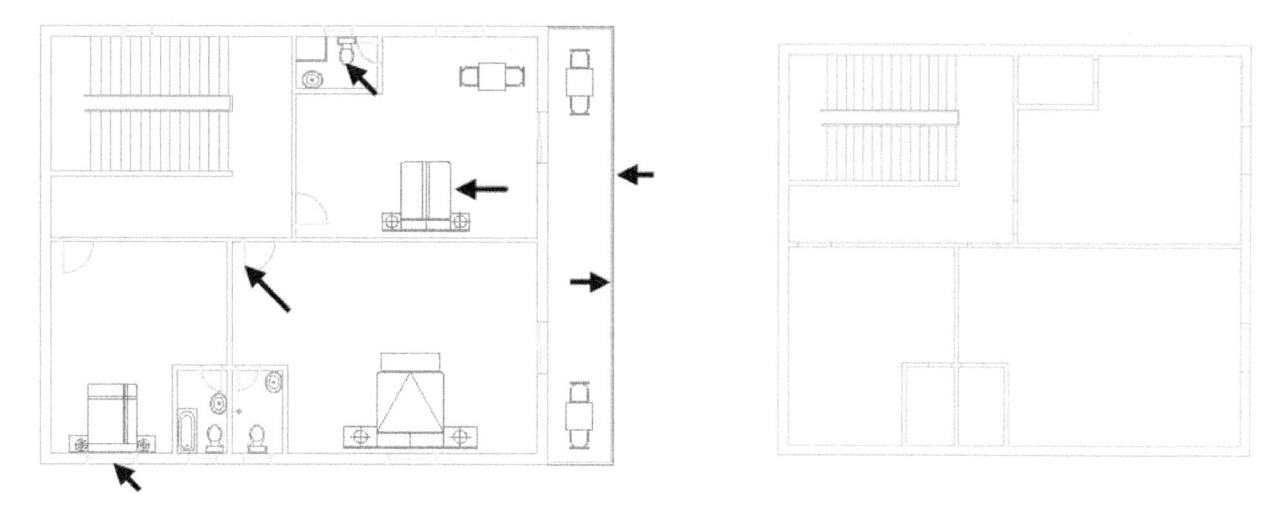

- Create a selection window over the first floor plan. On the ribbon, click **Home** tab > **Layers** panel > **Copy Objects New Layer**. Select any one of the 3D walls. Select the lower left corner point of the first floor, move the pointer toward right and click to place the copy.

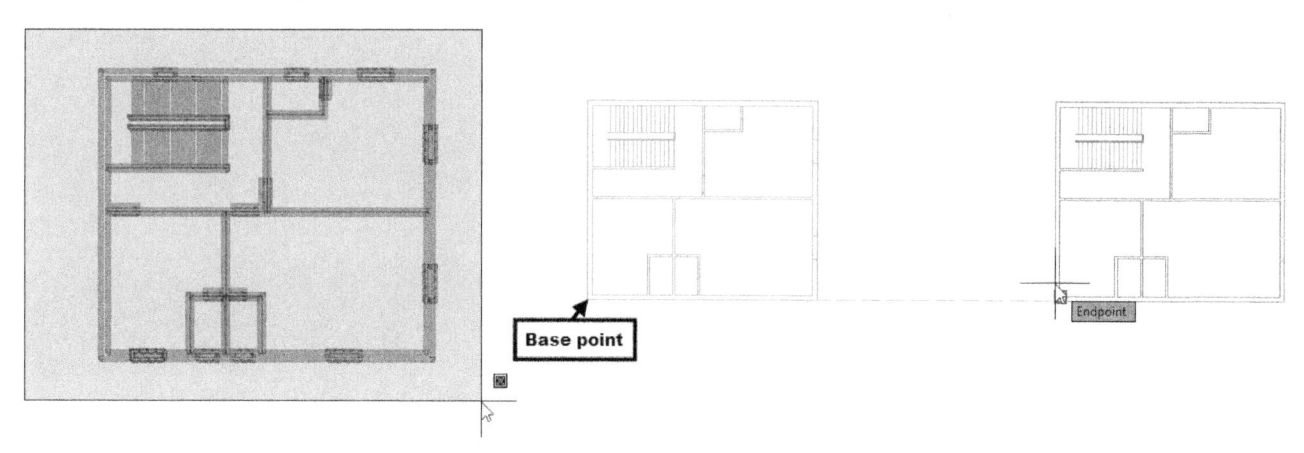

- On the **Home** tab of the ribbon, expand the **Draw** panel and click the **Region** tool. Create a selection window over the first floor plan, and then press Enter.

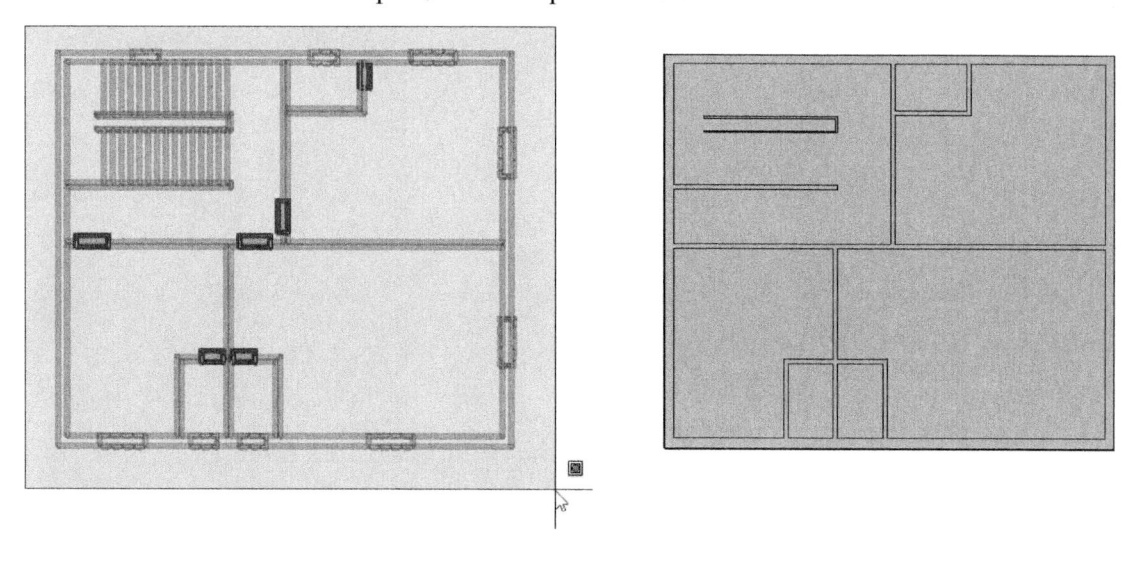

148 | Creating Architectural Drawings

- Type SU and press Enter. Select the outermost region and press Enter. Select the inner regions and press Enter.

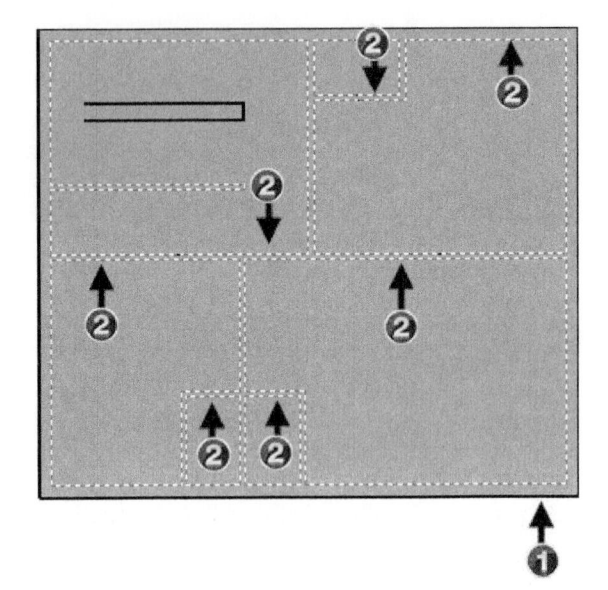

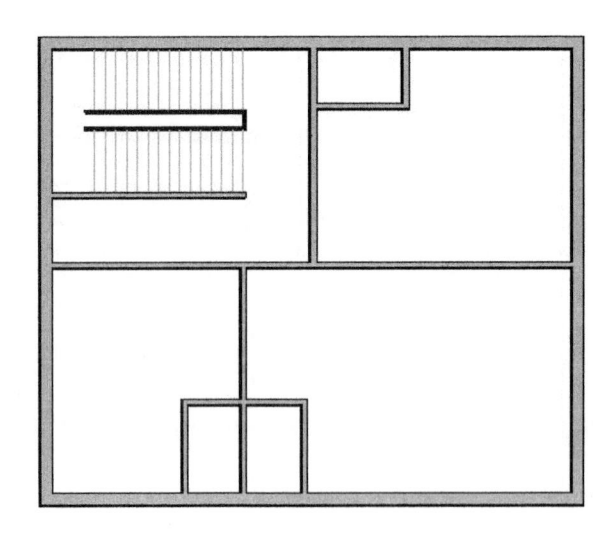

❶ Region to subtract from
❷ Region to subtract

- Change the view orientation to SE Isometric.

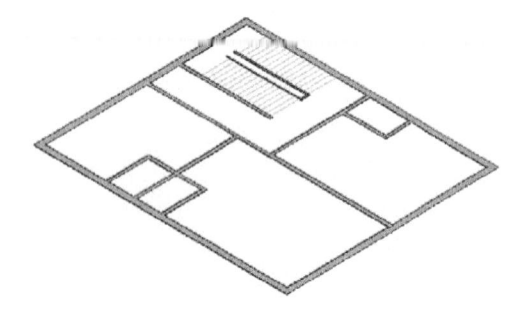

- Select the region in the stairs area. On the **Home** tab of the ribbon, expand the **Modify** panel and click the **Explode**. The selected region is exploded into individual objects.

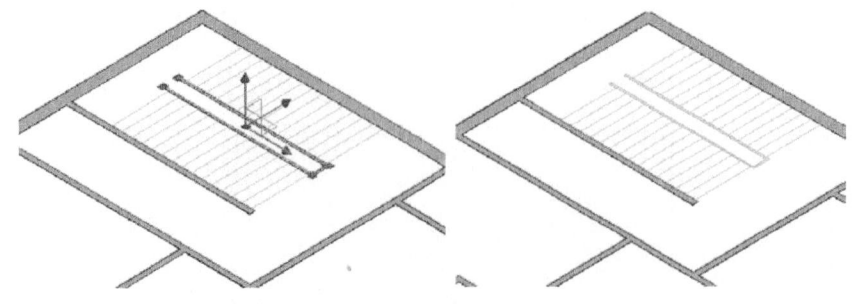

- Type EXT and press Enter. Select the region and press Enter. Move the pointer upward and select the point on the North elevation, as shown.

149 | Creating Architectural Drawings

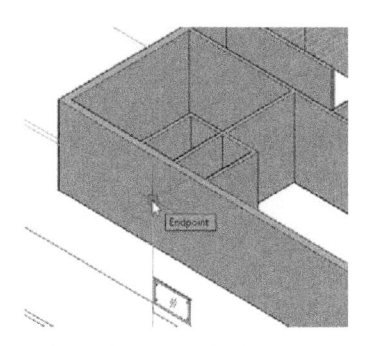

- Select the extruded solid, type M, and press Enter. Select the lower corner point, as shown. Select the corner point on the ground floor wall, as shown.

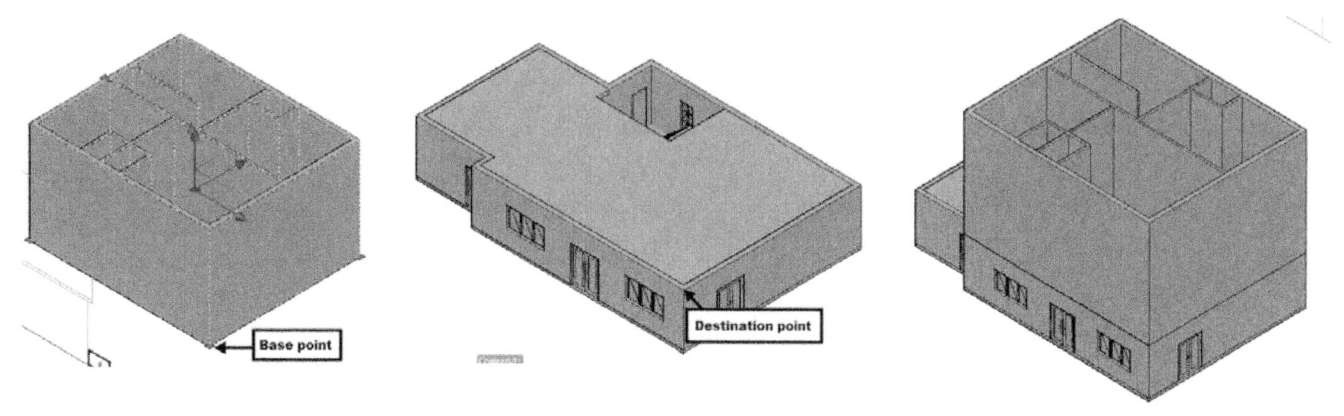

- Activate the **Presspull** tool and click on the top face of the walls. Move the pointer downward, Zoom to the North elevation and select the point, as shown.

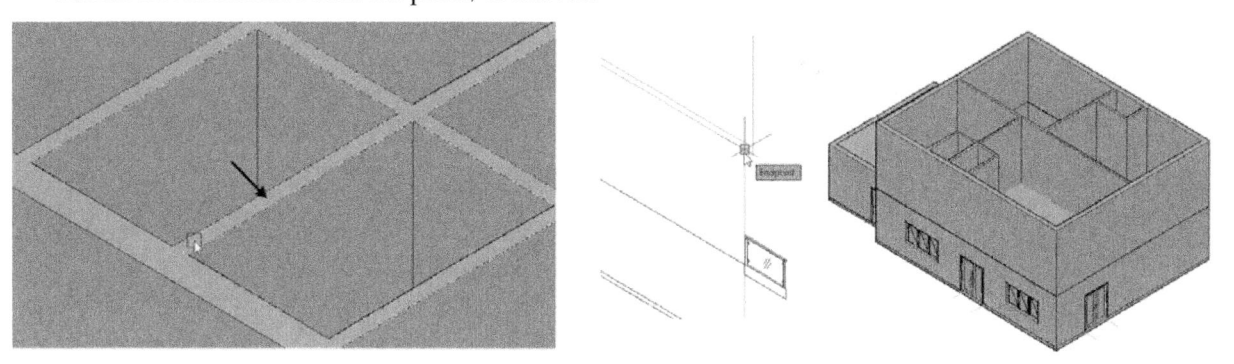

- Activate the **Rectangle** tool and create a rectangle on top face of the outer wall, as shown.

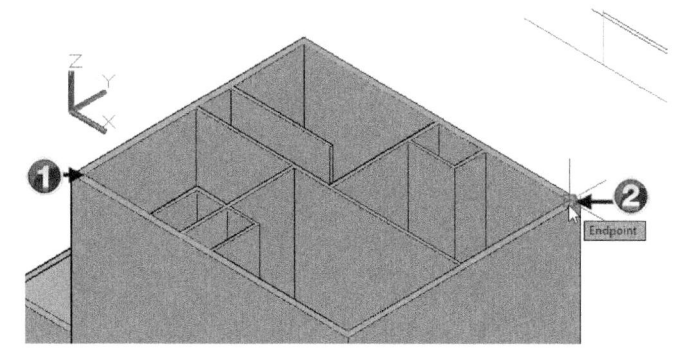

- Activate the **Presspull** tool and click on the top face of the inner wall, as shown. Zoom to the North elevation and select the point, as shown.

150 | Creating Architectural Drawings

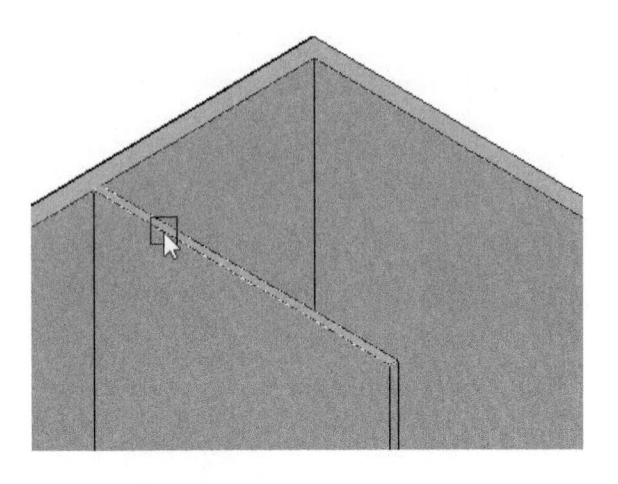

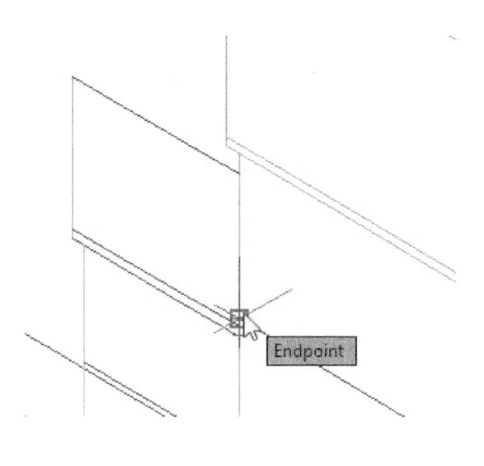

- Use the **Presspull** tool and decrease the height of the inner walls by 200 mm.

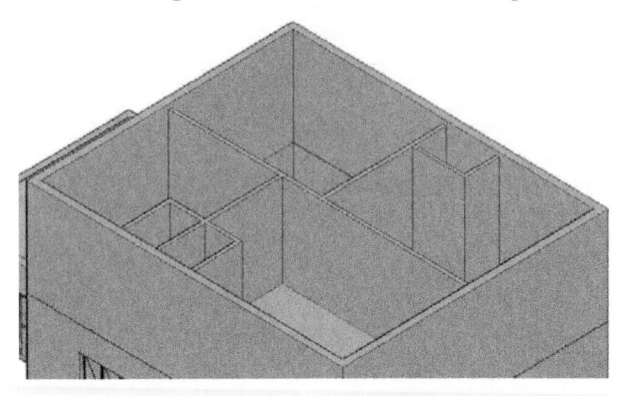

- Copy the 2D doors and windows from the elevation views onto the 3D walls.

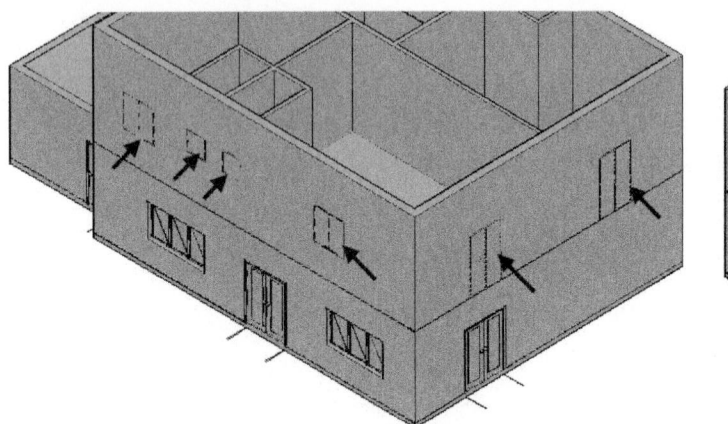

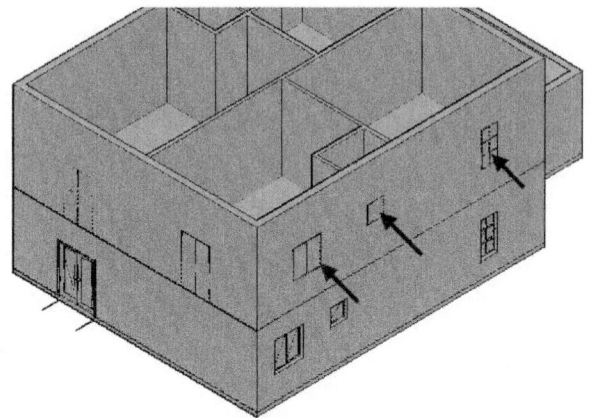

- Create the doors and window openings using the **Box** and **Subtract** tools.

151 | Creating Architectural Drawings

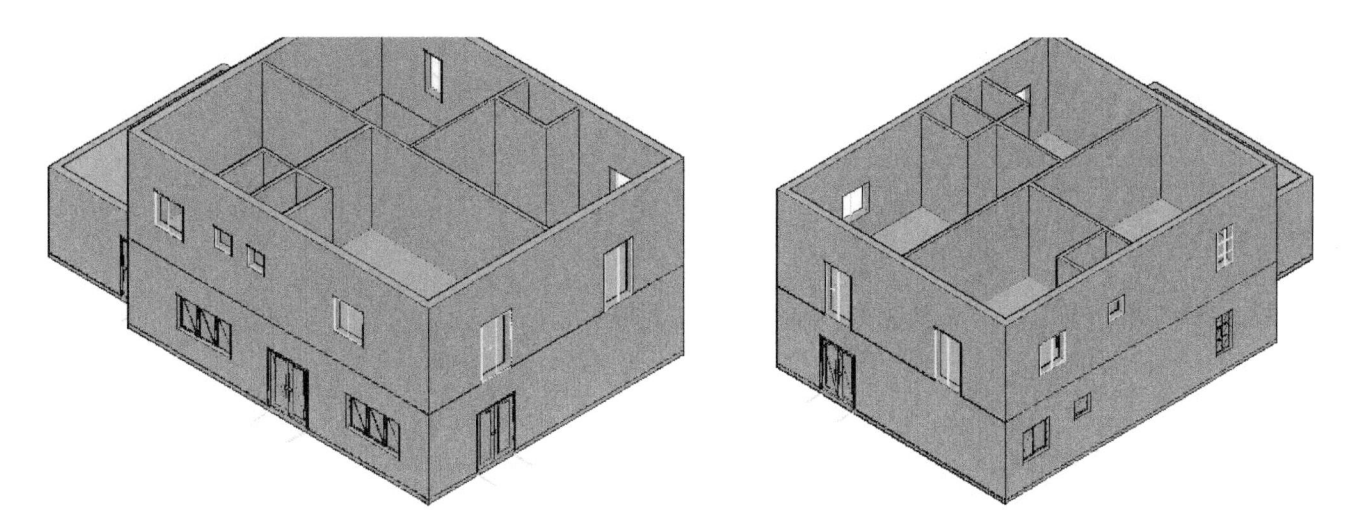

- Create boxes on the first floor plan, as shown. The height of the boxes is 2500 mm.

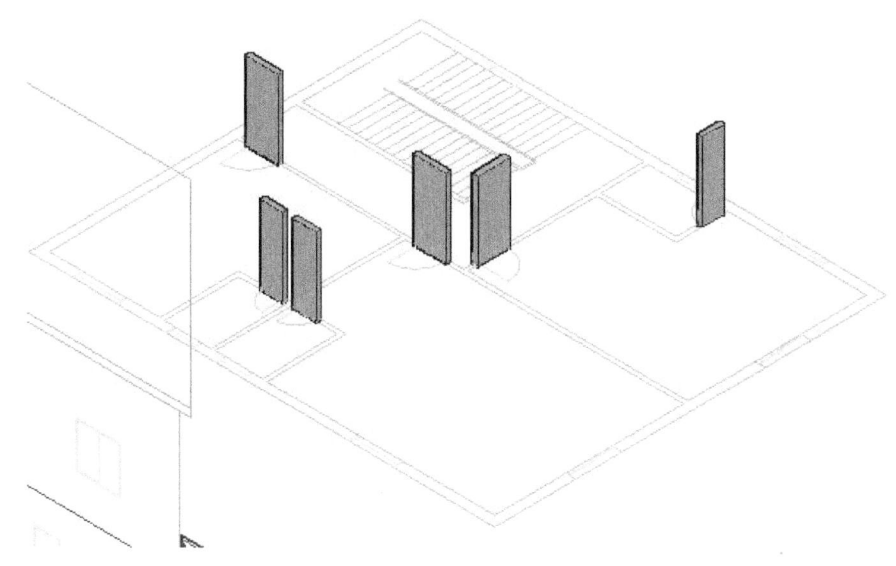

- Select all the boxes on the first floor plan, type M, and press Enter. Select the corner point on the first floor plan to define the base point, as shown. Specify the destination point on the 3D wall, as shown.

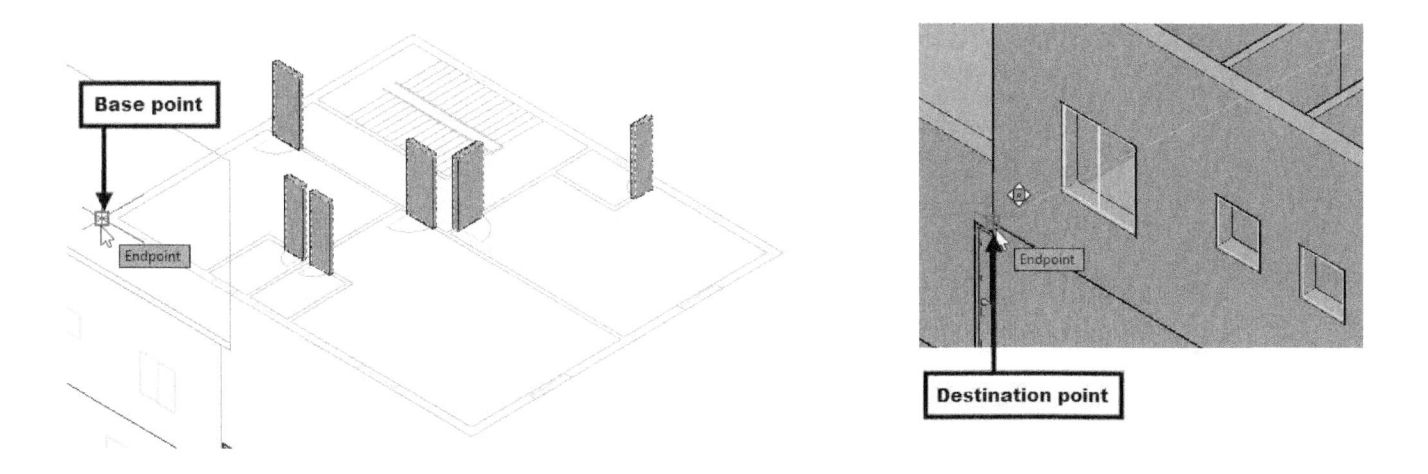

152 | Creating Architectural Drawings

- Subtract the boxes from the 3D walls.

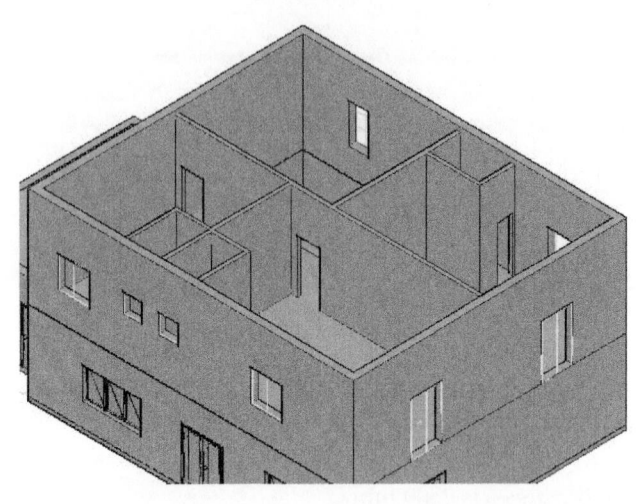

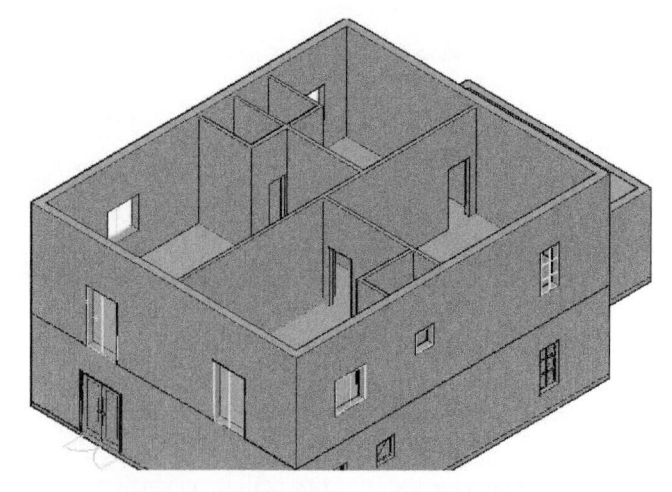

- Copy the doors and windows from the ground floor and place them on different door and window. Also, create sliding doors and bathroom doors. The procedure to create doors has been described already.

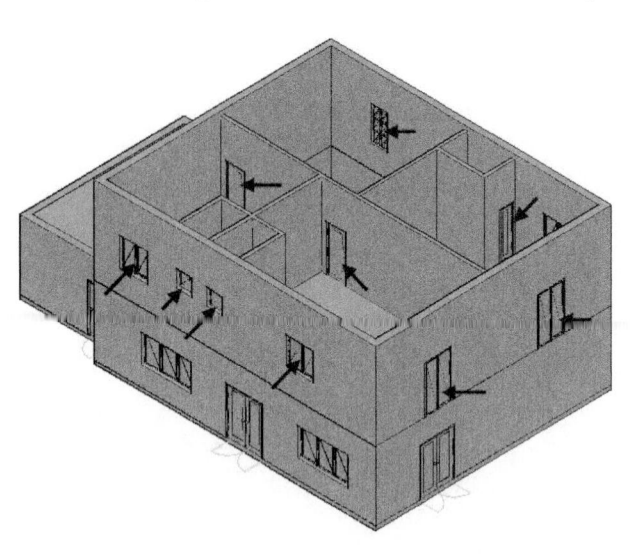

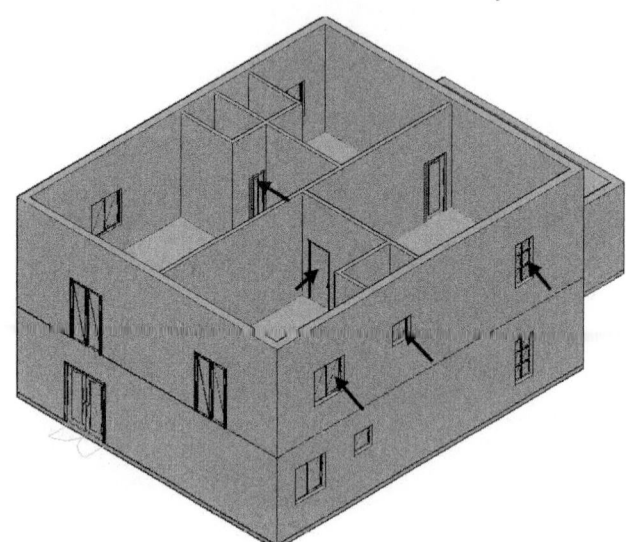

Tutorial 8: Creating the Balcony
- Create a new layer "3D-Balcony", set its color to green, and activate the layer.
- Zoom to the North elevation and create a selection window over the balcony. Type CO and press Enter. Specify the base and destination points, as shown.

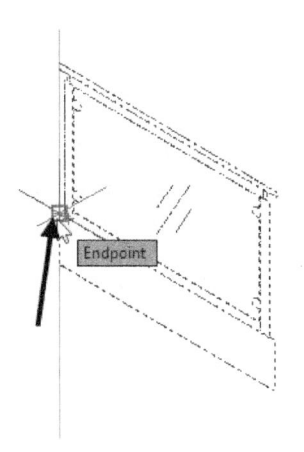

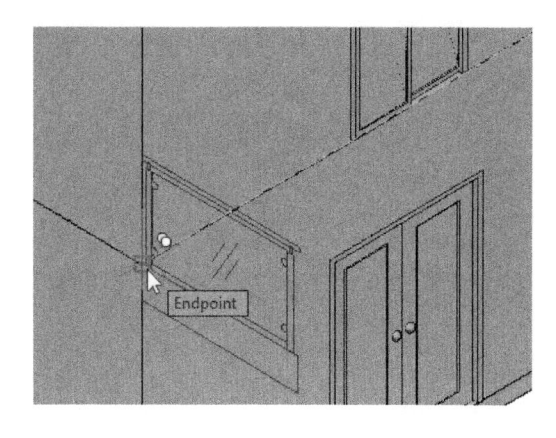

- Type EXT and press Enter. Select the large rectangle of the balcony and move the pointer toward right. Select the corner point of the ground floor wall, as shown.

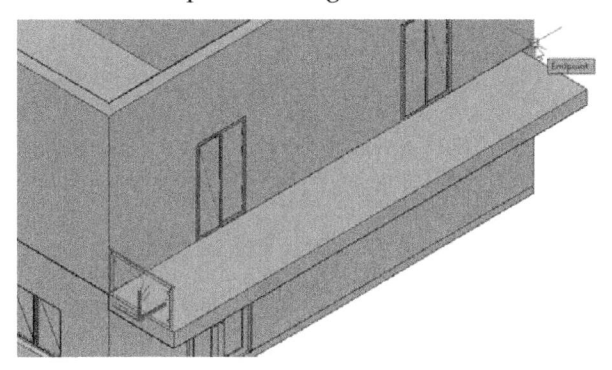

- On the ribbon, click **Home** tab > **Modeling** panel > **Primitives** drop-down > **Cylinder**. Select 2P from the command line. Place the pointer on the top face of the extruded solid, and select lower corner points of the rectangle, as shown. Move the pointer upward and select the top left corner point of the rectangle, as shown; the cylinder is created.

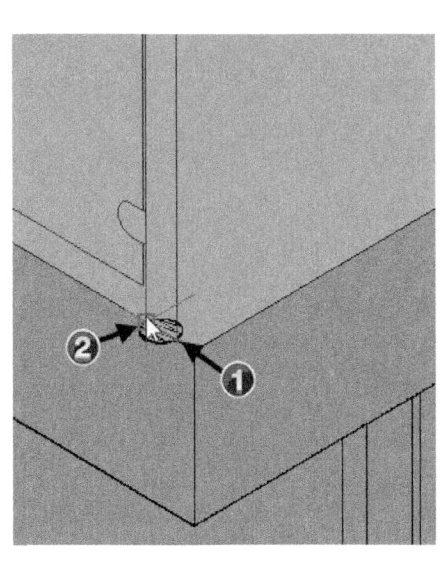

- Activate the **Cylinder** tool and create another cylinder, as shown.

154 | Creating Architectural Drawings

- Select the rectangular array of the sleeve. On the **Home** tab of the ribbon, expand the **Modify** panel and click the **Explode** tool.

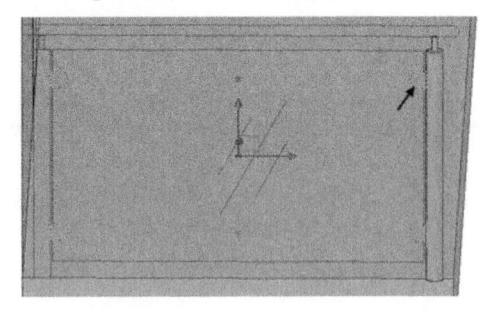

- On the **Home** tab of the ribbon, expand the **Draw** panel and click the **Region** tool. Select the arc and polyline of the sleeve and press Enter. Type EXT and press Enter. Select the region, move the pointer toward right, type 20, and press Enter.

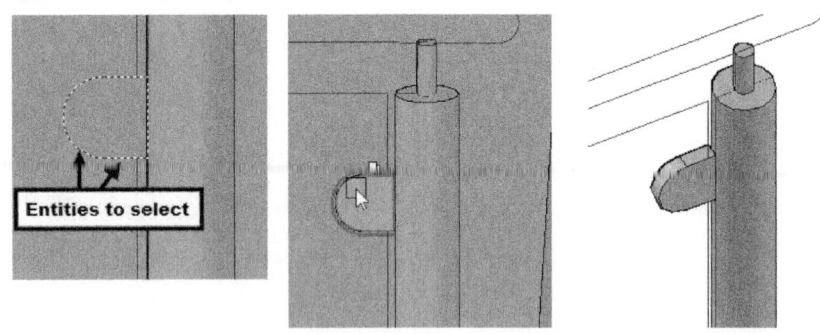

- Select the extruded solid. Select the Y-axis of the Move gizmo, move the pointer backwards, type 12, and press Enter.

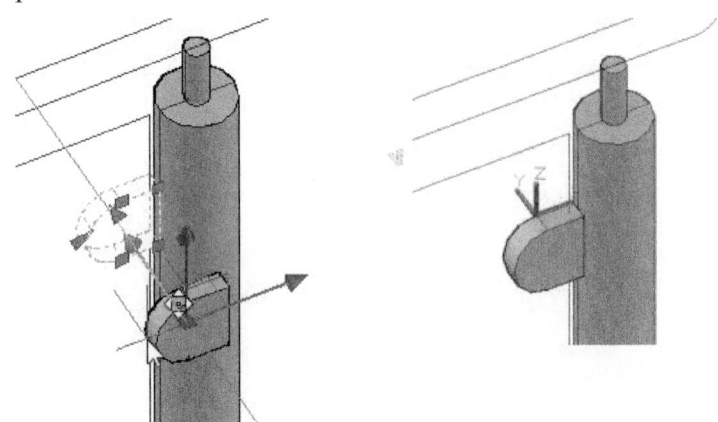

- On the ribbon, click **Solid** tab > **Solid Editing** panel > **Offset Edges** . Select the top face of the sleeve, and then select **Distance** from the command line. Type 4.5 and press Enter. Click on the top face of the sleeve to

155 | **Creating Architectural Drawings**

create an offset edge. Select the offset edge to display grips. Click on the midpoint grip of the width, move the pointer toward left and click; the rectangles is stretched.

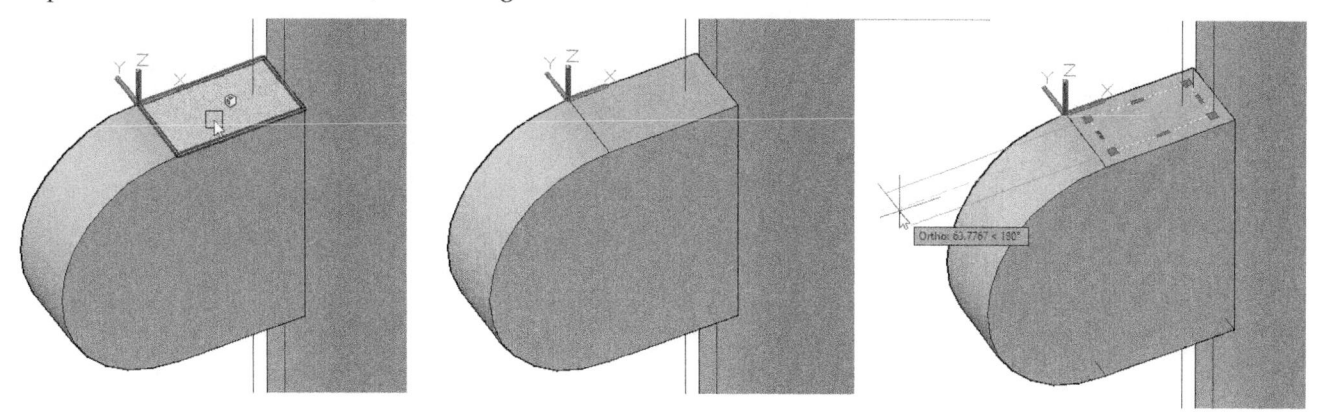

- Extrude the offset rectangle, and then subtract it from the sleeve.

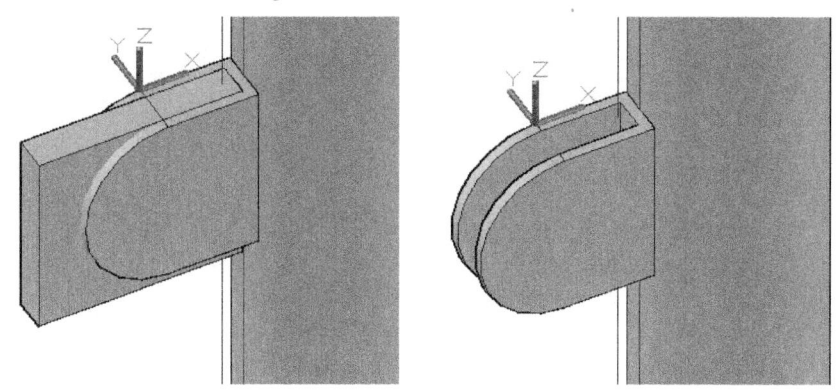

- Select the sleeve, type CO and press Enter. The midpoint of the top edge of the sleeve to define the base point. Move the pointer downward and select the corner pointer of the 2D sleeve as the destination point.

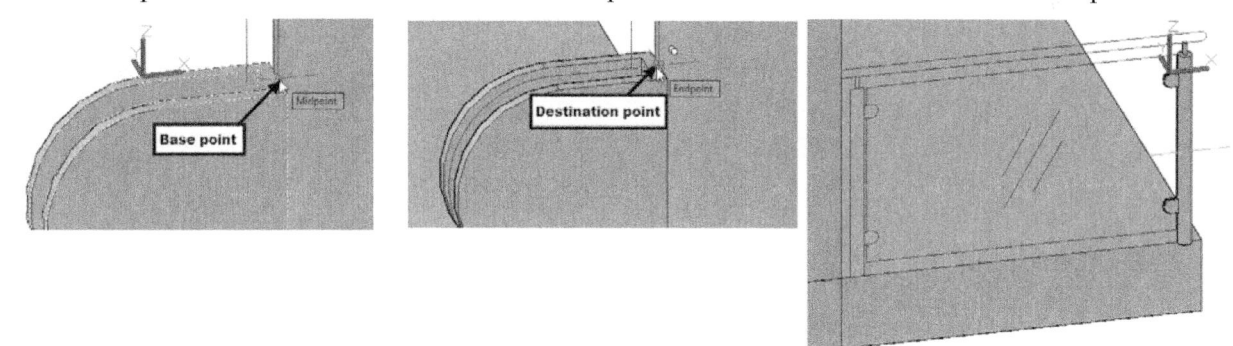

- Select the two cylinders and sleeves, and then click on the Y-axis of the Move gizmo. Move the pointer forward, type 90, and press Enter.

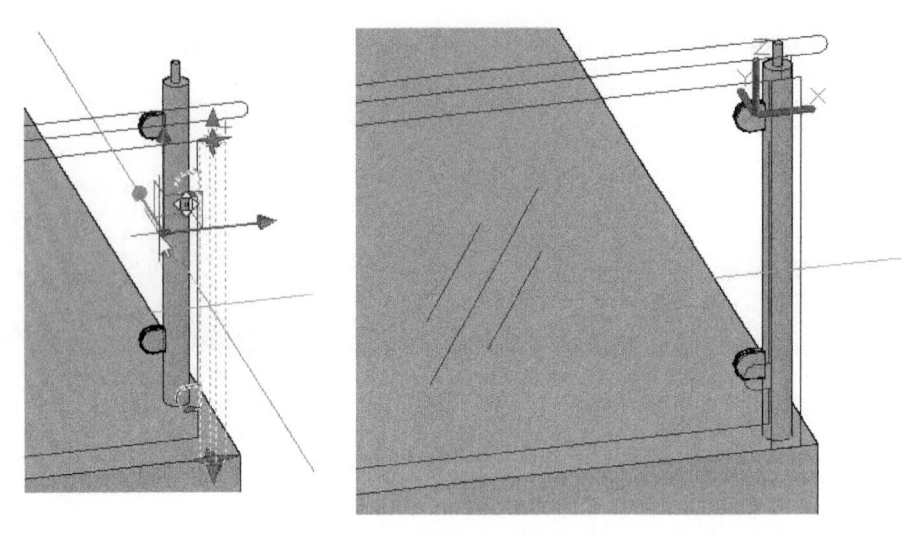

- Select the two cylinders and sleeves. Type MI and press Enter. Select the top edge of the balcony, move the pointer vertically upward, and click. Select **No** from the command line.

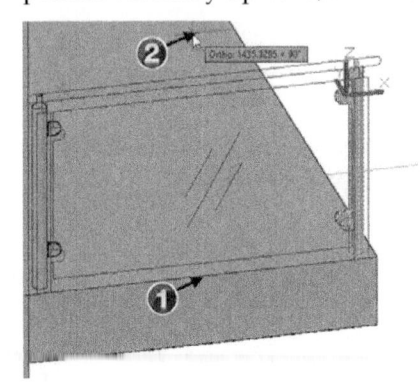

- Select the two sleeves on the right post, type RO, and press Enter. Select the center point on the top face of the cylinder. Select **Copy** from the command line. Type 270 and press Enter to create the rotated copies of the sleeves.

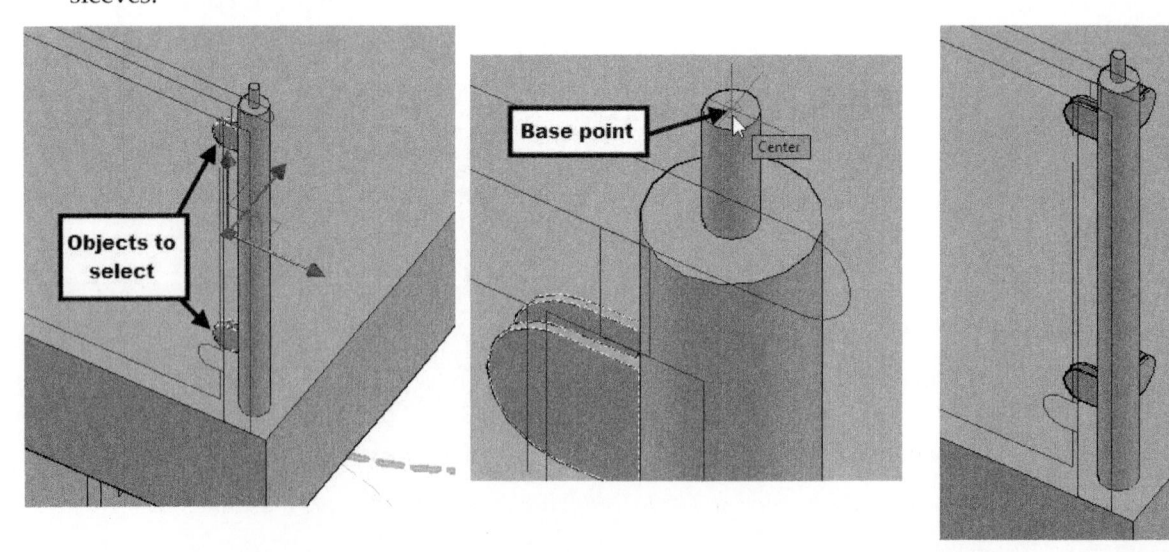

- Select the right side post and rotated copies of sleeves. On the ribbon, click **Home** tab > **Modify** panel > **Array** drop-down > **Rectangular Array**. On the **Array Creation** tab, enter 1 and 8 in the **Columns** and **Rows**

Creating Architectural Drawings

boxes, respectively. Enter 1820 in the **Between** box on the **Rows** panel. Click **Close Array** on the ribbon.

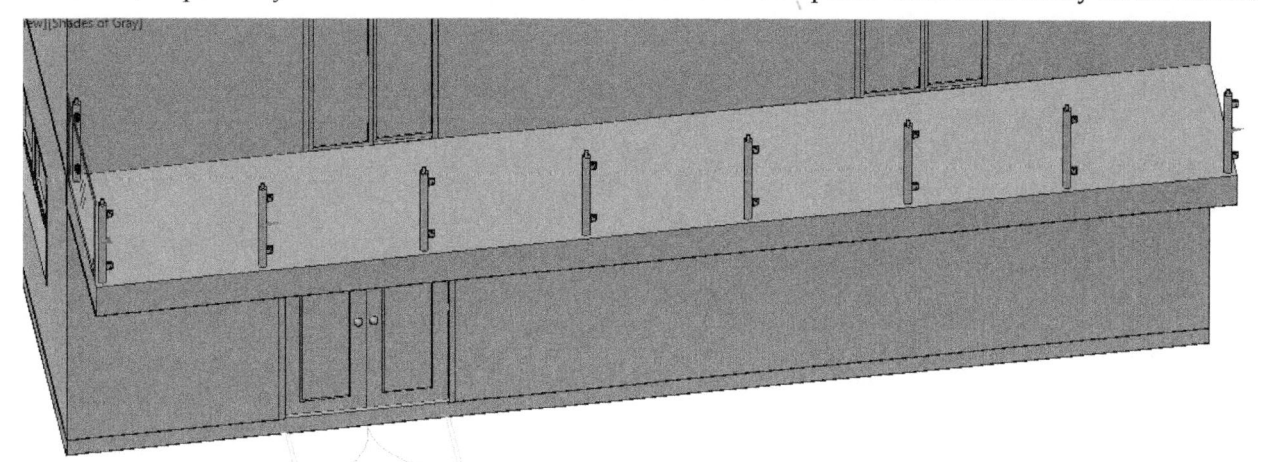

- Select the rectangular array created in the last step. On the **Home** tab of the ribbon, expand the **Modify** panel and click the **Explode** tool. The array is exploded into individual objects.
- Zoom to the second left post and select the two sleeves. Type MI and press Enter. Select the center point on the top face of the cylinder. Move the pointer backwards and click to mirror the sleeves. Select **No** from the command line.

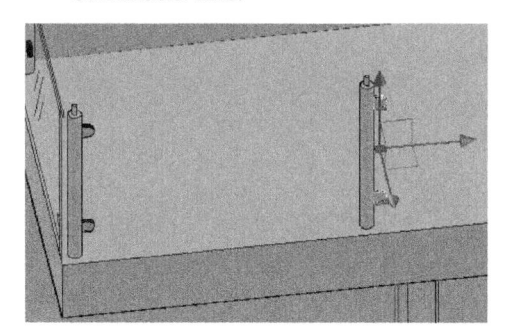

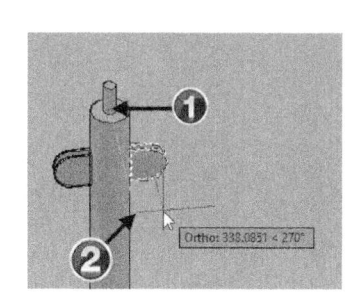

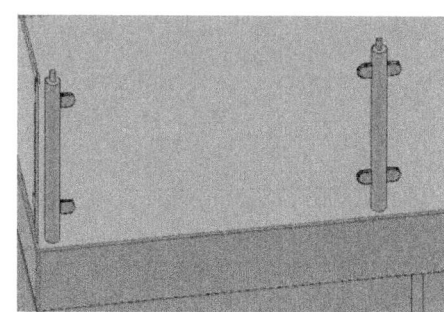

- Select the mirrored sleeves. On the ribbon, click **Home** tab > **Modify** panel > **Array** drop-down > **Rectangular Array**. On the **Array Creation** tab, enter 1 and 7 in the **Columns** and **Rows** boxes, respectively. Enter 1820 in the **Between** box on the **Rows** panel. Click **Close Array** on the ribbon.

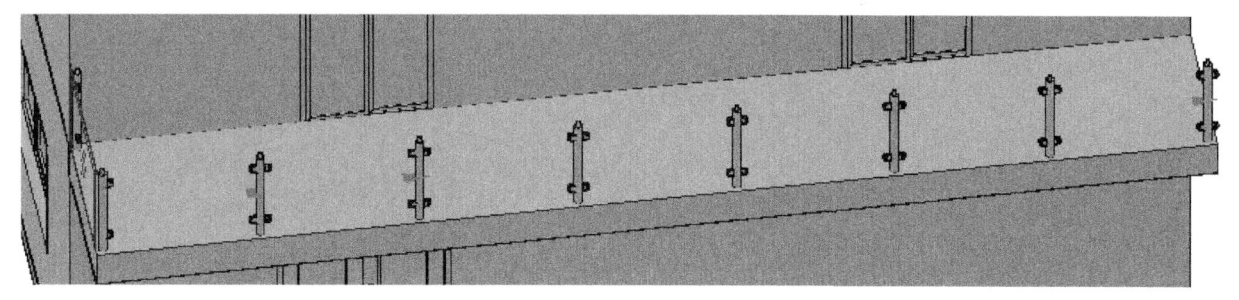

- Select the post next to the wall and the sleeves, as shown. Type **CO** and press Enter. Specify the base point by selecting the center point of the post, as shown. Move the pointer toward right and select the center point of the extreme right post, as shown.

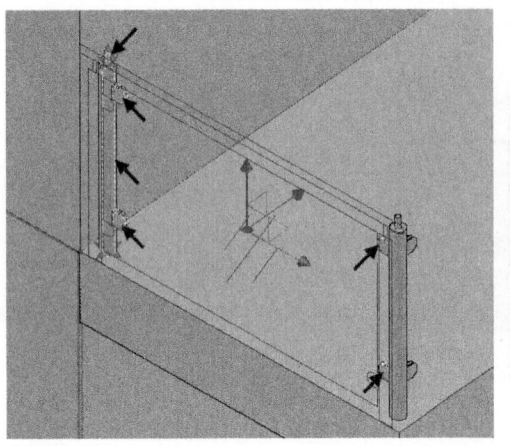

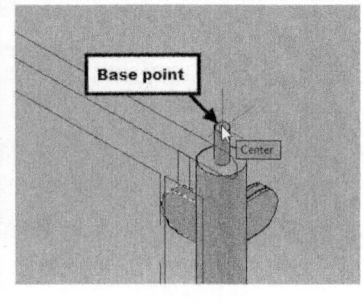

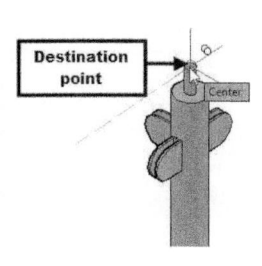

- Select the two unwanted sleeves on the extreme right post and press **Delete**.

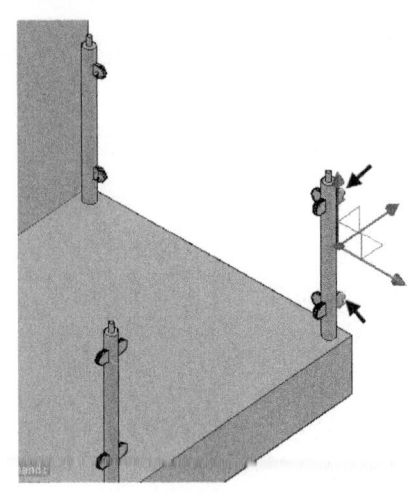

- On the ribbon, click **Home** tab > **Coordinates** panel > **3 Point**. Select the points on the side face of the balcony in the sequence shown below. The first point defines the UCS origin. The second and third points define the X and Y axes.

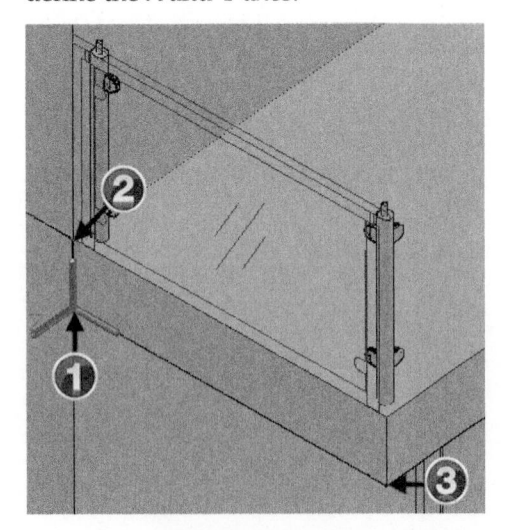

- Turn off the **Dynamic UCS** icon on the status bar. Activate the **Box** tool and specify the first and second corner of the box, as shown. Type -15 and press Enter.

159 | Creating Architectural Drawings

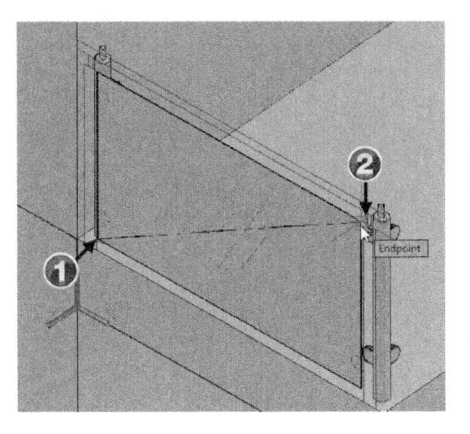

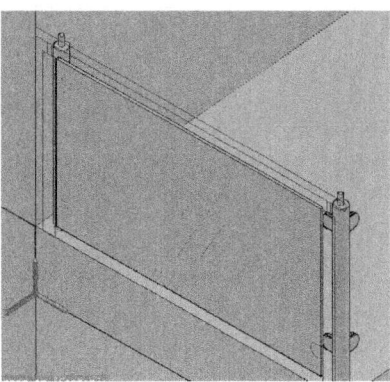

- Select the box to display the Move gizmo. Click on the Y-axis of the Move gizmo, move the pointer forward, type 82.5 and press Enter.

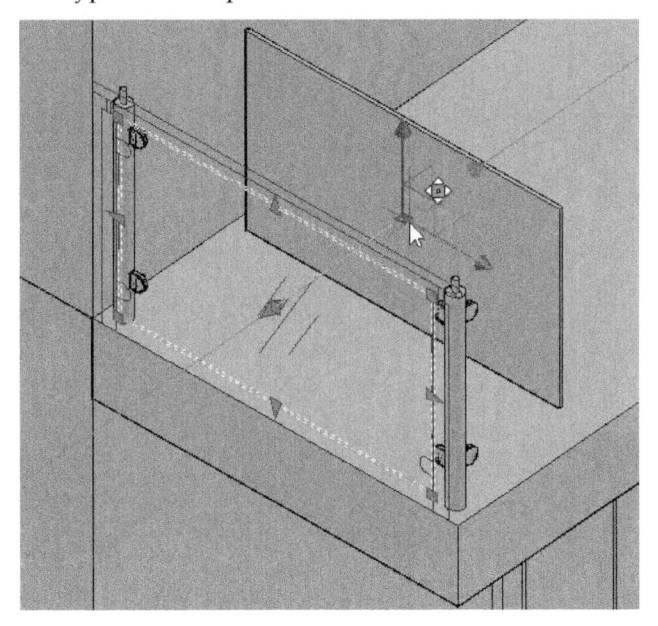

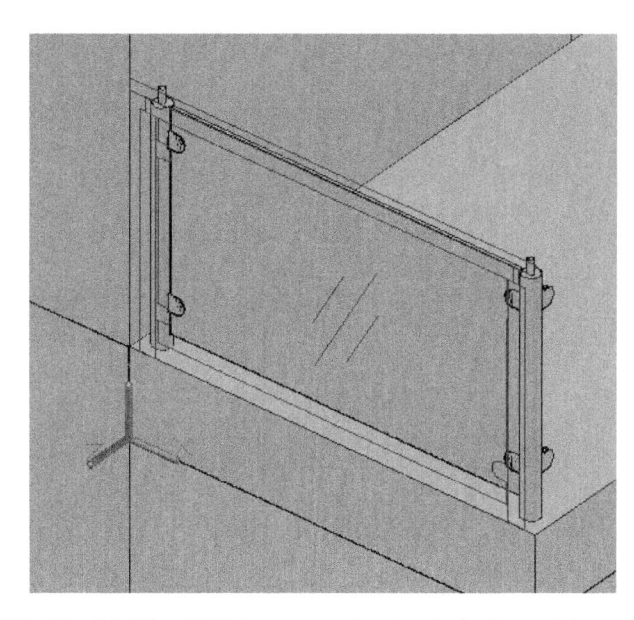

- On the ribbon, click **Home** tab > **Coordinates** panel > **UCS, World**. The UCS is restored to its default position.
- Select the box created in the earlier step. Type RO and press Enter. Select the center point on the top face of the cylinder. Select **Copy** from the command line. Type 270 and press Enter to create the rotated copies of the sleeves.

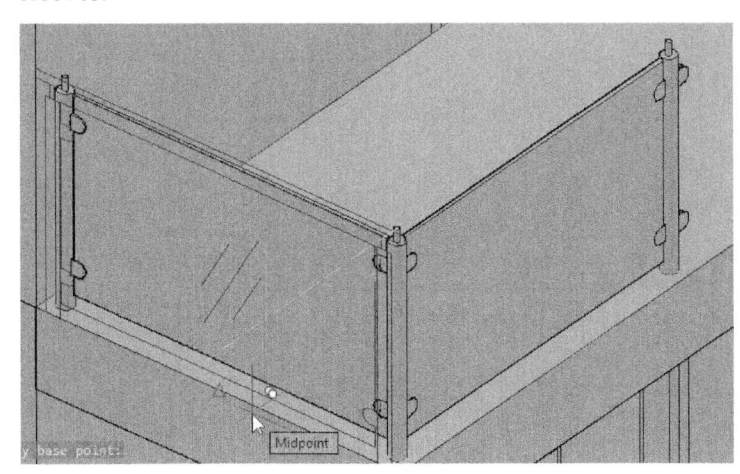

- Select the rotated copy of the box. On the ribbon, click **Home** tab > **Modify** panel > **Array** drop-down > **Rectangular Array**. On the **Array Creation** tab, enter 1 and 7 in the **Columns** and **Rows** boxes, respectively. Enter 1820 in the **Between** box on the **Rows** panel. Click **Close Array** on the ribbon.

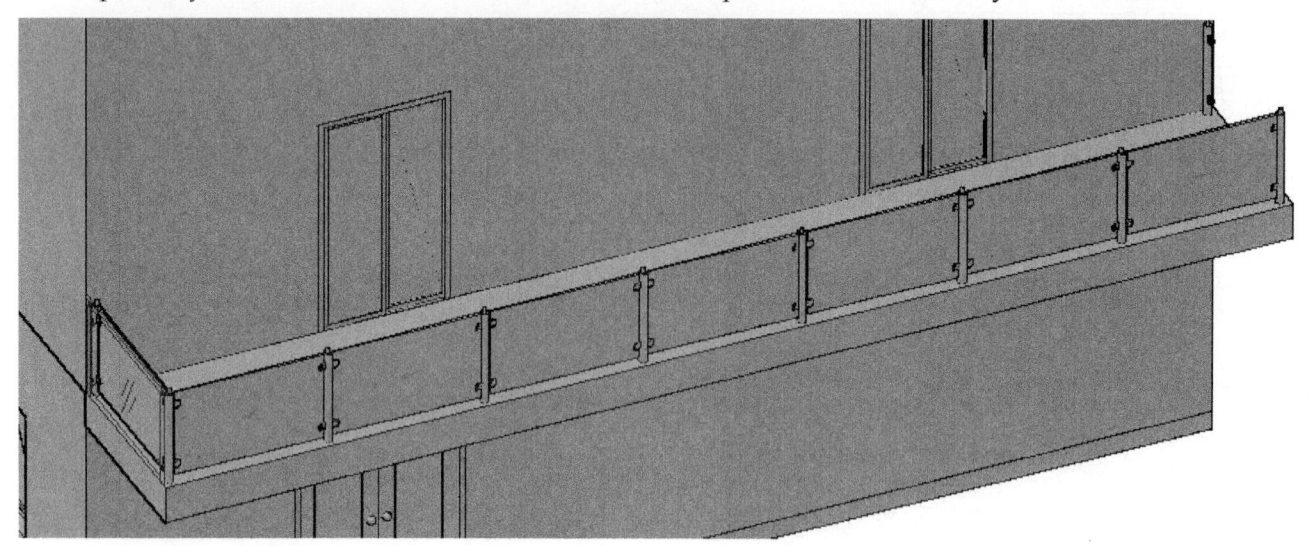

- Copy the box on the left end and place it on the right end.

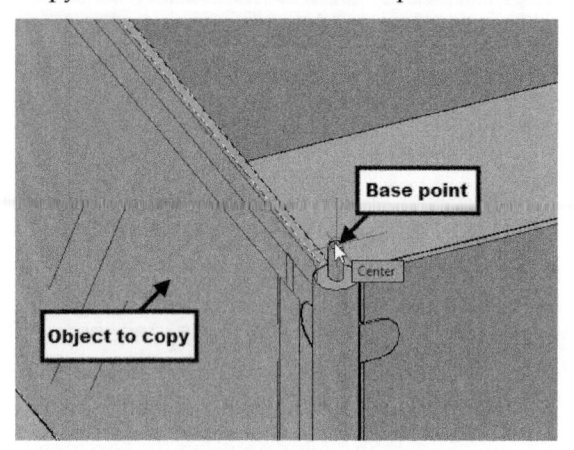

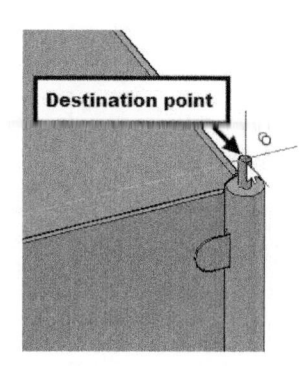

- Type PL and press Enter. Select the center points of the top face of the posts, as shown.

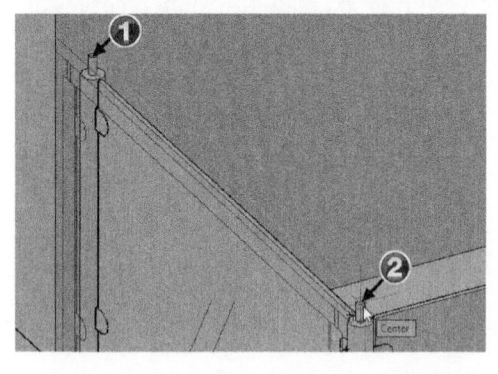

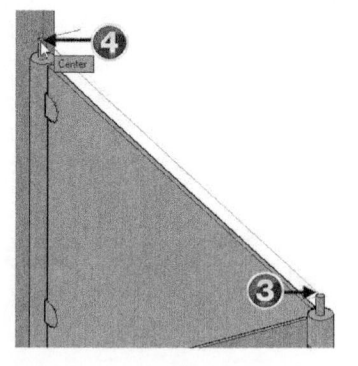

- On the ribbon, click **Home** tab > **Coordinates** panel > **Z-Axis Vector**.

161 | Creating Architectural Drawings

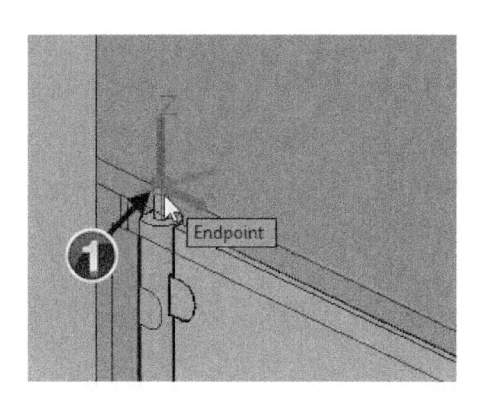

- Type C and press Enter. Select the origin point of the UCS. Type 25 and press Enter.

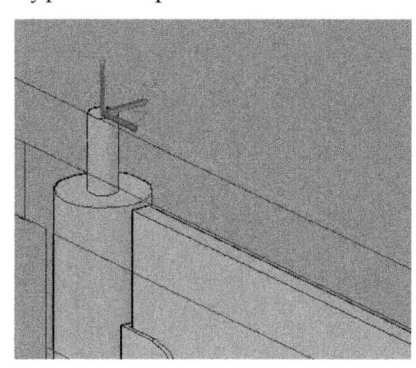

- On the ribbon, click **Home** tab > **Modeling** panel > **Extrude** drop-down > **Sweep**. Select the circle and press Enter. Select the polyline and press Enter.

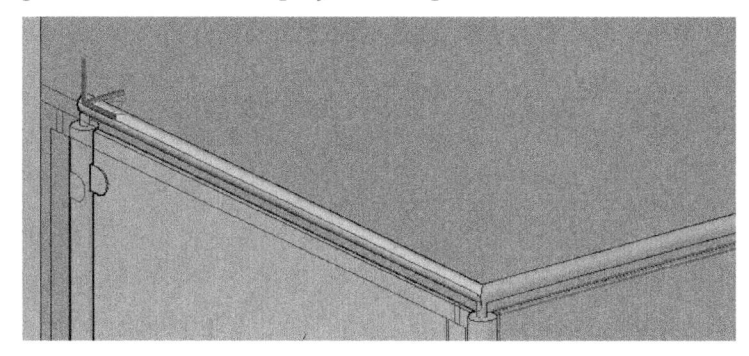

- Select the swept solid to display the Move gizmo. Select the Y-axis of the move gizmo, move the pointer upward, type 24, and then press Enter.

162 | Creating Architectural Drawings

- Extend the swept solid up to by using the **Presspull** tool.

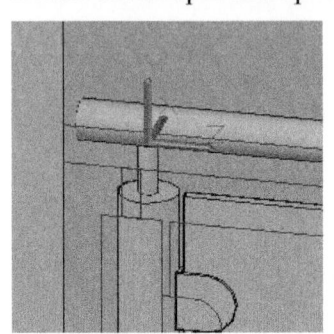

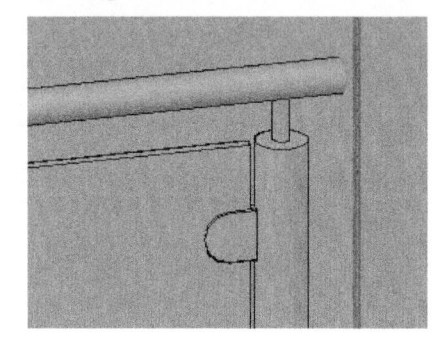

Tutorial 9: Creating the Staircase on the first floor

- Create the 200 mm thickness floor on top of the first floor. Create a 5438x1732x200 box at the corner of the floor, as shown. Create another box of 1732x3476x200 dimension. Subtract the box from the floor.

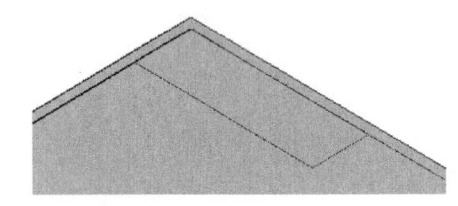

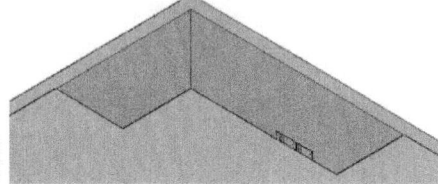

- Deactivate the **Dynamic UCS** icon on the status bar. On the ribbon, click **Home** tab > **Coordinates** panel > **UCS**↙. Specify the origin, X, and Y axes of the UCS, as shown.

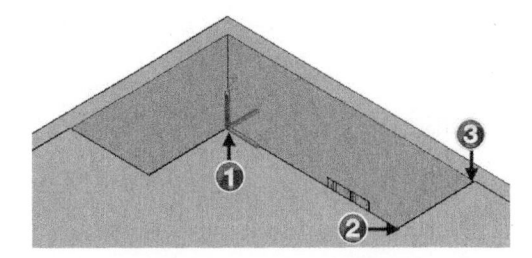

- Set the "3D-Stairs" layer as current.

163 | Creating Architectural Drawings

- On the ribbon, click **Home** tab > **Modeling** panel > **Primitives** drop-down > **Wedge**. Specify the first and second corners of the wedge. Move the pointer upward, type 3111, and press Enter.

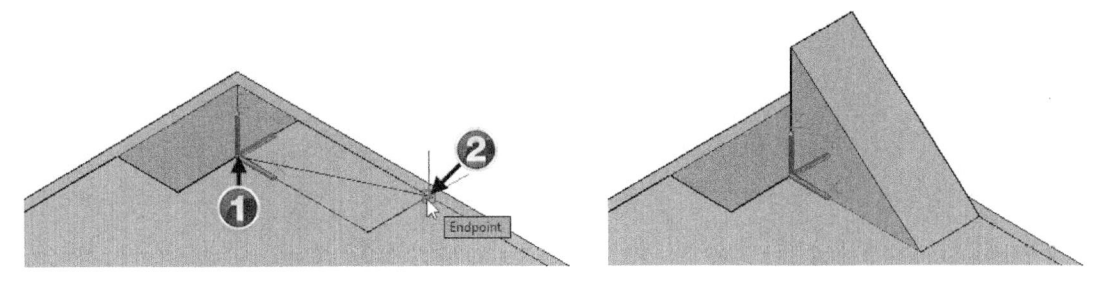

- Type **UCS** and press Enter twice to restore the **UCS** to its default position.
- Type L and press Enter. Select the end points of the inclined edge, as shown. Create a 1732x218x183 box on the top edge of the wedge. On the ribbon, click **Home** tab > **Modify** panel > **Array** drop-down > **Polar Array**. Select the box and press Enter. Select the line coinciding with the inclined edge. On the **Array Creation** tab, on the **Properties** panel, click **Measure Method** drop-down > **Divide**. On the **Items** panel, change the **Items** value to **18**. Click **Close Array** on the **Array Creation** ribbon tab.

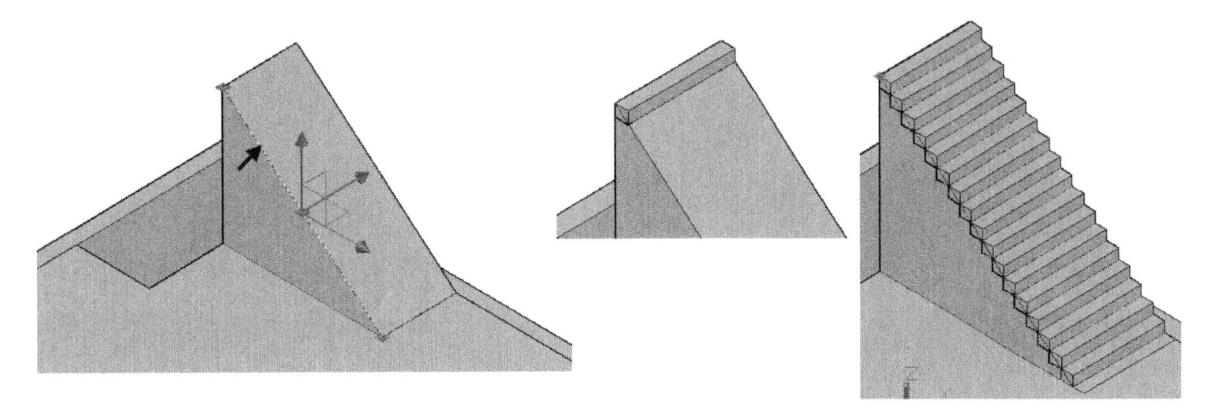

- On the **Home** tab of the ribbon, expand the **Modify** panel and click the **Explode** tool. Select the polar array and press Enter; the array is exploded into individual objects.
- Select the bottom most stair and press **Delete**.
- On the ribbon, click **Home** tab > **Layers** panel > **Isolate**. Select anyone of the stair and press Enter; all the layers except the layer of the selected object are hidden.
- Type UCS and press Enter. Select **Face** from the command line. Select the side face of the wedge, and then select accept from the command line. The UCS is positioned on the selected face.
- Offset the line used to create the path array by 450 mm. Use the **Presspull** tool to remove material on the wedge.
- Type UCS and press Enter twice to restore the UCS to its default position.
- Select the offset line and the line used to create the polar array. Press Delete.

- Type UNI and press Enter. Create a selection window over the stairs and press Enter.

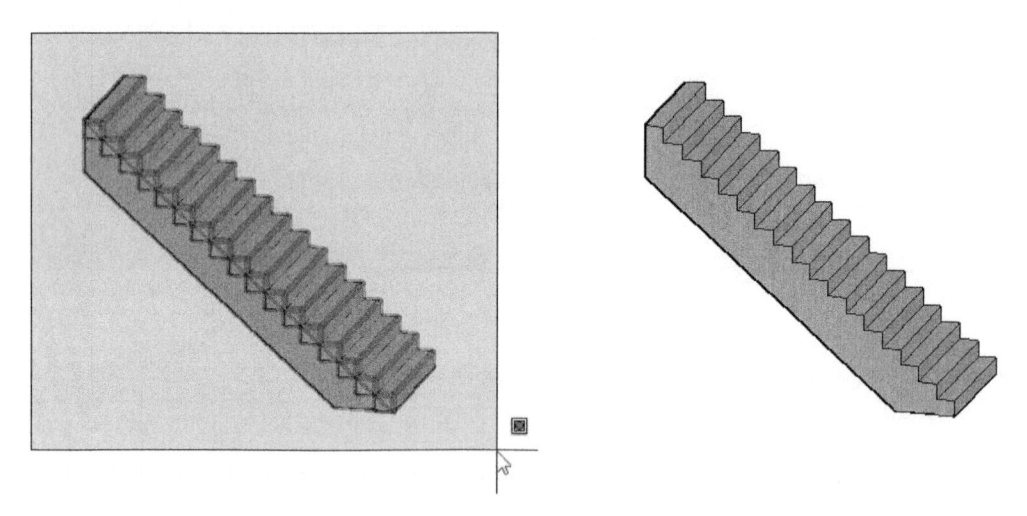

- Select the staircase, type M and press Enter. Specify the base points, as shown. Move the pointer downward, type 4572, and press Enter.

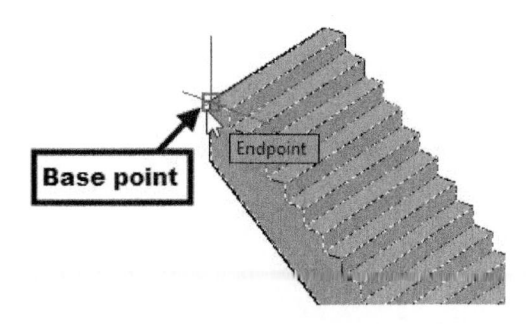

- On the ribbon, click **Home** tab > **Layers** panel > **Unisolate**. All the layers are turned on.
- On the ribbon, click **Home** tab > **Coordinates** panel > **UCS**. Specify the origin, X, and Y axes of the UCS, as shown.

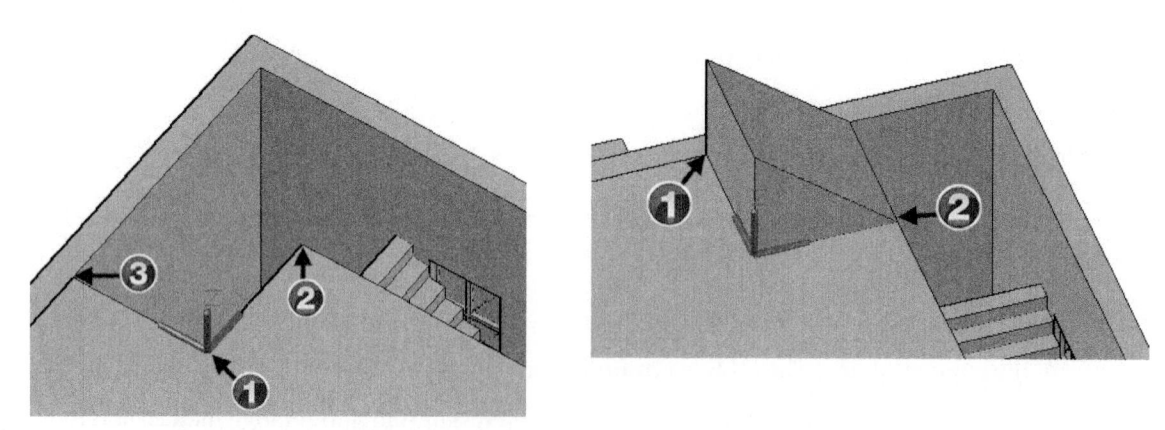

- Create the remaining 8 stairs on the wedge, as shown.

165 | Creating Architectural Drawings

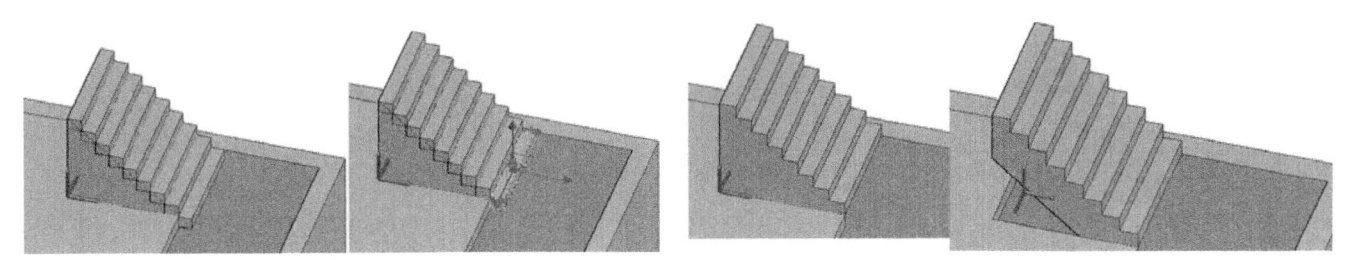

- Align the topmost stair with the ceiling, as shown. Type UCS and press Enter twice to restore the UCS to its default position.

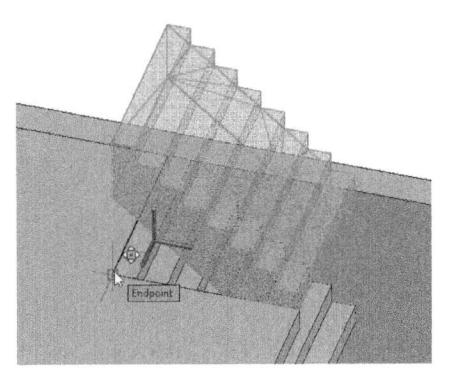

- Select the ceiling above the walls, and then select **Isolate > Hide Objects**. Create a 1732x1732x200 mm box on the top face of the walls, as shown.

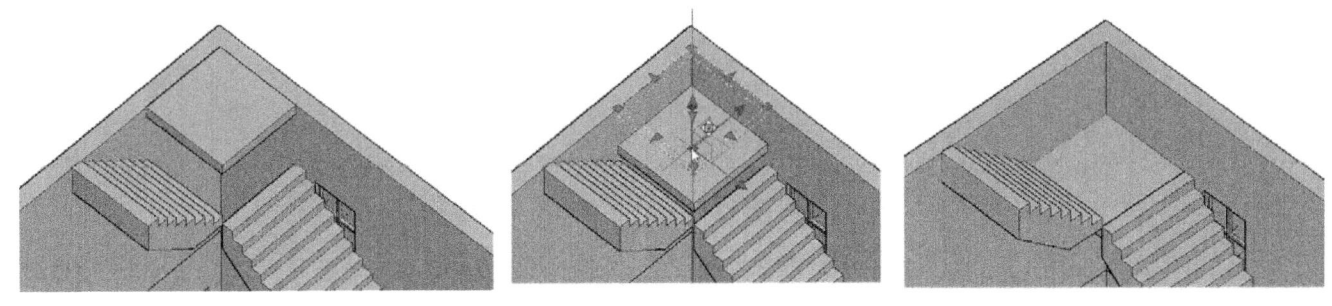

Notice that the staircase is placed in front of the window. You need to change the location of the window.

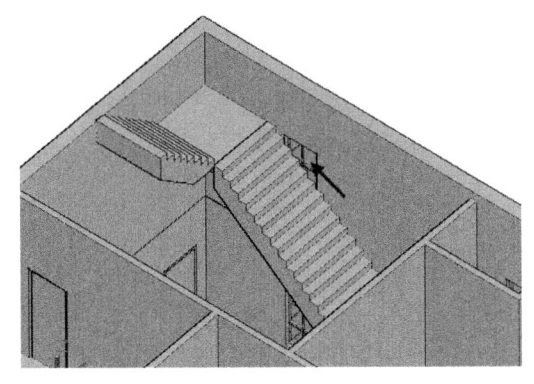

- Select the window, click on the X-axis of the move gizmo, and move the pointer toward right. Type 3710 and press Enter.

166 | Creating Architectural Drawings

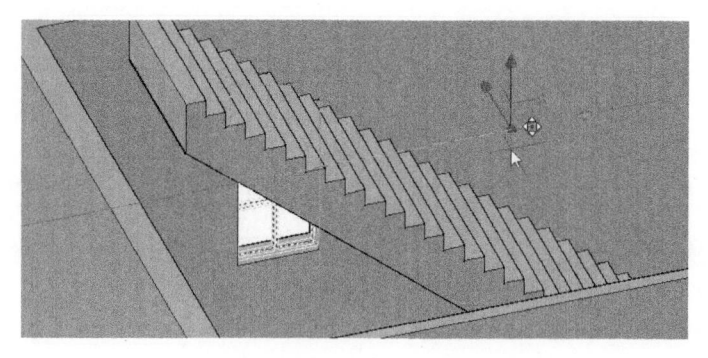

- Change the orientation to NW Isometric. Create a box on the window opening by selecting its corner points. The depth of the box is -320 mm. Create a copy of the box at 3710 mm in the positive X –direction. Subtract the box copy from the walls.

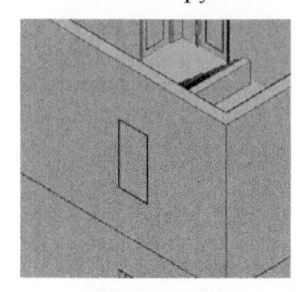

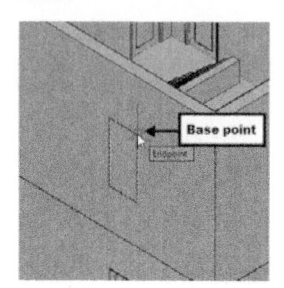

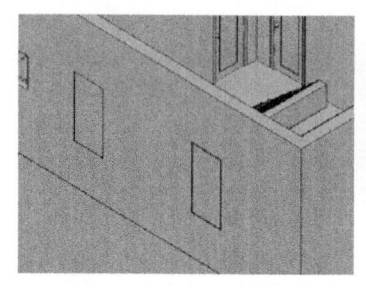

- Unite the box with the walls.

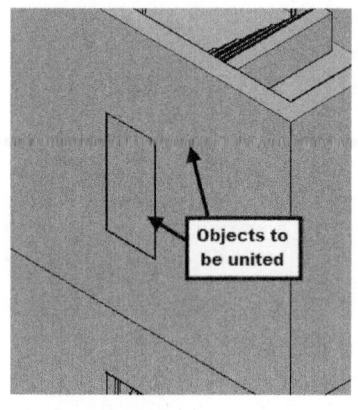

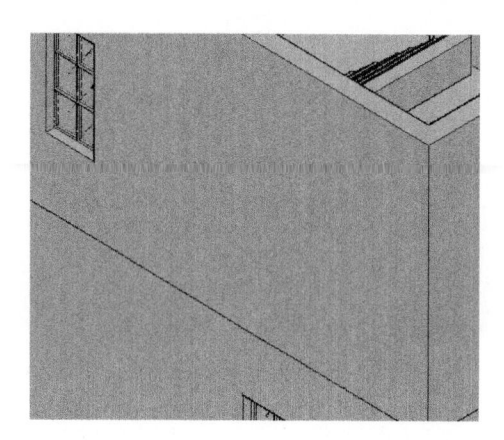

Creating Railing
- Create a new layer "3D-Railing" and set its color to Index color 12. Set the **3D-Railing** layer as current.
- Select the staircase on the ground floor. Right click and select **Isolate > Isolate Objects**; the selected object is isolated.

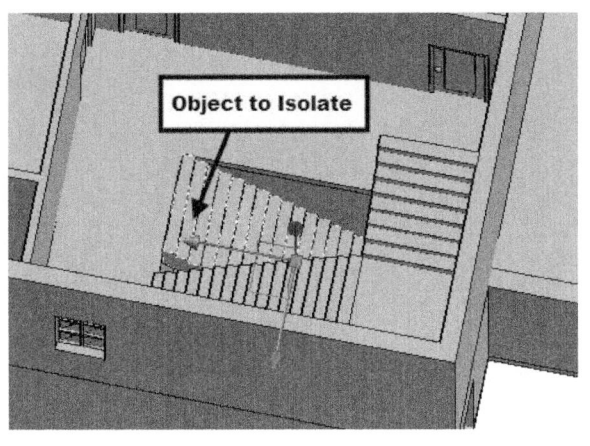

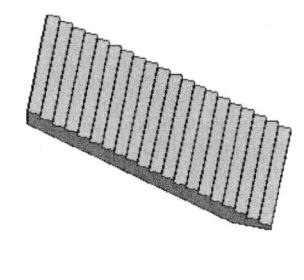

- Deactivate the **Dynamic Input** icon on the status bar.
- On the ribbon, click **Home** tab > **Draw** panel > **3D Polyline**. Specify the first and second points of the 3D polyline, as shown. Move the pointer horizontally toward left, type 450, and press Enter. Move the pointer backwards, type 450, and press Enter. Press Esc.

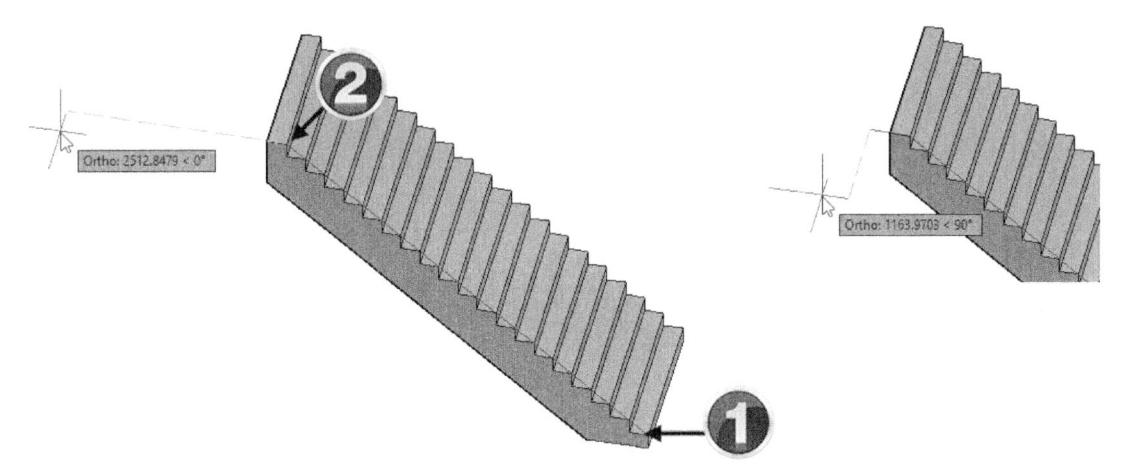

- Right click and select **Isolate** > **End Object Isolation**.
- Select the first floor walls and the ceiling on top of them. Right click and select **Isolate** > **Hide Objects**. Use the **Orbit** tool to rotate the model, as shown.

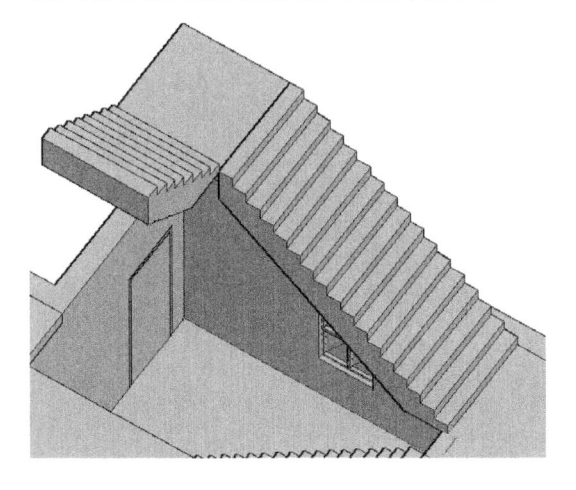

168 | Creating Architectural Drawings

- Type 3DPOLY and press Enter. Specify the eight points of the 3D polyline, as shown. Press Esc.

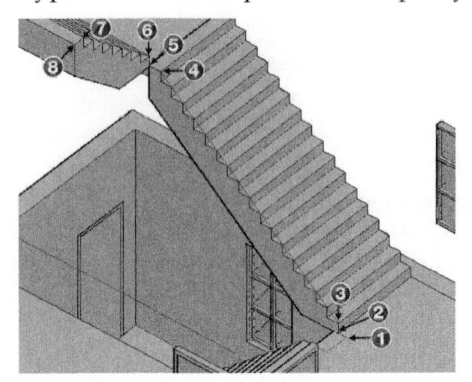

- Create a horizontal line by selecting the end points of the edge, as shown. Select the line and move it by 100 mm in the Y-direction, as shown.

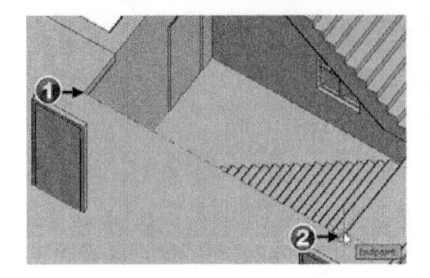

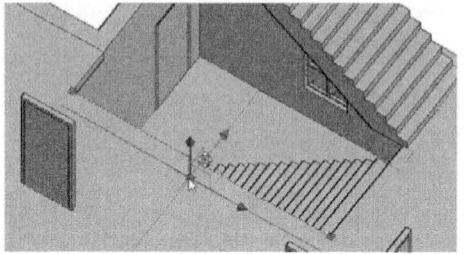

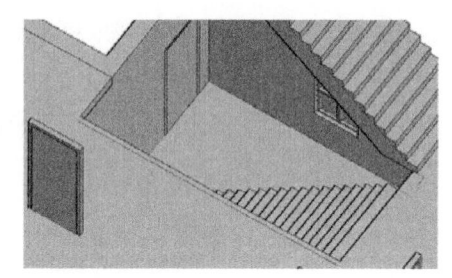

- On the **Home** tab of the ribbon, expand the **Modify** panel and click the **Join** tool. Select the two 3D polylines from the model space, and press Enter; the two polylines are joined together.

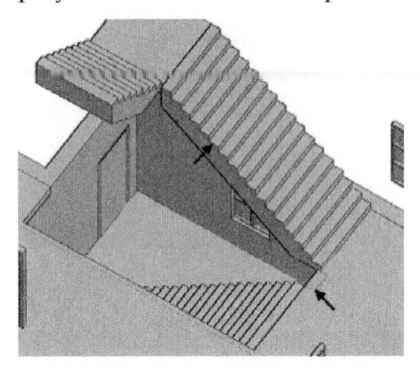

- Select the polyline, click on the Z-axis of the Move gizmo, and move the pointer upward. Type 1000 and press Enter. Likewise, move the horizontal line upwards.

Creating Architectural Drawings

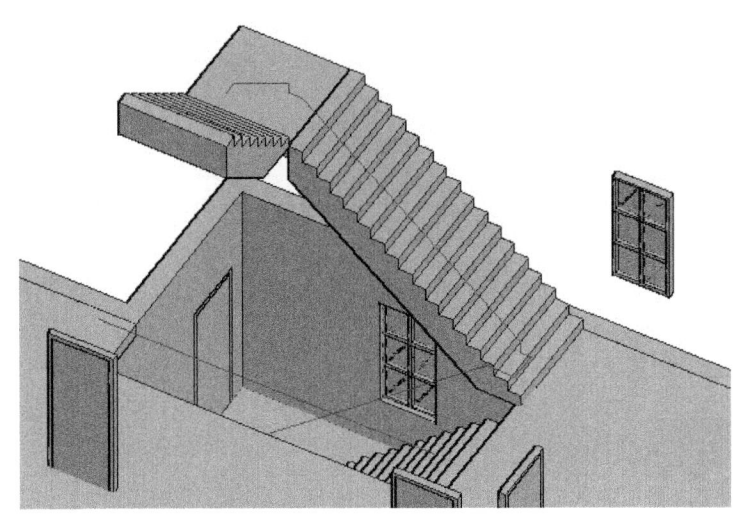

- Type the UCS and press Enter. Select Z-axis from the command line and the select the endpoint of the 3D polyline. Move the pointer forward and select the corner point of the polyline, as shown.

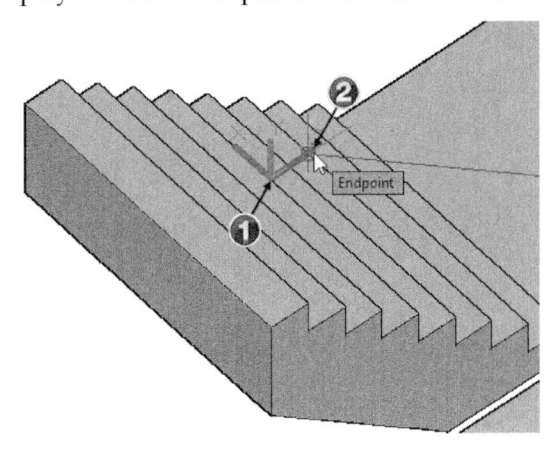

- Create a 100x100 filleted rectangle at the endpoint of the polyline, as shown. The fillet radius is 10 mm.

- Use the **Sweep** tool to create a swept solid, as shown. Likewise, create a rectangle at the endpoint of the horizontal line on the ground floor ceiling, and then sweep it.

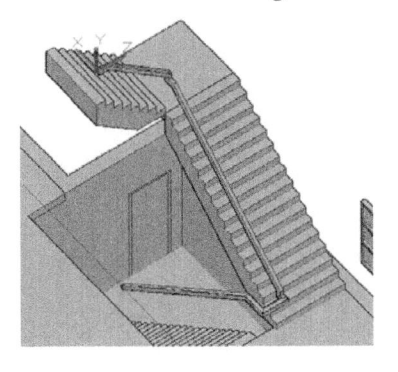

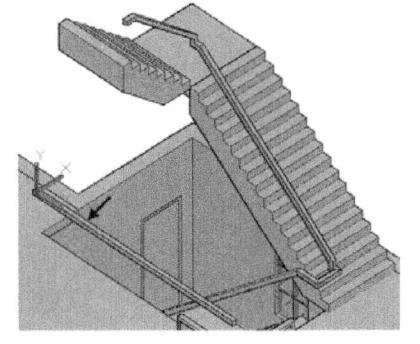

- Pull the side faces of the top two stairs up to 50 mm.

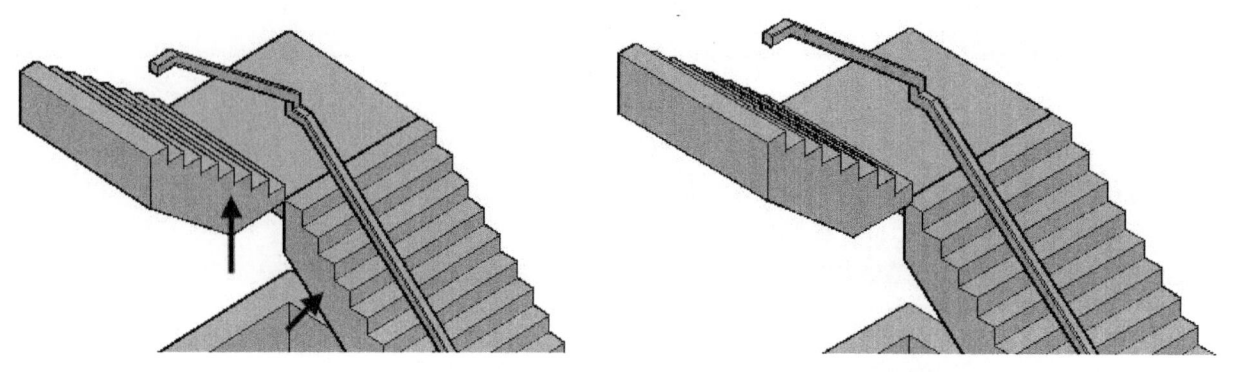

- Select the two staircases and railing. Right click and select **Isolate > Isolate Objects**. Change the view orientation to **SW Isometric**.

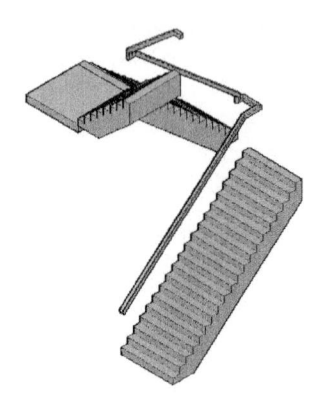

- Create an 80x80x1050 box on the bottom stair, as shown. Move the box 10 mm towards right and 69 mm backwards.

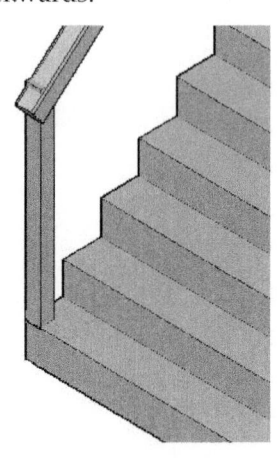

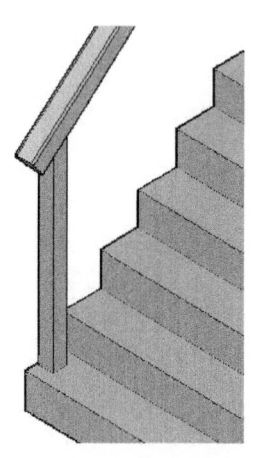

- Select the box, type CO, and press Enter. Specify the base point, as shown. Select **Array** from the command line. Type 7 and press Enter. Select the second point of the copy array, as shown; the copy array is created, as shown. Press Esc.

Creating Architectural Drawings

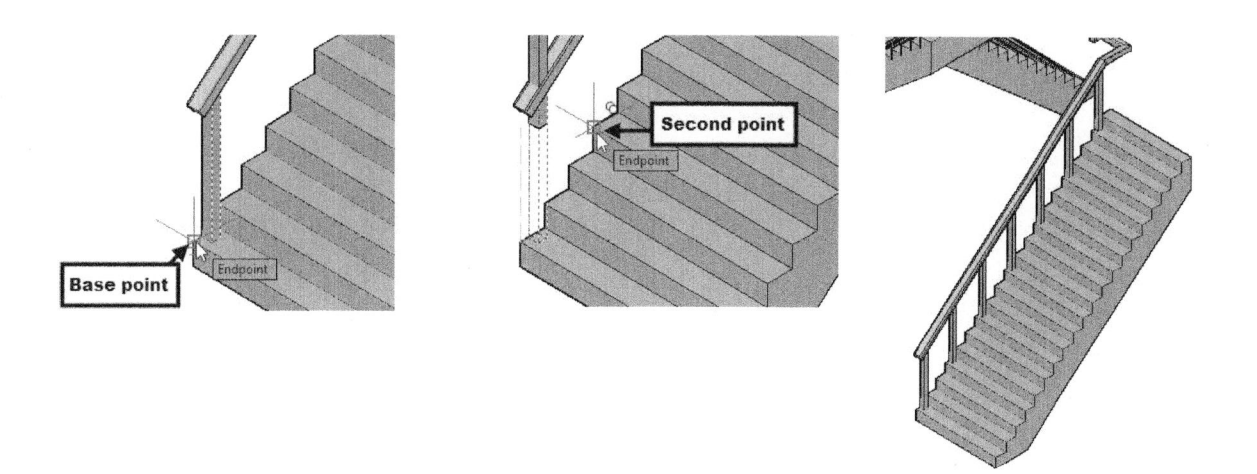

- Select the topmost box of the copy array, type CO, and press Enter. Specify the base and destination points, as shown.

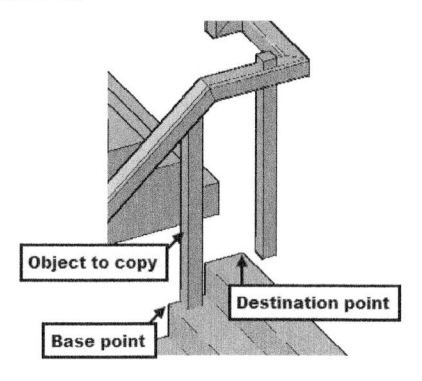

- Select the copied box, click on its arrow grip at the top, and move the pointer downward. Type 100 and press Enter.

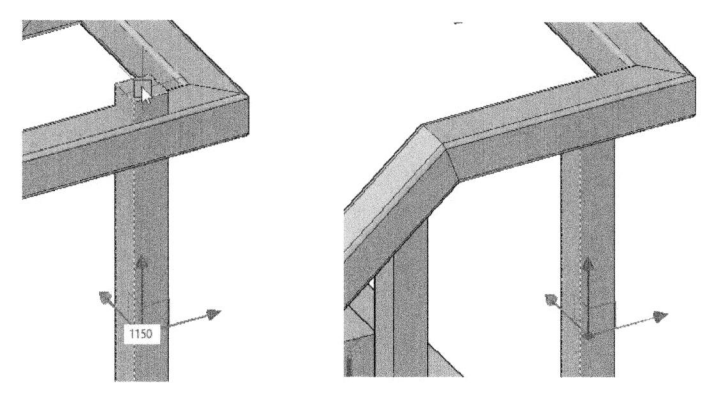

- Move the copied box by 150 mm in the X-direction.

172 | Creating Architectural Drawings

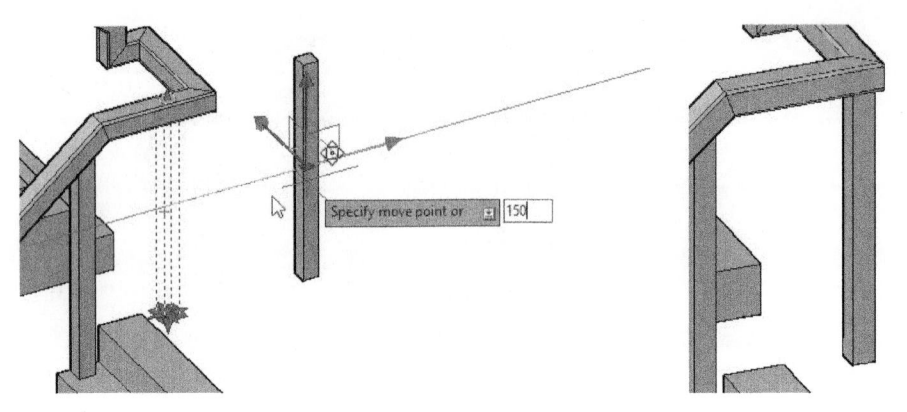

- Select the object which was moved in the last step, type CO, and press Enter. Specify the base point, as shown. Select the corner point of the stair, as shown; another copy of the box is placed at the selected point. Press Esc.

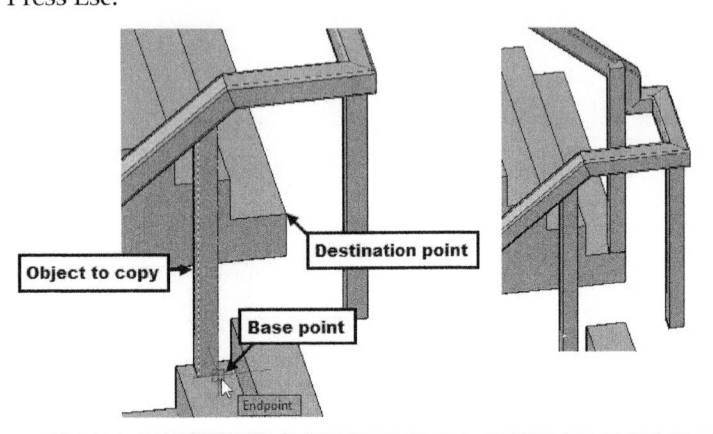

- Orbit the model, as shown. Move the box on the bottom stair 35 mm towards right and 69 mm backwards.

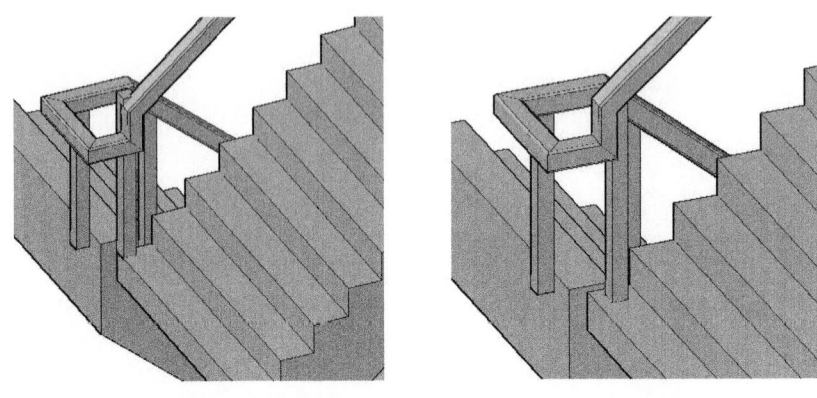

- Create the copy array of the box, as shown. Select the box located on the topmost stair, type CO, and press Enter. Specify the base point, as shown. Select the corner point of the bottom stair, as shown.

173 | Creating Architectural Drawings

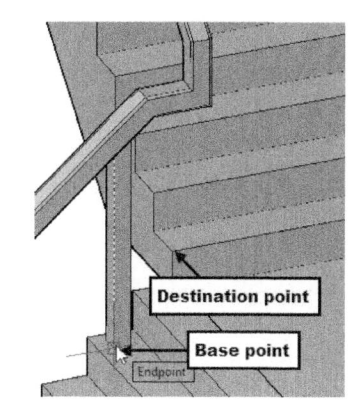

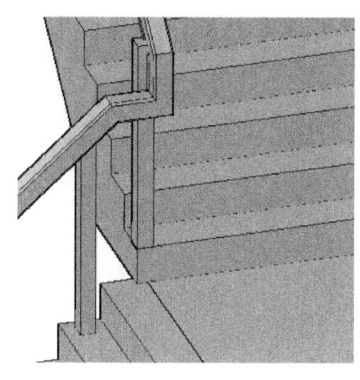

- Move the box on the bottom stair 35 mm towards right and 69 mm backwards. Increase the height of the box by 100 mm.

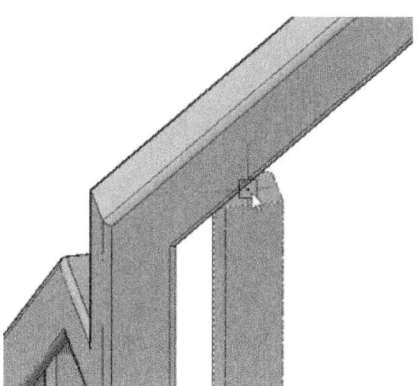

- Create the array copy of the box, as shown.

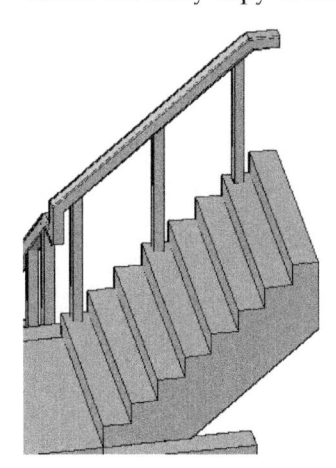

- Right click and select **Isolate > End Object Isolation**.
- Create a railing on the ground floor ceiling.

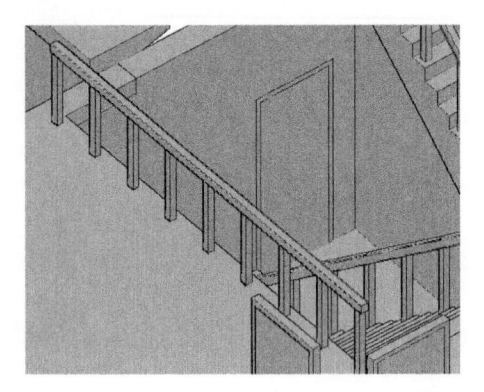

Tutorial 10: Creating the Roof

- Change the view orientation to **SE Isometric**.
- Create a new layer "3D-Roof". Change the layer color to green, and then set the layer as current.
- Select the roof entities of the Front elevation view, type CO, and press Enter. Specify the base point and destination point, as shown.

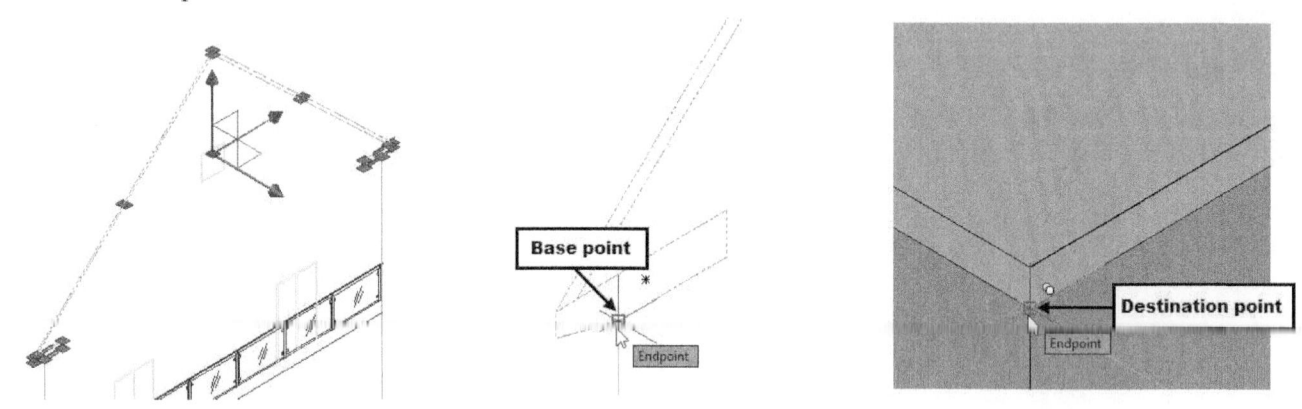

- Activate the **Extrude** tool and select the two entities of the roof, as shown. Press Enter and select the endpoint of the roof on the South East Elevation view.

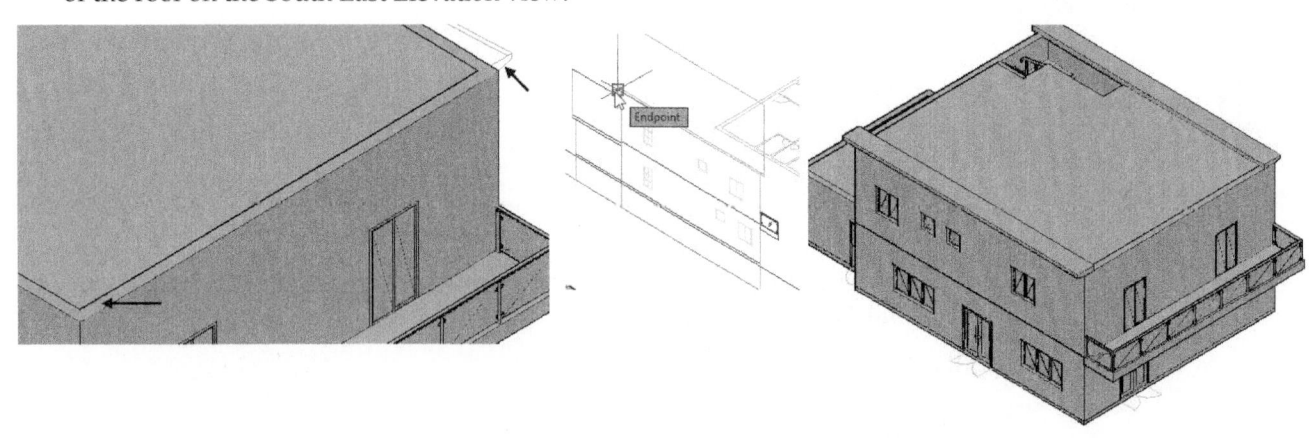

- Type L and press Enter. Close the openings of the roof, as shown.

175 | Creating Architectural Drawings

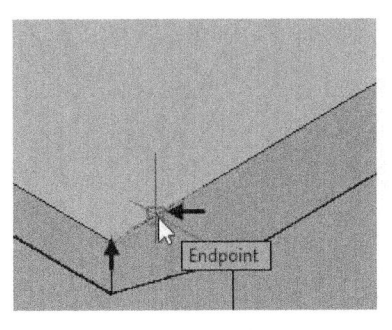

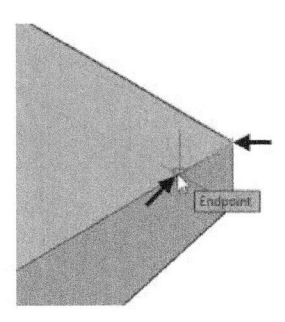

- Activate the **Dynamic Input** icon on the status bar. On the ribbon, click **Home** tab > **Draw** panel > **Polyline**. Place the pointer on the wall and select the corner point of the roof support. Select points in the sequence shown below. Select **Close** from the command line.

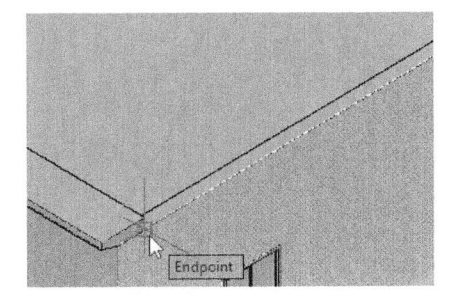

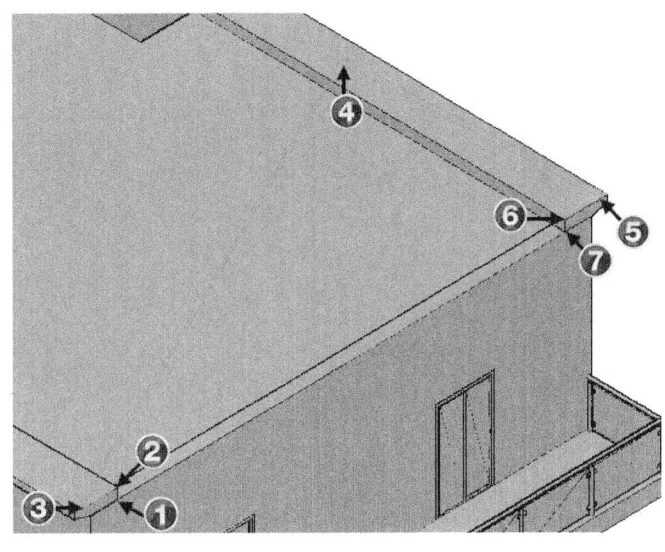

- Extrude the polyline up to 320 inward. Select the extruded solid, type MI, and press Enter. Select the midpoint the horizontal edge of the wall, as shown. Move the pointer vertically upward and click to mirror the extruded solid. Select **No** from the command line.

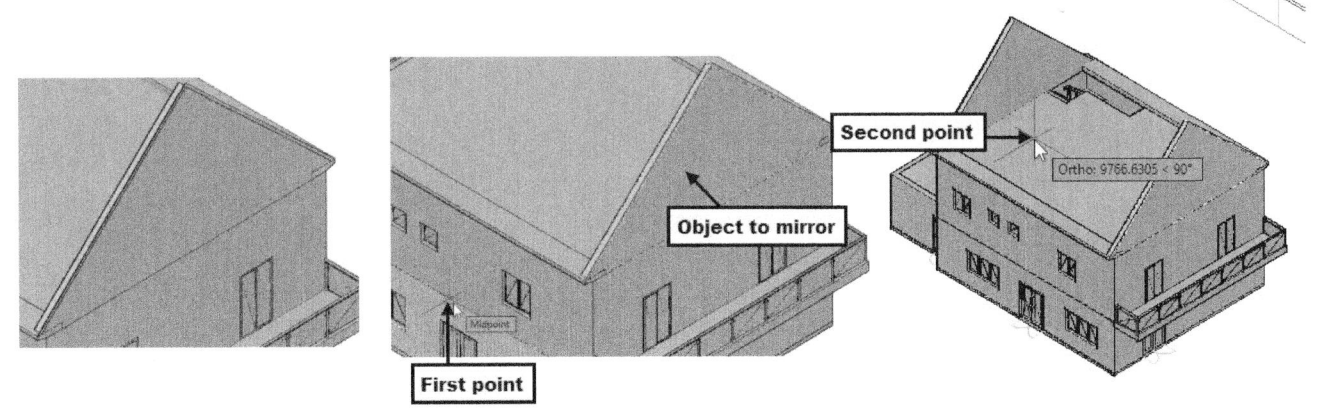

- Type REG and press Enter. Select the 2D lines of the roof, as shown. Press Enter to the convert the lines into a region.

176 | Creating Architectural Drawings

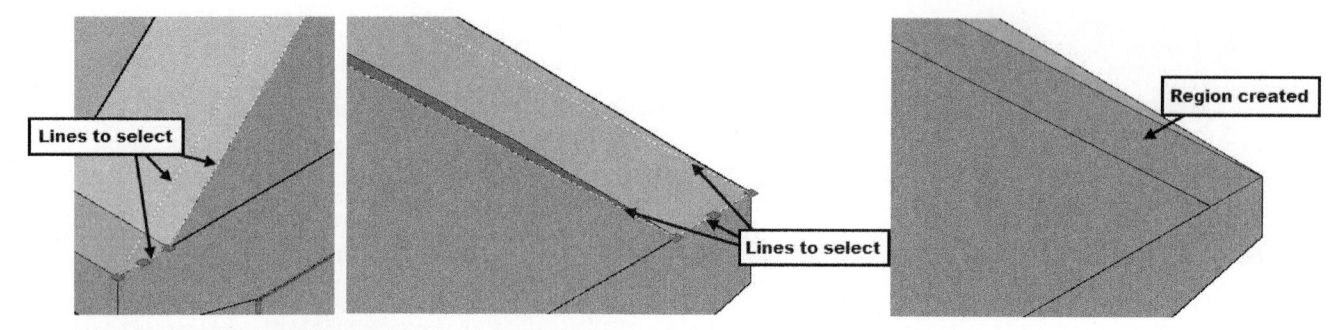

- Extrude the region up to other end of the roof support.

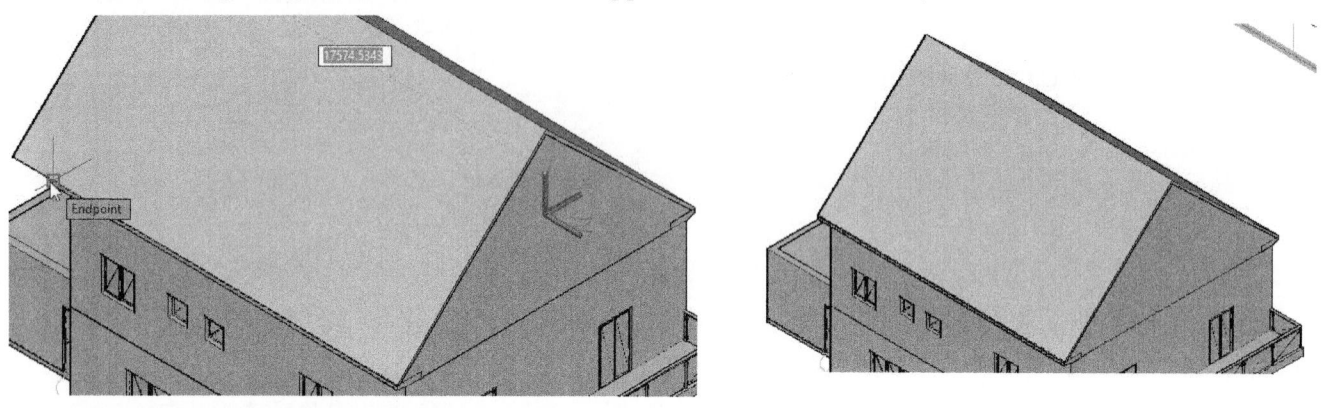

- Press-pull the front faces the roof and roof supports up to 406 mm.

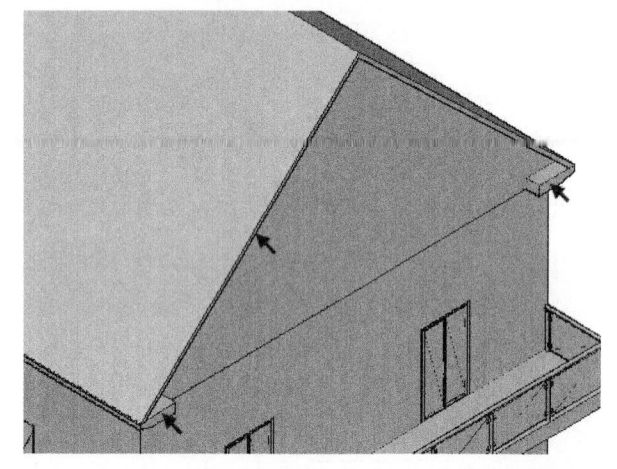

- Change the view orientation to **SW Isometric**. Press-pull the ceiling of the garage, and then create the roof, as shown.

Creating Architectural Drawings

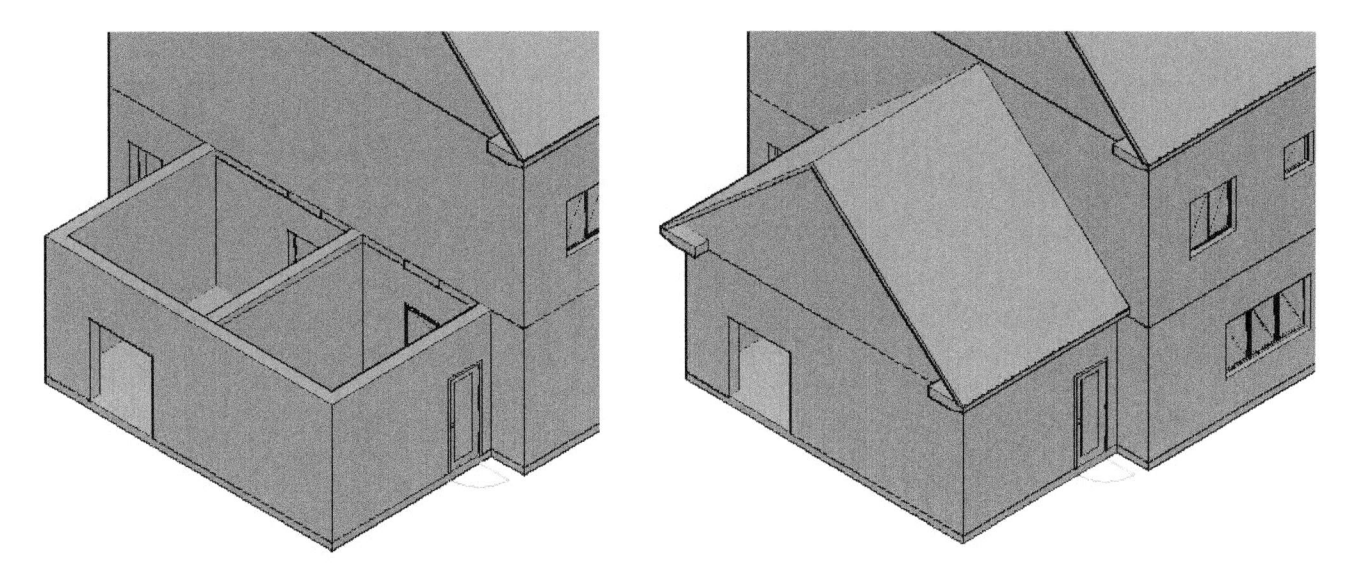

- Create windows on rear and front walls, as shown.

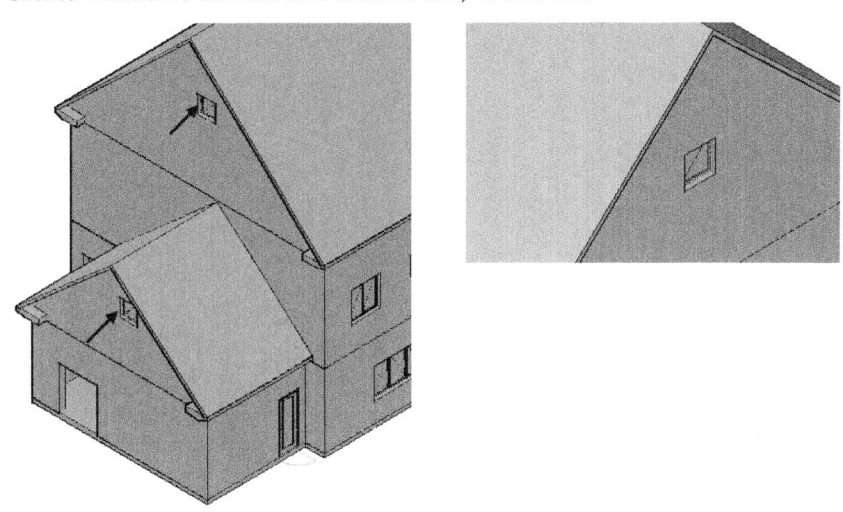

Tutorial 11: Creating the Terrain surface

- On the Quick Access Toolbar, click **Workspace** drop-down > **3D Modeling**.
- Download the Site_plan.dwg file the companion website and open it in AutoCAD.

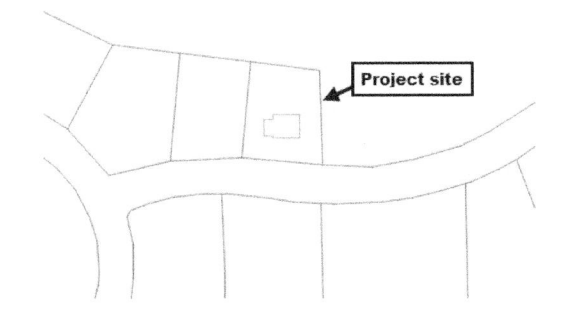

- Type REC and press Enter. Specify the first corner of the rectangle, as shown. Place the pointer on the two corner points, as shown. Select the intersection of the trace lines to specify the second corner. Offset the rectangle by the 1800 mm outwards.

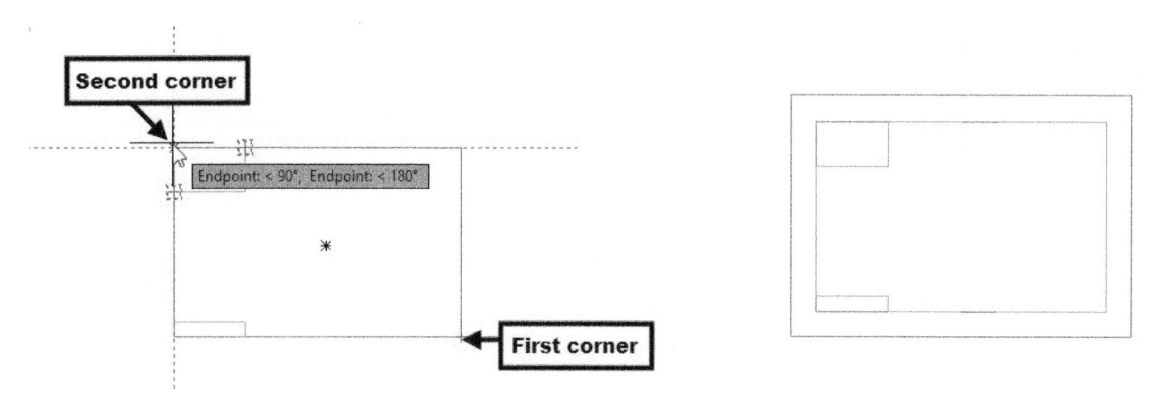

- Offset the left vertical line of the site boundary by 1400 mm inside. Again, offset the new line by 6096 mm. create two horizontal lines intersecting the offset lines. Trim the unwanted portions of the offset lines, as shown.

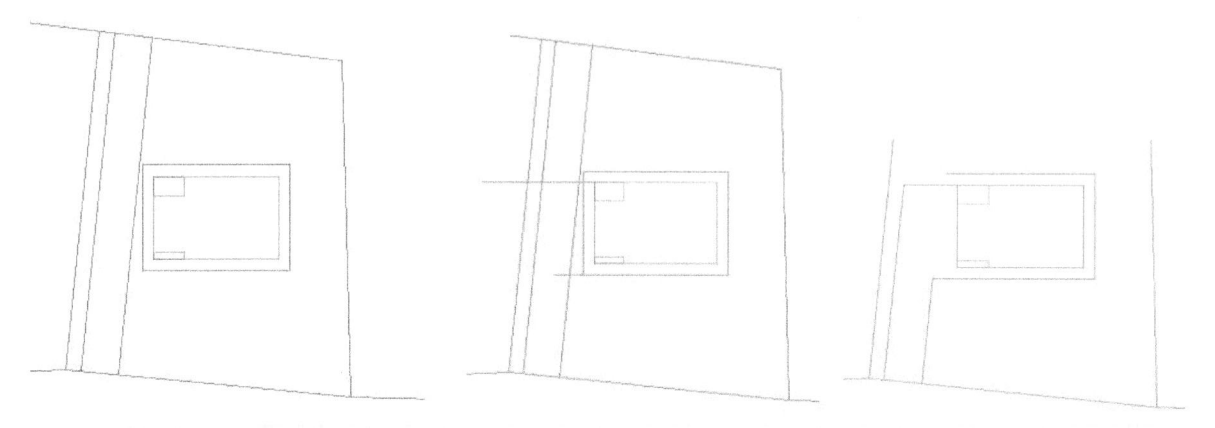

- Likewise, create other lines and trim the unwanted portions, as shown.

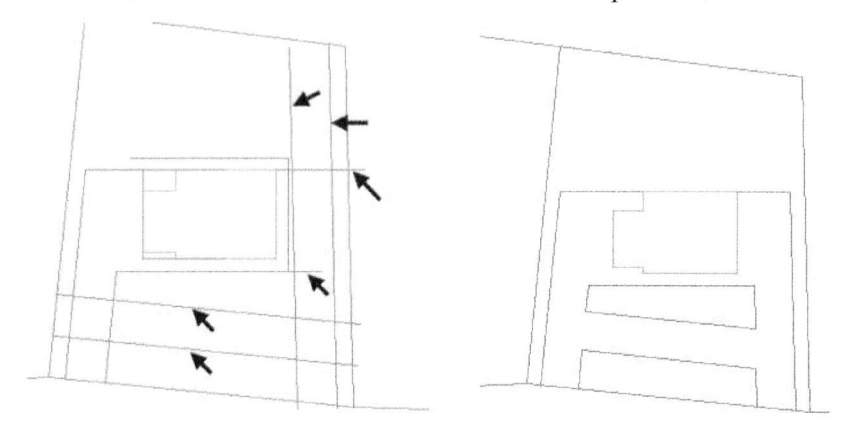

- Type L and press Enter. Press and hold the Shift key, right click, and select **From**. Select the corner point, as shown. Move the pointer on the horizontal line, type 7150, and press Enter; the start point of the line is specified. Move the pointer vertically downwards, and click to create a vertical line.

Creating Architectural Drawings

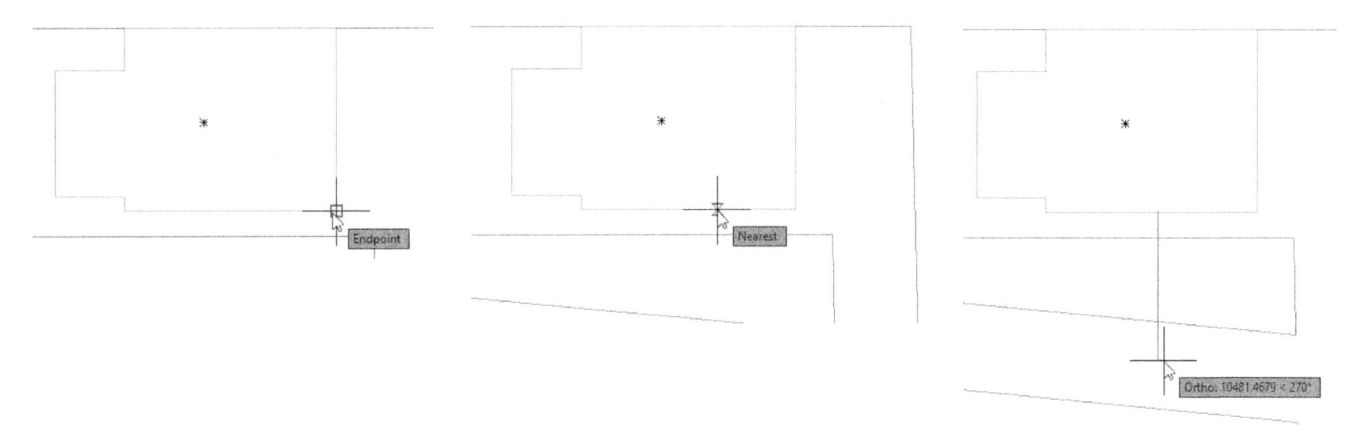

- Offset the vertical line 1200 mm on both sides. Trim the unwanted portions of the lines, as shown.

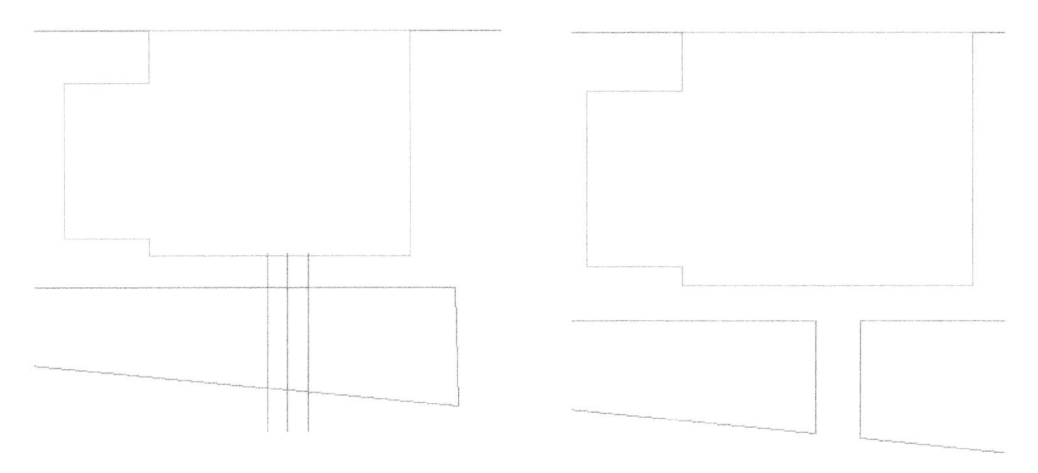

- Fillet the corner, as shown.

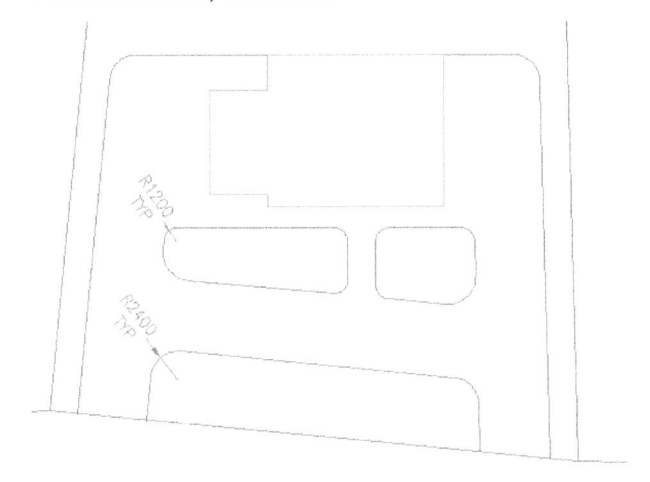

- Type F and press Enter. Select **Trim** from the command line, and then select **No Trim**. Select **Radius** from the command line, type 2400, and press Enter. Create four fillets, as shown. Use the **Trim** tool to remove the unwanted portions, as shown.

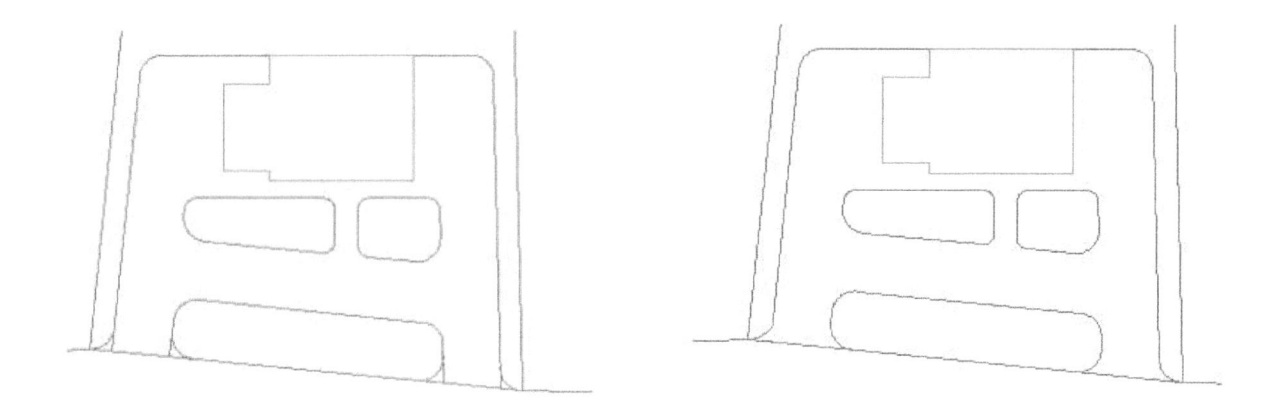

- On the ribbon, click **Home** tab > **Modify** panel > **Stretch**. Create a selection window from right to left, as shown. Press the Shift key and click on the unwanted entities from the selection set, as shown. Select the end point of the horizontal line and move the pointer upward. Type 1000 and press Enter.

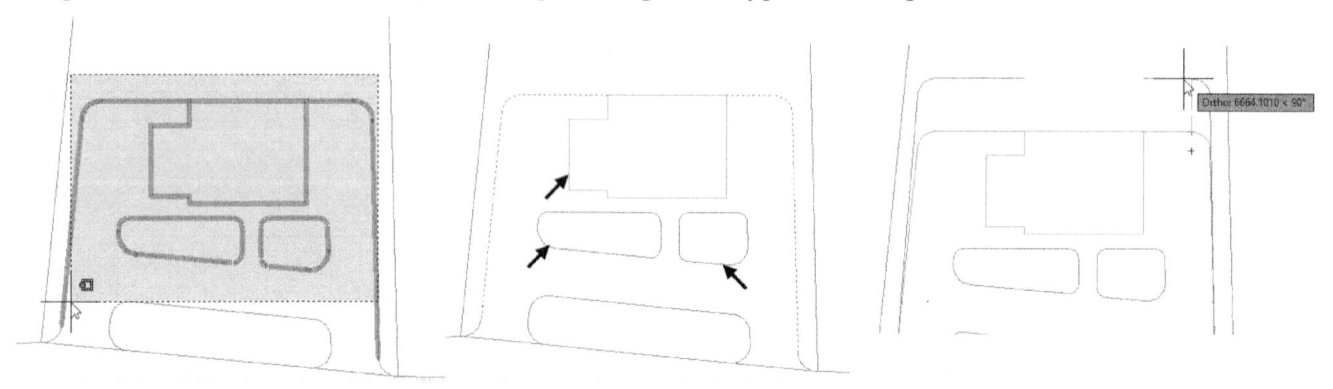

- Close the gap by connecting the two horizontal lines, as shown.

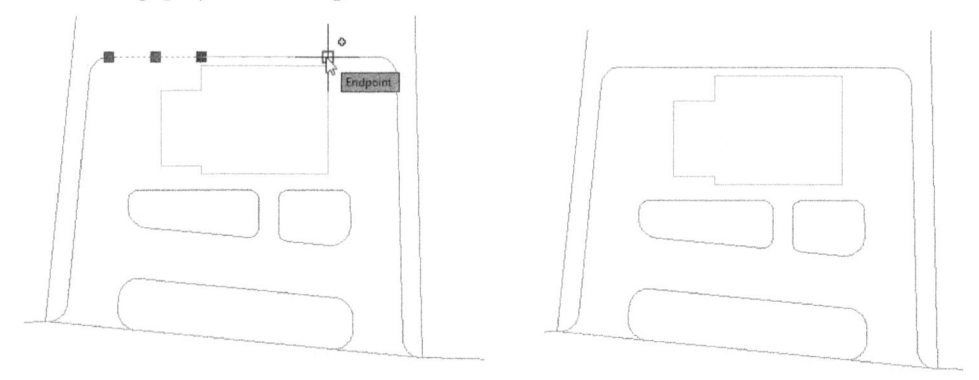

- Create a selection window over the site. On the **Surface** tab of the ribbon, expand the **Curves** panel and click the **Join** tool; the selected entities are converted into polylines.

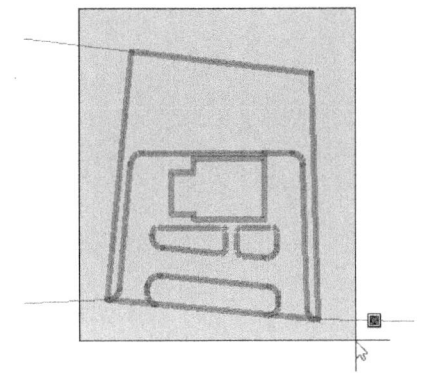

- Select the polyline, as shown. Click on the endpoint grip and select **Add Vertex**. Select the other endpoint of the polyline.

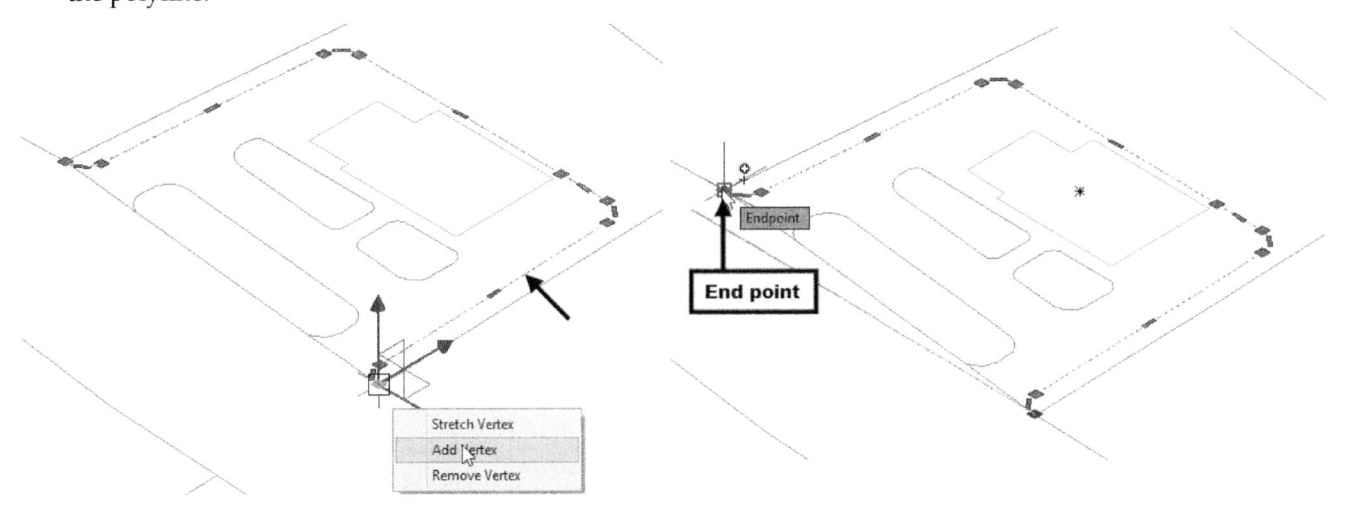

- On the **Home** tab of the ribbon, expand the **Modify** panel and click the **Edit Polyline** tool. Select the polyline, as shown. Select **Close** from the command line.

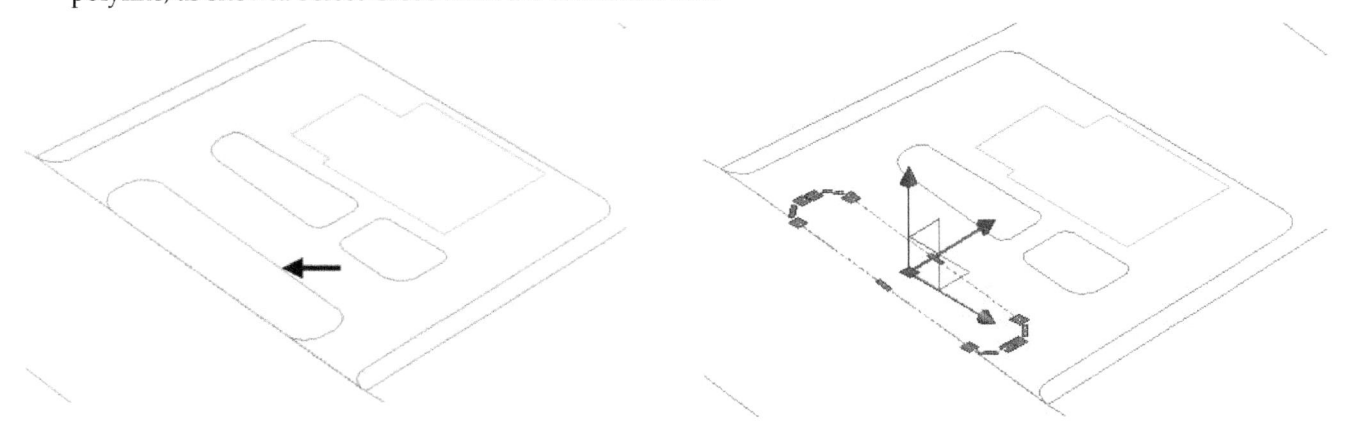

- On the ribbon, click **Surface** tab > **Create** panel > **Plane**. Select **Object** from the command line. Select the closed polyline and press Enter.

182 | Creating Architectural Drawings

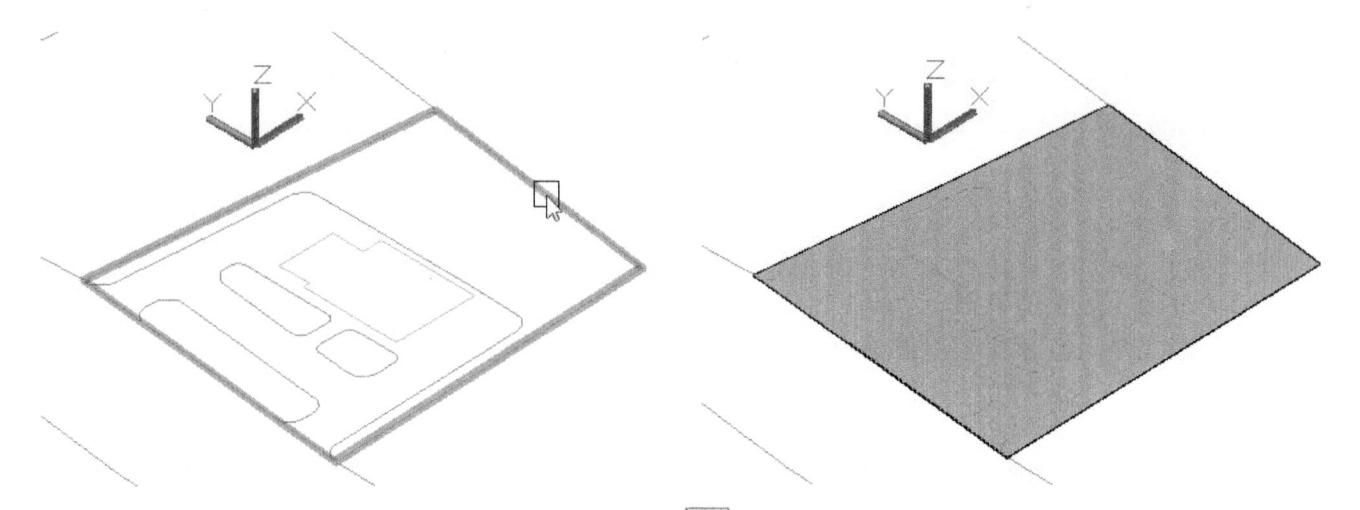

- On the ribbon, click **Surface** tab > **Edit** panel > **Trim**. Select the planar surface and press Enter. Select the polyline, as shown and press Enter. Click in the area enclosed by the polyline; the planar surface is trimmed.

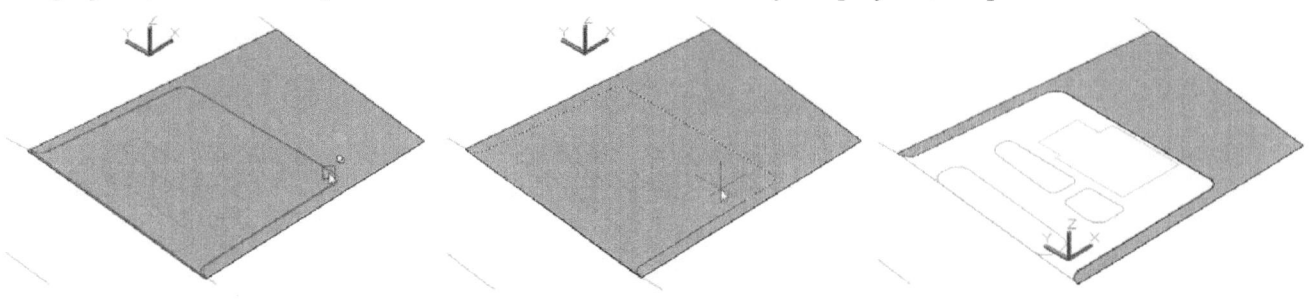

- Activate the **Planar** tool and select the polyline which was used to trim the surface in the last step. Press Enter to create the planar surface.

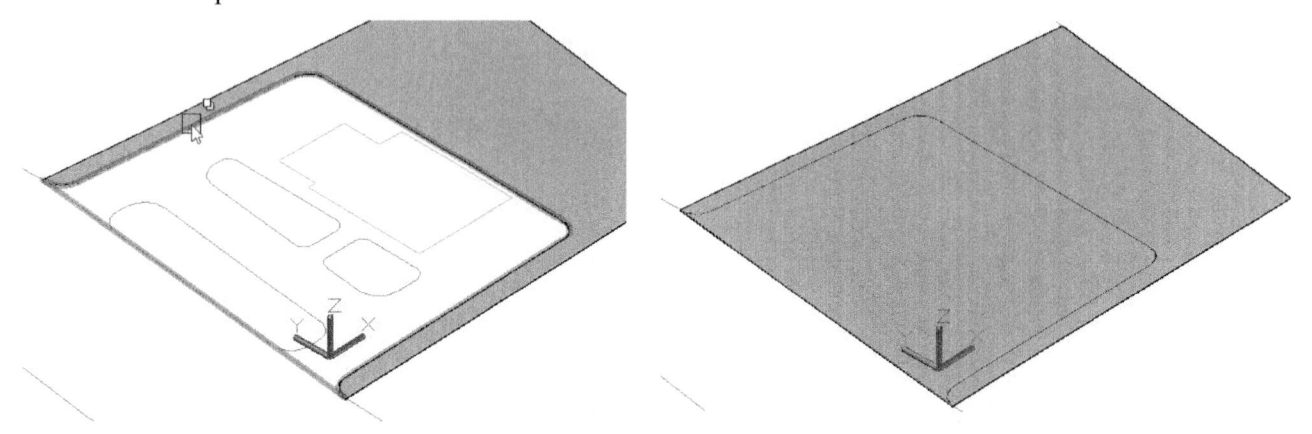

- Activate the **Trim** tool and trim the planar surface created in the last step.

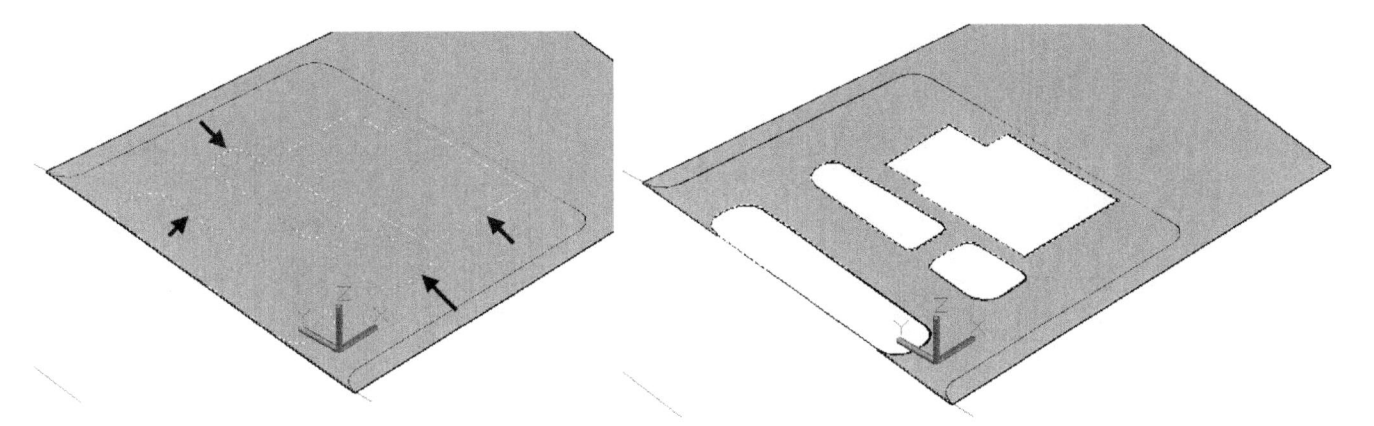

- Activate the **Planar** tool and select the polylines which was used to trim the surface in the last step. Press Enter to create the planar surface.

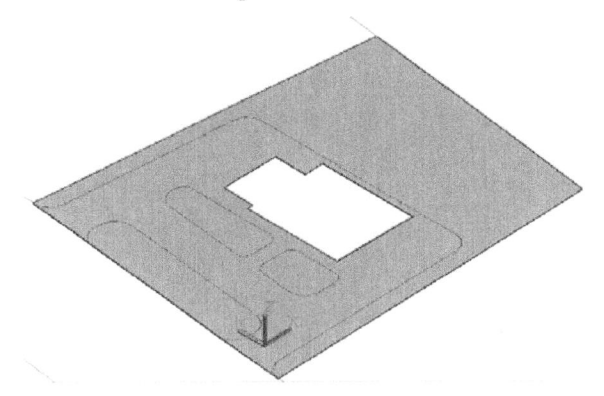

- Select all the planar surface, right click and select **Group > Group**. All the planar surfaces are grouped together.

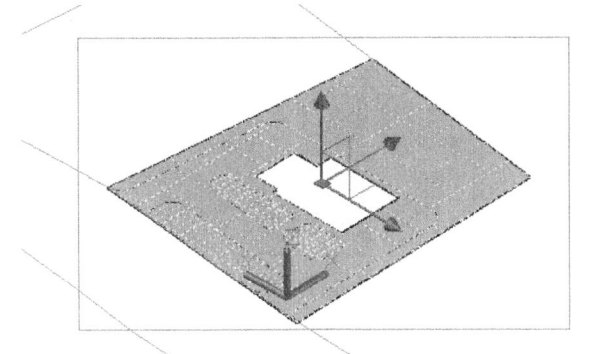

- Type **UCS** and press Enter twice. The UCS is restored to its default position.
- Type **COPYBASE** and press Enter. Select the corner of the subtracted region, as shown. Select the planar surface and press Enter.

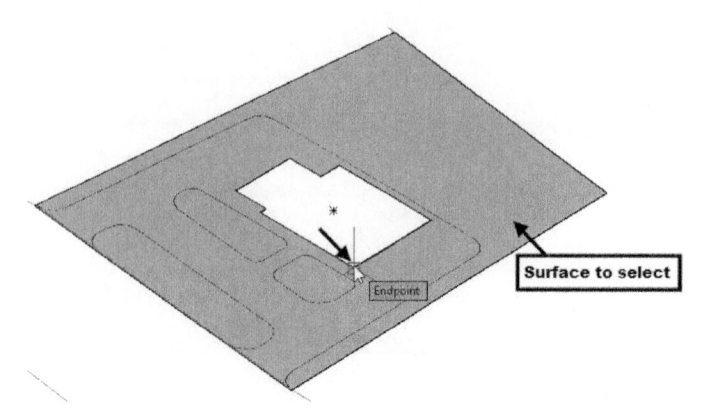

- Open the 3D-Modeling.dwg file.
- Press CTRL+V and select the corner point of the ground floor, as shown.

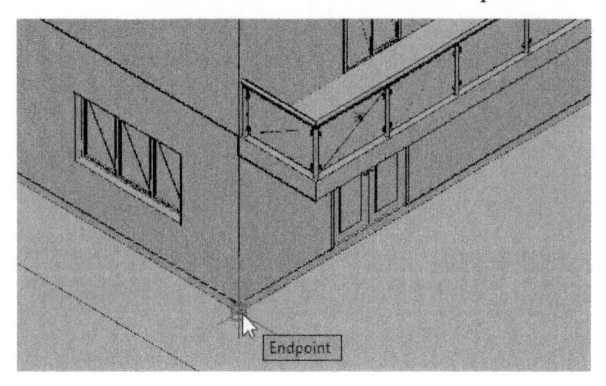

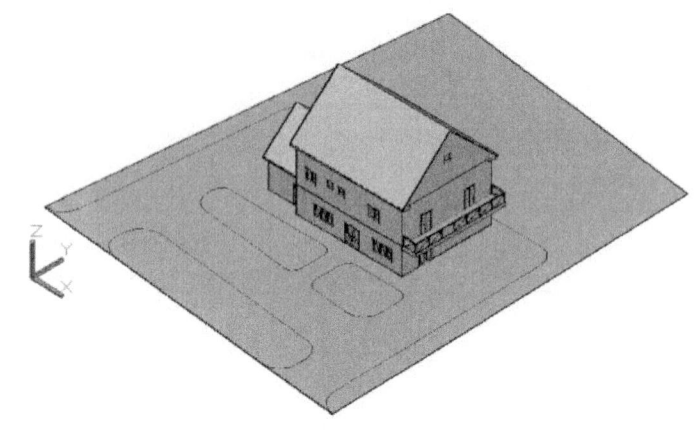

Part 3: Rendering

In this chapter, you will learn to do the following:
- Add Appearances and Textures to the model
- Apply Backgrounds and Scenes to the model
- Add Cameras and Lights
- Render Images

Tutorial 1: Adding Materials

Adding materials in the first step of the rendering a scene. Materials when applied appropriately will give a realistic appearance to the model. In this tutorial, you will add materials to 3D model. Before starting this tutorial, you need to make sure that the Autodesk material library is installed on your computer.

- On the ribbon, click **Visualize** tab > **Materials** panel > **Material Browser** . The **Material Browser** palette appears. It is divided into two portions: **Document Materials** and **Libraries**. The upper portion is called **Document Materials** and displays the materials used in the current document. The Libraries portion shows materials available in various libraries. By default, the **Favorites** and **Autodesk Library** are available in this portion. You can open existing libraries or create new one using the drop-down available at the bottom of the palette.

- On the Material Browser, click the **Changes your views** drop-down in the **Document Materials** portion and select **Thumbnail View**. Likewise, change the view in the **Libraries** portion to **Thumbnail View**.

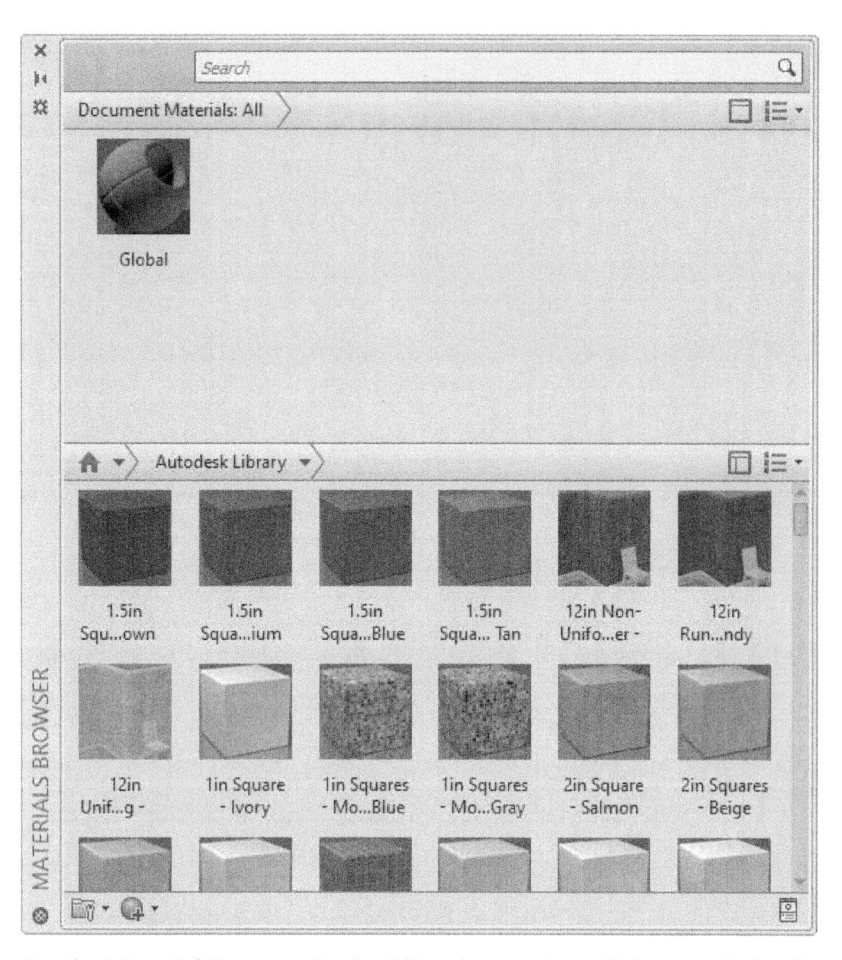

- On the Material Browser, in the **Libraries** portion, click **Autodesk Library > Wall Paint**. All the materials in the **Wall Paint** category appear. Place the pointer on the **Beige** material and select the **Add material** to document; the material is added to **Document Materials** portion. Likewise, add the White material to the **Document Materials** portion.

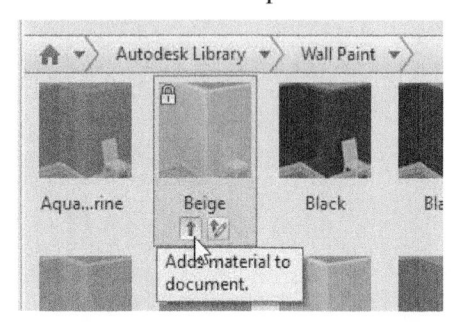

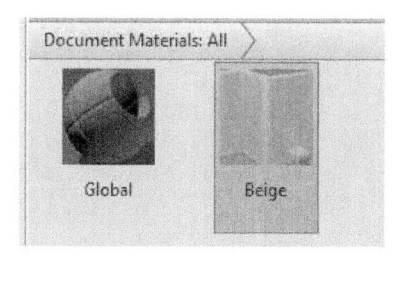

- Repeat the last step to add materials to **Document Materials** portion. The materials and their categories are given next.

Category	Material
Sitework	Grass – Dark Bermuda
	Cobble Stone – Herringbone
Glass	Dark Blue – Reflective

187 | **Creating Architectural Drawings**

Glass > Glazing	Clear
Siding	Horizontal 4in – White
Roofing	Shingles – Asphalt 3 – Tab Black
Paint	White
Metal > Steel	Stainless Steel -Bright
	Stainless Steel – Satin – Brushed
Wood	Teak

- On the **Visualize** tab of the ribbon, expand the **Materials** panel and click the **Attach By Layer** tool. The **Material Attachment Options** dialog appears.

  The dialog has two sections. The section on the left side has a list of materials available in the document and the right side section displays the list of layers. You need apply materials to the layers by dragging them from the material list and releasing them on the target layers.

- Scroll down in the material list such that the **Horizontal 4in –White** material is displayed. Also, scroll down the **Layer** list such that the 3D-Walls layer is displayed.
- Select the **Horizontal 4in-White** material, drag and release it on the **3D-Walls** layer.

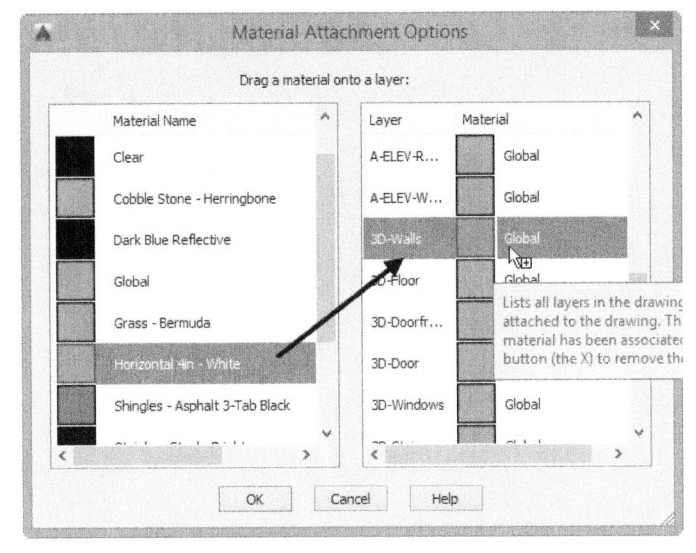

- Likewise, add materials to the other layers, as shown. Click **OK** on the dialog.

Material	Layer
Teak	3D-Doors
	3D-Doorframes
White (1)	3D-Windows

188 | Creating Architectural Drawings

Stainless Steel - Bright	3D-Balcony
Shingles – Asphalt - 3 Tab Black	3D-Roof

- On the ribbon, click **Visualize** tab > **Visual Styles** panel > **Visual Styles** drop-down > **Shaded with edges**.

The model is displayed with the materials.

- Select the planar surfaces of the sitework, as shown. On the **Material Browser** palette, in the **Document Materials** portion, right click on the **Grass- Dark Bermuda** material and select **Add to Selection**.

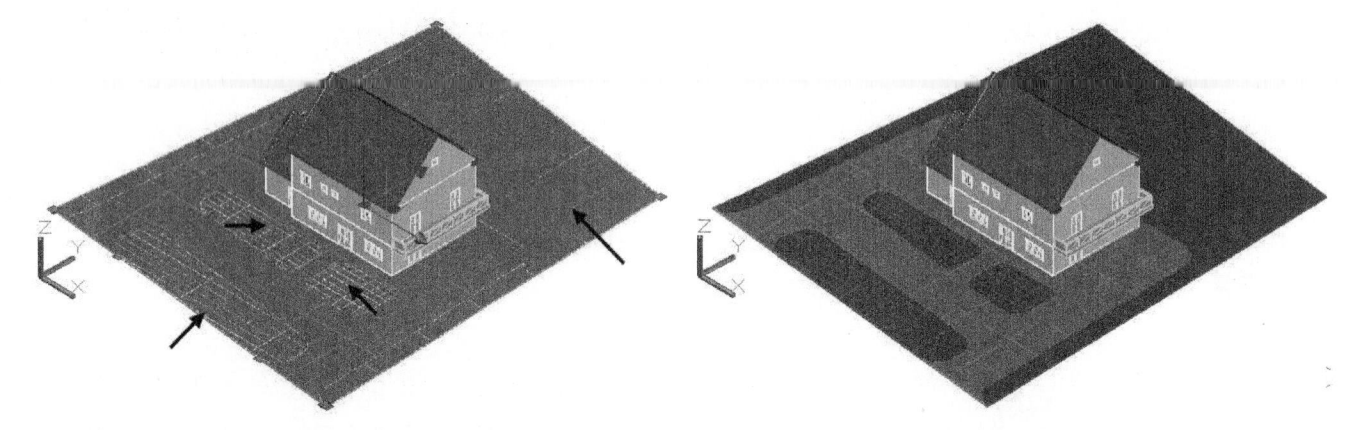

- On the **Material Browser** palette, in the **Document Materials** portion, select the **Cobble Stone - Herringbone** material, drag and place it on the remaining planar surface of the sitework.

Creating Architectural Drawings

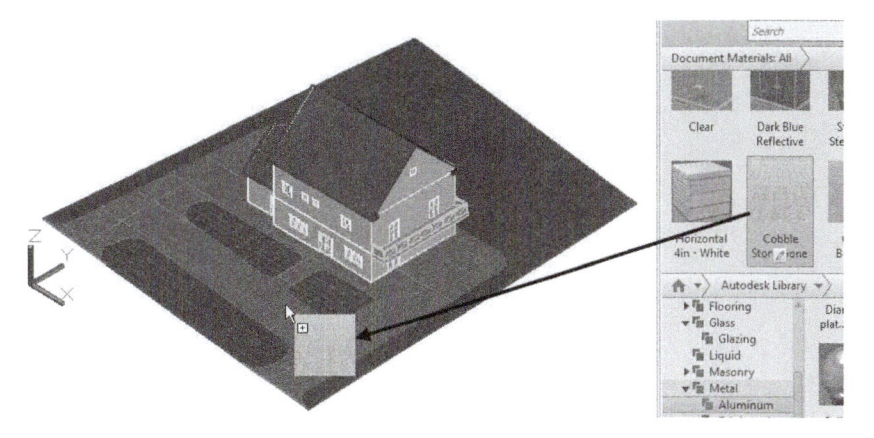

- Likewise, add materials to the other objects of the model, as shown. You need to explode the Rectangular pattern of the balcony glazing, and then apply the **Clear** material.

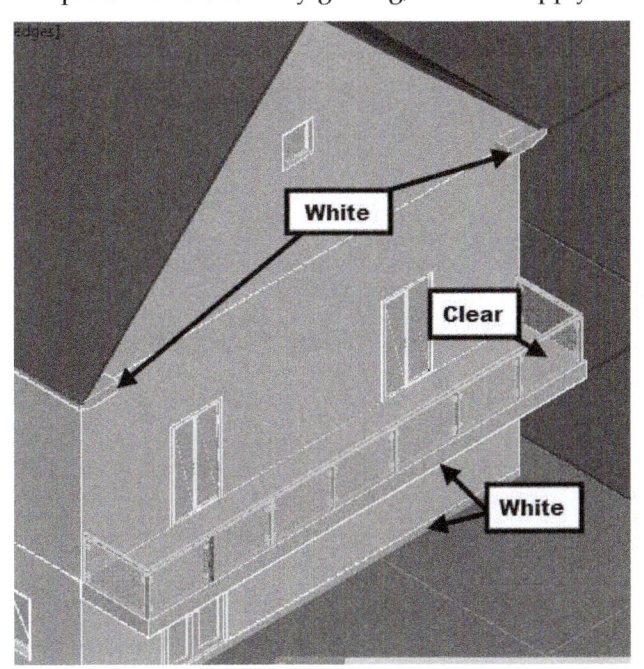

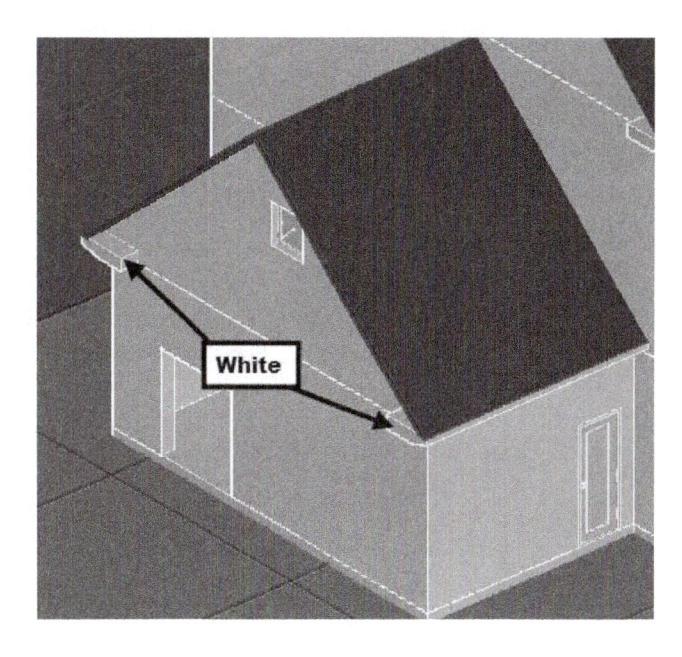

- On the ribbon, click **Home** tab > **Selection** panel > **Filter** drop-down > **Face**. Zoom to the windows and select the faces of the glazing. On the **Material Browser** palette, in the **Document Materials** portion, select the **Dark Blue Reflective** material and select **Add to Selection**. Ungroup the other windows sliding doors and add the **Dark Blue Reflective** material to the glazing.

190 | Creating Architectural Drawings

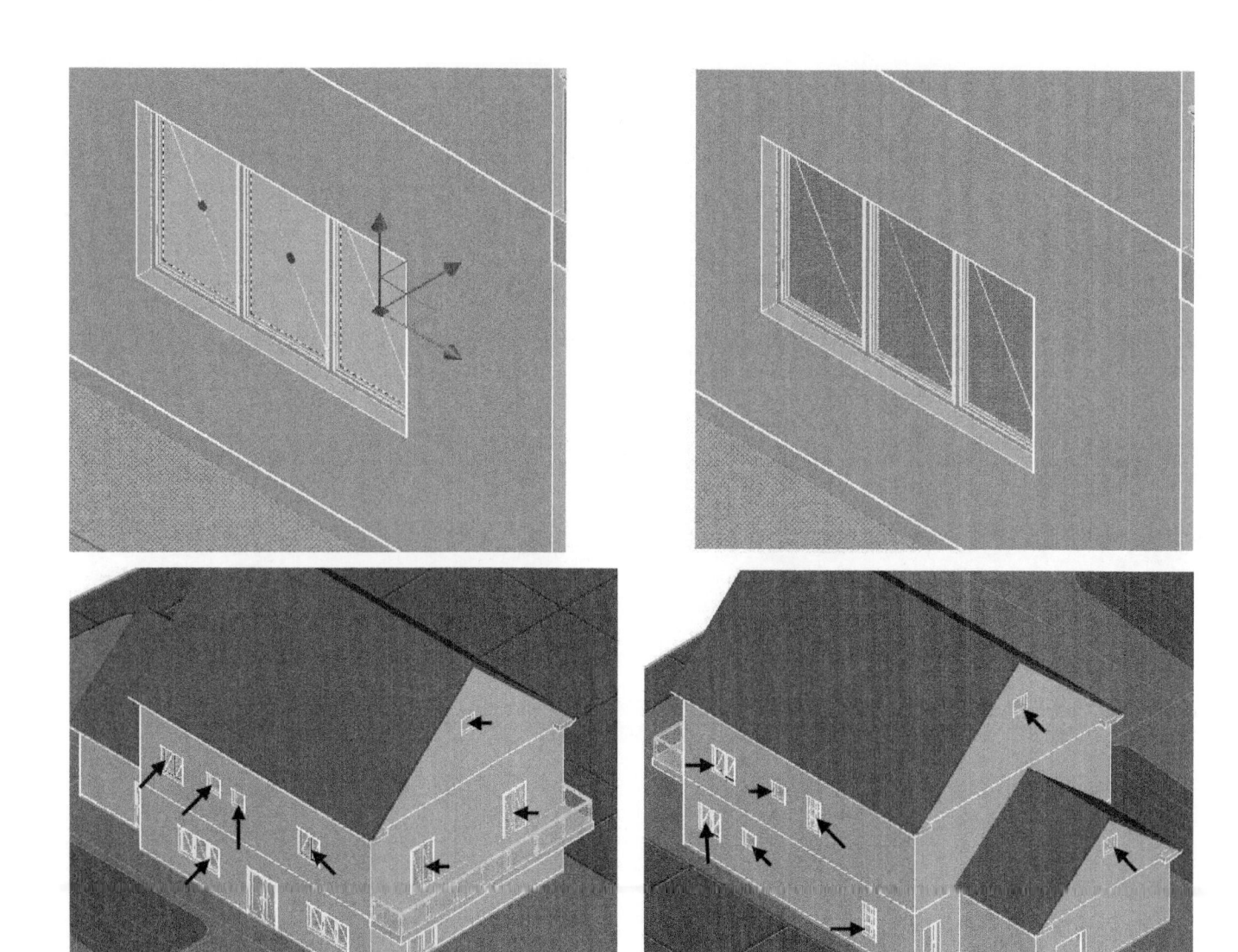

- Zoom to the double door and select the door handles. Select **Stainless Steel – Satin – Brushed Light** from the Material Browser.

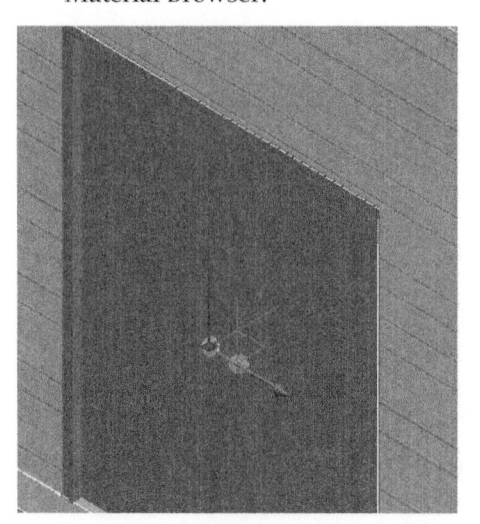

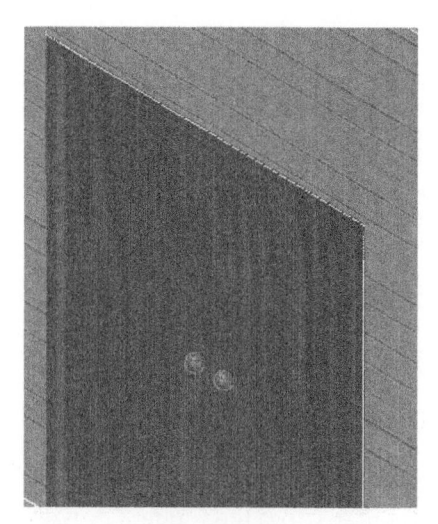

- Likewise, add the **Stainless Steel – Satin – Brushed Light** material to other door handles.

191 | **Creating Architectural Drawings**

- Save the model.

Tutorial 2: Adding Cameras

Cameras are used to define the viewpoint of a scene. You can add cameras in the graphics window and also define its target point.

- On the ribbon, click **Visualize** tab > **Camera** panel > **Create Camera**.
- Select the corner point of the planar surface of the site plan, as shown; the camera is fixed at the specified point and target is attached to pointer. Select the corner point of the window opening, as shown.

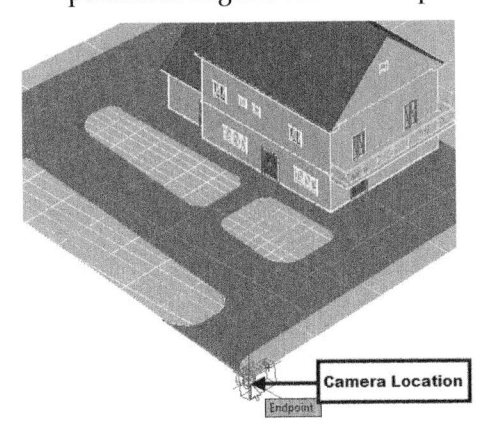

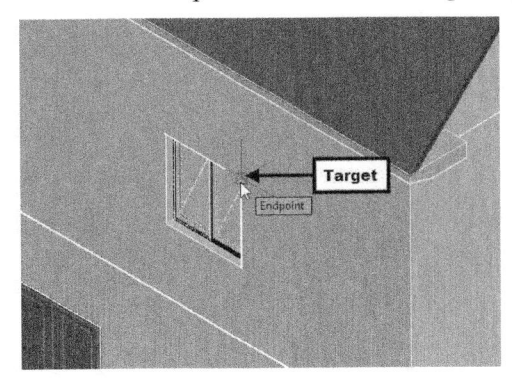

- Select **Name** from the command line. Type **Southeast camera** and press Enter.
- Select **Height** from the command line. Type 4200 and press Enter. Select **eXit** from the command line.
- Select **View Controls > Custom Model Views > Southeast Camera** from the In-Canvas controls.

Notice that the camera does not cover the entire model. You need to edit its location and target to cover the complete model.

- Select **View Controls > SE Isometric** from the In-Canvas controls.
- Zoom to the model and select the camera; the **Camera Preview** dialog appears.
- Select the Lens Length/ FOV grip and move the pointer upwards; the preview in the **Camera Preview** dialog is updated. Type 500 and press Enter. Close the **Camera Preview** dialog.

Creating Architectural Drawings

- Save the model.

Tutorial 3: Adding Lights

AutoCAD has a default lighting system in the model space. However, you can add new lights to the model. AutoCAD allows you to create four types of lights. Note that you need to turn off the default lighting to view the effect of the use-defined lights. To do so, expand the **Lights** panel and deactivate the **Default Lighting** icon. These lights are discussed next.

Point Light: The point light emits light in all directions from the location.

Spotlight: Spot lights are similar to the directional lights. However, they create brighter and sharp lights targeting a specific area.

Distant Light: The distance light emits light rays which are parallel to each other.

Weblight: Weblight can be used to create lights based on the data from the light manufacturers. This gives as precise output of the light similar to the real world lights. The data from the light manufacturers is provided in the IES format. The system computes the luminous intensity and direction of light using the data.

- Select **View Controls > Top** from the In-Canvas controls.

- On the **Visualize** tab of the ribbon, expand the **Lights** panel and deactivate the **Default Lighting** tool.

- On the **Visualize** tab of the ribbon, in the **Sun & Location** panel, click **Sun Properties** (Inclined arrow). On the **Sun Properties** palette, under the **Sun Angle Calculator** section, set the **Date** to 6/21/2015 and the **Time** to 11:00 AM.

- Under the **Sky Properties** section, change the **Intensity Factor** to 2.
- On the **Visualize** tab of the ribbon, expand the **Sun & Location** panel and select **Set Location > From Map** ; the **Geolocation – Online Map Data dialog** appears. Click **Yes** on the dialog; the **Autodesk – Sign In** dialog appears, if you are not logged into your Autodesk account. Sign into your **Autodesk** account; the **Geographic location – Specify Location** dialog appears.
- Type 41.273656, -96.207061 in the **Address** box. Click the **Drop Marker Here** button, and then click **Next**; **Geographic location – Set Coordinate System** page appears. Type 32165 in the search box and select the **BLM - 15** coordinate system. Click **Next**.

Tip: You can find the coordinate system closest to the site location by visiting www.epsg.io and typing the location address in the search bar.

- Select the lower left corner point of the house to define the location. Turn off the Ortho Mode. Move the pointer upward and click to define the north, as shown.

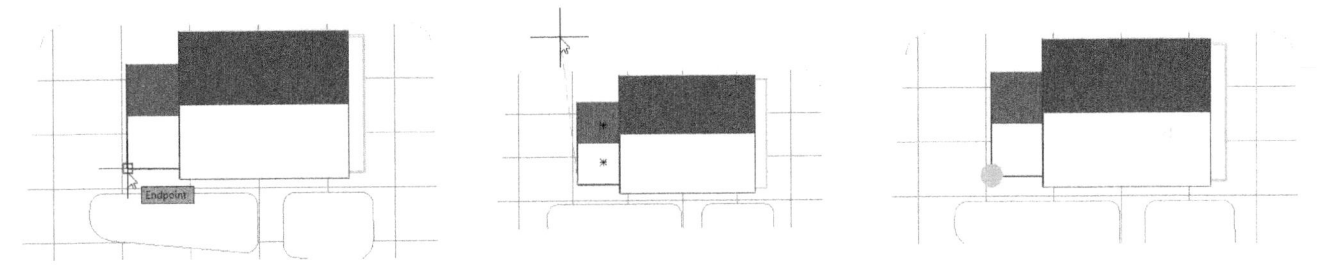

The **Geolocation** tab is added to the ribbon. You can use the tools on this tab edit or remove the location, change its orientation, turn on/off the map, and so on.

- Select **View Controls > Custom Model Views > Southeast Camera** from the In-Canvas controls.

- On the **Geolocation** tab of the ribbon, click the **Reorient Marker** tool. Select the corner point of the house, as shown. Press Enter to accept the earlier value of the North direction.

- On the ribbon, click **Visualize** tab > **Sun & Location** panel > **Sun Status** ; the **Lighting – Sunlight and Exposure** dialog appears. Select **Adjust exposure settings** from the dialog; the **Render Environment and Exposure** palette appears.

- On the **Render Environment and Exposure** palette, adjust the **Exposure** and **White Balance** values to 12 and 5500, respectively. Close the palette.

- On the ribbon, click **Visualize** tab > **Lights** panel > **Shadows** drop-down > **Full Shadows** .

- On the ribbon, click **Visualize** tab > **Sun & Location** panel > **Sky** drop-down > **Sky Background** .

- Save the model.

Tutorial 4: Rendering

Rendering is the process of generating Photorealistic images and videos.

- On the ribbon, click **Visualize** tab > **Render** panel > **Render to Size** . The **Render Window** appears, as shown. You can zoom in or zoom out of the image using the mouse. You can abort the rendering process by clicking the **Cancel rendering** icon.

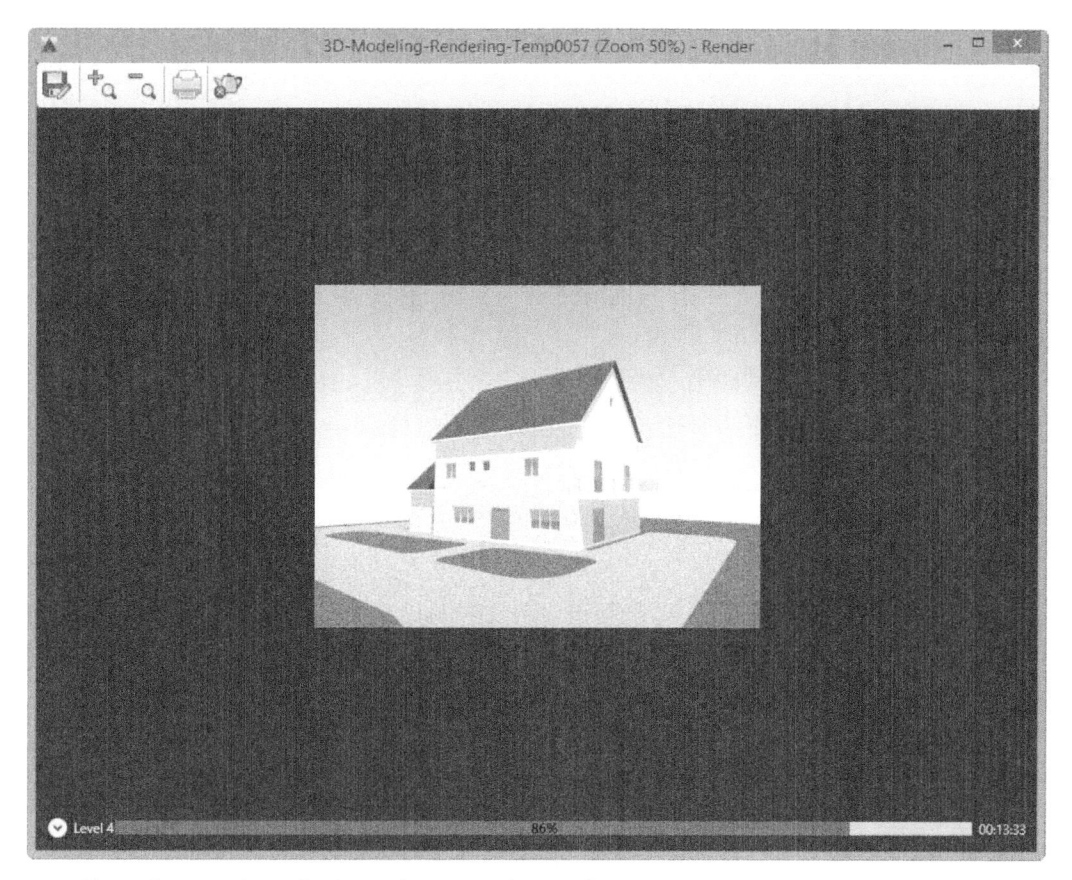

- Close the **Render window** after completing the rendering.
- Select **View Controls > SE Isometric** from the In-Canvas controls.
- On the ribbon, click **Visualize** tab > **Lights** panel > **Create Light** drop-down > **Point**. Select the point of the planar surface, as shown. Select **Intensity factor** from the command line. Type 60 and press Enter. Select **eXit**.

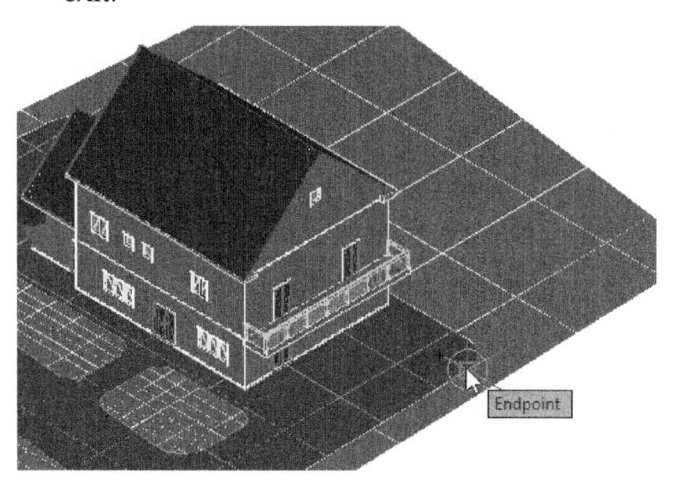

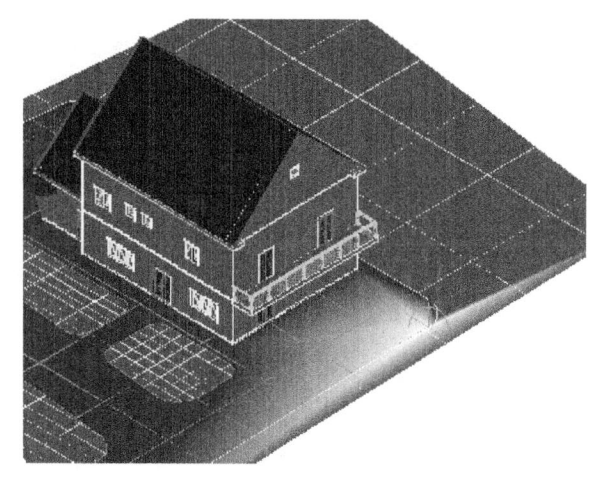

- Select the point light from the model space. On the ribbon, click **Home** tab > **Modify** panel > **Array** drop-down > **Rectangular Array**. On the **Array Creation** tab, change the **Columns** and **Rows** value to 1 and 3, respectively. Change the **Between** value on the **Rows** panel to -12000. Click **Close Array**.

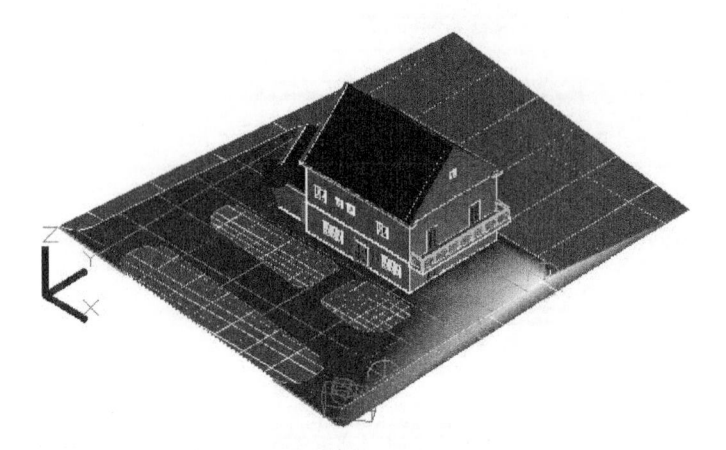

- Select the rectangular array, click on the Z-axis of the move gizmo, and move the pointer upward. Type 6100 and press Enter.

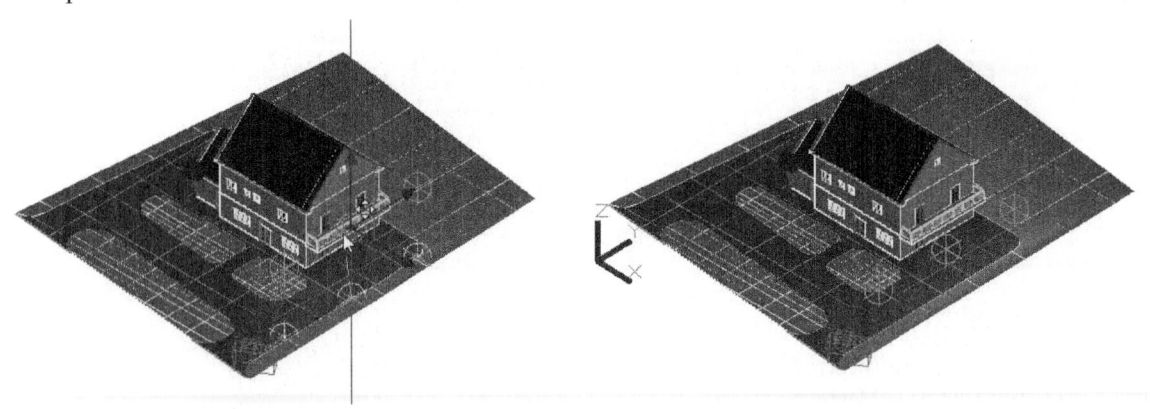

- Create another point light on the other side of the house. Create a line on planar edge, and then create the path array of point lights. Move the path array up to 6100 mm upward.

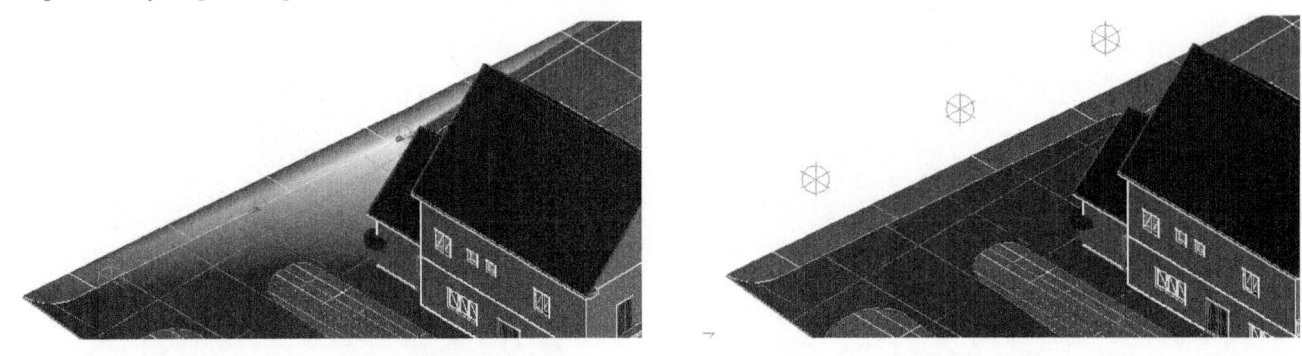

- Select **View Controls > Custom Model Views > Southeast Camera** from the In-Canvas controls.
- On the **Visualize** tab of the ribbon, in the **Sun & Location** panel, click **Sun Properties** (Inclined arrow). On the **Sun Properties** palette, under the **Sun Angle Calculator** section, set the Date to 6/21/2015 and the **Time** to 9:00 PM.
- On the ribbon, click **Visualize** tab > **Sun & Location** panel > **Sky** drop-down > **Sky Background and Illumination**.

197 | **Creating Architectural Drawings**

- On the ribbon, click **Visualize** tab > **Render** panel > **Render to Size** drop-down > **3300 x 2550 px (11 x 8.5 @ 300 dpi)**.

- On the **Render** panel, click **Render Preset** drop-down > **High**. Also, select **Render in Window** from the **Render in** drop-down.

- On the **Render** panel, click **Render to Size** to start the rendering.

- Click **Saves the rendered image** to file on the Render window. Go to a location on the drive and select **JPEG (*.jpeg; *.jpg)** from the **Files of type** drop-down. Type the name of the file, and then click **Save**. On the **JPG Image Options** dialog, set the **Quality** value to 100, and then click **OK**.

- Save and close the drawing file.

Creating Architectural Drawings

Printed in Great Britain
by Amazon